D1282305

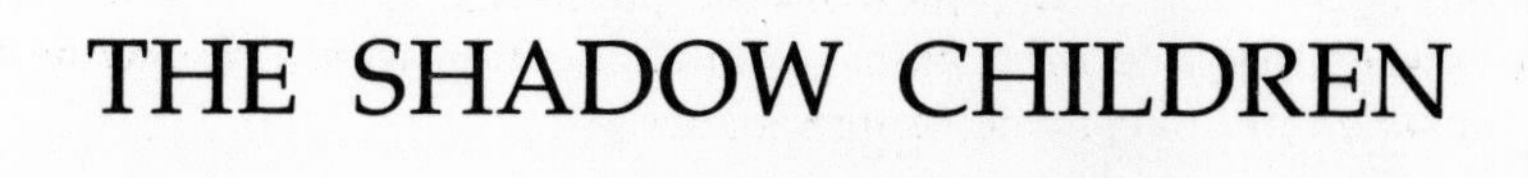
THE SHADOW CHILDREN

FIRST PRINTING

Library of Congress Catalog Card Number: 67-23849

Published by topaz Books
Five North Wabash Avenue, Chicago, Illinois 60602

Printed in the U.S.A.

THE SHADOW CHILDREN

A Book About Children's Learning Disorders

By

Careth Ellingson

This book is a product of the thousands of children, parents and teachers who have been living laboratories for the research and data which has gone into its making.

But, even more important than statistics, these same people have provided the one absolutely necessary factor—love. Parents love their children, teachers love those they teach, and children—they just love. A child's love is simple, unadorned, free from pretense or deceit and something all adults treasure.

I dedicate this book to children—and to the adults who love them.

Careth Ellingson
Coral Gables, Florida
1967

TABLE OF CONTENTS

FOREWORD

This is a book that had to be written. Over the years a substantial body of professional knowledge concerning children with learning disabilities has been developed. However, far too little of this knowledge has been readily available to those who need it most—the parents and teachers of the *shadow children*.

It is to this problem that the author addresses herself. As she notes in her introduction, this book makes no attempt to add to the sum of knowledge in the field. Rather it is a translation, for parents and classroom teachers, of the often technical professional literature that already exists. It is an attempt to describe in relatively simple language the problems faced by children with learning disorders, the nature of their disabilities, and the educational techniques that will help them become secure and productive individuals.

Until quite recently this book could not have been written. Learning disorders are the concern of professionals working in a number of different fields—medicine, psychology, education—and of specialists within each field. For many years experts in each discipline tended to pursue their own interests with only limited regard for the work of others in companion fields. As a result there was wide disagreement about terminology, the kind of treatment that would be most effective, and even about the nature of learning disabilities themselves. Today, however, the multi-disciplinary character of these disorders has been widely recognized and, increasingly, cooperative approaches by specialists of many kinds are the rule. It is the growing areas of agreement among the disciplines that are described here.

Mrs. Ellingson brings unusual qualifications to her assignment. She approaches her subject neither as an expert in a single professional field, nor as a journalist who has acquired a reporter's knowledge of learning disorders. Rather, she brings to her work wide knowledge and deep personal commitment to the *shadow children*. A dyslexic herself, she has for a number of years worked closely with professionals in the field, and has had an opportunity to observe at first hand many children with learning disabilities. At the same time, her personal interest has impelled her to read widely in the professional literature of the relevant disciplines in order to understand these disorders more fully and to discover the kinds of treatment that will ameliorate them. As a result, she brings to her task a unique combination of knowledge, experience, and insight into the problems faced by these children, their parents and their teachers.

This is a book that had to be written. It is important now that it be widely read.

—James Cass

THE SHADOW CHILDREN

1

INTRODUCTION

It is my firm belief that all children are the responsibility of all adults. It is true, however, that the major portion of responsibility for any given child falls on his parents and his teachers. Through the guidance of the home and the school—and in lesser degree, other institutions in society—the child is helped to develop into a civilized, educated member of the community. Even under normal circumstances, the process is hard on child and adult alike.

When we set up institutions to educate and civilize our young, we tend to think first in terms of those who fit the standard pattern—the normal children—and those who are different—the abnormal ones. We take care of both groups—and then feel that all are provided for. But with children, as with life, things are not that simple. There is a wide grey area between the black and white extremes—and it is in this no-man's-land that we find the grey or *shadow children.* Due to the subtle nature of their problems, they can neither function comfortably and securely in the world of the normal, nor expect the special treatment accorded the abnormal. They must live in a world whose demands they are unable to meet, through no fault of their own—and they must do so without understanding of the problems they face by their parents, their teachers, or even themselves.

Statistics are hard to come by in the field of minimal learning disorders. Experts can only estimate the numbers of children involved, and even the estimate varies with each expert. The figures given range from ten to thirty-five percent of all school age children who may suffer from a minimal learning handicap of some form and degree. If we use a conservative figure—seventeen percent (half of the maximum estimate)—we already have nearly six million children in trouble. The *shadow children* to be discussed in the pages of this book will comprise the major portion of these three million children.

These children are called by many names both in clinical and general language. Their disabilities and symptoms of disability take many forms. However, the one characteristic which all these children share is an inability to learn in the standard classroom environment. Oftentimes, one categorized disability will intertwine with another, thus adding to the primary, a secondary problem. Without professional diagnosis and treatment a child's problems can become increasingly complex as there are some problems that "feed" on these disorders. With the proper help, however, a child can be launched on the road to education and productive life. But where do parents start?

The most important single factor that is common to the plight of all these children is ignorance, but it is not the ignorance of indifference. Most parents love their children, most want to help them—if they can. But, they need information—layman's information—to give them clues to the nature of their child's problem, and a plan of action for ameliorating it. Too often the professionals have walled laymen off from the necessary knowledge through the use of clinical language. The purpose of this work is to help breach this wall. It is not a book of diagnosis or prescription; it is a book of information. For information, even of a preliminary sort, is the first major step we are able to take away from ignorance.

The whole area of minimal learning disorders is an emotion-packed problem for parents, doctors and educators. The mother pleads with pediatrician, "there's something wrong—I know it—find it for me." But, short of moving the child in question into his own home, the pediatrician is virtually helpless. He finds no gross abnormalities, he does not see the child in a classroom, and sometimes, of course, "mothers can be over-anxious." The teacher knows what the mother means, but she too is lost. She is likely to have more than one such child in her classroom—statistically, she can expect 5.1 in her classroom of 30. She may try, and usually does, but then, "maybe the child isn't really trying." And, the child doesn't know why he can't learn, why he can't live up to the expectations of his parents and teachers.

Some professionals are reluctant to label children with learning disorders. Certainly, no one wants to brand them with a frightening sounding name. Yet, clear distinctions exist and must be drawn among the different types of disabilities. All learning disorders cannot be approached in exactly the same manner. Therefore, labels are necessary in education. The point to remember, however, is that whatever label is applied to the children as a group, each one needs individual recognition, diagnosis and treatment. Too, the diagnosis of learning disorders is best approached on a multi-disciplinary basis. This simply means that the total child is considered in an evaluation. Obviously, this requires inter-discipline cooperation, careful attention to detail, and a thorough cross-correlation of all the data relating to the child.

A baby is born with a limited number of innate drives. All else is learned and, for some things, learned so quickly we do not realize they were learned. The difference in human babies and animal babies is the brain. At birth, an animal's brain has already reached almost its total size, output and capacity. This is not true of humans. Because of our brain, we are able to think, reason, analyze, originate, and our intellect is capable of new learning until the day we die. There is no argument that any organism capable of so much is very complex.

Conversely, to teach or civilize such an organism is an intricate coupling of brain and education. And, if the education of our offspring had not been an involved process to begin with, we adults, by now, have surely made it the most complicated of procedures possible.

In the past, if a child failed in school, he merely dropped out and apprenticed himself to a trade or found work that did not require intellectual skills. Most girls did not feel that a great deal of schooling was needed to outfit them for their roles as wives and mothers. But today, we have national campaigns against school drop-outs, and our girls consider college a necessity to proper marriage management, child rearing, and career opportunity.

Indeed times have changed, and with it attitudes regarding education. Now, the below-average child, upon recognition, is placed in a special education program, where the teachers bring to bear their special knowledge to shift the tactics of education. We recognize the limitations placed upon the capacity to learn by moderate or severe brain damage, retardation, blindness, deafness, and similar problems. The average child is provided with schooling that will effectively educate and civilize him into productive adulthood. And, the above-average child is actively encouraged to prepare himself for a career in any one of the many professions or occupations that require high intelligence and knowledge.

But, what of the child with a very mild or subtle learning handicap. His disability is not obvious, and usually, even if discovered, is not fully understood by a great many professionals and not at all by most parents. Where does he fit into the scheme of things? First of all, he is average or above in intelligence, so he does not qualify for special education. At the same time, he cannot learn without special help to acquire the proper tools with which to learn. Usually, therefore, he is either ignored or accused of being lazy and uncooperative.

A perfect example of this type of learning disorder is specific dyslexia. The child suffering from this disability is average or above in intelligence, but he cannot, try as he may, learn to do such a simple thing as read—without special teaching methods and techniques. "He cannot read"—it rolls off the tongue easily. Yet, reading, in our culture, is the key to all learning. Too often the dyslexic child is left to drift and fail, suffer and be ignored, tagged lazy and beaten, or, failing all else, eventually permitted to drop out of school.

These attitudes have been with us a long time. What is really encouraging is that they are changing—slowly to be sure, but changing. Once we Americans see and understand a problem, we do something about solving it. Parents, educators, doctors, researchers—all are becoming increasingly aware of the child with a subtle, difficult-to-diagnose learning problem. And knowledge is growing daily about these children. There have never been so many so eager for knowledge and for answers to the questions about this area of education.

This book is written for those who are totally uninformed about the subject of minimal learning disorders and how they handicap the education of children. It does not attempt to be original, but rather, it seeks to translate the clinical literature into layman's language. Thus, it should be considered a primer. For those readers who desire more understanding of the subject, the Suggested Reading List, in the back of the book, will help to further open the door to knowledge.

A note of caution to the reader about our joint responsibility to the individual child is needed. Because this book encompasses the problems of millions of children, it is, of necessity, a general book. The reader must always bear in mind that each child has his own set, or combination, of problems and circumstances. No two are identical. Each child is an individual and should, indeed must, be treated as such. Jumping to conclusions can be disastrous. If you have a child whose symptoms seem to be described here, your doctor, psychologist, guidance counselor, or school facility should be consulted. They and only they can diagnose his disability and treat it effectively. *Home diagnosis or treatment is in no way sufficient.* Learning problems do have definitive patterns and if the child's problem is accurately identified, he can be taught. *Professional* diagnosis and treatment is vital. Experience has shown that once parents realize that their child is not just being "bad-tempered or lazy" they will make every effort to find professional help. This book is specifically designed to help parents make a start on identifying the problem. The one prime concern throughout these pages has been to help the parent toward the first concrete conception of what may be a vague, uneasy sensing of a problem—an attempt to provide a small, flickering flame with which to light the *shadows*. If it serves this purpose, then I have done my job.

"These children are as handicapped by the ignorance surrounding their problem, as by the problem itself."

Frances K. McGlannan
Miami, Florida 1963

2

A FIRST COMMENT

This book, basically a translation of the clinical literature about children with minimal learning problems, has an unusual history. In 1963, I entered the field of learning disabilities as a non-professional and thereby changed my whole life. I gained a new sense and awareness of the potential of children. I also learned how easily this potential can be interrupted or held back, how much suffering can evolve from a learning handicap and then, gratefully, I learned how much can be done for such children.

Our children are our future—today's child will take over the stewardship of the world tomorrow. Therefore, what we do to them, for them, and with them, has great bearing on how our present-day adults will live out their lives. We are now educating our future lawmakers, civil servants, garage mechanics, corporation presidents, teachers—and criminals. By 1985, statisticians have projected we will have over sixty-three million children in our elementary and secondary schools. An increase of twenty-five million children in twenty years. When we educate a child, we are not merely trying to make sure that he will become a good mayor, or doctor, or businessman—rather, we are trying to make sure that he will become a productive adult, will add honor to his family unit, and have the ability to assume his inherent duties.

Working with or for children any length of time only serves to strengthen and reconfirm this sense of the future within our young.

In 1966, I co-authored an article on a very specific and publicly unrecognized learning disorder in children—genetic dyslexia. The reaction to this article was overwhelming. Thousands of letters from all over the world poured in requesting more information, expressing grateful thanks for highlighting the problem in layman's terminology, and asking for reprints.

When we sat down to discuss this parental and professional reaction to a single magazine article, Mr. Norman Cousins, editor of *Saturday Review,* in which the article appeared, expressed the opinion that a book would be necessary as an appropriate follow-up to the article. He said that it was obvious the public needed and wanted more information at the layman's level, and that it was equally obvious to him that I should be the one to attempt to supply this information. For a variety of reasons the idea of a book was set aside for some time. But, over a year later, with the mail still pouring in, and Mr. Cousins still firm in his belief that not only was a book necessary, it was a duty that must be performed—the task was started.

In retrospect, I can only be grateful for Mr. Cousins' faith and encouragement, and for his frank badgering in support of a book. Without his exhortations to effort, this job would not have been done. I hope the reader finds this book informative, but most of all, I hope Mr. Cousins will feel that his efforts in our joint behalf—reader and writer—have not been in vain.

Let us begin. . . .

Dear Mrs.

I am writing to you out of desperation in the hope that you may have the answer to my problem. My son is 16 years old and has just dropped out of high school to take a job in a filling station. The reason this bothers me so much is that I have been told that my son has an I.Q. of 125.

He has always had trouble with reading in school. Even now his reading is so poor that he finds it difficult to read anything above the third grade level.

He has always hated school and has been called "lazy" by his teachers. His teachers say that there is nothing wrong with him – that he just isn't trying. I know this isn't true. He has spent many hours with me talking about what he has learned or things he has heard or seen.

The last time he ran away from home was when he tried to read a book that his English class was discussing. He finally threw the book down in frustration and ran out of the house. It took us two days before we finally found him.

His writing is very sloppy. When he writes he reverses the position of letters in the words or makes many of his letters backwards.

I don't know if you can tell me anything that will be of help, but my husband and I are at wits end. We have lived with him and his problem for so many years, knowing there was something wrong, yet being told by his teachers that he was capable of the work.

We are terribly worried because he has started to hang out with a gang of kids, most of them high school dropouts too, who are always getting in trouble.

We love our son very much and we want, more than anything, to be able to help him.... we just don't know how.

Can you help me?

Mrs.

3

DYSLEXIA

"'ALTHOUGH SHARP AT ALL OTHER THINGS,' the boy could not read. He was thirteen years old; at thirteen years a boy's reading lessons should be over and done. Yet he could not read; or, if he might read at all, it was only such words as 'cat' and 'rat.'

"Therefore he died, which seems heavy punishment for being dull at his reading. The tramway which runs on Southend Pier is an electric tramway. It is fenced about with railings. What are railings that they should keep a boy from climbing over them? But, besides the railings, there were placards warning all who should approach of the dangers of the live rail.

"If the boy could have read the placards he would not have climbed the railing. But the placards told him nothing, he being able to spell out only the simplest words. So he climbed and took his death from the current.

"The world is like that, a perilous world for those who cannot learn to read. It must be so. We cannot fence every peril so that the unlettered may take no harm from it. There is free and compulsory education; at least everybody has his chance of learning his lessons in school. The world's business is ordered on the understanding that everybody can at least spell out words.

"We walk in obedience to the written word. All about us are boards and placards, telling us to do this thing or to keep from doing that other thing. Keep to the Right, we are bidden, or else we are to Keep to the Left. By this stairway we are to descend to enter the train that goes Westward; by that we go to the Eastward train. Way Out and Way In; Private; Trespassers will be Prosecuted; Pit Entrance; the street's name and the name of the railway station—all of these things are cried out to us by that wonderful device of letters, a babble of voices which make no sound.

"It is hard for us to understand the case of those to whom these many signs and warnings say nothing. They must move as though bewildered, as though they were blind and deaf. No warning touches them, not even that of the board which, like the board of the Southend tramway, cries Danger and Beware."*

In modern society, dependent as it is on the printed word, those who

* A partial reproduction of a story appearing in the Evening News, London, England, August 9, 1926, and written anonymously.[1]

cannot read easily, smoothly, without giving the act a second thought, are cut off irrevocably from most of the normal channels of learning and communication. Dyslexia, at this practical level, means that a child with average or above intelligence, cannot learn to function in today's world because he cannot learn to read.

Dyslexia is a medical term that is defined as lack of ability or inability to read. For many years definitions of the term have always included the words, "resulting from brain damage." Only in the past year has a definition of dyslexia appeared in a medical dictionary that did not include these qualifying words.

One of the major problems which has faced professional and nonprofessional alike whenever a discussion about learning disorders, and most especially dyslexia, arises is the terminology used. Differences arise among the three disciplines involved—education, medicine, and psychology. This is not necessarily the fault of the disciplines, it is rather more their burden. Just as word meanings vary in different sections of the country, so may the same word have a different meaning when it crosses discipline lines.

However, today throughout the world, responsible professionals have most widely accepted the assessment of the nature of dyslexia given in 1960 at the Johns Hopkins Hospital Conference on Dyslexia. The papers of this Conference, edited by John Money,[2] set forth that *specific dyslexia* is *a genetic, neurological dysfunction, uncomplicated by other factors.*

When we break down this rather technical definition, we find that dyslexia means, first, *that a child inherits from his parents, grandparents or a preceding generation, certain factors which play a special role in his problems, and these factors lead to a basic malfunction or immaturity of the neural system.* Even though the word malfunction is used, in genetic dyslexia it is not the malfunction of neural damage but rather slow or imperfect neural development. This makes it almost impossible for the child to acquire the skills he needs, in certain areas, at a level appropriate to his age. By age six, a child's body, nervous system, eyes, hands and mind have usually matured enough to make him capable of learning the skills that must be acquired in order to learn to read. For a dyslexic child, the hereditary factors retard this maturing process. Thus, these children are often described as "late starters" or "immature for their age," and parents and teachers take refuge in the hopeful phrase, "he'll grow into it."

And, second, this definition means that *there are no other intruding factors that complicate the child's problem.* That is to say, the genetic or specific dyslexia is the *primary* cause of the child's inability to learn to read—it is not the result of brain damage, retardation, psychopathology or poor teaching. This does not mean that a child suffering from specific dyslexia cannot have these other problems, but when a child does have one or more of these "intruding factors," then, with the exception of poor teaching, that becomes the primary cause for the child's inability to read, not the dyslexia.

The saddest aspect of genetic dyslexia is that, even today, with a wealth of clinical knowledge on the subject, we still do not have a wide public awareness of the problem or public school programs to teach these children. It is especially sad, because of all the learning disorders which may affect a child, dyslexia is the easiest to remediate. Today, a deaf or blind child can more readily receive a well-rounded education than a dyslexic child because their problems are easily recognized and widely understood. The dyslexic child's are not.

A child with dyslexia differs also from those with major impairments—severe retardation or brain damage, for example. These children really do not have any awareness of what they are missing and therefore have no sense of loss. But, a dyslexic is intelligent and knows that he is an object of ridicule by other children, his ego is battered by failure at school, and he is aware that his parents feel frustrated and heartbroken because of his inability to achieve. No wonder so many students draw the seemingly logical conclusion from all of this—that it is easier to run away from their problems that are symbolized by the school, than to stand fast and slowly sink in the quicksand of failure. It would seem almost as if self-preservation beckons our drop outs.

The history of medically recognized dyslexia may be traced to 1896, when an English physician, Dr. James Kerr,[3] cited a severe and specific learning disability in some children who were otherwise intellectually capable. Since that time, dyslexia has been known by a multitude of names: Specific Learning Disability, and Specific Language Disability (sometimes referred to as SLD), Hereditary Specific Language Disability, Congenital Word Blindness, Mirror Reading, and many others. It has also acquired a vast clinical literature of more than 20,000 professional articles on the subject. Very little of this clinical information has been made available in a form that is usable for the average classroom teacher, however, and even less has filtered down to those who are the most vitally concerned, the parents.

In the Scandinavian countries genetic or "family" dyslexia has long been recognized. A great deal of the original medical research was done there by Dr. Knud Hermann, of the University Hospital of Copenhagen. Dr. Hermann in his book, "Reading Disability,"[4] and in other published works, helped to clarify the concept of "family dyslexia" and the fact that it can be inherited. Then, in 1950, Dr. Bertil Hallgren of Stockholm, published a massive work on specific dyslexia,[5] pulling the then current literature together, adding detailed research findings and observations of his own. The result was an extremely comprehensive study on the whole area of inherited dyslexia. Later, the brilliance of Edith Norrie's teaching methods[6] was added to the work of these two men. Because of these workers and others, today, Scandinavia is fortunate in having recognized the dimensions of the problem and has developed a demography of the disability. Even more important, however, dyslexia is recognized for what it is—a genetic disability that can be treated with success—and there is no social stigma attached to the problem. Would that we could say the same for America!

From time to time, in the United States, there has been an upsurge of concern and questioning about these children. In 1925, Dr. Samuel T. Orton[7] did research on the neurological implications of dyslexia. Later, inspired by Orton's work, Anna Gillingham and others perfected some tutorial teaching techniques for them. As a result, we now have the famous Gillingham Method[8] and The Orton Society,[9] both major professional forces in this country.

But dyslexia is a complicated, often extremely subtle problem, requiring professional diagnosis and help from several disciplines. As a result of these complexities, after each upsurge of concern there has always come a general dissipation of professional interest in the field, leaving a relatively few dedicated people to carry on the fight.

Another major deterrent to effective action has been that only in recent years have we realized the multi-disciplinary nature of the disability—the fact that, "The eventual prevention of dyslexia lies in medicine, the diagnosis in the realm of psychology, while the 'cure' is the responsibility of educators."[10] The idea that a child with a reading problem needs, indeed is entitled to, the skills of all three disciplines is relatively new even to the people who want most to help these children. This recognition of the necessity for a team-type approach to learning disorders has been a major breakthrough for all concerned, parent, child, doctor, diagnostician, and teacher. With it, has come interdiscipline communication and cooperation, and for the first time in history there is a growing feeling of partnership in attacking a problem in which all are involved.

Now that the lines of communication are open among the disciplines, it is necessary that the information available be given to the professional teacher and the non-professional parent. It is no longer enough for researchers and college professors, pediatricians and neurologists, psychologists and psychometrists, to know about these children; everyone who has a dyslexic child, knows one, or works with one should understand the nature of the disability, and the approaches to its diagnosis and treatment. Even the children themselves need to know.

One of the first things that all those who have contact with dyslexic children should know is that this is not a rare disability; these children are not very special cases, and are not limited in number. Firm figures on the number of children in the country who encounter serious difficulty in learning to read, for whatever reason, are hard to find, and the estimates differ with each expert. However, a widely accepted minimum figure is that ten percent of all school age children, of normal or above intelligence, fall into the general category of reading retardation due to genetic dyslexia.

The evidence is overwhelming too, that for every girl afflicted with genetic dyslexia, there are more than fifteen boys affected. It can therefore safely be considered primarily a male problem. The reason for this seems to be that the female, physiologically, is the superior of the two sexes. The fact that girls mature at a more rapid rate and seem less inclined to pick up familial or genetic weaknesses appears to have a bearing on the lower incidence of female dyslexia. Another interesting aspect of this problem, which comes purely from personal observation and is unsupported by research data, is that there seems to be no middle ground for girls—they are either mild cases and learn to compensate for their problems, or they are extremely severe cases and require twice as long and twice the usual amount of help to overcome their problems. On the other hand, boys run the complete gamut from mild through severe. This, however, is a personal observation that remains to be proven by research.

Many factors appear to contribute to the dyslexic child's disability. Among these, researchers feel that there are certain familial (family) characteristics that are present, in some combination, not only in the child himself, but also in his family tree. One must bear in mind that in this connection a child's family includes his parents, his grandparents, both paternal and maternal, his aunts and uncles, as well as his own brothers and sisters. The family must be considered in its genetic entirety.

Left-handedness, ambidexterity and language disorders are three prime characteristics. In the simplest, most general terms, these are the kind of questions that should be asked: Did father have trouble in the early grades of school? Does mother's sister stutter? Is grandfather's handwriting still barely legible? Is brother a southpaw? Does mother or father still have to stop for a moment to ponder which is the left or right hand, especially when either is over-tired? Can the child swim like a fish, but cannot pick up a dime easily? Does twenty-year-old sister still knock over glasses at the dinner table?

Of equal importance, diagnostically, is a second list of familial characteristics. These include:

Families who demonstrate an allergenic history. The food or chemical allergies, also the asthmatics in the relationship, must all come under suspicion when the child and his family are investigated.

Families with an over-all poor medical history. (This, of course, does not include those who suffer from disabilities due to poor nutrition.) The reference here is to areas such as hyper and hypo glycemia,[11] petit mal, thyroxine imbalances, even supernumerary teeth. In short, general familial medical weaknesses.

Families with the "twinning factor" in present or preceding generations. The incidence of twins in the country is one in every eighty-eight births. In a recent study covering sixty-five families of children with genetic dyslexia (a total of 809 births registered in three generations), the incidence of twinning was nearly 2½ twins born in every eighty-eight births—about 293 percent above the national average.[12] These findings point to the need for intensive basic research on the biology of twinning and the correlation to dyslexia, since this may throw new light on the genetic factors that relate to the problem.

Dyslexia is the least severe of the disorders on the continuum of learning disabilities. A child with uncomplicated genetic dyslexia is the closest to a totally normal/average child. He literally is just one step over the line—and it is this "almost normalcy" which makes dyslexia a diagnostic nightmare, and has multiplied the dyslexic's problems in the search for public recognition and action.

One step further down the learning disabilities continuum, we meet the complicated or *complex* genetic dyslexic. In the past, all too often, the complex case of dyslexia has been generally misclassified as "an emotional block to learning," or, in the last decade, as minimal brain damage. For these cases, given the mis-diagnosis, too often the efforts at remediation have been unsuccessful.

Complex dyslexia requires more intense clinical teaching, a more exact determination of the problem areas to be remediated, and, quite often, medication to help in the learning process. To meet the necessity for more detailed information, diagnostically and clinically, neurologists oftentimes will use an electroencephalogram (EEG) as a diagnostic "tool." It is standard procedure to induce the sleep necessary for an EEG by drugs; however, some pediatric neurologists are currently doing "natural sleep" electroencephalograms and are finding the diagnostic rewards well worth the extra effort involved.

What sets a complex dyslexic apart from a child with uncomplicated dyslexia? To answer this question, we must again go back to the family. In her book, "Dyslexia—Theory Into Practice,"[13] Frances K. McGlannan sets forth the theory of *neurologically vulnerable families*. "The infants born of these dyslexia families," she notes, "are especially susceptible to trauma or insult and . . . all of the presenting symptoms in a dyslexic child; those of defective visual perception, insufficient memory for symbols, reversals, etc., are secondary systemic disorders stemming from the basic genetic anomaly." With the advent of this neurologic vulnerability and genetic anomaly theory, the questions are being asked, *why a genetic anomaly,* and, *what other results come from the genetics involved?*

The promulgation of this theory and the important questions arising from it offer a new and firm pathway for investigation by the sciences concerning this genetic pattern. Researchers with whom I have talked seem to feel that McGlannan's Theory is a substantial contribution to the understanding of the complicated mosaic of genetic dyslexia.

What exactly constitutes trauma—insult—and how do they differ? Trauma is injury, usually brought about my mechanical means. Insult is a nature-precipitated affront to the organism involved, in this case the child. Either insult or trauma can be the result of the many minor or major problems which may arise during the natal period, at birth, or afterwards. It is not necessary to belabor the manner in which an infant or child may suffer trauma or insult—anoxia, spotting during pregnancy, forceps delivery, high fevers, are some of the factors that could play a role. Many times the exact event is never successfully identified. The point is that the dyslexic child seems to be more vulnerable to *results*—that "something" happened to this child, who, if born of a different genetic background probably would not have been affected. As a result, the child was taken the next step into complex dyslexia. This "something" did not cause demonstrable neurological damage; it did, however, *compound* the child's basic dyslexia.

How is it compounded? What are the differences in symptoms? Again, it is a question of degree—an intensification of the perceptual deficiencies, and additional behavior problems. It is here that the hyper or hypo kinetic behavior enters the diagnostic picture. Physically, these youngsters may vascillate between two types, the withdrawn day-dreamer or the hyperactive child. The withdrawn child is often called "dull, disinterested," or "impractical." Teachers will say, "he doesn't seem to care if his work is right or wrong; he certainly is smart enough, but I just can't seem to motivate him."

The hyperactive children are the type that occur most frequently. These are the "ants in the pants" children. Those who are "silly" or "immature for their age." In infancy, they are the screamers, the short sleep children, the jiggling leg, wiggling foot, tapping fingers children—the ones who literally run from one activity to another. Their attention is shorter in the classroom. When they know the answer to a question, they cannot resist blurting it out immediately. Their arms and legs are not comfortable in a seat or in one position for very long. In many ways their hyperactivity is charming. The children seem to be so very full of life. They seem to race from one experience to another. But, the uncharming aspect is that they rarely finish any one project started. As they get older, and the failures and punishments mount up, the emotional overlay gets thicker, they increasingly will have catastrophic reactions to the simplest event. They may lash out in response to even a simple instruction.

So much of the clinical terminology used here is also used in reference to the child with minimal brain damage and/or dysfunction syndrome, that it is difficult to differentiate exactly between them solely from a description of the symptoms. Testing and analysis of test patterns will, in most cases, successfully identify the proper category.

There are two ways of giving actual help to these complex cases. One, of course, as with all learning disorders, is the proper educational remediation necessary for the problem. A child becomes an achiever rather than a non-achiever. Second, in certain cases, though not all, there are medications which will help the child with his inner controls, lengthen his attention span in the classroom, and generally "soften" him down. Much, I might add, to the relief of his parents, teachers, and himself. A doctor, most often a neurologist, must, as with all medication, make the decision as to what to use, what the dosage should be, and how long the medication should be continued. He will more than likely ask the parents to keep detailed notes and be extremely accurate with dosage timing. This is absolutely necessary to do complete justice to the child and the medication.

Genetic dyslexia results in a child being unable to read. Why? What is it that makes it impossible for a child of high intelligence to learn those academic skills that his less capable contemporaries master with comparative ease?

Over the years, a great deal has been learned about how the brain and nervous system function. Yet much remains to be discovered before this complicated process can be fully explained, and old theories are constantly being brought into question. For our purposes, however, a brief and admittedly oversimplified view of the brain and neural system will suffice.

The brain is divided into two hemispheres which control human thought, action and reaction. It is normal for either the left or right hemisphere of the brain to be dominant. This means that either the left or right hemisphere is the *controlling* one for both. The majority of people have a left hemisphere dominance which makes them right-handed; lesser numbers have a right hemisphere dominance and are left-handed. Others never achieve a true dominance, or it comes later in life than is normal. An infant is born without cerebral dominance, but by age two, usually, dominance is forming. As the child ages, the dominance becomes firmly established for life. When it does not, a flood of problems seem to follow. Problems which involve laterality, directionality, and the carry-through areas of horizontal spatial relations.

Humans normally make their dominant hemisphere do most of the work. Even though lack of dominance or mixed dominance can cause some severe problems, it is interesting that dyslexic children in this category almost seem to be trying to use both sides of their brains simultaneously—making full and complete use of their brains, not just a lazy side and a working side.

Cerebral dominance once again brings up the subject of the familial characteristics of genetic dyslexia since our hemispheric dominance makes us left-handed, right-handed, or ambidextrous. It is clear that the importance of inheritance keeps reasserting itself.

The most complicated function of the brain—this most complex of all human organs—is thinking. Thinking involves a multitude of factors that, with considerable accuracy, science is able to list separately. However, if any one factor is missing to any large degree, for any reason, we then have faulty or inconsistent thinking.

When we think, we use sensations, percepts, visual images, concepts, memory, all interwoven in some indefinable manner which creates the end product—thought. The simplest level of thinking is that of a child's, only because a child does not consciously want to think. That is to say, a young child does not set out to think; rather, he thinks in response to some need. Most thinking done by children is automatic, and is based on limited past experience, training, feelings, and needs or desires. As we age, our thought processes become more sophisticated and involve reasoning. And some individuals continue this process of development to the level of critical thinking and original discovery.

Most often in daily life we operate at the thinking level of judgment, memory, visual image, and concrete data sorting. However, to be truly successful we must use concepts and percepts in the more difficult process of inferential reasoning. A simple example of inferential reasoning would be to listen to one-half of a telephone conversation and deduce from that half what the whole conversation was about.

To a very large degree inferential thinking depends upon the ability to see or recognize the whole, even though only a part is available for inspection. Inferential thinking is based on an orderly array of concepts—which in turn are based on complete percepts. The dyslexic child gets into trouble at the "perceptual" level of thinking. As a result of these perceptual inadequacies he has a problem integrating parts into a whole. This, in turn, can release a "behavioral chain of events" causing the child to appear stupid or stubborn. If adults could accept the fact that these children often miss the "forest for the trees"—that they often cannot integrate the parts into a meaningful whole—especially before adolescence, many parent-child or teacher-child clashes would be avoided.

With maturation, the older dyslexic child usually learns to compensate for his perceptual inadequacies and uses his strong conceptual ability to bolster his faulty percepts. *And, it is this eventual conceptual strength that differentiates the dyslexic child from the minimally brain-damaged or psychotic child.*

Thinking and reasoning are necessary to true learning. Yet, it is possible to "learn" by rote memory alone. The fault with rote memory learning is that eventually something will happen to point out the lack of true learning.

I know of one mother who discovered her son's problem in a simple but startling manner. It was her practice to read with her son over the weekends. They would sit together, she holding the book for him while he read aloud and she turned the pages—a time honored form of "togetherness" for mother and child. The boy had been doing moderately well in first grade and was now reading well for his mother. He was half-way through the book, a typical soft-cover primer, when his mother became distracted, forgetting to turn the next two pages for him. Suddenly she realized that, even though she had stopped turning pages, he had not stopped reading! He was continuing as if she had indeed turned those two pages, *reading what was not there to read.* A whole book completely memorized for mother and teacher. The boy's mother checked the vocabulary level of the reader and purchased a different reader at the same level. When the child was asked to read the same words placed in a different order, in another book, he could barely stumble through four words. More than two-thirds of the first grade had passed and the boy had a sight reading vocabulary of four words—and neither the teacher nor mother had realized it! He had substituted memory for reading.

Paradoxically, another dyslexic child may have trouble with his memory for visual images. He can seemingly learn the image, but has trouble retaining it. The dilemma of dyslexia is the apparent inconsistencies. It is almost as if dyslexia is caused by short-circuits, but each child has shorted in different areas, in different degrees, and in different combinations of circuits.

But no matter what specific form the disability takes for a particular child, the one word which best describes the dyslexic child's major problem area is perception. *Perception is the key to reading.*

Marianne Frostig[14] describes and analyzes the five areas of *visual* perception in the following manner and explains the resulting disabilities as they appear in a child:

"PERCEPTION OF POSITION IN SPACE

"Perception of position in space may be defined as perception of the relationship of an object to the observer. Spatially, a person is always the center of his own world and perceives objects as being behind, before, above, below, or to the side of himself. A child with disabilities in his perception of position in space is handicapped in many ways. His visual world is distorted, he may be clumsy or hesitant in his movements, and he has difficulty in understanding what is meant by the words designating spatial position, such as in, out, up, down, before, behind, left, or right. His difficulties become most apparent when he is faced with academic tasks, because letters, words, phrases, numbers, and pictures appear to him distorted and confusing. To give the simplest and most frequently encountered example, a child with difficulties in perceiving the proper position of an object in relation to his body is likely to perceive b as d, p as q, on as no, 24 as 42, and so on. This, of course, makes it difficult for the child to learn to read, write, spell, and do arithmetic.

"PERCEPTION OF SPATIAL RELATIONSHIPS

"The perception of spatial relationships is the ability of an observer to perceive the position of two or more objects in relation to himself and in relation to each other. This ability to perceive spatial relationships develops later than, and grows out of, the simpler one of perceiving the position of an object in relation to one's body. Perception of spatial relationships is more complicated than the other perceptual processes. Disabilities in the perception of spatial relationships makes impossible the proper perception of the sequence of letters in a word, so that a child may read the word 'string' as 'stirring', or spell it 'siturg'. In attempting to solve arithmetic problems, he may be unable to remember the sequence of processes involved in problems of long division or fail to perceive the relative position of the digits in problems of multiplication. A myriad of other tasks, such as model making, map reading, understanding graphs, and learning systems of measurement, to name a few, may be equally difficult for him.

"PERCEPTUAL CONSTANCY

"Perceptual constancy is the ability to perceive an object as possessing invariant properties, such as shape, position and size in spite of the variability of the impression on the sensory surface (sensory surface= eyes, ears, hands, nose). This means that where constancy of shape is concerned, two or three-dimensional forms are recognized as belonging to certain categories of shapes, whatever their size, color texture, mode of representation, or the angle seen by the perceiver. A person with adequate perceptual constancy will recognize a cube seen from an oblique angle as a cube, even though the retinal image differs from that presented by the cube when seen squarely from the front.

"Three aspects of objects besides shape that may be visually perceived as constant are size, brightness and color.

"Size constancy is the ability to perceive and recognize the actual size of an object regardless of factors that may change its apparent size. For example, a person familiar with the standard size-football perceives one that is a field's length away as being the same size as if it were in his hands, despite the diminutive retinal image.

"Brightness constancy involves the ability to judge the lightness or whiteness of an object regardless of the amount of light reflected by it. A piece of white paper is perceived as white, even though the light that illuminates it may be unusually dim or bright.

"Color constancy involves the ability to recognize colors regardless of background or conditions of illumination.

"There is, as yet, no conclusive theory of how visual constancy is developed and of how or why different stimuli arouse the same percept, but obviously learning and experience are important factors. Of these four aspects of visual constancy—shape, size, color, and brightness—the first two are the most important for a person's adequate orientation in his environment. A color-blind person is only minimally handicapped, and even a totally blind person who has learned to judge size and shape through other than his visual senses can recognize his environment and adapt his actions to it. On the other hand, adequate perception of shape and size, whether obtained through visual experiences or through kinesthesis and touch, is essential if a person's physical surroundings are to appear relatively stable and predictable to him. A child with poorly developed shape and size constancy is not only likely to be made anxious by the general unreliability of appearances of his world, but he will also have major academic difficulties. Although he may learn to recognize a number, letter, or word, when he sees it in a particular form or context, he may be quite unable to recognize the same symbol when it is presented in a different manner. Such a child is constantly deceived by his senses. A word he knows well in one form or color or size or type of writing, or in conjunction with certain other words, may appear new to him when presented in another form, color, size or context. For a child with such a disability, learning to read, to work with symbols in any way, is most difficult.

"VISUAL-MOTOR COORDINATION

"Visual-motor coordination is the ability to coordinate vision with movements of the body or with movements of a part or parts of the body. Whenever a sighted person reaches for something, his hands are guided by his vision. Whenever he runs, jumps, kicks a ball, or steps over an obstacle, his eyes direct the movement of his feet. In such everyday activities as getting dressed, making a bed, carrying a tray, entering a car, or sitting down at the table, the eyes and the whole body work together. The smooth accomplishment of nearly every action depends upon adequate eye-motor coordination. This visual-motor coordination is also important to space perception and planning motor sequences. A child with defective or poorly developed visual-motor coordination is indeed handicapped in trying to adjust to the varied demands of his environment.

Though his academic learning may be less affected by a disability in the visual-motor area than by disabilities in other areas of visual perception, he will certainly have difficulty in learning how to write.

"FIGURE-GROUND PERCEPTION

"To understand figure-ground perception and its importance, it is essential to remember that we perceive most clearly those things to which we turn our attention. The human brain is so organized that it can select from the mass of incoming stimuli a limited number of stimuli, which become the center therefore of attention. These selected stimuli—auditory, tactile, olfactory and visual—form the figure in the person's perceptual field, while the majority of stimuli form a dimly perceived ground. For instance, a little girl bouncing and catching a ball in a play yard has her attention directed to the ball, which is the figure in the scene she perceives. Since other features of the play yard—sandbox, teeter-totter, flower bed, toy pail—are not the focus of her attention they form the dimly perceived ground, of which she is probably only sufficiently aware to avoid colliding with them. The figure is that part of the field of perception that is the center of the observer's attention. When the observer shifts his attention to something else, the new focus of attention becomes the figure, and the previous figure recedes into the ground. If the little girl puts down her ball and picks up the pail instead, the pail becomes the figure in her field of vision and the ball becomes part of the ground. Another important fact with regard to the figure-ground perception is that an object cannot be accurately perceived unless it is perceived in relation to its ground. The little girl would be unable to perceive the exact position of her bouncing ball and would have great difficulty in catching it if she did not see it constantly in relation to the ground formed by the surface of the play yard and adjacent objects. An observer can accurately judge the distance of an object, its size and even its shape, only if he perceives it in the proper relationship to its ground. A child with poor figure-ground discrimination of perception characteristically appears to be inattentive and disorganized. This is because his attention tends to jump to any stimulus that intrudes upon him—to something that moves or glitters or is brightly colored, for instance—no matter how irrelevant it may be to what he should be doing. Alternatively, his difficulty in screening out obtrusive stimuli may prevent him from separating himself from a particular stimulus, even though he ought to shift his attention to some other figure for purposeful activity. The child may be unable to draw a straight line between boundaries because one of the boundaries captures his attention and he directs his pencil towards and along it. Other difficulties arise in transferring the focus of attention from one stimulus to another and results in scanning problems. A child with poor figure-ground perception will appear to be careless in his work because he is unable to find his place on a page, skips sections, cannot find the word he is seeking in the dictionary, and is unable to solve familiar problems when they are presented on crowded pages, since he cannot pick out the relevant details. A typical complaint about such children, at home and at school, is that they seem unable to find anything, even when it is right in front of their noses."

The dyslexic child may have problems in any one or all five of the visual perception areas. Some, the visual-motor coordination areas, for example, affect him the least at early ages and not at all in daily functioning, but when he starts to learn to write his lack of visual-motor coordination becomes a major handicap. For others, figure-ground perception is consistently a problem.

It is obvious that all five areas of visual perception are significantly concerned with the perception of symbols. And, the ability to read depends upon the ability to perceive symbols. Our alphabet is really made of symbols—geometrical symbols—squares, triangles, circles, and straight lines.

Visual perception, however, has nothing to do with the eyes as organisms. Perfectly healthy eyes can still be unable to form correct or complete perception. On the other hand, a vision problem, due to ocular deficiencies, may be corrected with glasses, but the child will still have perceptual problems.

Proper visual perception and perceptual constancy means that a child who looks at a circle plus a straight line,○+|, circle to the left, equals a "d." This "d" may then be used in a multitude of words, and these words may then be used in a variety of sentences. But the "d," no matter where it is, is still "d." Also, the "d" remains "d" no matter what type style or size it is written in, no matter how many letters or words it is in the midst of. To paraphrase, a rose is a rose, whether in a vase or on a rose bush. The word "dog" is "dog," whether it appears on a flash card used by the teacher, is used in a book or newspaper, or is being put together by the student with individual cut-out letters.

If these five areas of visual perception are so difficult to achieve and have so much effect on a dyslexic child—and they have nothing to do with faulty vision—how then can a child ever learn to read if he is disabled in these areas? Faulty perception, in any of the five areas, can be improved, if not eventually corrected, by a carefully graded program to hasten the development of the child's perception. With the dyslexic child, faulty perception most often seems to be the result of his neurological immaturity. As we will see in the chapter on teaching, educators with special techniques build perceptual pathways into the child, and he learns. I fairly quake to make such a simple sentence out of what is probably one of the most complicated, tedious, and highly technical forms of education there is. However, Frostig gives us research and exercises in the areas of visual perception via her program for perceptual development.[15] This program of graduated exercises is designed to help the younger child gain visual perception and it may be considered a prime example of a fine technique. And yet, to look at it, or administer it to a child, it seems simple, and tedious, but—it works.

Another major area and form of perception that must be carefully considered with the dyslexic child is *auditory* perception. Remember the name—Specific Language Disability—mentioned earlier. If a child cannot properly perceive language as it is spoken to him, he cannot speak the language correctly, and therefore he cannot relate language sounds to the written symbols. He also cannot learn to blend the different symbol-sounds together. These auditory perception problems carry over into all phases of reading, writing and spelling. It is a question of input and output—what goes into the child through his ears is integrated and sorted, then comes out through his mouth or hand. Even though the original "input" may have been accurate, as it passes through the auditory system into the brain and out again, it is in some manner jumbled and in the split second it takes for input to become output, it becomes incorrect. Imperfect auditory perception is usually evidenced by poor auditory discrimination and this inability to discriminate between sounds demonstrates itself in very subtle and seemingly minor ways. However, what at age four or five is a minor problem, at age ten or twelve becomes acute.

The child with poor auditory perception is the child who retains his "baby talk" longer than other children, the child who constantly asks "what did you say?" Often, he will mimic, as if trying to sort out the sounds he has heard by repeating them. And, most especially, in a situation where the child is under stress, he has trouble expressing himself. In the case of auditory perception, as with visual perception, there is nothing organically wrong with the child's hearing.

Since the two main avenues of learning in the classroom are the eyes and ears, lack of auditory perception is an especially serious matter for the student because the visual perception problems are more quickly and easily recognized. It is here, in the classroom, that auditory discrimination becomes most important, and it is here the child will feel the loss the most.

In school, a child learns to "blend" sounds. This means that he takes one sound, slides another sound into the first, and arrives at a complete, new sound. For example—a child takes "at," adds "p," (he slides the "p" to "at") and comes up with "pat." He has blended sounds. Seems simple, doesn't it? A dyslexic child, however, can make a number of mistakes with this one three-letter word. He can reverse the "p" and get "q," he can place the beginning "p" at the end and get "tap," he can miss the sound and say "pee-at" or "pee-ut"—all this with just three letters and two sounds! Obviously, to the classroom teacher, auditory perception and discrimination are of vital importance in teaching a child.

In addition to these major areas of perception, there are other problems which may affect or hinder a dyslexic child. Among the most important are: *laterality, directionality,* and the resulting problems in *horizontal spatial relations*.

Laterality is the inner sense of one's own body symmetry—the ability to know automatically, from within oneself, leftness, rightness, or two-sidedness. It allows a child to perform smoothly with either hand or leg, or both.

Directionality is the projection of laterality into space—the awareness of left, right, up, down, in front of, and behind, in the world around us. It is the ability of the child to know when an object is to the left or right of himself. Later, he develops an awareness of the position of an object in relation to the position of another object, i.e., the chair is to my left, the table is to my right, therefore, the chair is to the right of the table. This is horizontal spatial relations.

Here is an example of how these areas work:

Laterality – in bowling, a child picks up a bowling ball in his right hand. He knows he has picked up the ball and he knows the ball is in his right hand.

Directionality – he then bowls the ball. He knows he has taken the ball, pulled it behind his body, then forward on the right side of his body, on out in front of him, and then has let go of the ball.

Spatial Relations – he watches the released ball go down the bowling lane, strike the pins, and move on out of sight.

Try to rethink this example, placing yourself in the position of a child with disturbed laterality or directionality. Not only would you be unable to know for sure in which hand you held the ball (you would just know you held the ball), you would be unable to judge your rate of swing or timing for release of the ball. Then you could not correct a mistake in form because you would not be able to tell accurately whether you bowled too far to the left or to the right of the pins. Under these circumstances, bowling wouldn't be much fun – would it?

The development of laterality and directionality produces deep automatic brain responses. When these responses are not automatic, when a child must consciously strive to make them function, it places a terrible burden on him.

And, when these automatic responses are interrupted, the resulting confusion has a direct effect on learning, most especially reading. The d-b reversals, writing, perceptual constancy, all require laterality and directionality to some degree. If a child cannot perceive left or right, up or down, how then can he "hold" the alphabet and learn to use it properly? How, indeed, can a teacher teach him when she is working against such odds?

An additional problem area for a dyslexic child may be his fine muscle control. His major muscles will respond easily and faultlessly when he swims, or plays baseball, but when he picks up a pencil to write he is in trouble. In fact, some educators say that teaching a dyslexic child cursive writing is one of the most difficult hurdles to overcome for both the teacher and child.

In this area, the child's rapid rhythmic movements will be slowed. For instance, if he holds both hands in front of him with his thumbs and index fingers touching and his other fingers raised, and he then attempts to open and close (flutter) both thumbs and index fingers rapidly at the same time, the flutter will be uneven or slow. Fine muscle control, with its primary effect on handwriting, is a great problem for the older child, as well as the younger. The younger child can use an extra large pencil or thick crayon. But, with the older student it is a different problem. Today, much of our education for the older student is based on writing rapidly in a classroom situation. Students are required to take lecture notes, and are given tests where neatness is important to the grade given. In short, a large amount of neatness is required of them. When this is coupled with a dyslexic's problems in spelling, the combination can make the difference between a passing or failing grade. In this situation, the real plight of the dyslexic is that if he were given the opportunity to take the same test verbally, or if he did not lose credit for spelling or poor writing, he would pass with flying colors. So often he knows the answers, is able to do the work, but is unable to spell the words correctly, or write them legibly.

Before we look at the symptoms of specific dyslexia as they appear in an individual child, let us review the fundamental elements which have been discussed thus far.

A developmental or complex case of genetic dyslexia must encompass two basic and primary criteria: these criteria are necessary as it is obvious that not all reading retardation is the result of genetic dyslexia.

First, the child must be average or above in intellectual capacity, and there must be no demonstrable evidence of brain damage, retardation, or psychopathology. (There are diagnostic techniques which enable the person testing a child to take into consideration poor or inadequate teaching and give a considered opinion about a child with a depressed I.Q.)

Second, the totality of the child's family history must be taken into consideration. His familial background must include one or more (preferably more) of the following: learning problems, language disorders, left-handedness, ambidexterity, "the twinning factor," and the "family vulnerability" syndrome. (These latter two items must be considered only as adjunct confirmation symptoms until further research studies are completed.) It must also be remembered, a child's family means his blood family, adopted children cannot be considered under the familial characteristics.

Although it is imperative that parents have full information about learning disorders, I must strongly emphasize that home diagnosis is perilous. Just because your mother's father was left-handed and a school drop-out, and your child does poorly in arithmetic, do not jump to conclusions—he may simply hate arithmetic.

We know now what most of the terminology of problem areas means and how dyslexia affects a child and his ability to learn to read. So now let us look at how these symptoms may appear in an individual child.

In researching the literature, there are many lists given of the symptoms that appear in an individual child. Because of its conciseness, I personally prefer Marion Fenwick Stuart's description of the symptoms of dyslexia presented in her book, "Neurophysiological Insights Into Teaching."[16] In this book, she speaks of the individual child and states:

"Among the characteristics which these children may exhibit singly, or in combination of degrees of difficulty varying from mild to extreme are:

"1] Poor visual perception and memory for words. In spite of normal vision, even after repeated effort, they cannot remember the words they have studied. Recognition is either absent or poor. Reproduction of words (spelling) may be phonetic because the visual memory for words is so uncertain.

"2] Poor auditory memory for words or for individual sounds in words. In spite of normal hearing, short auditory span may show up in speech or spelling or both. Many cannot distinguish between close gradations of sound.

"3] Reversal and confusion in direction. Right and left confusion may produce reversals of words, syllables or letters in reading, writing or speech. Examples are: "was" for "saw," "sowro" for "sorrow," "b" for "d," "p" for "q." (Hermann labels the confusion between letters "rotations" [b for d], and the reversed sequence of letters and syllables "reversals" [was for saw].) Not only may the confusion produce reversals, but also such reversals are usually more numerous and persist much longer than in other persons – far beyond what is considered to be normal learning time. Up and down confusion may produce inversion of letters, such as "m" for "w", or "p" for "d". Several other possibilities are: oral mix-up of whole sentences, mirror writing of sentences, or transposition of numbers.

"4] Poor recall for reproduction of simple figures. On being shown a picture of a simple figure such as the following ——————□, there may be inability to recall or reproduce this with any degree of accuracy – after removal of the picture (a series of pictures is used).*

"5] Ambidexterity. Uncertainty as to which hand is more comfortable to use may continue – a slowness in establishing habitual right or left-handedness. Or the use of the same hand for the same task may be inconsistent.

"6] Clumsiness, poor coordination. Early clumsiness in learning any gross physical act may be present, and coordination required for achieving finer motor skills, such as game skills, may show up later on as below average. They may, however, perform well in large muscle sports, such as swimming or football.

"7] Poor ability to reproduce rhythm sequences. Reproducing short rhythm patterns by tapping may be difficult.

"8] Speech disorders. Stuttering, lisping or lack of oral facility with language may be present or speech development may have been slow."

Stuart also cites two other factors as being of interest – hyperactivity and perceptual confusion resulting in poor Gestalt function. However, later research and literature indicate that these two factors become more important when one enters the realm of complex dyslexia.

It is obvious that genetic or developmental dyslexia is, even in its mildest form, an extremely complicated learning disorder in children. The question must then be asked, what happens to the child whose disability is never recognized or diagnosed? The feeling among clinical workers in the field seems to be that the dyslexia families, generally speaking, are high on the phylogenetic scales. Often, the children, even with their prob-

* See testing chapter for a series which may be used by parent, teacher or pediatrician.

lems, will have intelligence that will carry them through and help them learn to compensate for their handicap. Added to this, they are sensitive to their surrounding world, they seem to have an "inner awareness" of themselves that is unique. In fact, all things considered, they are unusual children, in the 'best' sense of the word. Even their problems are unusual.

But, what happens to the dyslexic child who, without problems, would be only average, and *with* problems is below average – the child who struggles his way through school, never really achieving? This situation becomes particularly acute for teenagers. By then, there may be such a thick emotional overlay, as the result of the years of frustration, failure and unhappiness, that it is difficult to tell which is the primary problem, dyslexia or emotion.

The emotional disorganization which comes to a child suffering with specific dyslexia can, at times, be overwhelming. When he is confronted by his parents, teachers, members of his peer group, in fact, a whole world that seems to feel he is deliberately "not trying", he must eventually react.

One must think at the child s level to understand what is involved when he is faced with teachers who do not understand why, in spite of his obvious intelligence, he will not learn. When he must cope with parents who feel that they have failed because he seems to misbehave wantonly. When he must live with a peer group that rejects him and sees, but does not understand, his great unhappiness with life.

Dr. L. P. Shirley,[17] writing in the California Medical Journal, summarizes the dyslexic child's reactions as follows:

"The child finds himself in a dilemma which he cannot understand and from which he can find no satisfactory avenues of escape. He finds himself the victim of concern, anxiety, and resentment, and perhaps punitive measures, with no way of finding relief, status or approval. He begins to feel alarmingly different from his classmates. He loses self-confidence and self-esteem. He may feel rejected, look down upon and disliked. In defense, he may break out with aggressive, hostile behavior. Or, he may become dominated by chronic anxiety, acquiring a variety of nervous habits, withdrawing from social activities, resorting to physical complaints or indulging excessively in day-dreaming. He may eventually succumb to defeatism, losing interest in school work, paying little attention to class activities and refusing to try. The longer he remains unable to progress in reading, the more deep-seated becomes his emotional disturbance and also his aversion to trying."

If we face the complexities of this issue frankly, we must realize that the fate of the dyslexic child depends far less on the severity of his problems than it does on our recognition and understanding. Even if the child were never to receive remedial help for his handicap; but if only those around him were sympathetically aware of the nature of his disability, this understanding would do much towards stopping the spiraling of the condition. Hermann says, "the most important thing is for all teachers, psychologists and doctors to realize the existence of these problems and their considerable dimensions."

To this list, we must add parents and the involved child.

4

DYSLEXIA CASE HISTORIES

THE FOLLOWING HISTORIES are composites based on actual cases. Of course, the names and locales have been changed. In some instances the long tedious detail has been shortened for easier reading. What *isn't* included is the heartbreak, the broken marriages, and the waste of childhood that came about as the result of the failures described here. But don't judge the adults involved too harshly. To most adults, our children are our prime incentive for continuing life's everday struggles and, when we fail with them, or they fail us, we flaggelate ourselves—and our children.

□ □ □

Jimmy started the first grade in September at age six years, one month. During his early years, his rate of development was a little slower in a few areas, but his parents checked from time to time with The Gesell Institute's Child Behavior Guide and when he didn't mature quite as fast as the average, they were assured by their pediatrician that children develop at different rates, as was clearly indicated in the book; that there was no real problem or cause for alarm.

When he entered school, most of his baby talk was gone. He did, however, still say "levermind" for "nevermind" and "put" for "pat." Nothing serious. He was a bright, outgoing child.

After the first two weeks of school his teacher said that Jimmy was going to be a leader of his class. In fact, he and another boy had quickly gone into competition for that unspoken leadership that emerges in all classrooms and neighborhoods. At the end of the first six weeks grading period, Jimmy's teacher sent a note home asking his mother to go over the alphabet with Jimmy at night as he did not seem to be able to "pull" the letters out when he needed them. So for the next week, Jimmy's mother worked with him every night and in the morning, just before school, he would be able to repeat the letters of the alphabet for her. With this accomplished, mother stopped the home lessons. In about three weeks Jimmy's teacher sent home one of his alphabet worksheets, along with a note asking why mother hadn't followed through on the home help. The work sheet looked like this:

Noʌ. 1Ɛ 19ƨƨ

My NAMe IZ JIMY

Before long a parent conference was requested. The teacher told Jimmy's parents it seemed that one day, especially in the morning when he was fresh, he would know the letters and the sounds they had studied. The next day he wouldn't. Of even greater concern to the teacher was that Jimmy was rapidly losing his place in peer group. His classmates were now reading in their first primer books, but Jimmy was unable to read or pronounce his words properly. Naturally, the other children in the class were beginning to make fun of him. His arithmetic was correct—except when he reversed his numbers and 2 became Ƨ. There were no other problems. Jimmy was well behaved, but the teacher did feel that "something was missing"—either in her, the child, or the home environment. Mr. and Mrs. E. agreed to work with him at home during the next six weeks.

Now a time of misery began for both Jimmy and his parents. His father could not understand why any son of his should not be able to learn the alphabet and was very inclined to blame his wife for "keeping Jimmy a baby too long." As a result, he didn't "understand his responsibilities" and "buckle down." A big order for a little boy, especially when daddy made it plain that he felt he was just a "six-year-old goof off." Mr. E. was not an unreasonable man. It would be difficult for any parent to understand why an obviously intelligent son could not function in, of all places, the first grade!

By mid-February, Jimmy was still not really reading. His parents lived in a state of almost constant battle over him. As one pushed and punished the child, the other was forced into the position of protecting and defending him.

Jimmy now hated school. He was beginning to retreat into his own private world since his two public worlds, school and home, were crumbling around his ears. The only time he was happy was when he was playing. The E's lived in Florida and Jimmy had learned to swim at an early age—and he loved it. He now wanted to spend all of his time in the pool—the pool, and his skill as a swimmer, became his refuge and sanctuary. He no longer was a leader in school, not even a good follower. At night his teacher went home and worried about what she was doing wrong.

Another conference was arranged and even though it was unusual to send a first grader to the school system's guidance department unless there was obvious impairment, Jimmy was referred. The guidance counselor explained that Jimmy was probably one of the "late bloomers" and that he would grow out of his problems. In the meantime, the parents were told to try to take the achievement pressures off of themselves and Jimmy. Give him time to grow, mature, come along at his own pace. His teacher was told to stop worrying—"he'll come along in the second grade." The school principal was advised to give him a social promotion. His tests showed him to be intellectually capable of the work, therefore it was felt certain that he would begin to progress "soon," and there certainly was no need to punish him for being "young."

This seemed to be sound, logical advice. All of the concerned adults followed it. Jimmy, unfortunately, couldn't. He stumbled through the second and third grades, never really achieving. By the fourth grade, he was a bitter, confused little boy. In his heart, he knew he was not stupid and, yet, he still had to struggle so very hard to make any headway in school. His parents could no longer hide their disappointment in him and in themselves. His whole world was permeated with a sense of useless struggle and frustration.

Jimmy never did "catch up." He went on to flunk several grades, ran away from home, was brought back, given psychiatric treatment, and at age seventeen, in the tenth grade, gave up for the last time. He quit school and is now working as a grocery clerk waiting to be called into the Army—if he can pass the induction tests.

Jimmy's I.Q., even with his problems, was 116—above average. What a waste, a sad, sad waste.

□ □ □

Danny, age nine, physical health excellent, I.Q. superior, was the third of four children. After three years in public school, Danny's world was truly chaotic. Educationally speaking, he suffered from severe reading retardation, and medically speaking, hyperkinetic behavior—but with a negative electroencephalogram. During the first two grades, he was always behind in his class, in the lowest reading group, and considered by his teacher to be a "problem child." By grade three, he began to feel that it wasn't worth trying because if he did well one day, his teacher would remark to the class that "Danny has decided he will join us in class today children, isn't that nice of him?" But his teacher should not be blamed for her lack of understanding. Danny was difficult to handle. One day he was the perfect student, the next, a whirlwind of disruptive activity, and then, for a day or two, a day-dreamer. The teacher was only human.

Danny's parents tried to be understanding and helpful, but his increasing irritability with his sisters and brothers, his emotional outbursts over minor matters, his growing rejection of controls—whether imposed with love or as punishment—coupled with his poor academic progress, triggered within the family circle serious consequences. The family began to operate around Danny, avoiding, at all costs, head-on collisions with him. And his teacher had adopted similar tactics at school.

Avoiding the problem, of course, was not the answer. It only confirmed Danny's image of himself as unloved, stupid, and a failure. But, Danny was not really stupid. His very intelligence made him aware of his family's rejection of him as a family member.

One day, Danny and his mother were shopping in the downtown area and they became separated. Danny wandered around for more than two hours, becoming more and more confused and frightened. When finally found by a policeman, Danny, age nine, could not tell him his correct address or telephone number. He kept reversing the digits. Nor could he write the information for the police, his handwriting was undecipherable. But, the most heartbreaking aspect was that Danny didn't *want* to tell the police who he belonged to or where he lived. He had decided that his mother had deliberately lost him because she no longer wanted him around. The police had to wait for Danny's mother to come to them.

Danny's attitude was horrifying to his parents, but in many ways his reasoning was logical. He had taken the information available to him—rejection by his parents and school—and reached the decision that he was no longer useful, desired, or needed by his world. And, at that stage, there was probably more than a grain of truth to this as far as his parents were concerned.

The evening of Danny's lost day, his parents decided he must go to a psychologist for help with his "emotional problems." In many ways it was a relief to his parents when the psychologist, after testing, diagnosed his problem as dyslexia, genetic in nature, with an emotional overlay, which he (the psychologist) felt sure would be completely alleviated with the proper and specialized scholastic help a dyslexic child needs.

Danny was sent to a private school that specialized in children with learning problems of his type. The school recommended psychotherapy for him as an adjunct to their program.

Nearly three years later, Danny is a different child. He is now a bright eyed, outgoing boy who is achieving in public school, is secure in his family's love, and ready to compete at a moment's notice with other boys his age. His parents are aware that with each new phase of Danny's development, they will all have some problems to face, but that these are mainly problems of logistics. As an example, when Danny is sixteen and wants to learn to drive, he will need help so that he will not turn left when he should turn right—in other words, he will probably wear a ring on his left hand. Try as he may, his handwriting will always be terrible, so he is learning to type instead. He has learned that if he doesn't understand a situation clearly immediately, he must ask questions so that he will. He has a bright, hopeful future. He will be able to use his superior intelligence to live a "normal," happy, productive life.

"We define the interjacent child as one who is in-between, marginal or weak but not altogether deficient in his aptitudes and the use of these aptitudes for successful learning. . . . These hazy defects and deficiencies are apparent in various modalities, sensory, neuromuscular, intellectual, social and other."

Edgar A. Doll, Ph.D.
Clinical Psychologist

5

MINIMAL BRAIN DYSFUNCTION

WHEN WE ENTER the area of brain dysfunction we are concerned only with the minimally handicapped child. This is the child who is intellectually capable, but due to some form of trauma is "different" from other children—the child who can function if the correct teaching techniques are used to overcome his perceptual difficulties and he is given guidance and taught inner controls for his conceptual and behavioral problems.

Often, as with the dyslexic, there is no suspicion of a serious problem with a child until he enters school. His mother may consider him a "holy terror" or "all boy," always into things, at times extremely difficult to handle. She may wonder why he reacts to situations in a certain manner, why he seemingly can trip on an eyelash, why he is always losing his belongings, why he forgets from one minute to the next—or his lack of self-control will bother her. But these manifestations are not serious—to a busy mother they are more bothersome than anything else.

It is when the child enters the world of the classroom that his "differences" will be more apparent and become a handicap.

Dr. Sam D. Clements[18] gives us an excellent definition of "minimal brain dysfunction" as we use the phrase here. He states that this term "refers to children of near average, average or above average general intelligence with certain learning or behavioral disabilities ranging from mild to severe, which are associated with deviations of function of the central nervous system. These deviations may manifest themselves by various combinations of impairment in perception, conceptualization, language, memory and control of attention, impulse or motor function. These aberrations may arise from genetic variations, biochemical irregularities, perinatal brain insults or other illnesses or injuries sustained during the years which are critical for the development and maturation of the central nervous system, or from other organic causes as yet unknown. The definition also allows for the possibility that early severe sensory deprivation could result in central nervous system alterations which may be permanent. *During the school years, a variety of learning disabilities is the most prominent manifestation of the condition which can be designated by this term.*" (author's italics)

No attempt will be made here to cover all of the possible sources of brain dysfunction beyond a brief listing of the more generally known causes of trauma. It must be borne in mind that in many cases the "why" is never known. However, medical knowledge today usually makes it possible for doctors to give a qualified opinion as to whether or not a child falls within the range of the pattern for this syndrome.

The most commonly known causes or etiologies are: premature birth, anoxia, Rh factors, fetal injury, or illnesses with concomitant high fevers. Usually, when it is believed that the occurrence happened during the natal period it is called *insult;* at birth most often it is called *trauma;* and, after birth, most often the term used is *damage*. From the time an embryo is conceived, until death, we are all subject to the possibility of brain damage. However, Dr. Nicholson J. Eastman[19] states, "In the majority of cases, *at least two thirds,* something unfavorable to the fetus takes place sometime between the moment of conception and the moment of birth, that is, during fetal life."

As with most learning disorders or disabilities, terminology is always a major problem. Every discipline, in fact every professional, seems to have a favorite term to describe the minimal brain damage or dysfunction syndrome. Some of the names applied and used interchangeably to describe this disorder are:

Aggressive Behavior Disorder
Aphasoid Syndrome
Association Deficit Pathology
Attention Disorder
Auditory Handicap
Brain Dysfunction
Cerebral Dysfunction
Cerebral Dyssynchronization
Character Impulse Disorder
Choreform Syndrome
Clumsy Child Syndrome
Conceptually Handicapped
Diffuse Brain Damage
Disorders of Attention
Disorders of Concept-formation
Disorders of Impulse Control
Disorders of Motor Coordination
Disorders of Perception
Distractibility
Dyscalculia
Dysgraphic
Dyssynchronous
Hyperexcitability Syndrome
Hyperkinetic Behavior Disorder
Hyperkinetic Behavior Syndrome
Hyperkinetic Impulse Syndrome
Hyperkinetic Syndrome
Hypokinetic Syndrome
Interjacent Child
Mild Neurosensory Defects
Minimal Brain Damage
Minimal Brain Dysfunction
Minimal Brain Injury
Minimal Cerebral Damage
Minimal Cerebral Injury
Minimal Chronic Brain Syndrome
Minor Brain Damage
Neurophrenia
Organic Behavior Disorder
Organic Brain Dysfunction
Organic Driveness
Organic Language Disorder
Organic Language Dysfunction
Perceptual Cripple
Perseverative
Psychoneurological Learning Disorders
Scatter Child
Visual-motor Perceptual Lag

Obviously so many names for the same general disability leads to confusion—especially when, in the majority of cases which fall under one of these descriptions, *the child does not necessarily display any visible handicap.*

How then will the problem make itself evident in the child? To answer this, we can again turn to Dr. Clements writing with Dr. John E. Peters,[20] who list the outstanding manifestations to be found in some combination or form in a particular child:

"Specific Learning Deficits—the child cannot read at grade or age level, a mildly stressful situation may bring out typical dyslexic errors; spelling poor; difficulty with arithmetic; difficulty with abstractions and whole-part relationships; difficulty in mastering tasks which are dependent on good visual-motor coordination.

"Perceptual-Motor Deficits—printing, writing and drawing poor; poor and erratic performance when copying geometric figures.

"General Coordination Deficits—the child is often described as awkward or clumsy, this may appear in either fine muscle performance or in over-all coordination, or both.

"Hyperkinesis—the child appears to be in constant motion, flitting from one object or activity to another, or may be merely restless or fidgety; we have considered that the child's "driveness" may be manifest also as voluble, uninhibited speech, or as disorganized thinking, even in the absence of outward hyperkinesis.

"Impulsivity—the child cannot keep from touching and handling objects, particularly in a strange or overstimulating environment; he may speak without checking himself and even say insulting things; his impulsivity easily leads him into conflict with the demands of conformity as established by family, school and society.

"Emotional Lability—the child may be 'highstrung,' irritable, aggressive or easily moved to tears; he may have quick changes from high temper to easy manageability and remorse; he may be panicked by what would appear to others as a minimally stressful situation, however, some of these children are sweet-tempered, even in the presence of a frustrating inability to read—in such cases, the underlying temperament and benign environmental influences may have made the difference.

"Short Attention Span and/or Distractibility—the child is unable to concentrate on one thing for very long; he especially loses interest when abstract material is being considered."

The doctors go on to discuss neurological signs and electroencephalograms, which must always be considered when evaluating a child.

Because of the special nature of the disability, and the necessary approaches to overcoming it, the term most often used concerning these children by doctors and educators is *management.* I don't find this an attractive term, but it is accurately descriptive of what is necessary for the child, *and parent.* If parents train themselves to observe, they will soon be able to see how their child reacts to a given situation. They learn what routines the child cherishes and help him stay within his needed boundaries; they can guide the child as life's changes require him to change his routines of living. Usually, it is the very minor incidents which will set the child off—the major ones, by the very fact that they are major, are more easily understood and easier to cope with—but the minor can be truly devastating. The best rule probably is to "keep the pressures off and the routines intact."

The problem is that the child is inadequately empowered for coping with the variety of life situations. It is hard to realize this since he looks normal, reacts in most things in fairly standard fashion, and was born of normal parents. He moves along smoothly and then some minor incident induces a catastrophic reaction. Sometimes it is a situation that pyramids – a question is asked of him, his answer is not appropriate, the questioner chides him for being silly, not trying or having a smart-alecky attitude. The child does not understand this response and feels maligned – he tried to answer the question to the best of his ability – so he becomes infuriated at being wrongfully accused and reacts with a torrent of anger.

An example, which is unusual because it involves two entirely different reactions to an almost identical situation, concerns two girls, both with brand new dresses which they thought particularly beautiful and wore to school to show off. A friend of one of the girls, in a fit of jealousy, said, "I have a new dress too, but it is too good to wear to school. If your mother lets you wear yours, I'll bet it didn't cost much." The other girl's friend said, "Oh, it's a beautiful dress, but aren't you hot in those long sleeves?" The first girl's mother literally had to hide the dress in order to wash it – the girl refused to wear anything else, she wanted to wear it to school, church and play. The second girl very carefully and deliberately poured paint all over her dress so that it was ruined. Both girls over-reacted. What is also unusual is that we would expect the reactions in the two girls to be reversed. In the context of the two incidents, each reaction can be considered violent – a violent stubborness carried much further than necessary in one girl, and, for the other, an act of physical violence to the dress.

As you can see, when the terms "violent" or "catastrophic reaction" are used, they do not necessarily mean physical violence. They can also mean the violence of a prolonged out-of-proportion reaction. This, too, is true violence – ask any parent or teacher who is responsible for such a child.

Another example is the boy in a classroom where all of the students were doing quiet work at their seats. Suddenly the boy turned around and hit the girl sitting next to him. When the teacher interceded, he accused the girl of hitting him first and asserted that he would not stand for that type of treatment. The girl was crying, the whole class was in an uproar and the boy was loudly defending his action. It was useless to explain to him that even if the girl had hit him first, he should have raised his hand and reported to the teacher, not hit first, then tell later. After the class had calmed down, the teacher proceeded to investigate. The girl stoutly maintained she had not hit him – the boy just as vehemently maintained he had been hit. Wisely, the teacher reconstructed the scene and discovered that it was she (the teacher) who was the culprit. Teachers, in a class for children with learning disorders, teach from behind the children so that when a child makes a mistake it is corrected immediately, thus mistakes are not reinforced by repetition. In walking behind the children, checking their work, the teacher had accidentally brushed against the boy's back, the child had reacted instantly, striking out without thought of who might have hit him, or what the consequences of his action would be for himself.

The child with minimal brain dysfunction suffers more from his impulsiveness and inability to see the whole of a situation than from any other aspect of his handicap. It is here that he loses friends, is shut off from his peer group, and invites punitive measures by his parents. Depending upon his age, his behavior is variously described as anti-social, strange, nutty, childish, bratty, socio-pathic, or stupid.

The neurologically involved child is unable to think abstractly and use percepts and concepts in the automatic interaction that is necessary. When an individual is incapable of abstract thinking, he is unable to perceive or function in his environment at the level that is expected of him. He constantly operates, or attempts to operate, on faulty or inconsistent data. As a consequence of these difficulties, the child behaves in a fashion that is alternatively devastating, frustrating, heartbreaking, sometimes funny, and, all too often, demanding of punishment from the adult world. Hyperactivity, distractibility, inflexibility and disinhibition—all may be displayed. And, because they are the most subtle, or the least concrete, manifestations of the over-all problem, they are the most difficult for teacher and parent to understand, to learn to cope with, and to help the child solve.

Hyperactivity in infancy may be manifested by children who are described as poor feeders, criers, light or restless sleepers. Some parents describe one child as seemingly "more needful of attention" than their other children. One case history tells of an infant who would sleep soundly in her mother's arms until the mother attempted to lay her in her crib, when the child would immediately cry like a banshee, no matter what time of night it was. The child was awake most of the day, but would still only sleep in her mother's arms at night. After six weeks, the mother was close to collapse. The notations in this case history show that the child was in excellent health, in fact, the only other infant symptom was an allergy to milk which made it necessary to feed the child a formula that consisted of soybean milk. Later, as the child grew, she did well in school, had few problems but, when she walks, her left foot swings too far in, she cannot stand being shouted at, requires routine in her life, still needs a great deal of physical reassurance and love. Her mother knows that if the child goes to a movie in the evening, she will need at least an hour or two afterwards to settle down to sleep. The infant was a high forceps delivery, after a long labor period, and she comes from a "neurologically vulnerable" family. But, it is a fortunate family because the mother and father have trained themselves to watch over her and help her. Her problems are so minor, and each year lessens them, that no doctor could give a diagnosis of minimal brain damage, but there is obviously some neurological involvement. For this case, there are no concrete problems in the academic area, just in the day-by-day living.

This case is a very mild example of minimal brain dysfunction. In most cases the symptoms are much more apparent, and less easily handled. There are guide-lines, however, that can be useful to parents and teachers, no matter how mild or serious the child's disorder.

Routine is vital to these children. Any disruption of their cherished patterns of living can be a great burden for them. A calm, orderly life is what they desire the most—and certainly this is one of the easiest contributions adults can make to their welfare. If, for example, a parent feels the urge to move furniture around, he should wait until the child is home and can help. This will aid him in re-establishing a new routine in his mind in respect to furniture placement. This is especially vital where the child's own room and personal belongings are concerned. Above all, he should not have surprises or drastic changes sprung on him. A little forethought in any given situation will help immeasurably. These children need reliable routine to use as a base of security and a stepping stone throughout their daily lives.

A *consistent approach* to all dealings with the child will, in the long run, be more of an aid to the adults concerned than to the child. These children are very inclined toward "scatter" and must have their wishes, needs and routines cared for in a consistent day-in-and-day-out manner. To give in to special requests, or change the rules from day to day, will only complicate the problem, deepen the "scatter," and turn a minor problem into a major one.

Careful giving of one-step instructions is mandatory. We constantly force children to sort out our instructions from a flood of words. We love our children, but when we want them to do something, we often get our own personalities and prejudices involved. "Come wash for dinner" is much more easily understood than, "Darling, dinner is almost ready, please come in and wash. Make sure you get your hands clean—we're having your favorite, steak and corn on the cob—etc."

Giving tasks where the child can "shine" is important to all children, but evidence shows it is especially vital to these children. They have trouble achieving academically. We must strive, therefore, to replace this constant failure with solid achievements that bring a sense of belonging and usefulness.

Don't give choice commands, most especially in the non-pleasure areas. A child may be allowed to pick out the coloring book he wants, but he should not be given a choice as to whether he will take a bath now or later. This is the realm of life functions and daily tasks and consistency is necessary here.

Watch your voice level and tone. These children should not be yelled at, nor should they be spoken to in a monotone, or a "put upon" tone of voice. Proper modulation and emphasis can give the child clues to what you want from him, thus helping to sort out the words. Remember, he badly needs all the help he can get.

Don't convey your anxiety to your child. At the same time, don't try to ignore his disability. He knows that something is wrong, and he needs to know, too, that you are concerned. Excess tension will not help; warm understanding and frank discussion of the problem, at a level appropriate to the child's age, will. Communication with those outside the family is also important. Some parents feel it necessary to tell all their neighbors, relatives, friends and fellow workers that their child is "not really stupid, but just suffers from minimal brain damage." Unfortunately, we have a long way to go in our culture for a full and unconcerned acceptance of anything that varies from the norm. To advertise indiscriminately that a child is "different" can only add to his burden, as well as to the whole family unit's. Both adults and children can be cruel, even when they don't intend to be. At the same time, the family should not attempt to hide the problem. Rather, a judicious blend of frankness and discretion is likely to prove most helpful to all concerned.

A well informed professional, when he evaluates a child, is able by combining the results of a child's testing protocol, the patterning on the scored results, and the medical and scholastic history, to give a "considered" opinion on the child's disability. Because of the child's intelligence, and the frequent lack of specific medical evidence, it would be helpful if more psychometrists and psychologists were more aware of the minor subtleties of the pattern of symptoms. This is especially true because a doctor, when he cannot secure the necessary medical evidence in his office, has nothing further to use for diagnosis as he must abide by the demonstrable medical facts. Therefore, it is quite possible for the most capable doctor to fail to arrive at a correct diagnosis—simply because of the lack of concrete medical evidence.

In this connection, Dr. Paul Ellwood, speaking at a convocation on learning disabilities at Pittsburgh in February, 1967, made the valid point that pediatricians, as well as other medical men, must recognize the role of educators and psychologists in helping to diagnose minimal learning disabilities. He noted that it is the clinical teacher or psychologist who can, in many instances, identify and describe for the doctor diagnostic specifics about a child's problem—that they are often in a better position than the doctor himself to perform this function. This is a new and startling view of the position of the doctor as a partner on the multidisciplinary diagnostic team that is required.

For the parent whose child is diagnosed as suffering from minimal brain dysfunction, the first step should be complete acceptance of the child and his handicap. Before the child can learn to accept himself and achieve the inner controls necessary to overcome his problem, his parents must acquire their own set of inner controls.

Once a child's disability is diagnosed, there are facilities for educating him that specialize in the methods that will help him to learn. True, such facilities are all too rare in this country. We need many more as well as the highly trained clinical personnel necessary for staffing them. But we do have the knowledge to educate our minimally handicapped children of average or above intelligence. Nevertheless, even in educating these children, the role of the parents is still vital.

Studies of orphans being raised in an institutional environment have shown that they can be fed, bathed, educated, given playtime, properly cared for in all ways, and still remain unhappy, listless, uninterested in the world around them. They are not healthy, happy children. What they lack is love. Yet when these children are given individual attention, individual love, and are made to feel an individual sense of worth—in spite of their handicap of environment—they become happy, well-adjusted children.

For the child with minimal brain dysfunction, the same holds true. The educators can help the child to learn, but it is the parents who have to make him whole, happy, secure in the knowledge that he is loved.

When the child first goes to school, in kindergarten or first grade, the teacher knows very soon that she has a problem child in her class. This is the child who spills all the finger paints, climbs to the top of the tree, has six minor tussles with other children in one day, is the first out of the door at the end of the day by dint of pushing and shoving. Or, she knows he's there because he is painfully afraid, can't seem to remember class routine from one day to the next, has difficulty changing activities or has trouble with organized games.

Usually, in her parent conference, the teacher tries to spare the parent's feelings with phrases such as: "Derek is so interested in discovering the world, but he needs some organization to his searchings." Or, "Tom's social and tidiness habits need a little maturing." Or, "Jim has trouble keeping up with the class – he's still young for his age."

If, after a child has reached the age of six years, nine months, and the teacher still says that he is "a little immature for his age" – or any of the other phrases so common to the language of education – remember that these phrases are often used to buffer the parent – and the teacher – from the reality of the situation. They should be a warning to the parent to "perk up his ears" and listen to what the teacher is *really* saying. Get to the bottom of the dialogue. This doesn't mean he should berate the teacher for being too harsh or for attempting to hide something. Instead, he should cooperate. Ask for specifics. It may be that the child is simply a holy terror, or he may be in trouble. In either case, full cooperation between parent and teacher is needed.

Too often, because education is ostensibly free, and also compulsory, teachers are expected to take full responsibility for the education of all children assigned to them, and parents feel they have no responsibility in the matter beyond attending PTA functions, or watching to make sure their tax dollars are spent efficiently.

A case in point concerns a parent whose child has been in nearly every public school in the city where they live. At each school, an attempt has been made to help her child, who not only manifests the usual ills of the spoiled brat, but also seriously needs extra academic help. He has received "social promotions" because the mother insisted. The mother refuses to have a parents conference without a witness being with her, stating clearly to the teacher that Mrs. _______ is present as a witness to what the teacher says. She always comes with a list of questions, detailed in all respects. The mother has further made it a practice over the years to write many letters to the school principal, with carbon copies for the teacher of the year, outlining the way her child is to be handled. At the end of the year, she threatens a lawsuit if the letters are forwarded to the new school, using as her excuse that the child is entitled to start over with a "clean slate."

Once, an attempt was made to help him with his speech and reading problems, which meant he had to work in a tutorial situation – and really work. He told his mother that they were doing this to punish him and she immediately demanded that the school stop the tutorial help. Her attitude was, "her child did not need extra help, he was passing, wasn't he?"

There are many case histories of children who could have done so much more, truly achieved their potential, if only their parents had asked for help at an early age. If, rather than ignoring signs, they had accepted the limitations of their child, aided the teachers, and avoided either rejecting him or babying him into neurosis. Children are like trees. When young, they can be bent, they can bear a lot, and like a young willow snap back and continue to grow. But the older they get, the more difficult it becomes for them to change. *The optimum age for education for any child with a learning disorder is between five and eight. He can absorb more at a faster rate than at any other time in his life.*

Drs. L.J. Hanvik and H.B. Hanson[21] state, "the physical aspects of milder brain injuries in children have a good chance of being 'healed over' through forces of growth and development but resulting psychological scars could be severe and permanent if not properly understood and treated."

The teenager will have areas of competence due to maturation factors, together with areas of incompetence. If his environment has been hostile to him, he will have a deepening emotional overlay. As we already know, the major problem these children must overcome in their handicap is behavior. When an emotional overlay is added, a whole new set of circumstances must be dealt with. Sometimes, the overlay can result in severe consequences; more often though, because of their intelligence, the children are not physically dangerous to themselves or others.

The interplay of emotional overlay and handicap can have amusing and yet somehow sad results. An example of this is the teenage boy who went sailing with his father. They both used the one man racer-type of sailboat. The father suggested a race – out to the buoy and back. The boy immediately began to have maneuvering troubles, sliding off several times, and so on. The father was most patient, in fact, because he knew his son to be a good sailor, teased him slightly about his tacking problems and suggested they start the race over. Instead the boy slid off the boat, swam to shore, got dressed, went home and for the next two days would not speak to his astounded father. The boy had reached the stage where he could not tolerate a minor failure, even in an area where he knew himself to be competent.

These children can be so easily discouraged and given to great sadness about their incapabilities. From the younger years, on up into teenage life – until the protective shell forms – they will literally and figuratively "cry a lot."

The role of medication is generally accepted as an important aid in specific cases. It is not, however, a cure-all that eliminates the problem. Medication can give some children an "edge" on their problems, particularly in the areas of hyperactivity and attention span. It can, however, be used safely only under the most careful medical supervision.

Two other problem areas for some of these children are defective memory and perseveration.

The factor of defective memory can make learning a nightmare for the child. At times, it would seem that all the child has worked so hard to learn during the week is wiped clean from his memory over the weekend. He must start afresh each Monday and then the nightmare begins, because he is aware that he learned the work last week, knows that it is his failure, and hates himself for it.

Perseveration is the inability to stop a task or activity when it should be stopped; and it can reach into every area of the child's life—even his play. The child will hammer a nail long after it is in place. He will draw his picture right off the paper. He repeats the last word in a sentence time and again until it becomes almost a stutter. In a sequential situation, for example during a game, he will get stuck in the middle, repeating again and again, unable to continue. Perseveration sounds like one of the most terrifying of all the symptoms, but in reality it is the easiest to handle. In the paperwork, the teacher can simply lay her hand across the child's work, lifting his hand up and restarting him on the next line of the task. With the verbal perseveration, touching the child's lips with a finger will most often stop him. At play, or in a similar circumstance, a physical touch, a hug, a whisper in the ear, clasping both his hands gently in yours will almost always help. Most of the situations take only common sense, firmness, and, above all, gentleness.

And finally, we come to the one pervading over-all aspect of minimal brain dysfunction. In its severest forms, the clinical name applied is The Aphasias. In the milder forms with which we are concerned here, it is called the Aphasoid or Aphasic factor. Aphasia refers to language in all its uses of interpretation and transfer into verbal and auditory input and output. In severe cases a child is unable to speak or comprehend what is spoken to him. There are many different forms, degrees, and types—thus the applied plural—aphasias. For the children with whom we are concerned here, however, the problem is one of improper speech development and a deeper auditory perception problem than has been mentioned before. As a result, it is necessary for the child to have clinical speech and hearing added to his education program. It will take longer to go shorter distances in the classroom with this child. *All children with learning disorders have this aphasic tendency*—it is a question of degree and type. Stammering, cluttered speech, inability for immediate recall, difficulty with blending sounds, difficulty in imitating sounds, lack of ability to discriminate sounds, and many other examples, all come under the heading of an aphasoid factor. The professional literature on the subject gives the impression that it is the result of a deep "inner brain" malfunction or lesion, however, there is not complete agreement on the exact cause or etiology involved. The literature details the "gross" aspects of the disability mainly in the form of "gross" symptomology and when we try to define what is usually considered a major disability in terms of the subtler or minimal impairments, the terminology becomes inexact and confusing. It must suffice here to say that a minimal form of the aphasias is a factor, a major factor, which must always be considered in any given child's evaluation.

These, then, are the manifestations of minimal brain dysfunction. There is, however, a final point to be made. One of the most difficult aspects of having a child with this form of learning disorder is that there is nothing that can prepare a parent for this enventuality. There are many defects that a parent can assume may appear at birth. A good example is hereditary color blindness; another is hemophelia. Based on family history, background, and characteristics, knowledgeable parents are even able to consider whether a son might have a tendency toward genetic dyslexia. But, cerebral dysfunction or damage cannot be predicted—whether minimal, moderate, or severe. A mother can have a successful pregnancy and delivery and then, as a result of illness during infancy, accompanied by high fever, find her perfect child is damaged. True, the damage may be very slight, but it has changed the child. He no longer has full and complete use of all his human faculties. His responses are now slightly different, he is now a hurt child, and a family with a hurt child is a hurt family.[22]

These hurt children may be found anywhere. There are no protective boundaries of race or color, socio-economic status, or national origin, ethnic or cultural lines that are free of the possibility. Throughout man's history we have had, in all degrees and types, brain-injured individuals. Fortunately, over the years, we have gained knowledge of the problem, especially about these very limited types of dysfunction. We know now that the hyperactivity of these children is the result of a problem, not the problem itself; the emotional overlay comes from the years of failure, but that, too, is a result, and it only becomes the problem when it is so firmly set we cannot break through it to help the child start achieving.

Today, a firm diagnosis of minimal brain dysfunction is not the end of the world for either the parents or, more important, the child. With appropriate educational facilities and techniques, and proper parental attitudes, the child will progress, slowly to be sure, to productive adulthood. In this process, the main burden falls on the parents rather than the child or his teachers. It is their ability to overcome their feeling of dismay; to ignore for the time being their sense of expectancy for achievement from the child, that will make the greatest difference. Above all, parents should remember the admonition, *don't rush, time is in your child's favor.*

Parents may react in a variety of ways when confronted with actual diagnosis; I have seen fathers cry and mothers go into deep depression. Often parents, after the initial shock, will frantically berate themselves and each other in the belief that it must be their fault. Still others will turn to the child for expiation of what they consider to be their guilt, or throw up their hands in total defeat. Still others will use their child's disorder as the reason for their own failure to cope effectively with the multitude of daily problems we all must meet. For some strange reason, we Americans place all learning disabilities, and most especially the brain disorders, into a category that seems to reflect on our moral terpitude, our standing in the community, our family and personal image—a whole complex of reactions—none of which have anything to do with the problem. No martyrs, nor the guilt-ridden or belligerent, are needed.

All of us tend to try to "stretch our children"—because of their intellectual capacity these children may be stretched—it must be done, however, with controls on the child, teacher, and most of all parent, else all may spin out of control.

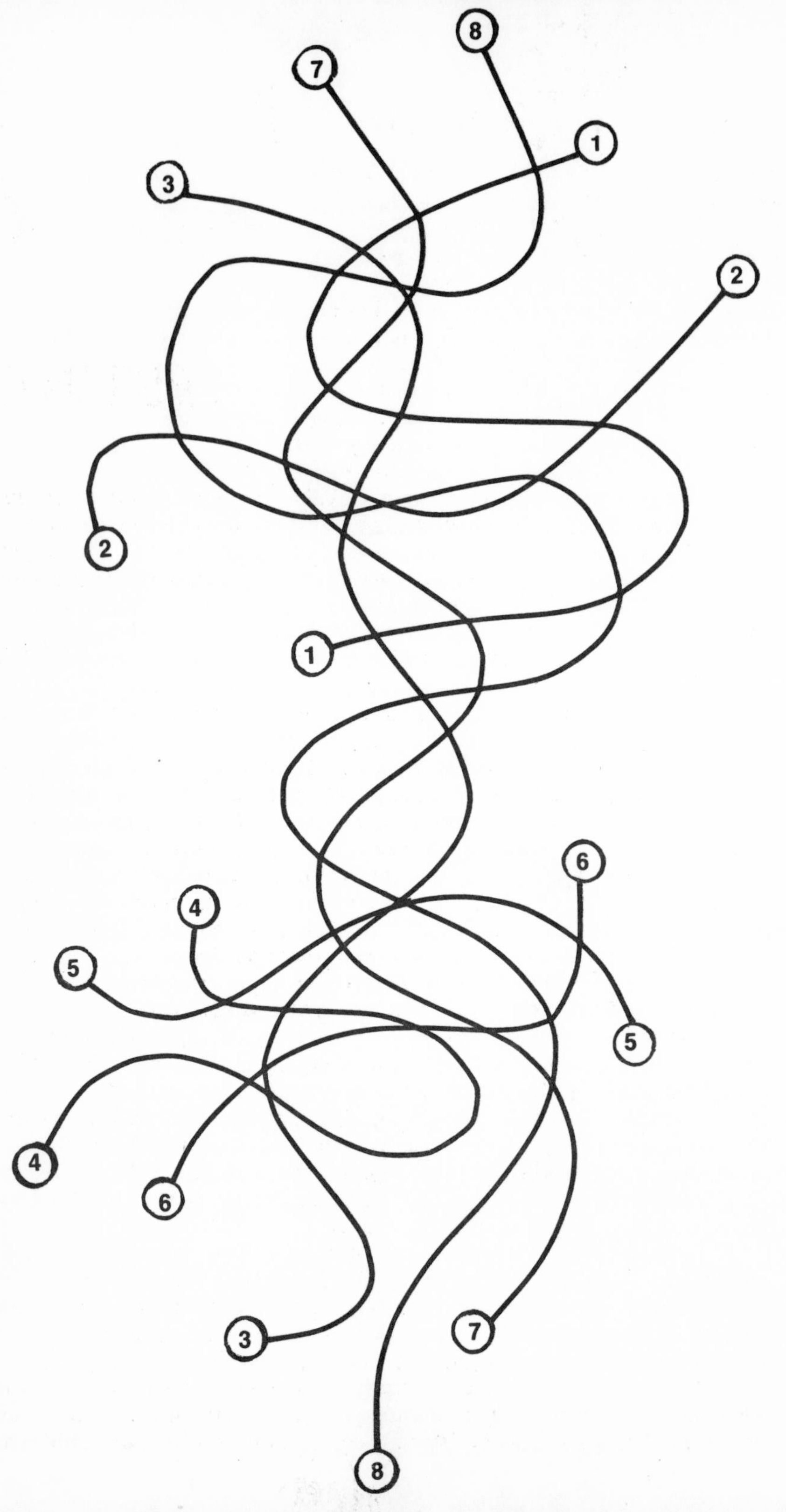
8
7
1
3
2
2
1
6
4
5
5
4
6
3
7
8

6

TESTING

Before a teacher can teach a child with a minimal learning disorder, and before a parent can change the home environment for his child, they both must know exactly where the child's problem areas lie. Some professionals object strongly to any attempt to "tag" a child or to put a label on his problems. They contend that in doing so the child is harmed irreparably—that the "tag" will follow him throughout his life, adversely affecting his chances for marriage, children, employment and social life. This is a valid argument that responsible adults must take into consideration. However, there are two sides to the question. We must consider the benefits to be derived and weigh them against the harm that may be done. When, for instance, we consider a child with minimal brain dysfunction—we have a child who is smart, capable of learning, whose main manifestations of "difference" are hyperactivity and behavioral problems from within himself; if he is educated to full capacity, and learns that the world is not his enemy because he has a problem, he can become a productive adult. But, instead of this, if we fail to diagnose his problem or try to ignore it—fail, in effect, to identify his disability and put a label on it so that it can be effectively treated—we not only do a disservice to the child, but deny him the opportunity to grow into a successful adult.

Testing and the resulting diagnosis are absolute necessities if these children are to be aided. Testing can, however, be expensive, time-consuming, and, most of all, frustrating. For laymen, it presents an unknown, complicated, and sometimes frightening field. The purpose of this chapter is to present information—some in detail and some in general terms—that will make it possible for the reader to make at least a preliminary judgment as to whether a particular child will be well served by testing, as well as what rights and responsibilities a parent has to the child, to himself and to the persons testing his child.

It is important for both parent and child to enter a testing situation with proper attitudes. It is very possible that all their fears are unfounded. But, whether unfounded or not, there are several basic "do's" and "don'ts" that parents should remember as they enter a testing situation. First, no matter what a parent feels may or may not be wrong with his child, he should not attempt to develop his own preconceived ideas of what the problem may be: remember it is the professional evidence on which the diagnosis must be based. Second, don't surprise the child with the testing. If it is a younger child, a simple explanation is all that is necessary: "Tomorrow we are going to meet a nice man who will have some games for you, and ask you some questions." For the older child who knows he has a problem, a simple statement of fact is all that is really necessary: "Tomorrow, we will try to find out what the problem is and how to solve it." Do not frighten the child, do not make him feel his whole life hangs in the balance, do not make him feel that he must perform well or this will be another case of failure for him. But, most of all, do not surprise him. Cancel the appointment if the child does not feel well or was sick the night before. Tell the tester if the child is taking any form of medication. Don't lie—either by omission or commission—when relating the family history and the child's problems, behavior and attitudes. Full and complete knowledge of all relevant facts is the surest pathway to accurate diagnosis and treatment.

A perennial question concerns the age at which testing should be done. The answer, as with remediation, is the earlier the better. A child may be tested for severe handicaps at any age. For educational purposes, there is general agreement that the minimum age at which the testing will truly be valid is approximately five years, nine months. The instruments most widely used today are based on the six-year norms. Testing between the ages of six and eight is extremely valuable, not only for what can be done for the child immediately, but a cumulative test record will be very useful to those working with the child later. A great deal can be told, for instance, by how a child performs on the Wechsler Intelligence Scale for Children at age seven and how the same child performs on the same test at age ten. Therefore, parents should not only initiate testing early, but always keep a record of where the child has been tested, so that it will be possible to refer back to the test results in succeeding years.

There are many testing instruments to choose from and the choice of which to use for an individual child changes with age, presenting symptoms, private or public facilities, and individual preference of the tester. Every parent has the right to ask first what the testing battery being given his child will consist of. When he is told his child will undergo a "psychological study," he should inquire exactly what instruments will be used. Remember, the instruments that are used and the resultant protocol (diagnostic picture) are the basis on which the diagnosis is made—the diagnosis that will be the key to remediation of the child's problems. Each child is entitled to have the very best tests available used for the diagnosis which may make such drastic changes in his life.

Every parent has the right to inquire about the tester's qualifications, his background, the degrees he holds, and his experience. He also has the right to inspect the tester's professional credentials. This is especially important when dealing with private facilities or individuals since many of our states have no system of professional licensing in the field and issue only standard commercial business or occupational licenses. Therefore, an individual's claim that he does psychological testing or educational evaluation testing does not guarantee that he is adequately trained and fully qualified to do so. Those who are qualified will not object to a parent's questions; the others are likely to be evasive.

A parent also has the responsibility to question in detail the basis on which the diagnosis was made and to receive proof that it is justified by the evidence. I know of numerous cases where parents have received no less than five different "diagnoses" for one child. However, once satisfied that a professionally competent diagnosis has been made, the parent has the continuing responsibility to follow through on the referrals recommended for further testing by allied disciplines or medical "check-outs," as well as the recommendations for scholastic help. One case comes to mind, of parents who, whenever they have the opportunity, question the qualifications of the facility which is handling their son. They accept the diagnosis given, place the child in a clinical school, and the boy progresses well. But, they keep themselves and their child constantly stirred up by asking uninformed outsiders for opinions regarding the school. They question the child endlessly and drag him from one facility to another, seeking confirmation of the diagnosis. They have not stopped "running" long enough to try to understand and accept the child as he is, give themselves credit for doing all they possibly can for him, and give their full and unqualified support to the facility which they themselves selected. In the process, they make it far more difficult for the boy to progress and for those at the school to help him overcome his problems.

Once a diagnosis is accepted, fully confirmed with facts and data, and a program is begun, faith and trust must take over. No matter what the problem may be, the remedial facility must always have supportive help from the home environment. If the child has to fight his parents, as well as his problems, he is wasting his strength in non-productive activity.

Another pitfall for parents is the cost of testing, diagnosis, and remediation. In every field, the price of goods and services increases when the purchaser needs something outside of the normal or standard. This rule holds true in the field of education as it does in business or industry. But there are reasonable limitations to this increase in cost. Just as one would not pay a usurious rate of interest no matter how much he needed to borrow money, so the parent must become aware of the reasonable price limitations in his geographical area for the services he requires. He must be equally suspicious of the low cost and exceptionally high cost facilities. After all, we usually get exactly what we pay for in this world and there are no bargain basements for learning disorders. It is very difficult to generalize on the subject of costs because they do vary widely in different parts of the country, and for different kinds of public and private agencies. However, anything from $35.00 to $100.00 for testing, diagnosis and referral would be within reasonable limits for a private facility. For this, the parent should receive an intense, well-defined testing battery, a parent conference, possibly referrals for other forms of testing (i. e., neurologist, endocrinologist, psychiatrist, etc.), and a detailed statement of what should be done for the child based on his test protocol and subtest patterning.

For schooling or remediation, the average price runs from $200.00 to $350.00 per month for a full clinical program, where the child is offered a complete academic program. Unfortunately, there are too few facilities of this kind in the country. Most often, a parent must find the necessary remediation with a private school that offers tutoring as an adjunct to its program, or a private tutor. For these, the charges are hourly and may run from $5.00 to $12.00 per hour. Prices charged by public agencies, university reading clinics, and similar facilities vary greatly because they are governed by the kind of financial support the facility receives and the purposes for which it was established. All of these figures are very rough, designed to provide guidelines, not to set limits.

As with testing, again, the parent has every right to inspect the school or tutoring rooms personally in order to ascertain whether the child will be taught in an environment that is appropriate for clinical teaching. Of course, credentials must be inspected, and the parent should find out whether the teachers who will be working with his child have clinical backgrounds and degrees in reading, or are regular classroom teachers without special training who take on the extra job of tutoring in the afternoon.

The time of day a child will receive his tutoring is also important—the younger child has gone far past his "peak" by one o'clock in the afternoon, while an older child can still function at four o'clock—especially if his problems are not too severe. Not infrequently a child is tested at a university reading clinic, then referred to a private school for a complete program because it is felt that just afternoon tutoring would not be sufficient. This is probably the best referral a parent can receive. Universities are always very careful about the schools to which they refer students, especially when they are private facilities. Not all agencies, diagnostic clinics or schools will accept a child for testing or schooling unless the referral comes from another professional source—the parent cannot just walk in off the street.

It is becoming progressively more common throughout the country for testing agencies to insist that both parents be present—even in the case of divorce—at the parent conference. It is in this conference, where the child's test results are discussed, that all fears, questions, uncertainties, and acceptance or rejection of the problem comes. Professionals have discovered that a mother who goes home and explains the problem second-hand to the father oftentimes fails to make the problem clear. As a result, father may be very reluctant to give his full cooperation and support since he has not had the opportunity to have his specific questions and doubts answered. This state of mind can, in turn, lead to a generally mistrustful attitude toward the treatment recommended for the child, or doubt that a problem even exists. Many times, it is the father who bears the more traumatic burden when a son, possibly his only or eldest, gives evidence of a learning problem. And, it may very possibly be the father who first asks the most important question of all. Why test? Why go to the expense, trouble and trauma of testing? To answer this question for parents, let us look at three children, all male, all seemingly average, all the same age. They all demonstrate an Intelligence Quotient of 110. None bears any outward sign of handicap. One would assume that, barring minor social and cultural differences, they would all be able to achieve at about the same level. Of course, one may be better in arithmetic, another in science, due to individual talents and interests, but in general, they should be about equal in performance. This, however, is not the way it works out. Each child has very particular strengths, weaknesses and handicaps—and it is these factors that are discovered and assessed by testing. Boy A came from a "neurologically vulnerable" family and when tested was discovered to have auditory and visual perception problems. Boy B was discovered to have some severe hyperkinetic problems, but it was felt his behavioral problems were the result of home environment, and boy C was perfectly average with the exception of a minor neurological maturation lag, which was rapidly disappearing with age.

These strengths, weaknesses and handicaps compose the child's *triangle of learning potential.* And this triangle of learning potential may be thought of as a child's prescription for learning—the prescription blank is written by testing and diagnosis—the prescription is filled by our teachers.

A parent is vitally interested in the diagnosis of his child because it identifies his disability, but the educators of the child use the evaluation for other purposes. They are interested in the diagnostic breakdown—strengths, weaknesses, specific type of handicap. An educator will look at the sub-test patterning (each testing instrument usually consists of sub-tests which make up the whole instrument), and how the individual instruments have meshed together for a complete protocol. It is this that tells the teacher exactly what techniques to use for the individual child. And, it is this knowledge that will enable the teachers to teach each of the three boys to his full capacity.

One of the most troublesome questions a parent can meet is when he should consider testing for his child. What signs can he look for? Does his child really need testing? Parents, of course, cannot diagnose, they can only decide to seek a professional for diagnosis. Many of the clues that parents need have already been listed, and the profile of family symptoms that may be checked has been discussed. Let us now look at some of the everyday behavior and physical manifestations that may help parents in reaching their decision.

The following items, which may be used as a check list, are predominantly from the Peterson-Quay-Werry-Weiss-Peters Scales and are basically adjectives which parents and teachers will immediately recognize as descriptive of some children. The lists are loosely grouped (author's grouping) according to type. They should be read carefully and thoughtfully—not just scanned. Some of the behavior items are found in all children at one time or another. In reviewing these lists, one must bear in mind the degree and number of items "ticked off." There is a great deal of difference between "occasionally" and "usually." Parents should also remember that what is unimportant at age six may be very important at age eleven.

Group No. 1	Never	Occasionally	Usually
Disruptiveness, tendency to annoy and bother others			
Restlessness, inability to sit still			
Attention-seeking, show-off behavior			
Short attention span			
Fighting			
Temper tantrums			
Tension, inability to relax			
Disobedience, difficulty in disciplinary control			
Uncooperativeness in group situations			
Hyperactivity—always on the go			
Distractibility			
Destructiveness in regard to his own and/or others' property			
Profane language, swearing, cursing			
Nervousness, jitteriness, jumpiness, easily startled			
Irritability, hot-tempered, easily aroused to anger			
Excessive talking			
Requires adult supervision or attendance constantly			
Inability for quiet play			
Constantly changing activity			
Disrupts others' play			
Interrupts teacher and other children excessively			

Group No. 2	Never	Occasionally	Usually
Doesn't know how to have fun, behaves like a little adult			
Feelings of inferiority			
Crying over minor annoyances and hurts			
Preoccupation—in a world of his own			

Social withdrawal, preference for solitary activities

Easily flustered and confused

Reticence, secretiveness

Hypersensitivity, feelings easily hurt

Anxiety, chronic general fearfulness

Excessive day-dreaming

Depression, chronic sadness

Passivity, suggestibility, easily led by others

Sluggishness, lethargy

Specific fears, e.g., of dogs, of the dark, of going to sleep at night

Group No. 3	Never	Occasionally	Usually
Dislike for school			
Jealousy over attention paid other children			
Prefers to play with younger children			
Inattentiveness to what others say			
Truancy from school			
Laziness in school and in performance of other tasks			
Irresponsibility, undependability			
Negativism, tendency to do the opposite of what is required			
Prefers to play with older children			
Fluctuating performance			
Socially inept behavior			
Seeks parental attention excessively			

Group No. 4	Never	Occasionally	Usually
Thumb sucking			
Skin allergy			
Headaches			
Dizziness, vertigo			
Difficulty in bowel control, soiling			

Nausea, vomiting as associated with emotional stress

Masturbation

Hay fever and/or asthma

Clumsiness, awkwardness, poor muscular coordination

Stuttering

Drowsiness

Enuresis (bed wetting)

Stomach aches, abdominal pain of undefined character after illness is ruled out

Group No. 5	Never	Occasionally	Usually
Tics			
Difficulty in settling down for sleep			
Inadequate amount of sleep			
Restlessness during sleep			

Professionals use these, or similar scales, for a careful and detailed analysis of a child's behavior, but parents can also use them effectively in the more general assessment regarding their decision for or against testing. If, for instance, a parent has to check more than four items in any two groupings, he should add this information to the details given on the specific problems described in the chapters on dyslexia and minimal dysfunction. He should also check over the family patterns, the birth and infancy history of the child, his achievement levels in school and, by then, the parent should have a fairly clear picture of whether or not his child might be in trouble.

For the reader with a younger child, the following partial screening for perception instrument is given. This is only a part of an entire instrument and it is the Visual Retention Section. The instrument was designed for use by doctors in their offices, classroom teachers, and knowledgeable parents. The instructions are simple and the correction is even simpler. If a child has had one year of kindergarten, and cannot complete this test properly, he should be watched for the possibility of future trouble. If a child has completed the first grade and cannot complete the test properly, he should be tested. If a child is older and cannot complete the test properly, run, do not walk, to the nearest testing facility. Needless to say, the instructions must be followed to the letter and the test should not be used over and over on the same child.

PRELIMINARY SCREENING
—(Visual Retention Section)

DIRECTIONS FOR ADMINISTERING

Materials:

1] Numbered set of 12 designs

2] Structured test sheets (pages 1 & 2) for each child. These sheets are for the reproduction of the symbols and sequences

3] Crayon or pencil

Procedure:

1] Small groups—preferably 6

2] Have students judiciously spaced—so they are unable to see each others performance—but able to have a clear view of the stimulus cards

* 3] This is a screening test of visual retention, therefore a distracting activity has been introduced. To implement this distraction, the examiner is asked to stand at the side of the room.

* 4] The students are instructed to put pencils down on table or desk, turn bodies (not just heads) to the side to view the design.

* 5] The design exposure is approximately 10 seconds—after which students turn back to their tables, pickup pencils and draw the design in designated numbered section corresponding to design number

6] Clear instructions re the proper section of the page to be used, should be given before design exposure. Assistance may be freely given after exposure of the design if child is confused as to "where to draw his design"

* 7] Allow approximately 15 seconds for simple design performance (1 or 2 symbols) approximately 20 seconds to reproduce the more complex design series (3 or more symbols)

*Pertinent to individual administration

top

top

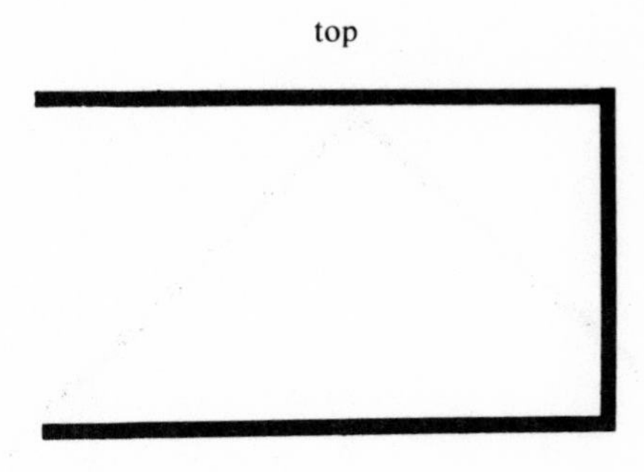

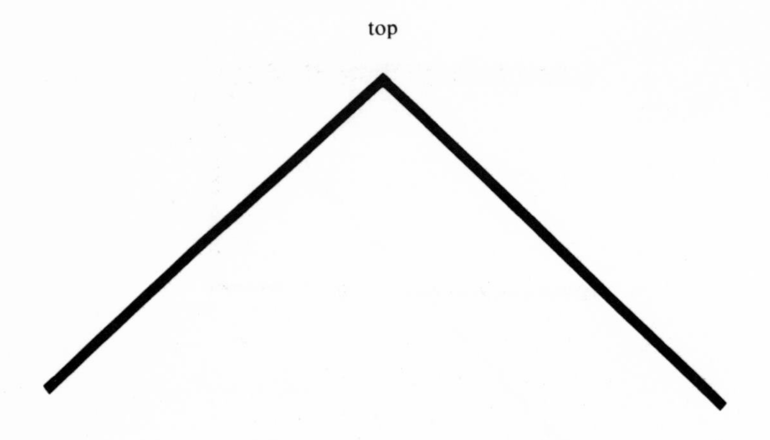
top

top

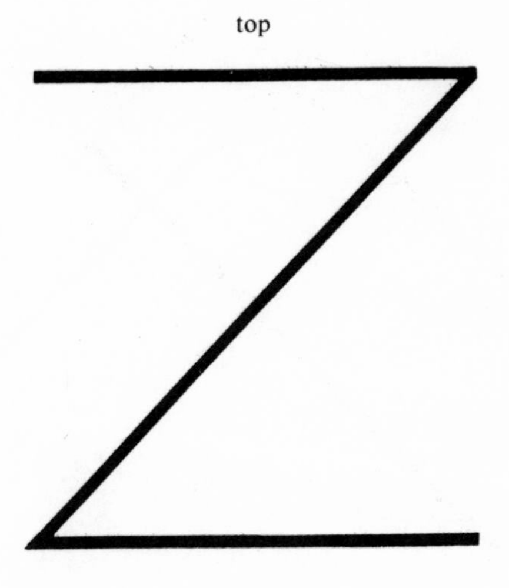

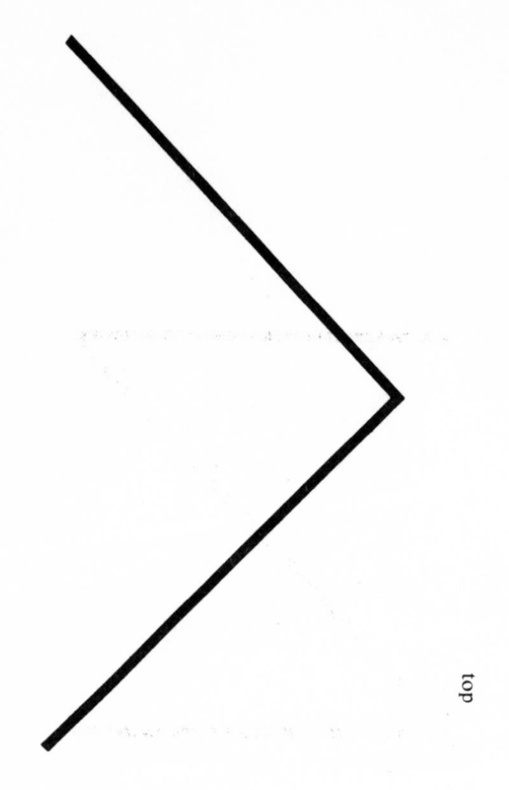
top

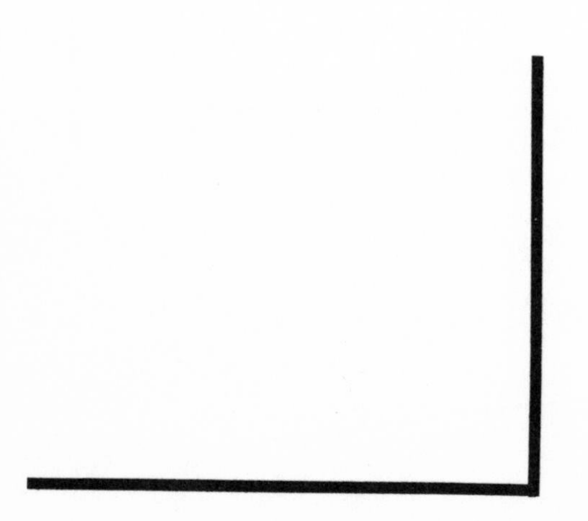

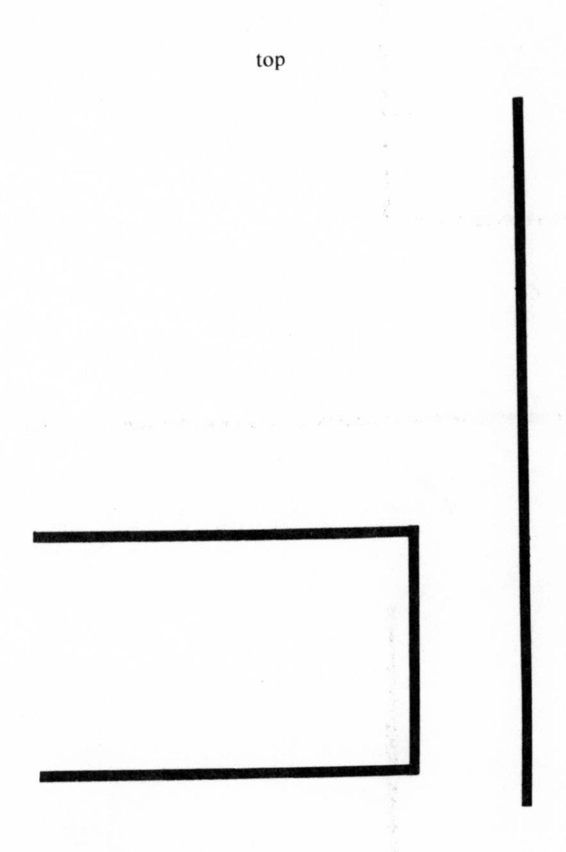
top

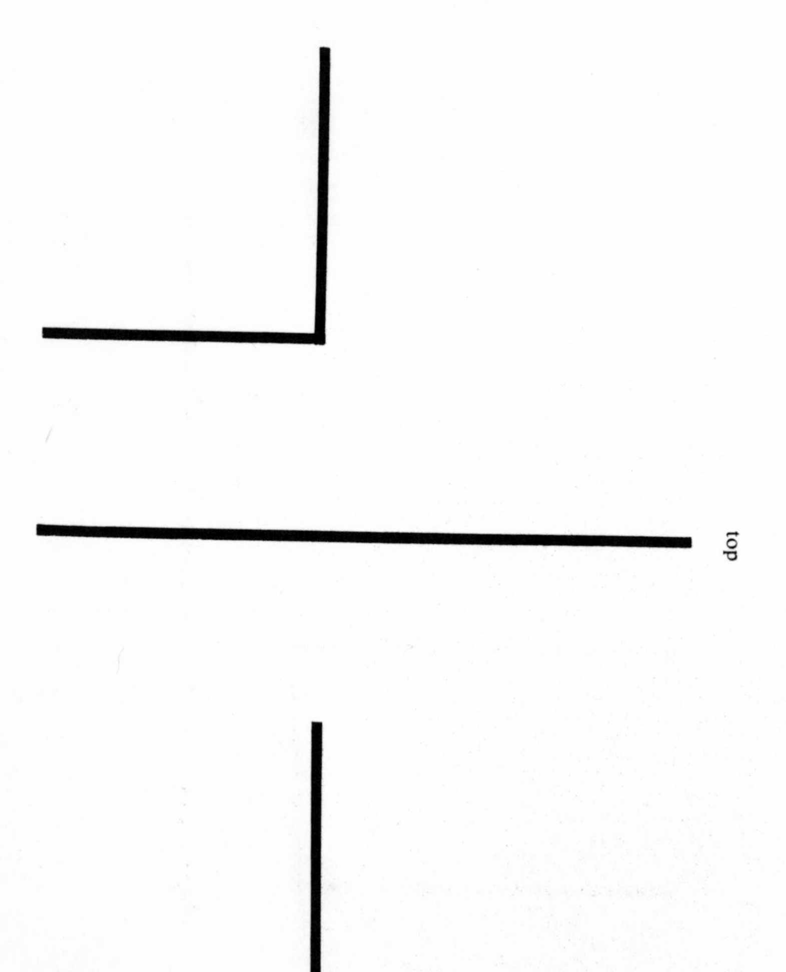
top

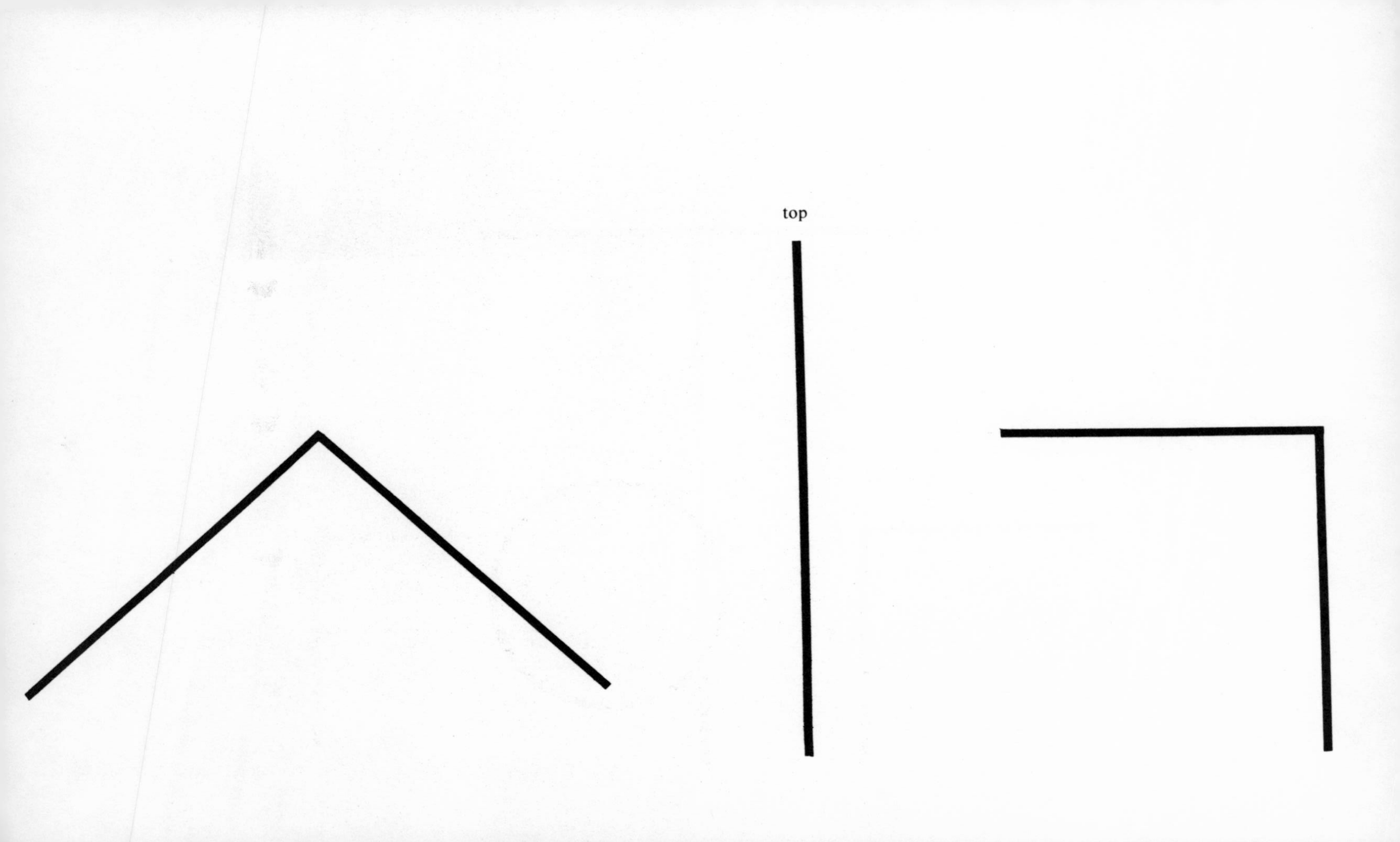
top

top

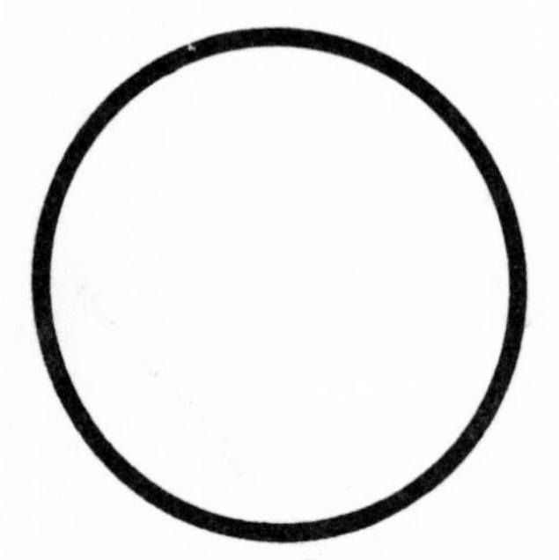

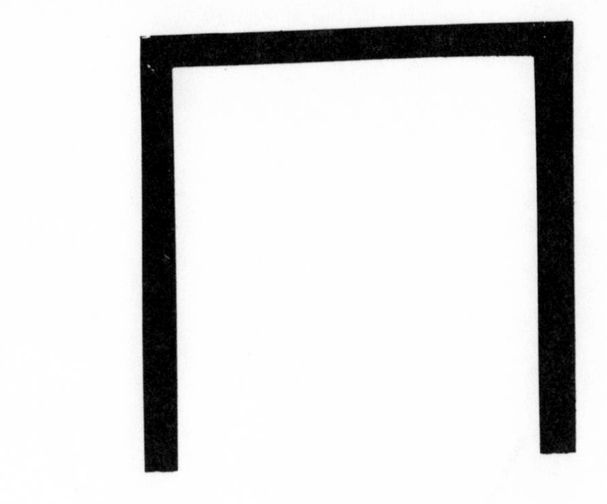

top

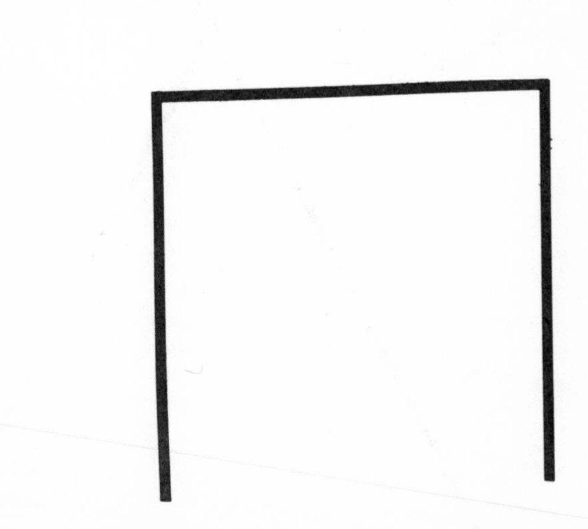

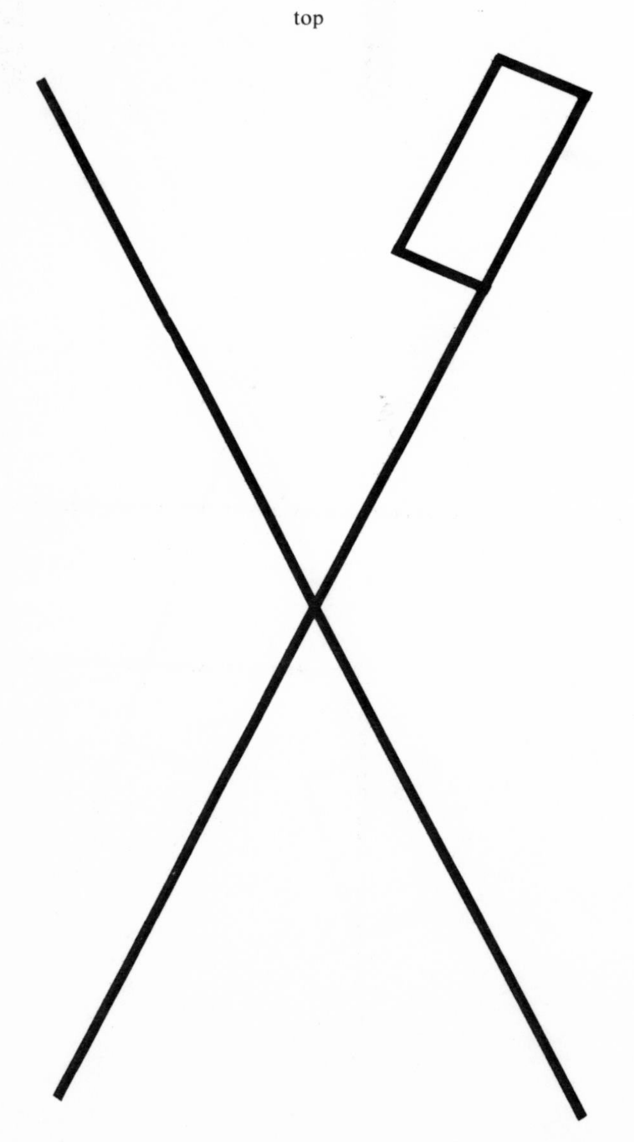
top

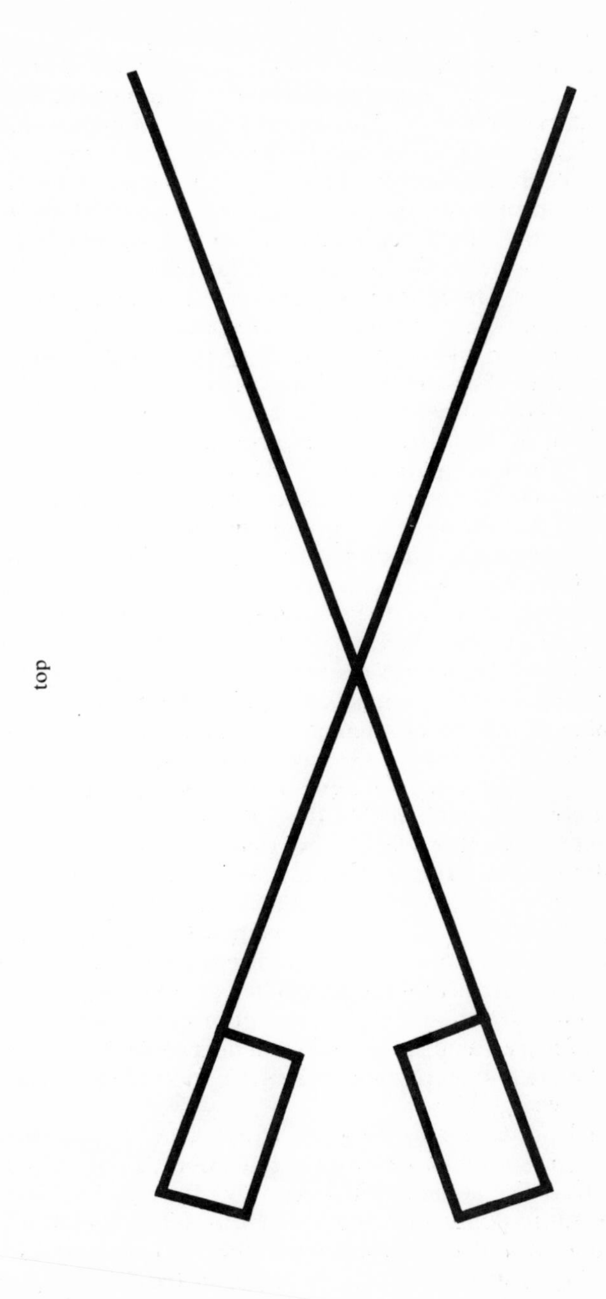
top

It is natural, when one thinks of testing, to think automatically in terms of I.Q. or Intelligence Quotient. For many years it was believed that an I.Q. score was a permanent and immutable statistic that very rarely, if ever, changed. This has been proven untrue. It must be understood that an I.Q. score can be translated to mean "current operating level." Within reasonable limits, the existing score on an individual can fluctuate up or down the scale. Age, newly gained knowledge, environmental factors—both deprived or abundant—health, etc., all may play a role in a present or future score. In his book, Diagnostic Psychological Testing,[23] Dr. David Rapaport comments regarding the nature of intelligence and the determinants of intelligence test achievement. "When a subject takes an intelligence test, his performance represents his efficiency of functioning then and there. This may or may not be an adequate sample of his general efficiency; or, in other words, of the intellectual assets potentially at his disposal. His present life-situation, or even present testing situation, may temporarily encroach upon and diminish his efficiency. On the other hand, the store of intellectual assets potentially at his disposal is not necessarily a final and unchangeable characteristic. The environment in which he grew up, including home, region and country, with its barrenness or stimulating character, had its influence. The degree of schooling and the profession chosen may have expanded or constricted the development of the endowment and range of efficiency. An emotional or organic disturbance may have caused an arrest or setback of the level of efficiency. Thus, in the intelligence test performance, a number of influences interact, yielding the results obtained."

Traditionally, exact I.Q. scores are never given to parents regarding their child, to the individual who was tested, or to the teacher working with a child. It was felt that this information was not only unnecessary to give to a parent or teacher, but that in many cases the knowledge could be harmful. The basic reasoning behind this attitude seems to have been that most testing protocols were evaluated only from a psychological viewpoint, and that the score was regarded as final and static. In recent years, however, since it has been discovered that the *same* protocol can also be evaluated from the additional, or other, viewpoint of remediation for specific areas—and that this form of evaluation may, in the long run, prove of more value to the child and his problems—the emphasis is being placed more and more on giving information to the parent and teachers of the involved child.

An I.Q. score may be given in any one of three ways: as an actual numerical figure; as descriptive adjectives; or in population percentile rank. To arrive at percentile rank—take the possible range of intelligence of the entire population and divide it into one hundred compartments—the population is then dropped into these compartments. This population "drop" is broken down, for example, in the following manner: those at the lowest percentile rank, or compartment, in terms of intelligence, number one percent of the total population; conversely, those in the highest percentile rank, or compartment, still in terms of intelligence, also comprise one percent of the population. However, professionals refer to those individuals in this highest one percent as being at the ninety-ninth percentile rank, i.e., *Very Superior,* and those in the lowest one percent as being at the first percentile rank, i.e., *Defective.*

Different intelligence tests will have minor variations for the norms bearing this in mind—the following table gives the numerical score, comparable descriptive adjective, and the equivalent percentile rank. The reader will note, that the scoring for *Average* can run from ninety-one to one hundred and ten, but the percentile rank for *Average* changes drastically as the numerical score goes up or down.

Numerical Score	Descriptive Adjective	Percentile Rank	
Below 65	defective	1 and 2	–population 50%
66 to 79	borderline	3 to 8	
80 to 90	dull normal	9 to 24	
91	average	25	
94	average	30	
96	average	35	
98	average	40	
99.7	average	45	
101.4	average	50	
103	average	55	50% population+
105	average	60	
106	average	65	
108	average	70	
110	average	75	
111 to 119	bright normal	76 to 91	
120 to 127	superior	92 to 97	
128 and over	very superior	98 and 99	

An important facet of this Intelligence Quotient—one which is often unrecognized by laymen and even some professionals—is that, that intangible entity, concept formation and abstract thinking, which we have traditionally thought of as I.Q., is not the essential requirement for learning in the first grade and a goodly portion of the second grade. Visual and auditory perception is what is really vital for these early grades, for without these perceptions, the child is unable to acquire the skills necessary to adequate learning. For example, a high degree of inferential reasoning is certainly not required to understand the content of first grade readers, i.e., "Dick and Jane ran down the hill." What is required is the ability to see and perceive the symbols, and to hear the fine nuances of sound in our language. Care must be taken, however, not to infer or apply this premise when a clear-cut diagnosis of retardation has been given—the guiding professionals for these children must be the mentors of their programs and prognoses.

We have now arrived at the final necessary information. That of the exact instruments which may be used for diagnosis. What these instruments are called, what they test for, what the tester learns from them.

Naturally, it would be impossible to relate all of the tests in use today, so I will confine the listing to those which are most commonly used by the majority of qualified professionals. If at least four to six of the tests listed are not utilized on the child for his evaluation, it might be advisable to check further into the facility doing the testing. The list is not in alphabetical order, nor is it in order of importance, quality or desirability, with the exception of the first seven tests. These seven I personally consider absolutely necessary to proper evaluation for a child with a minimal learning disorder. Being quite aware that some professionals may argue with my choices, I bow to their professional discernment and preferences. However, the particular professionals who have guided me in this feel no sense of irresponsibility on my part for putting one instrument above another—when the choices are taken in the context of use for which this list is intended. The list is intended to familiarize the reader with some of the language of testing. I have talked with hundreds of parents who, after their parent conference, were so terribly confused by the language that they were literally incoherent. They knew their child had a problem, but they had no real understanding of its scope or depth. And, most often, this confusion was caused by their inability to sort the clinical names and terminology successfully. The following paragraphs are devoted to brief and very general descriptions—all of the instruments listed, with one exception, must be administered by a psychologist, psychometrist, or comparable professional.

The Wechsler Intelligence Scales—there are three different instruments for the different age levels: for ages four years to six years, six months, the W.P.P.S.I. (Wechsler Pre-School and Primary Scales of Intelligence [pronounced wipsey]); for ages five years to fifteen years, eleven months, the W.I.S.C. (Wechsler Intelligence Scale for Children, [pronounced wisk]); and for sixteen years to over 75 years, the W.A.I.S. (Wechsler Adult Intelligence Scales [pronounced wais]). These tests are designed to test "mental age" intelligence regardless of chronological age. There are five sub-tests each for two sections—Verbal and Performance—with two alternate sub-tests available for each section. The tester receives the scoring as three numerical scores: 1) for the Verbal; 2) for the Performance; and 3) for the Full Scale I.Q. The WISC sub-tests for the Verbal Section are: Information, Comprehension, Arithmetic, Similarities, Vocabulary, and Digit Span. This Section tests for the child's word usage, whether it is mature, immature, and accurate; that his information is at, below, or above expected levels; his common sense and social awareness; his logical or illogical approach to a task; and his ability to comprehend relationships at the concrete as well as the abstract level. The sub-tests for the Performance Section are: Picture Completion, Picture Arrangement, Block Design, Object Assembly, Coding and Mazes. This Section tests for: the child's ability to find and use details logically; his part-to-whole, space perception and orientation; and his visuo-motor coordination. The Wechsler tests are highly sophisticated instruments and have the extra value that when the sub-tests are graphed, a knowledgeable clinical educator can remediate from their patterning.

The Marianne Frostig Developmental Test of Visual Perception—this fine instrument tests for the development and maturity of the five areas of perception, which are position in space, horizontal spatial relationships, perceptual constancy, visual-motor coordination, and figure-ground perception. The child may then go into the Frostig Exercises for Perceptual Development for remediation.

Bender Visual Motor Gestalt Test—in performing this instrument the child is required to reproduce a series of designs. How the child reproduces the designs, how accurate his reproduction of the designs is, are interpreted in terms of the Gestalt laws of perception and organization. The term Gestalt is best illustrated by taking the letter A, which, when taken apart is three straight lines—two slightly tilted from the vertical, the third horizontal. If a child is able to put the three straight lines together in proper position, he has formed a Gestalten. If he errs, the degree and type of errors are the basis for scoring this instrument.

The Detroit Tests of Learning Apitudes—this instrument may be given by a knowledgeable classroom teacher and tests for exactly what the title connotes. The sub-tests test for items such as pictorial and verbal absurdities. motor speed, auditory attention span, social adjustment, orientation, free association, number ability, ability to follow oral directions. All of these are aptitudes necessary to daily classroom performance. The scoring is received in the form of years and months. As an example, the child's chronological age may be six years, seven months, but he is only able to perform some of the sub-tests at the neurological age level of four years, two months. Thus, the teacher learns in what classroom areas the child is able to perform at his expected levels or those in which he is deficient.

Eisenson's Examining for Aphasia—this instrument performs a systematic exploration of the language functions of the child. It also may be related to the necessary remedial work.

The Wide Range Achievement Tests—the sub-tests cover the academic skill of the child in the areas of oral reading, spelling and arithmetic computation. It is considered a clinical evaluation of the levels of achievement for these areas. The test emcompasses kindergarten through college levels.

Wepman Test of Auditory Discrimination—this test does exactly what its title states—it tests the child's abilities in the areas of auditory discrimination, i.e., can the child discriminate between the "fine" sounds of the English language like T and D.

Goodenough-Harris Drawing Test—this is a non-verbal intelligence test which is scored on the basis of the child's drawings.

Otis Mental Ability Tests—this is a group instrument that measures I.Q.

Raven Progressive Matrices—a non-verbal instrument to test intelligence by requiring that the child solve problems presented in abstract figures and designs.

Cattell Infant Intelligence Scale—this is the downward extension of the Stanford-Binet Intelligence Scale. Its age range is from three to thirty months.

Gesell Developmental Schedules—this instrument is designed to test the pre-school child in the areas of motor development, adaptive behavior, language development, and social behavior.

Benton Visual Retention Test—this instrument tests the child's visual retention abilities, i.e., memory for designs and sequence of designs.

Harris Tests of Lateral Dominance—this instrument requires the judgment of the examiner as it is a combination of tests that test for lateral dominance. It is important in screening for maturational lag.

Vineland Social Maturity Scales—this instrument is designed, in progressive stages, to measure competency from infancy to adulthood in the areas of developmental history, growth—both improvement and deterioration, social education, vocational and educational guidance, as well as an insight into mental aberrations.

Make a Picture Story (Maps)—this is a projective technique wherein the child's inner picture of his world is brought forth via the use of background, placement of figures, and verbalizations.

Thermatic Apperception Test (T.A.T.)—this may be used on children and adults and is considered a projective test which delves into the areas of dominant drives, emotions, sentiments, complexes, and conflicts within the person being examined.

Durell Analysis of Reading Difficulty—this instrument diagnoses reading disabilities at three levels, non-reader or pre-primer, primary, and intermediate grade levels. The areas covered by the sub-tests are: oral reading, silent reading, listening comprehension and others.

Gray Oral Reading Tests—a verbal test, wherein the child reads paragraphs while the tester makes notations on his check sheet regarding the different kinds and types of errors made. In this manner, the child's reading level may be found.

Iowa Silent Reading Test—a non-verbal test for the first part, then the child must answer questions regarding what he has read. It checks for reading rate, comprehension, word meaning and information location.

Wide Range Vocabulary Test—a quick, concise estimator of the child's level of verbal or scholastic intelligence.

The Oseretsky Tests of Motor Proficiency—an instrument designed to test motor proficiency of children ages four through fourteen. It tests via the various sub-tests and exercises for general static coordination, dynamic coordination of the hands, general dynamic coordination, motor speed, simultaneous voluntary movements and assocated involuntary movements. It is of especial use to educators in evaluating a child's manual ability, skill and motor equilibrium.

Illinois Test of Psycholinguistic Abilities—an instrument still in research form and commonly refered to as the I.T.P.A. Basically, it is the newest of the intelligence tests and it is considered that its sub-tests give a definition to the specific problem areas as well as the strength areas for the tester. The score is received in terms of language age, i.e., above, below, or at the child's chronological age. The sub-tests cover the areas of auditory decoding and vocal association; visual decoding and motor association; motor encoding; and the sequential and automatic abilities for the vocal and visual-motor areas.

The reader must be aware that there is no such thing as the perfect testing instrument or testing situation. For instance, some of the instruments in most common use for children are standardized or have norms for adults. Some were standardized in foreign countries, yet are used frequently here in America. Some may have intra-test deviations which the testor must take into consideration when he evaluates the scoring. These, and many other factors play an inescapable role in testing and diagnosis. However, until we have perfect humans to devise and administer perfect tests, the many fine, albeit imperfect instruments, must suffice for our needs.

Ideally, all children should be thoroughly tested and evaluated near the end of their sixth year and that testing should continue throughout their academic life at approximately four to five year intervals. These evaluations can be valuable guidelines for parents, and useful tools to understanding a child. They are, I am convinced, well worth the financial investment involved. However, if a note of caution seems to pervade this chapter—an apparent reluctance to recommend testing for children until the necessity is entirely clear—it is only because I have been very conscious of the cost involved.

J. Piaget tells us, "we can foresee a good deal of progress in pedagogy, hand in hand with child psychology. . . . I am convinced that further progress in this field of psychology will have many repercussions on educational methods."[24] To Piaget's words, I would only add, it is not really enough to have education and psychology walk hand in hand—we must ask the parent to walk in cadence too.

I plage allegins to the
flag of the Uneit State's
of Amaca. And to the
Repulick for wich it
stands one nation
under god undavisabul
and justist for all

7

TEACHING

TECHNIQUES FOR TEACHING all of the children discussed in these pages are similar in nature – they vary only in the complexity of the methods required in a given case, and the length of time necessary for remediation. Just as learning disorders themselves present a continuum from mild to severe, so there is a continuum of teaching techniques – the more severe the problem to be remediated, the more intense must be the application of teaching methods and programming for the child.

Most clinical methods are logical, step-by-step progressions which help build neural pathways within the child. As with diagnosis, the earlier the child suffering with a learning disorder receives the special teaching attention he requires, the easier it is for teacher and child. The length of time necessary for such special teaching varies with the individual child and depends upon the type and degree of severity of his handicap. Any learning disorder requires very specific methods of teaching, and teaching techniques must vary or change to meet the specific nature of the individual child's strengths and weaknesses.

Patience is the key word in discussing remedial techniques. Time is necessary, but time is relative. What seems endless to one parent may appear quite reasonable to the next. For parents who have watched their child suffer through six grades of failure, a three-year remedial program to bring him up to grade level seems short. On the other hand, the parent who discovers that his first grader has problems, may find it difficult to understand why it takes three years to set him firmly on the path to normal learning. Suffering makes for patience.

As we discuss the different avenues of learning for the child with learning disabilities and the different techniques that can be used to help him, I will digress from time to time, to bring in an explanation of a clinical technique or principle that can be put to use immediately in a public classroom or home environment. These are simple, everyday ideas or ways of handling a situation that will not necessarily "cure" the problem, but will help to alleviate some of the day-to-day difficulties that parents, teachers and children have to meet. Some of these should, in the considered opinion of many experts, be used in all classrooms, for they could help all children regardless of their capabilities.

One of the major advances in teaching for these children, especially the specific dyslexic, has been achieved in just the last three years.

Heretofore, clinical techniques have always been used on a one-to-one (tutorial) basis, or at the most, one to four (one teacher, four children). It is now clear, however, that the tutorial or clinical methods that are necessary for working with these children can successfully be used with groups in the classroom, and can cover the full range of standard school curriculum. This does not mean, to be sure, classrooms containing thirty to forty children. It does mean that it is possible to teach eighteen to twenty-two children in a class. In addition, we now know that with the addition of a few relatively simple techniques to our present first and second grade school classrooms, it would be possible to give approximately one-third of our children who will be our future reading retardation problems that "extra lift" which might enable them to learn without remedial techniques. At the same time, we would be applying methodology that would immeasurably help the whole class with the learning process. This capacity to take these tutorial methods and principles into larger groups in the classroom has enormous ramifications for our educational system.

If we can make it economically feasible to handle these children within the framework of our public schools, we will be able to reduce the rate of school drop-outs. When these children achieve instead of fail in school, they will stay in school. And the effects of a successful effort in this direction will touch not only the children themselves, but everyone who has contact with them.

When approaching the teaching of children with learning disabilities, the immediate classroom environment is of crucial importance. Distractibility is the keynote here. Because children with learning disorders are easily distracted, it is necessary that the room in which a child is taught be free of unnessary accouterments on the walls, the desks—and even the teacher. The point is that the teacher should not have to *compete* for the child's attention. Noise, a smudge on his paper, pictures on the walls, a tapping pencil, a left-over lesson on the blackboard, teacher's bracelet that jingles, all are distractions. In a clinical school or tutorial room these things are not permitted.

It is truly amazing how many distracting objects are hung on the walls and blackboards of a typical classroom today. This one factor affects not only the children with learning problems, but all children—especially in the first three grades. All of the teaching aids, progress charts, maps and other paraphernalia of modern education, are all fine, in their place. But, their place should be in a drawer or cupboard when not in use. It is important to reduce the number of visually stimulating, and therefore distracting, objects in any classroom, but it is absolutely imperative that they be eliminated entirely for the children we are discussing here.

Noise is another distracting factor which intrudes upon the learning process for all children. In any classroom of twenty-five to thirty children there is more than enough noise generated just by the children themselves to make concentration difficult. Why then must we add traffic noise, the class next door, the class upstairs, movements in the hallways, all the unnecessary noise that intrudes upon a child sitting in a classroom trying to learn.

The seat placement of a child with a learning disorder is also extremely important to him and to his teacher. Oftentimes, the simple act of moving a child to make it easier for him to see and hear will help him to learn. Traditionally, teachers have placed the class trouble-makers directly in front of them so that they can exercise better control over them. This practice is not always fair to the child who desperately needs to sit directly in front of the teacher. To a child with an auditory perception problem, the teacher's instructions can become a horror for two reasons. First, of course, he is not able to hear her properly—remember this is a child whose translation of the auditory sounds is impaired.

Second, there is the problem of instruction sorting. For parents and teachers alike—the number of words used to tell a child what to do is, at times, truly remarkable. A mother, when dinner is ready, is likely to go to the door and call, "Billy, come in now and wash your hands for dinner." As the child approaches, she continues, "be sure you use soap, and don't dirty the guest towels, use the blue towel I put on the bowl for you. Wipe your feet before you come in." Then, as the child goes by her, she says, "did you do your homework, you didn't tell me how school was today. Oh, do hurry up, you're always so slow and dinner will get cold!"

If, instead of all these words, she would simply go to the door and say, "Billy, dinner, come wash," life would be infinitely simpler for Billy—and for mother too. What happens is that Billy gets so lost in trying to sort all of the words, instructions, and questions, he doesn't wash well, uses the wrong towel, and comes to the table with a disquieting sense of undefined frustration. His mother can't understand his sudden change of humor, sees that he used the wrong towel, tracked dirt across the kitchen . . . result, dinner just has to be unpleasant.

This same situation can occur in a classroom. A teacher may constantly be interrupted, or interrupt herself, while giving class instructions. "Now, class, take out your social studies book—Johnny, who gave you permission to sharpen your pencil?—turn to page one hundred—yes, Mary, you may be excused—page one hundred and three, and today we will study about vol—Eugene, stop that racket!—volcanoes." A trial of fortitude, a true test of sorting ability, for teacher and child. It is almost certain that the child, and his lesson, will come out second best.

Another dimension to proper seat placement for a child is his position in relation to the blackboard. It can be agony for a child who can barely use the alphabet, to have to stretch constantly, fight glare, and decipher chalk shadings from a distance. Even under the best circumstances he will have trouble, but with poor placement in the room his problems are multiplied.

If just these three simple reforms, uncluttered classrooms, noise abatement, and proper seat placement, were initiated in every classroom in the country it would be a major step toward remediation of one-third of our reading problems. And, there is nothing here that in some way can not be applied to a home situation.

Ideally, and most certainly for best results, a child with a learning disorder should attend a school where the full curriculum is taught on the basis of the special clinical methods he so badly needs. However, in our country today, there are too few such facilities for the minimal learning disorders. If we are to adequately teach these children, we must institute programs in the public schools for them.

Presently, if a child is receiving any help at all, it is likely to be in a tutorial situation. This means that the child either goes to a private tutor or to a university-affiliated reading clinic. After school hours, or sometime during his school day, he is removed from his classroom to receive tutorial instruction. But even for the lucky children who are receiving such help, there are serious drawbacks. If a child is tutored after school hours, he is tired, has had his fill of school by then, and is long past his optimum learning time of the day. Most tutorial situations encompass only reading and other language skills. The child does not receive any help in the other areas of the curriculum. He still must function without aid in social studies, arithmetic, history, science, etc. And, if he is taken out of class for tutoring, he is made to feel "different" from the other students with whom he must function socially—always an added burden to a child already in trouble.

Researchers feel that the basic problem for the dyslexic child is that of a massive neurological immaturity, and for the minimally damaged child, a need to overcome or work around a particular type of problem.

Reading, or the act of reading, is the ability to identify and combine properly the sight, sound, and meaning of a letter of the alphabet, or sequence of letters. This identifying and combining is accomplished via perception of symbols (i.e., letters), comprehension and association of what has been read. Frequently, these types of minimal, often subtle, problems will not become evident in a child until he enters first grade. Let's investigate a six or seven-year-old as he enters the first grade.

We automatically assume that a first grader has either reached, or very nearly reached, a stage of neurological development that is comparable to his chronological age level. He is given work to do based on this assumption. But, what happens to him if his maturity is that of only a four-year-old? He is defeated before he starts. The simplest techniques of perception, that other children have learned, are denied him. The classic example, which we have noted earlier, is the b—d reversal and the p—q inversion.

Let us transfer these perceptual errors into another area of childhood experience. Consider one of the first objects a child meets as an infant—a cup. We can make an interesting analogy to the b-d-p-q problem. Take an ordinary kitchen cup, hold it in your hand as if to drink, now reverse the handle to the left, it is still a cup—now hold the cup upside down, handle to the right, then to the left—still a cup. In other words, no matter where the handle is—up, down, left, or right, the object is still a cup. Now again look at the letters b-d-p-q, all are really only a circle with a straight line. It is where the circle is placed that changes the use and sound of the circle and straight line—yet the cup didn't change when you moved the circle—

or handle—around.[25] We expect children, with this concrete knowledge of a cup, to enter a classroom and almost instantly be able to master this whole new concept, without telling them that the rules have been changed, and changed drastically! A formidable prospect for a child without perception problems, let alone those with perception problems.

What else do we do to or expect of our first graders? The following pages are devoted to a listing of the skills that are considered necessary to the development of good reading *at the first grade level.* It will be instructive to consider the variety of skills we expect of a six or seven-year-old. Most children, to be sure, master them with relative ease, but it is easy to see the many points at which a child with perceptual problems may encounter trouble.

IN THE AREAS OF VISUAL PERCEPTION AND DISCRIMINATION A CHILD MUST BE ABLE TO:

do *directional drills*
understand *differences in geometric forms*
have ability to do *sequential geometric form drills*
see and understand *likenesses in abstract figures*
know his *position of body in space*
know laterality—*his right from his left hand*
have *visual discrimination for objects*
have *visual discrimination for details in pictures*
have the *ability to complete pictures*
have *visual discrimination for gross symbols*
be able to perform *perceptual constancy drills*
discriminate the *differences in form and position of objects*
have *perception of spatial relationships*
have ability for *comparing and constrasting configuration of words*
be able to perform *figure-ground perception*
be able to perform *visual-motor drills*
discriminate *differences in gross symbols*
discriminate *differences in horizontal and vertical lines and curves in making words*
discriminate *likenesses and differences in word configurations*
be able to perform *matching drills with initial letters*
have *discrimination of small symbols*
be able to perform *word pattern matching drills*
have *visual discrimination of words of similar appearance*
understand *differences in consonant blends*
be able to perform *matching drills for word patterns—short vowel plus one consonant*

IN THE AREAS OF AUDITORY PERCEPTION AND DISCRIMINATION A CHILD MUST:

understand *common words as spoken*
be able to perform *listening drills for differences in words*
be able to *reproduce pronounced three syllable words*
be able to perform *rhythmic training drills*
be able to perform *digit drills for attention span*
have *recognition of rhyming elements*
be able to *reproduce rhyming sounds*
be able to recognize *words to rhyme with pictures*
be able to *perceive rhythmic phrases*
have *recognition and discrimination of common sounds*
have *recognition and discrimination of similar sounds*
give *initial consonant sounds to pictures*
be able to *hear similarities in initial consonant sounds*
be able to *match first sounds of words*
be able to *hear and reproduce the sounds of K, Q, V, X, Z*
be able to *hear first, last and middle sounds in words*
be able to *hear vowel differences*
be able to *hear and reproduce all consonants*
be able to *hear and reproduce short vowels*
be able to *hear and reproduce long vowels*
be able to *hear and reproduce consonant blends*

IN THE AREA OF COMPREHENSION A CHILD MUST:

be able to *classify common objects*
have a *concept of when, where, what and who*
have *ability to tell time*
understand *sequence of events*
have ability to *anticipate holidays, etc.*
have a *concept of directional words—stop, go, etc.*
have a *concept of up, down, first, last, etc.*
be able to *interpret pictures*
be able to *follow a picture sequence*
be able to *draw conclusions*
be able to *interpret punctuation*
understand and use *capital and small letters as an aid to learning*
be able to *use capital letters for names and beginning of sentences*
understand *use of word "and" to connect two ideas*

have *developing weather concepts*
be able to *match color names to colors*
be able to *associate action with words, come, run, etc.*
have developing *knowledge of community workers*
understand *difference between fact and fantasy*
understand *meaning of first grade vocabulary*
have a *visualization of what is read*
be able to *follow one step directions*
be able to *classify ideas*
be able to *perform and comprehend similar word drills*
understand *sentence meaning*
have *meaningful use of new words*
have *concept of singular and plural*
be able to *identify individual items included in a general term*
be able to *answer questions based on reading*
be able to *select a sentence to answer a question*
be able to *select a phrase to complete sentence*
be able to *follow two-step directions*
be able to *select quotations*
be able to *give antecedents of pronouns*
have *awareness of sentence structure*
be able to *visualize the thought in a story*
be able to answer *inferential questions based on reading*
be able to give *appropriate abbreviations*
have *concept of true and false*
understand *opposite thoughts connected by "but"—compound sentence*
have *ability to use context clue for meaning of new word*
understand and use *compound words*
have a *concept of subject and predicate of sentence—"who" did something?—"what" did he do?*
have *concept of use of possessive—mine, yours, etc.*
have *concept of words that can be used as both noun and verb*
be able to *determine which sentence tells about some point in story—relevancy*
have *ability to select title*
have a *concept of first, next, last*
be able to *comprehend what punctuation means to sentence structure—paragraph structure*

IN THE AREA OF STRUCTURAL ANALYSIS A CHILD MUST BE ABLE TO:

use *short vowel sounds*
use *long vowel sounds*
use *consonants in final position*
perform *blending of short vowel and final consonant*
perform *blending of consonants in initial position*
word patterns—*short "a" plus tongue consonants*
word patterns—*short "a" plus labial consonants*
word patterns—*short "a" plus throat consonants*
word patterns—*short "a" plus throat consonants*
word patterns—*short vowels plus single tongue consonants*
word patterns—*short vowels plus single labial consonants*
word patterns—*short vowels plus single throat consonants*
use of *digraphs—sh, th, wh, ch, ng, ck*
use of *dipthongs—ōō, ŏŏ, oi, oy, ou, ow, au, aw*
use of *blends—mp, sp, pl, spl, nt, tr, bl, st*
use of *blends—all "r" and "l"*
use of *final y*
use of *y as i*
use of *y as e*
use of *two vowel rule—ōa*
ability to *add "s" to verb*
be able to give *word classifications—ight, etc.*
use of *vowels plus "r"—er, ir, ur, ar, or*
use of the *silent final e rule*
use of *ack, all, ay, oy endings*
the *three sounds of "ed" endings—ed, d, i*
use *of "all" and "old" words*
use *of rhyming phonograms*
use *of final "ll" and "ck"*
use *of abbreviations—Mr., Mrs.*
use *of "a" as a prefix*
concept *of inflectional endings—s, ed, ing*

The author gratefully acknowledges the use of the McGlannan School's unique report cards from which the above lists were taken. The school's first grade report card is twenty pages long and is part of a complete breakdown of skills expected of children at each of the elementary grade levels.

There are four avenues of learning though which a child learns and the teacher may teach, and children with learning disorders need to employ them all. Educators abbreviate these four avenues as V.A.K.T.—

V = visual, A = auditory, K = kinesthetic, and T = tactile.

The first two, visual and auditory, of course, are the basic means of learning for all of us. It is the eyes and the ears that are primarily used in classrooms today. A child with a learning disorder, however, must also have the other two avenues used in the teaching and learning process if he is to learn effectively.

Kinesthetic adds a motor activity to the learning process. An example is tracing or outlining a large letter or word—and doing it over and over again. The letter or word must be large enough to use the arm muscle as opposed to standard writing where just the finger and wrist muscles are used. Muscular (motor) activity of this kind reinforces what the eye is seeing. When a child uses a large primary crayon or chalk to trace a word, it helps him coordinate what his eye is seeing with what his hand is doing—it is almost as if there is a physical "pull" that reaches into the brain. Teachers of these children sometimes regret the fact that we no longer use individual slate boards in our schools as in the past. The use of individual slates is probably one of the best examples of kinesthetic teaching that at one time was in common use for all children.

Tactile means touch and describes methods that employ the sensory modality of touch for learning. These methods are similar to the ways in which we teach blind children—and the way infants learn about the world around them. When a baby is beginning to discover the world, he not only smells, tastes, looks at, and listens to an object, but he also touches it all over, feels it with his hands. In this way he becomes aware of its form, depth, size, shape and character.

When these two avenues to learning, the kinesthetic and the tactile, are added to the visual and auditory, the child with a learning disorder is aided immeasurably.

To further help a child with a learning disorder, one more factor must be added. *Association.* Proper association is often overlooked as an aid to learning even in some clinical schools, and most school workbooks on the market today seem to ignore this very important facet of learning. For example, when teaching a child the initial sound "ã" as in age or aid, workbooks will often instruct the child to underline, circle or X all of the words containing this sound on a page. *This method does not reinforce the child's association of the letter with the proper sound.* An X or a circle has nothing to do with the sound "ã". Instead, the child should be instructed to trace the letter with his pencil, verbalizing the sound at the same time, thus achieving association for him.

A favorite anecdote among the group I have worked with concerns a boy who, after painstaking care, finally learned the composite parts of the word "until," but still could not "pull" the word instantly from memory when he tried to read it. Finally, he said to his teacher, "if I could just *see* an 'until', I know I could remember it." What was necessary to complete the boy's mastery of the word was an associative method. The boy was instructed to draw, from within himself, his idea of the word—to make a picture to go with a sentence using the word. The boy then carefully drew a picture of a herd of cows, pastureland, a fence with a gate, and a farmhouse in the distance, with the cows going through the gate toward the farmhouse. He then wrote his sentence, "I will wait until the cows come home." For this boy, with this word, "until the cows come home" provided the needed association and visual memory that firmly "set" it in his mind. From then on, whenever he came across the word, no matter how different or complicated the context, he could look at it and say, "Oh yes, that's until—until the cows come home." This achievement is not inconsequential. The child had used all of his avenues of learning—then added association and was able to read, write, spell, and comprehend the word "until."

The details of specific teaching methods are too long and too complicated to pursue here. However, an overview of this entire V.A.A.* K.T. approach to teaching and learning may be obtained from a brief description of the way the letter A might be taught.

Visual—the child looks at the letter "A," he attempts to learn to recognize it in all its forms, lower case, upper case (capitals), different type styles, different sizes, at the beginning of a word, in the middle of a word, at the end of a word, wherever it may be, and in whatever form it may appear. Thus, when an "A" is seen, he will immediately recognize it.

Auditory—the child then learns the different sounds of "a," and how those sounds change with the placement of it in conjunction with other letters. He learns to blend these different sounds properly with other sounds, i.e., "a" blends into "at," "at" blends into "pat," "ā" blends into "āge," "āge" blends into "gāge" and so on.

Kinesthetic—the child traces the letter "a"—first with a heavy black crayon, eyes open. He is then asked to reproduce the letter, again with black crayon, eyes closed. In both case he says the sound aloud as he traces it.

Tactile—the child then traces over the heavy crayon residue with his index finger, eyes closed. He may also turn to letters cut from wood—with these, he is able to learn the front, back and shape of the letter with his hands. He will run his index finger through the groove left in the wood block from which the letter was cut. Or, he may use a replica of the letter made from pipe cleaner material and pasted on a small cardboard square, again tracing with his finger over the configuration of the letter. He can trace the letter and make copies of it from clay. He becomes totally familiar with the "feel" of the letter, using his sense of touch.

Association—from within himself, the child must form an association to go with the letter "a." He makes words, then sentences, then a whole story of the sight, sound and use of the letter. He will draw an association picture for the letter—thus, we start with "a," go on to "at," on to "pat," thence to "my mother will pat my head" and on to a picture of mother patting him on his head. Association must always come from the child, not the teacher. It does no good for a teacher to suggest "an example of

* Association[26]

this word would be: mother will pat you on the head." The child must think it out for himself.

This is a very brief overview of the teaching techniques employed for these children. However, it is clear that the process is long, complicated and tedious. In fact, it is hard to find a "happy" adjective to apply to these methods, *but the fact remains that they work—they will teach a child to read.*

The average child only requires mainly visual and some auditory techniques to learn. Other children must have all four avenues opened up in order for them to learn. Some only need all of them some of the time. Each child is different—and this is the best reason I know why parents should not attempt to teach their own children. A parent who is not a teacher or a clinician cannot possibly know which methods are necessary for a specific child. These specialized techniques are designed to give a child "total involvement" in the process of learning and *must* be applied by qualified persons. This does not mean, however, that parents should never attempt to help their children at home. The many studies of children who have learned the alphabet or the fundamentals of reading at home indicate that no harm is done—*unless the child is unable to perform and thus is placed in a stressful situation.*

Once a child is able to read, he operates at three levels: first, the *functional level* or level at which he is able to read independently. Second, his *instructional level* or the level at which he is operating in the classroom situation. And, finally, his *frustration level* or the level to which the teacher is slowly introducing him, and the level at which he still misses at least half of what he reads. A child should never attempt to function outside a classroom at any but the *functional level* and parents who do not understand this do their children a great disservice.

One might well ask if all the time and effort necessary for V.A.A.K.T. teaching is worth the results. The answer must always be yes. Every parent and every teacher wants the children they are dealing with to become productive adults. The greatest harm done to these children and to the adults concerned with them is that we lose their productivity. The dyslexic and the minimal dysfunction problems we are speaking of have high potential. These are the children who can learn, are intellectually capable, and can contribute productively to society. We are literally "throwing these children away" when we do not teach them in the manner they need to learn.

It appears we do not at present have facilities for helping these children in our school systems for two reasons—ignorance and economy. Few educators know how much can be accomplished with a minimum of time and effort and a slight alteration of or addition to our present programs. Actually, a few of our far-sighted public school systems are already accomplishing much in this area through what is known as "unit teaching." Let us see what can be done with "unit teaching" in a particular subject—geography.

Geography is built upon time lines and sequences that cannot be "seen" and upon geographic locations that are simply lines on a map.

When a child with impaired visual perception looks at a map of the continents, it may appear to him to be a mere collection of symbolic designs. "Looking" therefore does not necessarily mean that the child "sees" that Africa is larger than Australia, or that England has a jagged coast while Florida's is smooth. But, if a child is permitted to trace the continents, color them, cut them out, paste them on a styrofoam globe, and then take string and attach his own longitude and latitude lines—when he is through, he will know the difference between the Near East and Far East, and the Gulf of Mexico and the Black Sea. He has used all of his avenues to learning—visual, auditory, kinesthetic and tactile.

Earlier in the chapter a listing of first grade skills which are necessary to reading was given, but what clues can a parent or teacher look for in these children who have such subtle impairments? What indications will there be of more than normal learning difficulty? What errors will the child himself make? There are a number of possible areas of error that interested teachers and parents should be aware of.

Incorrect pronunciation of vowels or consonants, i.e., rug for rag, or fad for fat; difficulty with phonemes; perseveration of words or sounds; lack of comprehension of what is being read; complete omission of words, word endings or beginnings, or when going from one line to the next, omission of complete lines of type; difficulty with "sound alike" words; and, of course, reversals or inversions.

Some of these difficulties are fairly normal for any young child. It is when the child has reached the last one-third of the first grade or above, and they still persist or show no sign of improving, that we must look long and hard at the child to see if he is in trouble. *We must not wait, as is the present common practice, until the child is in the third or fourth grade.*

When discussing the education of any child, we must also take into consideration what the child is not allowed to do in most of our classrooms today. There are many learning aids which can come automatically from the child himself which will help him learn. He will work out for himself techniques that help him read more effectively. Unfortunately, however, these techniques are not accepted by current educational theory and they are usually denied to the children. J. F. and S. R. Jastak give us an excellent overview of what today's school child "dare not do."[27]

"The literature on reading instruction contains various prescriptions as to what children should not be encouraged to do in learning to read. Sometimes such prescriptions are in the form of indirect allusions that children are slowed down when they use certain ways of learning.

"Among the taboos are pointing with the finger, moving lips, oral reading, reading without comprehension, spelling aloud before reading, reading without inflection, phonic reading, breaking words up into syllables, etc. These interdictions are taught with complete confidence in their validity without evidence that they are bad habits except that they 'slow children down.' Furthermore, they are applied as absolute rules to persons of any age and at any point of the learning stage. We have heard of supervisors and reading specialists visiting classrooms for the sole purpose of checking whether any of the children move their lips or point with their fingers while reading. Teachers whose children move their lips are condemned as inferior and are given poor professional ratings. This strange behavior on the part of supervisors and reading experts causes more retardation in reading than any moving of the lips or pointing with the finger has ever done. It can be demonstrated that some children who point with their fingers read faster and more accurately than when they do not point. The fallacy of 'being slowed down' stems from the observations that good readers do not point with their fingers but poor readers do. It is known however to students of statistics that correlation is not causation. The poor reader, finding that he loses his way or that his performance is not what it should be, hits upon the device of using his finger to help himself. Pointing with the finger becomes an important temporary aid in overcoming the coordination difficulties that exist in poor readers. Pointing with the finger is not a cause but an effect of reading disability. It is helpful in the early stages of learning to read and is spontaneously abandoned as the skill of reading gains in efficiency.

"If the inversion of cause and effect were carried to its logical extreme, one might be justified in concluding that only those children would learn to read fast whose fingers are cut off, whose lips are taped, and whose vocal chords are paralyzed."

Everyone who has a child who is having difficulty in learning to read, must agree with the Jastaks—anything that helps a child to learn should be used.

Some educators complain that many of the remedial techniques for children with learning disorders are akin to kindergarten methods, child-like in conception and usage. It almost seems that they assume that if it is "simple" it is no good. This is far from the truth. Determining what techniques are appropriate for a particular child's special form of disability is a very complex problem indeed. Yet the individual techniques may be relatively simple. The problem is not complexity, but time and proper choice, they are tedious and time-consuming and necessitate extreme caution in their coordination.

Since time is money, and educational reality demands that costs be taken into consideration, let us look at the economics involved in diagnosing and teaching children with minimal learning disorders.

If, at the kindergarten level, all children were screened for possible perceptual problems, a substantial portion of the problem children would be identified. In the chapter on testing and diagnosis a simple ten-minute screening instrument is included that can be given to children by trained volunteers, a pediatrician in his office, or when the children register in the spring for the first grade the following September.

Then, if these children who gave evidence of perceptual problems were given Frostig's Perceptual Training Program[28] over the summer months, or as an adjunct to the kindergarten program, one-third of the problem children would be on their way to remediation. The next one-third, when they enter the first grade, will still need a continuing program of perceptual training, possibly some remedial tutoring, and most certainly sympathetic teachers. The other one-third will require intensive training and should be referred to the school guidance department immediately. It is cheaper in the long run to screen, test, and remediate at the very early ages, than to wait until later in the child's life—even until grade three or four. It is the usual procedure today to wait until a child reaches the third or fourth grade before his problem is acknowledged. By then, an emotional overlay is very likely to have developed which must be broken through before the child can be successfully taught—and at that late date, it takes longer. All experts agree that the optimum age for remediation is between five and eight years.

For children already in a school where no program for diagnosis and treatment is available, an awareness of the problem on the part of the classroom teachers, initiation of some of the simpler techniques, and a testing program for the children who have been receiving social promotions through the grades can be helpful to many. In many schools the introduction of ungraded reading levels has proved a useful innovation. A child works his way up, at his own pace, through the different levels, without the competitive pressure to keep up with his class.

At the college level, a greater recognition of the needs of these students is badly needed and would be a major step in the right direction. Too often it is assumed that a student who cannot compete with his contemporaries simply isn't capable of "college level work." Yet this is not always true. On a history exam, for example, if the student knows the answer, but cannot spell quickly and accurately, he may fail the timed tests he is given—even though he may have mastered the subject thoroughly. I am not suggesting that colleges should change their curriculums, or that students should not meet the college's standards. I am suggesting that some—perhaps many—students fail, not because they are incapable intellectually or academically, but because they have difficulty in performing the mechanical functions required in modern test-taking as fast and accurately as their more fortunate contemporaries. Better understanding of their plight could salvage many of these young people.

Too often, I'm afraid, we are unaware of a rather subtle change that has taken place in our educational system during the last ten years. We have accelerated the curriculum at every level to the point where a first grader now meets a program that contains much of what used to be required of third graders. In other words, the first grade today is keyed to eight-year-olds, rather than six-year-olds. This is not necessarily wrong, especially for very bright children. But it does place a heavy burden on children with learning disorders, as well as on the less capable.

There is obviously no real barrier to teaching children suffering with these minimal learning disorders. The basic prerequisite is a teacher with knowledge of the problems, appropriate treatment techniques, and patience and ingenuity in adapting techniques to the individual child. A second and equally vital necessity is parents who understand the problems and are willing to learn along with their child. But, before either teacher or parent can cope with these disorders effectively, a massive effort must be made among both laymen and professionals to achieve recognition, funding, and most of all acceptance of the needs of the children.

8

A FINAL COMMENT

This book has been an attempt to stimulate dialogue: dialogue between reader and author, and a beginning dialogue between parents and the professionals who are concerned with – and necessary to – these children.

In re-reading the manuscript I find that it is studded with many if's, but's, cautions and concerns. There are several reasons why this should be so. First, our school system was designed to serve the "normal" child – that theoretical "average" who never existed. In the course of the past generation or more we have paid lip service to the concept of individual differences – but only rarely have we matched our words with comparable action. To be sure, in recent years we have given greater attention to those children who diverged furthest from the norm – the very bright, and those who suffered from serious learning disabilities – but even here our record has been spotty. We have done even less in providing for the differences of that infinitely varied group we call "normal" – and virtually nothing for those with minimal learning disorders – our *Shadow Children*. For a nation that possesses the greatest financial and intellectual resources in history, this is a sorry record.

Second, wide knowledge of the nature of minimal learning disorders has been inhibited by lack of communication among the disciplines concerned – and sometimes by the professional vested interests involved. Certainly the multi-disciplinary character of the literature on the subject does present a legitimate obstacle to professional understanding, but too often lack of understanding seems to come from a willful disregard of the easily available facts.

At a mental health conference in the spring of 1967, for instance, a reputable psychiatrist made the unqualified assertion that all learning disorders can be traced directly back to mental illness. And, a director of speech correction for a New England public school system, in a Spring 1967 issue of a national magazine, called dyslexia "a fancy and fashionable word, pseudo-scientific labelling." She then recounted the case history of a young girl who displayed many of the classic symptoms of dyslexia. It is not possible, of course, to diagnose the case of this child at long distance, but there is far too much data on the record for any professional's assertion that dyslexia is "a fancy and fashionable word" to be anything less than irresponsible. Yet her case, and that of the psychiatrist, highlight the problem of professional knowledge in the field of learning disorders. One was a specialist in the field of speech, the other in psychiatry, and most of the literature on the subject comes out of the fields of neurology, clinical reading and research, psychology, optometry, and related professional areas.

These problems present special difficulties for parents of children with learning disorders. Fortunately, the number of school systems attempting to learn about and provide care for the *Shadow Children* is slowly growing, and the number of unaware and uninformed professionals is rapidly decreasing. But parents must also face another serious obstacle to adequate treatment for their children—the limited number of facilities prepared to work with handicapped children, and the consequent overcrowding. Nearly every facility, whether public or private, has a waiting list—many of them unbelievably long. It is especially difficult for parents to find a facility that offers a full curriculum for children with minimal learning handicaps. Many clinics are only able to provide tutorial help, and can handle only fifteen to twenty-five children a year. This situation makes particularly disheartening the news received during 1967 that the Johns Hopkins Reading Clinic and Research Facility, under the direction of the great John Money, must close due to lack of funds. It may seem unusual to fret about the closing of one research-clinical facility—but this is not just any facility. It was the Johns Hopkins unit that sponsored the 1960 Conference on Dyslexia, and it was the report of that conference which once and for all took specific dyslexia out of the "pseudo-scientific" or "brain damage" categories. It clearly, concisely and finally, after years of confusion, exactly defined the nature of this minimal learning disorder. The clinic lost the federal funds that supported it, apparently because the federal bureaucracy cannot understand that in order to do research on minimal learning disorders, one does not sit in a laboratory with test tubes, one sits in a clinic room with children. In order to provide clinical research, the facility must offer clinical services—the children are the test tubes. Put as gently as possible, this attitude, which has closed down one of our country's finest facilities, is tragically short-sighted.

* * *

One final note to parents—if you discover that you have a child with a learning disorder, remember, it is not the child's fault, nor is it yours. It is not the end of the world for you or your child—in fact, the discovery is likely to turn out to be the beginning of a new world for you both.

GLOSSARY

Ameliorate: To make better or improve, a relieving of the problem.

Anomaly: Anything unusual or irregular or contrary to the general rule. A departure from the norm.

Anoxia: Lack of or failure to properly use the necessary amount of oxygen in the blood.

Chronological Age (Also: Mental Age, Neurological Age, Language Age): All of these ages have meaning for testers and educators. A child's *chronological age* refers to his actual age in years and months, *mental age* refers to his intelligence age in years and months, and his *neurological age* refers to his neurological maturity age. These ages are used in a correlated sense, i.e., a child may be six years, seven months chronological age, but only able to perform neurologically at the age level of a four year, five month old, and yet his mental age may be equal to or above his chronological age. The *language age,* again refers to the child's ability to use, as well as, speak the language as compared to his other age levels.

Continuum of Learning Disabilities: This continuum means, start with the premise all children are normal/average, and the sequence deviations, degree of deviations therefrom are the continuum.

Electroencephalogram: A method of recording the electrical activity of the brain, especially of the cerebral cortex. The electrical impulses are detected by means of wires attached to the scalp and are recorded graphically in waves—thus, the term "gram." Commonly referred to as EEG.

Etiology: An assignment of cause; in medicine the theory of the causes of a disease.

Familial: Pertaining to the family.

Genetic: Having to do with the principles of heredity and variation in animals and plants of the same or related kinds.

Hyperkinetic: Overactive movement.

Manifestations: Apparent to the eye or to the mind, clearly seen or demonstrated.

Maturational Lag: This denotes the degree, or lag, the child may demonstrate in his neurological age versus his chronological age. Also, in psychology this may refer to his social adjustment level versus his chronological age.

Natal: Relating to birth.

Neonatal: Relating to the period immediately succeeding birth and continuing through the first month of life.

Neural: Pertaining to the nervous system.

Perinatal: Occuring, or pertaining to, before, during, or after the time of birth. (Also: PRENATAL).

Phoneme: In linguistics, a phoneme is one of the basic sound units of speech. There are, in the English language, supposed to be forty-four phonemes.

Phylogenetic Scales: The scales used by researchers as characteristic of the race or species history, rather than individual history.

Physiology: This is a science which deals with the normal functions of living things or their organs. When we say physiologically speaking, we mean, the norms for female versus male, i.e., strengths, weaknesses, etc., indicate the female is stronger.

Projective Technique: In testing, there are many tests wherein the tester is given guidelines for scoring, but the must take into consideration of multitude of other factors concerning the person being tested as an individual – then make their judgment.

Protocol: The overall pattern of the child's handicap, his diagnosis, all that is known about a particular child.

Reading Retardation: In education it is usually considered that a child suffers reading retardation if he is two or more years behind grade level in his reading abilities. This term is applied regardless of the cause or reason for the reading retardation.

Remediate (Also: Remedial, Remediation): To remedy, to help, to relieve, a pedagogical term used to indicate the relieving, but not necessarily the curing of an educational problem.

Syndrome: A group of symptoms or signs, which when considered together characterized the handicap, disorder, disability, etc.

SUGGESTED READING LIST

Abrahamson, E. M., Pezet, A. W.
Body, Mind and Sugar
Holt, Rinehart and Winston
New York, New York

A Briefing for Parents: Your Child's Intelligence
National Education Association of the United States
Washington, D. C.

Almy, A., Chittenden, E., Miller, P.
Young Childrens Thinking
Forward by J. Piaget
Teachers College Press
Columbia University, N. Y., N. Y.

Bender, L.
Specific Reading Disability as a Maturational Lag
Orton Society Bulletin 7:9-18

Benton, A. L., Bird, J. W.
The EEG and Reading Disability
Amer. Journ. of Orthopsychiatry 33:529-531

Bloom, Benjamin S.
Stability and Change in Human Characteristics
John Wiley & Sons, Inc.
New York, New York

Clements, S. D.
Minimal Brain Dysfunction in Children: Terminology and Identification
Task Force I document of the national project on MBD in children.
Washington, D. C., March, 1966

Clements, S. D., Peters, J. E.
Minimal Brain Dysfunction in the School-Age Child
AMA Arch. of gen. psych.

Conference Papers—International Approach To Learning Disabilities
Association for Children with Learning Disabilities. Tulsa, Oklahoma
(This is a parent organization which has a multi-disciplinary advisory board. It is suggested that all interested parents contact A.C.L.D. for parent information.)

Crider, B.
The Lack of Cerebral Dominance as a Cause of Reading Disability
Childhood Education 10:238-39, 270

Critchley, Macdonald
Developmental Dyslexia
William Heinemann Medical Books, Ltd.
London, England

Cruickshank, W. M., Bentzen, F. A., Ratzbury, F. H., Tannhauser, M. T.
A Teaching Method for Brain-Injured and Hyperactive Children
Syracuse University Press
Syracuse, New York

Cruickshank, W. M.
The Teacher of Brain-Injured Children
Syracuse University Press
Syracuse, New York

DeWitt, F. B.
Academic Therapy Quarterly
San Rafael, California
(This quarterly is published for interested professionals and parents.)

Dolch, E. W.
A Manual for Remedial Reading
Garrard Press
Champaign, Illinois

Eastman, N. J.
The Brain Damaged Child; Why Does He Happen?
The Dallas Med. Journal

Eisenberg, Leon
Reading Retardation
Pediatrics Journal 37:2, 352-366

Eustis, R. R.
Specific Reading Disability: a familial syndrome, associated with ambidexterity and speech defects and a frequent cause of behavior problems
New England Journ. of Medicine 237-243

Experiences of a Sufferer From Word Blindness
British Journ. of Ophthalmology
London, England

Explorations in Educational Techniques
Report under ESEA 89-10 Title I Project
St. Charles Community Schools
St. Charles, Michigan

Fernald, G. M.
Remedial Techniques in Basic School Subjects
McGraw Hill Book Co.
New York, New York

Filbin, R. L.
A Prescription for Johnny Who Can't Read
Elementary English 34:559-561

Fisher, D. C.
A Montessori Mother
Holt, Rinehart and Winston, Inc.
New York, New York

Frostig, Marianne
Exercises for the Development of Visual Perception (exercises and manual)
Follett Publishing Company
Chicago, Illinois

Gallagher, J. R.
Specific Language Disability: Dyslexia
Orton Society Bulletin 10:5-10

Getman, G. N.
Pre-School Perceptual Skills: An aide to first grade achievement
Optometric Weekly 53:1749-1753

Gillingham, A., Stillman, B. W.
Remedial Training for Children with Specific Disability in Reading, Spelling, and Penmanship

Hallgren, Bertil
Specific Dyslexia
Acta psych. neur., Suppl 65, 1-287

Hanvik, L. J., Hanson, H. B.
The Child With A Possible Organic Brain Injury
Washburn Memorial Clinic
Minneapolis, Minn.

Harris, A. J.
Lateral Dominance, Directional Confusion and Reading Disability
Journ. of Psychiatry 44:283-294

Hellmuth, J., Straug, B.
Learning Disorders—Two Volumes
Seattle Seguin School, Inc.
Seattle, Washington

Hellmuth J., Straub, B.
Educational Therapy
Seattle Seguin School, Inc.
Seattle, Washington

Hermann, Knud
Reading Disability
Charles C. Thomas, Publisher
Springfield, Illinois

Ilg, F. L., Ames, L. B.
The Gesell Institute's Child Behavior
Dell Publishing Co., Inc.
New York, New York

Ilg, F. L., Ames, L. B.
School Readiness
Harper & Row, Publishers
New York, New York

Jastak, J. F. and S. R.
Wide Range Achievement Test—Manual of Instructions
Guidance Associates
Wilmington, Delaware

Johnson, D. J., Myklebust, H. R.
Learning Disabilities
Grune & Stratton
New York, New York

Kawi, A. A., Pasamanick, B.
Prenatal-Paranatal Factors in the Development of Childhood Reading Disorders
Monograph Soc. Res. Child Development 24, No. 4, 1-80

Kephart, N. C., Radler, D. H.
Success Through Play
Harper and Row, Publishers
New York, New York

Kerr, James
The Lancet
London, England

Koppitz, E. M., Mardis, V., Stephens, T.
A Note on Screening School Beginners with the Bender-Gestalt Test
Journ. Educ. Psych. 52:80-81

Krise, E. M.
Reversals In Reading: a problem in space perception
Journ. of Nerv. and Mental Dis. 89:164-173

Lewis, R. S.
The Brain Injured Child
National Society for Crippled Children and Adults
Chicago, Illinois
(This organization should be contacted by interested parents.)

Lewis, R. S., Strauss, A. A., Lehtinen, L. E.
The Other Child
Grune and Stratton
New York, New York

Malmquist, E.
Factors Related to Reading Disabilities in the First Grade of the Elementary School
Almquist and Wiksell
Stockholm, Sweden

McGlannan, Frances K.
Dyslexia—Theory Into Practice
The Professional Press, Inc.
Chicago, Illinois

Money, John
Reading Disability Progress and Research Needs in Dyslexia
The Johns Hopkins Press
Baltimore, Maryland

Money, J.
The Disabled Reader, education of the Dyslexic child
The Johns Hopkins Press
Baltimore, Maryland

Montessori, M.
The Montessori Method
F. A. Stokes Company
New York, New York

Orton, Samuel T.
Reading Disability
Genetic Psychology Monographs 14:335-453
Pomfret, Conn.

Rapaport, David
Diagnostic Psychological Testing
The Year Book Publishers, Inc.
Chicago, Illinois

Redl, F., Wineman, D.
Children Who Hate
Collier Books
New York, New York

Reed, S. C.
Parenthood and Heredity
John Wiley & Sons, Inc.
New York, New York

Robinson, H. M.
Why Pupils Fail In Reading
The University of Chicago Press
Chicago, Illinois

Russell, D. M.
Children's Thinking
Ginn and Co.
Boston, Mass.

Scheinfeld, Amram
Your Heredity and Environment
J. B. Lippincott Company
Philadelphia, Penn.

Schubert, D. G.
The Doctor Eyes the Poor Reader
Charles C. Thomas, Publisher
Springfield, Illinois

Segal, M. M.
Run Away, Little Girl
Random House
New York, New York

Siegel, E.
Helping the Brain Injured Child
B.I.C.,
New York, New York
(This is a parent organization which has a multi-discipline advisory board. It is suggested that all interested parents contact The Brain Injured Child Association for parent information.)

Silver, A. A. and Hagen, R.
Specific Reading Disability: Delineation of the syndrome and relationship to cerebral dominance.
"Comprehensive Psychiatry"

Strauss, A. A., Kephart, N. C.
Psychopathology and Education of the Brain Injured Child – Two Volumes
Grune and Stratton,
New York, New York

Stuart, M. F.
Neurophysiological Insights Into Teaching
Pacific Books
Palo Alto, California

Vernon, M. D.
The Psychology of Perception
Penguin Books
Baltimore, Maryland

Wellington, C. B. and J.
The Underachiever: Challenges and Guidelines
Rand McNally
Chicago, Illinois

REFERENCES

[1] Critchley, Macdonald, *Developmental Dyslexia,* William Heinemann Medical Books, Ltd., London, England.

[2] [25] Money, John, *Reading Disability Progress and Research Needs in Dyslexia,* The Johns Hopkins Press, Baltimore, Maryland.

[3] Kerr, James, *The Lancet,* London, England.

[4] Hermann, Knud, *Reading Disability,* Charles C. Thomas, Publisher, Springfield, Illinois.

[5] Hallgren, Bertil, *Specific Dyslexia,* Acta psych. neur., Suppl 65, 1-287.

[6] Norrie, Edith, A young Danish woman, who was unable to read. She taught herself through the phonics organization approach to language. *Orblinde Undervisning med fonetisk saellekasse,* Nyt Nordisk Forlag Arnold Busck, Copenhagen, Denmark.

[7] Orton, Samuel T., *Reading Disability,* Genetic Psychology Monographs Pomfret, Conn.

[8] Gillingham, A., Stillman, B. W., *Remedial Training for Children with Specific Disability in Reading, Spelling, and Penmanship.*

[9] Orton Society, Publishes a bulletin of great help to teachers, medical researchers, and psychologists, as well as laymen. Pomfret, Conn.

[10] [12] [13] [26] McGlannan, Frances K., *Dyslexia – Theory Into Practice,* The Professional Press, Inc., Chicago, Illinois.

[11] Abrahamson, E. M., Pezet, A. W., *Body, Mind and Sugar,* Holt, Rinehart and Winston, New York, New York.

[14] [15] [28] Frostig, Marianne, *Exercises for the Development of Visual Perception* (exercises and manual), Follett Publishing Company, Chicago, Illinois.

[16] Stuart, M. F., *Neurophysiological Insights Into Teaching,* Pacific Books, Palo Alto, California.

[17] Shirley, L. P., California Medical Journal.

[18] Clements, S. D., *Minimal Brain Dysfunction in Children: Terminology and Identification,* Task Force I document of the national project on MBD in Children, Washington, D. C., March, 1966.

[19] Eastman, N. J., *The Brain Damaged Child; Why Does He Happen?* The Dallas Med. Journal.

[20] Clements, S. D., Peters, J. E., *Minimal Brain Dysfunction in the School-Age Child,* AMA Arch. of gen. psych.

[21] Hanvik, L. J., Hanson, H. B., *The Child With a Possible Organic Brain Injury,* Washburn Memorial Clinic, Minneapolis, Minn.

[22] Segal, M. M., *Run Away, Little Girl,* Random House, New York, New York.

[23] Rapaport, David, *Diagnostic Psychological Testing,* The Year Book Publishers, Inc., Chicago, Illinois.

[24] Almy, A., Chittenden, E., Miller, P., *Young Childrens Thinking,* Forward by J. Piaget, Teachers College Press, Columbia University, N. Y., N. Y.

[27] Jastak, J. F. and S. R. *Wide Range Achievement Test—Manual of Instructions,* Guidance Associates, Wilmington, Delaware.

DIRECTORY INTRODUCTION

THE FOLLOWING DIRECTORY attempts to list for the first time the many public and private agencies that provide the testing, diagnostic and educational services so badly needed by the *Shadow Children*. Every effort was made to compile as complete a listing as possible. Almost inevitably, however, a first attempt of this kind—especially in so complex a multi-disciplinary field—will fall short of the ideal. Very possibly some excellent facilities have been missed in this first effort. If this proves to be the case, we will welcome their cooperation in making sure that they are included in future editions of the directory.

No attempt is made here to list individuals who offer diagnostic or educational services, nor are the many fine foreign facilities included. All this will come at a later date. The public school systems that provide services for children with minimal learning disorders have not been included since it is assumed that parents and professionals are already aware of such facilities in their local schools.

Each of the facilities listed here completed a lengthy questionnaire detailing the services it offers. We are indebted to them for their investment of time and effort in providing information about themselves—and thereby contributing directly to the usefulness of the directory. [The facilities did not, of course, pay for their listing.] The process of gathering the facts and statistics was handled by the market research firm of Rome Arnold & Company (Chicago), and the author and publisher gratefully acknowledge their help in handling so ably this pioneering task.

The facilities receiving questionnaires were carefully selected. All of the data provided here, however, was supplied by the units themselves and the author and publisher can take responsibility only for the accuracy with which it has been reproduced. We will, therefore, welcome reports from parents and professionals who use this directory on those facilities that demonstrate high quality in the services they provide.

And finally, we would like to express our grateful appreciation to all those professionals who have contributed their time and effort to making this directory a useful tool in helping children with learning disorders to achieve successful and productive lives.

DIRECTORY

ALABAMA

Auburn University
School of Education
Reading Clinic
Auburn, Alabama
Director: Dr. Gary D. Spencer

DIAGNOSTIC FACILITIES: *Diagnostic facilities offered:* dyslexia (genetic or developmental), minimal brain damage syndromes, slow learner, psychiatric disorders. *Referral sources:* school—public, parent. *Ages accepted:* 6 years to 20 years (rarely over 20 years). *Waiting period for first appointment:* Autumn—6 weeks, Spring—2 months, Summer—1 month. *Staff and orientation:* a total child, multi-discipline team approach; with emphasis in the educational area. *Professional services available:* neurology, psychology, audiometry, visual training. *Average annual case load:* 100—majority in the psychiatric category.

TESTING FACILITIES: Strong testing program available.

EDUCATIONAL FACILITIES: *Remedial/developmental facilities:* dyslexia (genetic or developmental), minimal brain damage syndromes, slow learner, emotionally disturbed (moderate). *Instruction levels:* primary, elementary, junior and senior high, above 18—attending college. *Curriculum:* tutorial only; summer only. *Waiting period for enrollment:* summer—all year. *Average annual enrollment:* 40 students—majority in the emotionally disturbed category. *Program limits:* a student may be enrolled for the complete summer program. *Staff:* majority of staff have completed pertinent graduate courses and have had 2 or more years practical experience.

Huntsville Achievement School
212 Eustis Street (Box 835)
Huntsville, Alabama 35804
Director: Dr. Jane C. Aycock

EDUCATIONAL FACILITIES: *Remedial/developmental programs offered:* the aphasias, dyslexia (genetic or developmental), speech (developmental), minimal brain damage syndromes, slow learner, emotionally disturbed (moderate). *Instruction levels:* pre-school, primary, elementary. *Curriculum:* full day—full curriculum, annual basis. *Waiting time for enrollment:* No waiting period. *Average annual enrollment:* 1966-67 total—30 students. *Individual tutoring:* No information given.

TESTING FACILITIES: Testing program with off-campus referrals made.

FACULTY: School oriented to inter-discipline cooperation. *Professional services available to faculty:* neurology, psychology, audiometry, pediatric, ophthalmology, visual training, optometry. *Faculty-student ratio:* 1:8. *Faculty qualifications:* Not given.

SPECIAL INFORMATION: Program of development is oriented to the work of Kephart; classroom environment and teacher planning schedules adapted from Cruickshank.

Shades Cahaba Elementary School
Aphasoid School
3001 Montgomery Highway
Homewood, Alabama
Director: Mrs. Margaret G. Vines

EDUCATIONAL FACILITIES: *Remedial/developmental programs offered for:* the aphasias, dyslexia (genetic or developmental), speech (developmental), minimal brain damage syndromes, slow learner, emotionally disturbed (moderate). *Instruction levels:* pre-school, primary, elementary, and junior high. *Curriculum:* full day—full curriculum; annual basis. *Waiting period for enrollment:* no waiting period to date/have been able to take children upon completion of diagnostic testing. *Average annual enrollment:* 44 students. *Individual tutoring:* included automatically in students curriculum.

TESTING FACILITIES: Mental ability testing program available, with referral.

FACULTY: School is oriented to inter-discipline cooperation. *Professional services available to faculty:* (referral to on-campus Medical Center) neurology, psychology, audiometry, pediatric, ophthalmology, visual training, optometry, psychiatric, endocrinology. *Faculty-student ratio:* 1:10. *Faculty qualifications:* entire staff has had specialized training in remedial reading; graduate level training has been had by 50% of staff in reading; 10% of staff, in speech; 25% of staff in learning disabilities.

SPECIAL REQUIREMENTS: All testing (other than mentioned above) administered at on-campus Diagnostic Clinic.

SPECIAL INFORMATION: Consideration being given to change in terminology, re: name of Aphasoid classes. Discussion being given to the name of—*Classes for Children with minimal brain damage or with Specific Learning Disabilities.*

Smaban Psychiatric Clinic
Medical College
Reading Disability Center and Clinic
Birmingham, Alabama
Director: Charles L. Shedd

DIAGNOSTIC FACILITIES: *Diagnostic facilities are offered for:* the aphasias, dyslexia (genetic or developmental), speech (developmental), minimal brain damage syndromes, slow learner, and psychiatric disorders. *Referral sources:* pediatrician, school—public and private, psychiatrist, psychologist, parent. *Ages accepted:* all ages. *Waiting period for first appointment:* varies. *Staff and orientation:* a total child, multi-discipline team approach. *Professional services available:* neurology, psychology, audiometry, pediatric, ophthalmology, psychiatric, endocrinology, speech pathology. *Average annual case load:* No figure given.

TESTING FACILITIES: Not given.

EDUCATIONAL FACILITIES: None available.

University of Alabama
College of Education
Reading Laboratory
University, Alabama
Director: Frederick L. Westover

DIAGNOSTIC FACILITIES: *Diagnostic Facilities are offered for:* reading disability. *Referral sources:* pediatrician, school—public and private, parent. *Ages accepted:* 6 years—20 years. *Waiting period for first appointment:* Autumn—1 month, Spring— 1 month, Summer—1 month. *Staff and orientation:* psychological, educational. *Professional services available:* psychology, audiometry. *Average annual case load:* 150.

TESTING FACILITIES: Testing program available.

EDUCATIONAL FACILITIES: None available.

SPECIAL INFORMATION: Referrals made to other diagnostic facilities for language disorders and learning disabilities.

University of Alabama Medical Center
Department of Pediatrics
Clinic for Developmental and Learning Disorders
1919 Seventh Avenue, South
Birmingham, Alabama
Director: Dr. John W. Benton, Jr.

DIAGNOSTIC FACILITIES: *Diagnostic facilities offered:* minimal brain damage syndromes, slow learner, psychiatric disorders. *Referral sources:* pediatrician, psychiatrist, health agencies. *Ages accepted:* 3 years to 12 years. *Waiting period for first appointment:* approximately 3 months. *Staff and orientation:* emphasis in the neurological, psychological, pediatric and educational areas—with referral when needed. *Professional services available:* neurology, psychology, audiometry, pediatric, ophthalmology, psychiatric, endocrinology, genetics. *Average annual case load:* 245—majority in the slow learner category.

TESTING FACILITIES: Strong testing program available.

EDUCATIONAL FACILITIES: None available now, will be added in 1968.

ARIZONA

Arizona State University
College of Education
Department of Elementary Education
Reading Center
Tempe, Arizona 85281
Director: Dr. N. J. Silvaroli

DIAGNOSTIC FACILITIES: *Diagnostic facilities offered:* dyslexia (genetic or developmental), minimal brain damage syndromes, slow learner, psychiatric disorders. *Referral sources:* pediatrician, psychiatrist, psychologist, parent. *Ages accepted:* 6 years to 20 years. *Waiting period for first appointment:* Autumn—4-6 weeks; Spring—4-6 weeks; Summer—4-6 weeks. *Staff and orientation:* emphasis in the psychological and educational areas. *Professional services abailable:* neurology, psychology, audiometry, pediatric, ophthalmology, visual training, optometry, psychiatric. *Average annual case load:* 80-majority in the slow learner category.

TESTING FACILITIES: Strong testing program available.

EDUCATIONAL FACILITIES: *Remedial/developmental facilities:* dyslexia (genetic or developmental), minimal brain damage syndromes, slow learner, emotionally disturbed (moderate and severe). *Instruction levels:* primary, elementary, junior and senior high. *Curriculum:* tutorial only; annual basis. *Waiting period for enrollment:* Autumn—4-6 weeks; Spring—4-6 weeks; Summer—4-6 weeks. *Average annual enrollment:* 80 students—majority in the slow learner category. *Program limits:* 1 academic semester is the maximum time a student may be enrolled for a remedial program. *Staff:* majority of staff have completed pertinent graduate courses and have had 2 or more years practical experience.

Cerebral Palsy Foundation of Southern Arizona Inc.
3825 East Second Street
Tucson, Arizona
Director: Col. F. C. Skillman

EDUCATIONAL FACILITIES: *Remedial/developmental programs offered for:* the aphasias, dyslexia (genetic or developmental), speech (developmental), minimal brain damage syndromes, emotionally disturbed (moderate and severe). *Instruction levels:* pre-school. *Curriculum:* Full day—full curriculum; annual basis. *Waiting period for enrollment:* September —1 to 2 months; January—2 months. *Individual tutoring:* included automatically in students curriculum. *Average annual enrollment:* 126 students.

TESTING FACILITIES: Testing program with referral.

FACULTY: School oriented to inter-discipline cooperation. *Professional services available to faculty:* neurology, psychology, audiometry, pediatric, ophthalmology, visual training, optometry, psychiatric, endocrinology, orthopedic. *Faculty-student ratio:* 1:5. *Faculty qualifications:* 12% of the staff have had specialized training in remedial reading; graduate level training has been had by 12% of the staff in speech, by 12% of the staff in reading, and by 25% of the staff in learning disabilities; Master Degrees are held by 12% of the staff in speech.

Children's Evaluation Center of Southern Arizona
1 South Quadrante Street
Tucson, Arizona
Director: Dr. J. C. Heinlein

DIAGNOSTIC FACILITIES: *Diagnostic facilities offered for:* the aphasias, speech (developmental), minimal brain damage syndromes, slow learner, psychiatric disorders. *Referral sources:* pediatrician, school—public and private, psychiatrist, psychologist, parent, other child agencies. *Ages accepted:* 3 years to 9 years. *Waiting period for first appointment:* Autumn—1 month, Spring—1 month, Summer—1 month. *Staff and orientation:* a total child, multi-discipline team approach for diagnosis of mental retardation. *Professional services available:* neurology, psychology, audiometry, pediatric, ophthalmology, psychiatric, endocrinology, nutrition. *Average annual case load:* approximately 60 cases per year.

TESTING FACILITIES: Testing program available—with further testing by referral.

EDUCATIONAL FACILITIES: None available.

Northern Arizona University
Department of Special Education
Flagstaff, Arizona
Director: M. G. Beals

DIAGNOSTIC FACILITIES: *Diagnostic facilities offered:* the aphasias, dyslexia (genetic or developmental), speech (developmental), minimal brain damage syndromes, slow learner. *Referral sources:* pediatrician, school—public, psychiatrist, psychologist, parent. *Ages accepted:* 3 years to 16 years. *Waiting period for first appointment:* none. *Staff and orientation:* emphasis in the psychological and educational areas. *Professional services available:* psychology, audiometry, pediatric, ophthalmology, visual training, psychiatric. *Average annual case load:* figures not available—new program.

TESTING FACILITIES: Testing program available.

EDUCATIONAL FACILITIES: *Remedial/developmental facilities offered:* speech (developmental), minimal brain damage syndromes, slow learner, emotionally disturbed (moderate). *Instruction levels:* pre-school, primary, elementary, junior and senior high, adult rehabilitation. *Curriculum:* full day—full curriculum; annual basis and summer program. *Waiting period for enrollment:* none—at this time. *Average annual enrollment:* no figures at this time—new program. *Program limits:* no maximum time a student may be enrolled for a remedial program. *Staff:* majority of staff have completed pertinent graduate courses and have had 2 or more years practical experience.

University of Arizona
College of Education
Reading Service Center
Tucson, Arizona 85721
Director: Dr. George Becker

DIAGNOSTIC FACILITIES: *Diagnostic facilities offered:* dyslexia, minimal brain damage syndromes, slow learner. *Referral sources:* pediatrician, school—public and private, psychiatrist, psychologist, parent. *Ages accepted:* 6 years to over 20 years. *Waiting period for first appointment:* Autumn—4 months; Spring—4 months; Summer—4 months. *Staff and orientation:* a total child, multi-discipline team approach; with emphasis in the neurological, psychological, educational, and psychiatric areas. *Professional services available:* psychology, audiometry, visual training, optometry. *Average annual case load:* 16—majority in the dyslexia and minimal brain damaged categories.

TESTING FACILITIES: Strong testing program available.

EDUCATIONAL FACILITIES: *Remedial/developmental facilities:* dyslexia (genetic or developmental), minimal brain damage syndromes, slow learner, emotionally disturbed (moderate). *Instruction levels:* primary, elementary, junior and senior high, above 18-attending college, adult rehabilitation. *Curriculum:* tutorial only; annual basis. *Waiting period for enrollment:* Autumn—6 months; Spring—6 months; Summer—6 months. *Average annual enrollment:* 30 students—majority in the slow learner category. *Program limits:* no maximum time a student may be enrolled for a remedial program. *Staff:* majority of staff are currently enrolled in graduate school.

SPECIAL INFORMATION: At present, the Service Center is primarily oriented to training of advanced graduate students under the supervision of the clinical psychologist and several senior staff members.

University of Arizona
Department of Psychology
Psychological Clinic
Tucson, Arizona
Acting Director: William L. Simmons, Ph.D.

DIAGNOSTIC FACILITIES: *Diagnostic facilities offered:* minimal brain damage syndromes, slow learner, psychiatric disorders. *Referral sources:* pediatrician, school—public and private, psychiatrist, psychologist, parent. *Ages accepted:* all ages. *Waiting period for first appointment:* Autumn—2 weeks; Spring—none; Summer—2-3 months. *Staff and orientation:* emphasis in the psychological area. *Professional services available:* psychology, psychiatric. *Average annual case load:* 20—majority in the psychiatric disorders.

TESTING FACILITIES: Testing program available.

SPECIAL REQUIREMENTS: Acceptance limited to those who meet training needs for clinic staff.

SPECIAL INFORMATION: Clinic run solely for the purpose of training graduate students in clinical psychology.

EDUCATIONAL FACILITIES: None available.

ARKANSAS

University of Arkansas
Department of Psychiatry
Division of Child Psychiatry
Medical Center
Little Rock, Arkansas
Director: John E. Peters, M.D.

DIAGNOSTIC FACILITIES: *Diagnostic facilities offered:* dyslexia (genetic or developmental), minimal brain damage syndromes, slow learner, psychiatric disorders. *Referral sources:* pediatrician, school—public and private, psychiatrist, psychologist, parent. *Ages accepted:* 3 years to 16 years. *Waiting period for first appointment:* none given. *Staff and orientation:* a total child, multi-discipline team approach. *Professional services available:* neurology, psychology, pediatric, psychiatric, endocrinology. *Average annual case load:* 200.

TESTING FACILITIES: Testing program available

EDUCATIONAL FACILITIES: None available.

SPECIAL INFORMATION: A proposed Child Study Center is anticipated for the Fall of 1968, and this facility will offer educational programs.

CALIFORNIA

The Boyden School
1760 Third Avenue
San Diego 1, California
Director: H. W. Mitchell

EDUCATIONAL FACILITIES: *Remedial/developmental programs offered for:* minimal brain damage syndromes, slow learners, emotionally disturbed (moderate). *Instruction Levels:* junior high, senior high, above 18-college preparatory. *Curriculum:* tutorial and full day-full curriculum; annual basis. *Waiting time for enrollment:* usually none. *Average annual enrollment:* 23 students; majority in the slow learner and emotionally disturbed (moderate) categories. *Individual tutoring:* presented as an adjunct to the curriculum.

TESTING FACILITIES: Testing program available.

FACULTY: School is oriented to inter-discipline cooperation. *Professional services available to faculty:* none available, but recommend parental investigation and abide by recommendations of their professional choice. *Faculty-student ratio:* 1:8. *Faculty qualifications:* 2 members of staff have had specialized training in remedial reading; 10% of staff have had graduate level training in reading; 20% have had graduate level training in learning disabilities; 10% of staff hold Masters Degrees in reading.

California Pediatric Center
1415 South Grand
Los Angeles, California
Director: Geraldine M. Mellon

DIAGNOSTIC FACILITIES: *Diagnostic facilities offered:* speech (developmental), slow learner. *Referral sources:* not given. *Ages accepted:* from new-born to 18 years. *Waiting period for first appointment:* none. *Staff and orientation:* a total child, multi-discipline team approach; with emphasis in the neurological, psychological, pediatric, and educational areas. *Professional services available:* neurology, psychology, audiometry, pediatric, ophthalmology, psychiatric. *Average annual case load:* not given.

TESTING FACILITIES: Not given.

EDUCATIONAL FACILITIES: None available.

SPECIAL INFORMATION: Center is a community out-patient clinic.

California State College at Long Beach
Educational Psychology Clinic
Long Beach, California 90804
Acting Director: Dr. L. Stacker

DIAGNOSTIC FACILITIES: *Diagnostic facilities will be offered for:* the aphasias, dyslexia (genetic or developmental), speech (developmental), minimal brain damage syndromes, slow learner, psychiatric. *Ages accepted:* not given. *Waiting period for first appointment:* unavailable at this time. *Staff and orientation:* will be for a total child, multi-discipline team approach in the initial diagnosis. *Professional services available:* information unavailable at this time. *Average annual case load:* no figures on average annual cases at this time.

TESTING FACILITIES: Plans for a strong psychological testing program.

EDUCATIONAL FACILITIES: No information given-possibly not available.

SPECIAL INFORMATION: All above information is tentative, program is in the development stage, with plans to have an operative clinic by the Spring term of 1968.

California State College at Los Angeles
Department of Associated Clinics
5151 State College Drive
Los Angeles, California
Director: Richard G. Cannicott

DIAGNOSTIC FACILITIES: *Diagnostic facilities offered:* the aphasias, dyslexia (genetic or developmental), speech (developmental), minimal brain damage syndromes, slow learner. *Referral sources:* pediatrician, school—public and private, psychiatrist, psychologist, parent. *Ages accepted:* 3 years to 16 years. *Waiting period for first appointment:* Autumn—3 months, Spring—3 months, Summer—3 months. *Staff and orientation:* a total child, multi-discipline team approach in the areas of speech, reading, psychology, hearing, and guidance; with an emphasis in the psychological and education. *Professional services available:* psychology, audiometry, diagnosis of speech and reading difficulties. *Average annual case load:* 285—majority in the speech category.

TESTING FACILITIES: Testing program available.

EDUCATIONAL FACILITIES: *Remedial/developmental facilities:* the aphasias, dyslexia, speech, minimal brain damage syndromes, slow learner, emotionally disturbed (moderate). *Instruction levels:* pre-school, primary, elementary, junior and senior high. *Curriculum:* weekly appointment basis or enrollment for a college quarter; all outpatient clinic facilities. *Waiting period for enrollment:* Autumn—6 months; Spring—6 months; Summer—6 months (waiting period dependent upon which clinic needed). *Average annual enrollment:* 300 students—majority in the speech category. *Program limits:* varies from 1 quarter to 3 years—depending on the nature of impairment. *Staff:* majority of work is done by graduate students in training under the supervision of approximately 20 Ph.D.s in several disciplines.

SPECIAL INFORMATION: Associated Clinics is a college professional training facility and service of clients is a by-product of this training.

California State College at Los Angeles
Department of Psychology and Special Education
Learning and Behavior Problems Project
Los Angeles, California 90032
Director: Alice C. Thompson, Ph.D.

DIAGNOSTIC FACILITIES: *Diagnostic facilities offered:* the aphasias, dyslexia (genetic or developmental), speech (developmental), minimal brain damage syndromes, slow learner, psychiatric disorders. *Referral source:* anyone may request, but all must channel through public school. *Ages accepted:* 3 years to 20 years. *Waiting period for first appointment:* Autumn—2 months, Spring—2 months, Summer—2 months. *Staff and orientation:* a total child, multi-discipline team approach; with emphasis in the neurological, psychological, pediatric, educational, and psychiatric areas. *Professional services available:* neurology, psychology, audiometry, pediatric, ophthalmology, visual training, optometry, psychiatric, endocrinology. *Average annual case load:* 75—majority in the minimal brain damaged category.

TESTING FACILITIES: Strong testing program available.

EDUCATIONAL FACILITIES: *Remedial/developmental facilities:* minimal brain damage syndromes, slow learner, emotionally disturbed (moderate and severe). *Instruction levels:* primary, elementary, and senior high. *Curriculum:* full day-full curriculum; annual basis. *Waiting period for enrollment:* Autumn—1 year, Spring—1 year, Summer—1 year. *Average annual enrollment:* not given. *Program limits:* no maximum time a student may be enrolled for a remedial program. *Staff:* majority of staff are currently enrolled in graduate school and have had less than 2 years practical experience.

SPECIAL INFORMATION: Project is sponsored by the Los Angeles County schools.

Children's Hospital and Adult Medical Center of San Francisco
Department of Child Development Center
3700 California Street
San Francisco, California
Director: Morrison F. Gardner
Medical Director: Jerome P. Mednick, M.D.

DIAGNOSTIC FACILITIES: *Diagnostic facilities offered:* the aphasias, dyslexia (genetic or developmental), speech (developmental), minimal brain damage syndromes, slow learner, psychiatric disorders. *Referral sources:* pediatrician, school – public and private, psychiatrist, psychologist, parent, Health and Welfare department. *Ages accepted:* 3 years to 16 years. *Waiting period for first appointment:* none. *Staff and orientation:* a total child, multi-discipline team approach. *Professional services available:* neurology, psychology, audiometry, pediatric, ophthalmology, visual training, psychiatric, endocrinology, all laboratory work. *Average annual case load:* 552 annually – majority in the minimal brain damaged category.

TESTING FACILITIES: Testing program available.

EDUCATIONAL FACILITIES: *Remedial/developmental facilities:* dyslexia (genetic or developmental), speech (developmental), minimal brain damage syndromes, slow learner, emotionally disturbed (moderate and severe). *Instruction levels:* pre-school, primary, elementary, junior high. *Curriculum:* tutorial only (for the primary, elementary and junior high levels) (educational evaluation for pre-school level); annual basis. *Waiting period for enrollment:* none. *Average annual enrollment:* figures not given. *Program limits:* no maximum time a student may be enrolled for a remedial program. *Staff:* majority of staff have completed pertinent graduate courses and have had 2 or more years practical experience.

SPECIAL INFORMATION: The dyslexia, speech, brain damage, and slow learner children's time of enrollment not considered full-time, for their enrollment varies as to their needs. The emotionally disturbed (moderate and severe) children are treated in hospital's Child Guidance Clinic.

Children's Hospital Medical Center
Northern California Regional Child Development Center
51st and Grove Streets
Oakland, California
Director: Richard Umansky, M.D.

DIAGNOSTIC FACILITIES: *Diagnostic facilities offered:* the aphasias, dyslexia (genetic or developmental), speech (developmental), minimal brain damage syndromes, slow learner. *Referral sources:* pediatrician, school – public and private, psychiatrist, psychologist, parent, physician. *Ages accepted:* infant to 7 years. *Waiting period for first appointment:* 2 – 4 weeks. *Staff and orientation:* a total child, multi-discipline team approach. *Professional services available:* neurology, psychology, audiometry, pediatric, ophthalmology, psychiatric, endocrinology. *Average annual case load:* not given.

TESTING FACILITIES: Testing program not listed; medical and psychological examinations.

EDUCATIONAL FACILITIES: None available.

Children's Hospital of Orange County
Department of Speech and Language
1109 West LaVeta Street
Orange, California 92668
Director: Max Nelson, Ph.D.
Speech Pathologist: Sister Ann Monica

DIAGNOSTIC FACILITIES: *Diagnostic facilities offered:* the aphasias, dyslexia (genetic or developmental), speech (developmental). *Referral sources:* pediatrician, school – public and private, psychiatrist, psychologist. *Ages accepted:* 3 years to 20 years. *Waiting period for first appointment:* approximately 2 weeks. *Staff and orientation:* a total child, multi-discipline team approach. *Professional services available:* neurology, psychology, audiometry, pediatric, ophthalmology, psychiatric. *Average annual case load:* approximately 600.

TESTING FACILITIES: Testing program available—geared to the individual.

EDUCATIONAL FACILITIES: *Remedial/developmental facilities:* the aphasias, dyslexia (genetic or developmental), speech (developmental), minimal brain damage syndromes. *Instruction levels:* not given. *Curriculum:* tutorial only. *Waiting period for enrollment:* waiting list of 80, as of May 1967. *Average annual enrollment:* 40 students. *Program limits:* no maximum time a student may be enrolled for a remedial program. *Staff:* majority of staff have completed pertinent graduate courses.

DeWitt Reading Clinic
1543 Fifth Avenue
San Rafael, California 94901
Director: Frances B. DeWitt

EDUCATIONAL FACILITIES: *Remedial/developmental programs offered:* dyslexia (genetic or developmental), minimal brain damage syndromes, emotionally disturbed (moderate). *Instruction levels:* pre-school through above 18-college preparatory. *Curriculum:* tutorial only and half day; annual basis. *Waiting period for enrollment:* 3-4 weeks. *Average annual enrollment:* no figures given. *Individual tutoring:* all programs are individual.

TESTING FACILITIES: Testing program available with outside referral.

FACULTY: School is oriented to inter-discipline cooperation. *Professional services available to faculty:* neurology, psychology, pediatric, ophthalmology, optometry, psychiatric. *Faculty-student ratio:* 1:1. *Faculty qualifications:* entire staff has had specialized training in remedial reading; graduate level training has been had by the entire staff in reading and learning disabilities.

SPECIAL INFORMATION: Facility is involved in a two-fold program of therapy, that is, movement efficiency and communication efficiency. The child's program begins with movement efficiency and integration of modalities. This is carried on concurrently with a program of communication efficiency which is a program to develop the language areas—reading, writing, and spelling. Clinic is planning a new program for movement efficiency which will be presented in small groups to all students before entering the communication efficiency program. The new program was to be initiated in June (1967), tailored around the Barsch movigenic curriculum.

Escalon, Inc.
230 S. Holliston Avenue
Pasadena, California 91106
Director: Alice C. Thompson, Ph.D.

EDUCATIONAL FACILITIES: *Remedial/developmental programs offered:* the aphasias, dyslexia (genetic or developmental), speech (developmental), minimal brain damage syndromes, slow learner, emotionally disturbed (moderate). *Instruction levels:* pre-school, primary, elementary, junior high. *Curriculum:* tutorial only, half day, full day-full curriculum; annual basis. *Waiting time for enrollment:* September semester—none, January semester—none, and Summer program—none. *Average annual enrollment:* 148—majority in minimal brain damage syndromes. *Individual tutoring:* No information given (see special information).

TESTING FACILITIES: Strong testing program.

FACULTY: School is oriented to inter-discipline cooperation. *Professional services available to faculty:* neurology, psychology, audiometry, pediatric, ophthalmology, visual training, psychiatric, endocrinology. *Faculty-student ratio:* 1:5. *Faculty qualifications:*

1 member of staff has had specialized training in remedial reading; 1 staff member has had graduate level training in reading, 1 member in speech, and 3 members in learning disabilities; 1 staff member holds a Masters Degree in learning disabilities.

SPECIAL INFORMATION: Besides regular curriculum, afternoon remedial services are offered to children who are still within the public schools. While facility does not provide individual tutoring for students, each child's activities are individually programmed within the class room.

Glendale Adventist Hospital
Department of Speech and Audiology
1509 E. Wilson
Glendale, California
Director: Kenneth R. Lutz, Ph.D.

DIAGNOSTIC FACILITIES: *Diagnostic facilities offered:* the aphasias, speech (developmental), minimal brain damage syndromes, psychiatric disorders. *Referral sources:* pediatrician, school—public and private, psychiatrist, psychologist, parent, physician. *Ages accepted:* all ages. *Waiting period for first appointment:* Autumn—3 weeks, Spring—3 weeks, Summer—3 weeks. *Staff and orientation:* a total child, multi-discipline team approach; with emphasis in the neurological and psychological areas. *Professional services available:* neurology, psychology, audiometry, pediatric, psychiatric. *Average annual case load:* 145—majority in the aphasias category.

TESTING FACILITIES: Strong testing program available.

EDUCATIONAL FACILITIES: *Remedial/developmental facilities:* the aphasias, speech (developmental), minimal brain damage syndromes, slow learner. *Instruction levels:* pre-school, primary, elementary, junior and senior high, adult rehabilitation. *Curriculum:* tutorial only; annual basis. *Waiting period for enrollment:* Autumn—4 weeks, Spring—4 weeks, Summer —4 weeks. *Average annual enrollment:* 90 students. *Program limits:* no maximum time a student may be enrolled for a remedial program. *Staff:* majority of staff members have completed pertinent graduate courses.

SPECIAL INFORMATION: Facility operates in conjunction with the rehabilitation unit of the hospital and provides inpatient service for hospital patients in general, and rehabilitation unit patients specifically.

Harbor General Hospital
Department of Pediatrics
1000 W. Carson Street
Torrance, California
Director: Kenneth Zike, M.D.
Department Director: Joseph W. St. Geme, Jr., M.D.

DIAGNOSTIC FACILITIES: *Diagnostic facilities offered:* the aphasias, dyslexia (genetic or developmental), speech (developmental), minimal brain damage syndromes, slow learner, psychiatric disorders. *Referral sources:* pediatrician, school—public and private, psychiatrist, psychologist, parent. *Ages accepted:* 3-6 years and 16-20 years. *Waiting period for first appointment:* 3 weeks. *Staff and orientation:* a total child, multi-discipline team approach; with emphasis in the neurological, psychological, pediatric, educational and psychiatric areas. *Professional services available:* neurology, psychology, audiometry, pediatric, ophthalmology, visual training, psychiatric, endocrinology, occupational therapy. *Average annual case load:* 470 plus 400 re-visits—majority in the brain damage category.

TESTING FACILITIES: Strong testing program available.

EDUCATIONAL FACILITIES: None available.

SPECIAL INFORMATION: Facility is open to visitation by any professional (physician, educator, psychologist), but does not offer a formalized training program for other than physicians.

The Langley Porter Neuropsychiatric Institute
Department of Psychiatry
Children's Service
401 Parnassus
San Francisco, California 94122

DIAGNOSTIC FACILITIES: *Diagnostic facilities are offered for:* the aphasias, dyslexia (genetic or developmental), speech (developmental), minimal brain damage syndromes, slow learner, psychiatric disorders. *Referral sources:* pediatrician, school—public and private, psychiatrist, psychologist, parent. *Ages accepted:* 3 to 18 years. *Waiting period for first appointment:* varies—intake offered within 2-3 weeks. *Staff and orientation:* psychiatric. *Professional services available:* neurology, psychology, audiometry, pediatric, ophthalmology, visual training, optometry, psychiatric, endocrinology, all resources of the University of California, Medical Center. *Average annual case load:* 60-70 cases.

TESTING FACILITIES: Strong testing program available.

EDUCATIONAL FACILITIES: *Remedial/developmental programs offered:* the aphasias, dyslexia (genetic or developmental), speech (developmental), minimal brain damage syndromes, slow learner, emotionally disturbed (moderate and severe). *Instruction levels:* preschool, primary, elementary. *Curriculum:* full day-full curriculum; annual basis. *Waiting time for enrollment:* intake never closed—no waiting list kept. *Average annual enrollment:* 12-intake students. *Program limits:* no maximum time a student may be enrolled for a remedial program. *Staff:* majority of staff members have completed pertinent graduate courses and have had two or more years practical experience.

SPECIAL REQUIREMENTS: Children admitted because of severe emotional disorder—total therapeutic effort includes educational program.

SPECIAL INFORMATION: Adult Services offered also, but handled separately from Children's Services. Future plans include greater expansion into the areas of special learning problems.

The Laurence School
6428 Woodman Avenue
Van Nuys, California 91401
Director: Marvin Jacobson

EDUCATIONAL FACILITIES: *Remedial/developmental programs offered:* the aphasias, dyslexia (genetic or developmental), speech (developmental), minimal brain damage syndromes, emotionally disturbed (moderate and severe). *Instruction levels:* pre-school, primary, elementary, junior high. *Curriculum:* full day-full curriculum; annual basis. *Waiting period for enrollment:* January—2 months. *Average annual enrollment:* 100 students. *Individual tutoring:* included automatically in students curriculum.

TESTING FACILITIES: Strong testing program available.

FACULTY: School is oriented to inter-discipline cooperation. *Professional services available to faculty:* neurology, psychology, audiometry, pediatric, ophthalmology, visual training, psychiatric. *Faculty-student ratio:* 1:4. *Faculty qualifications:* graduate level training has been had by 3 staff members in reading, by 1 staff member in speech; Master Degree is held by 1 staff member in speech.

Los Angeles Rehabilitation Center
Department of Language Therapy
1225 N. Mission Road
Los Angeles, California 90033
Director: N. W. Freestone, Ph.D.

DIAGNOSTIC FACILITIES: *Diagnostic facilities offered:* the aphasias, dyslexia (genetic or developmental), speech (developmental). *Referral sources:* pediatrician, school—public and private, psychiatrist. *Ages accepted:* all ages. *Waiting period for first appointment:*

Autumn – 1 week; Spring – 1 week; Summer – 1 week. *Staff and orientation:* a total child, multi-discipline team approach. *Professional services available:* neurology, psychology, audiometry, pediatric, ophthalmology, visual training, optometry, psychiatric, endocrinology. *Average annual case load:* no figures given.

TESTING FACILITIES: Testing program available.

EDUCATIONAL FACILITIES: *Remedial/developmental facilities:* the aphasias, dyslexia (genetic or developmental), speech (developmental), minimal brain damage syndromes. *Instruction levels:* primary, elementary, junior and senior high, adult rehabilitation. *Curriculum:* tutorial only; annual basis. *Waiting period for enrollment:* Autumn – 1 week; Spring – 1 week; Summer – 1 week. *Average annual enrollment:* 65 students – majority in the aphasias and speech categories. *Program limits:* no maximum time a student may be enrolled for a remedial program. *Staff:* majority of staff have completed pertinent graduate courses and have had 2 or more years practical experience.

Los Angeles Rehabilitation Center
Division of Speech and Reading
1225 Mission Avenue
Los Angeles, California 90033
Director: N. W. Freestone, Ph.D.

EDUCATIONAL FACILITIES: *Remedial/developmental programs offered:* the aphasias, dyslexia (genetic or developmental), speech (developmental), emotionally disturbed (moderate). *Instruction levels:* all ages – from pre-school through over 18-college preparatory. *Curriculum:* tutorial only; annual basis. *Waiting period for enrollment:* none. *Average annual enrollment:* 55 students – majority in the aphasias category. *Individual tutoring:* presented as an adjunct to the curriculum.

TESTING FACILITIES: Testing program available.

FACULTY: School is oriented to inter-discipline cooperation. *Professional services available:* psychology, audiometry, pediatric. *Faculty-student ratio:* 1:3. *Faculty qualifications:* Director has Doctorate in speech and reading.

Marianne Frostig Center of Educational Therapy
7257 Melrose Avenue
Los Angeles, California 90046
Director: Marianne Frostig, Ph.D.

EDUCATIONAL FACILITIES: *Remedial/developmental programs offered:* the aphasias, dyslexia (genetic or developmental), speech (developmental), minimal brain damage syndromes, slow learner, emotionally disturbed (moderate and severe). *Instruction levels:* preschool, primary, elementary, junior high. *Curriculum:* full day – full curriculum; annual basis. *Waiting time for enrollment:* September session – one month; January – no waiting. *Average annual enrollment:* 245 students; majority in the minimal brain damage syndrome, dyslexia (genetic or developmental) categories. *Individual tutoring:* included automatically in students curriculum.

TESTING FACILITIES: Strong testing program available, with school psychology staff doing evaluation.

FACULTY: School is oriented to inter-discipline cooperation. *Professional services available to faculty:* neurology, psychology, audiometry, pediatric, ophthalmology, visual training, optometry, psychiatric. *Faculty-student ratio:* 1:4. *Faculty qualifications:* entire staff has had specialized training in remedial reading; entire staff has had graduate level training in reading and learning disabilities, 3 staff members have had graduate level training in speech; 2 staff members hold Masters Degrees in speech, and 4 members hold Masters Degrees in learning disabilities.

SPECIAL INFORMATION: A tutorial program is offered to the public school children needing special help.

Michael Kent School
1845 W. LaPalma Avenue
Anaheim, California 92801
Director: Marge Bengston

EDUCATIONAL FACILITIES: *Remedial/developmental programs:* the aphasias, dyslexia (genetic or developmental), speech (developmental), minimal brain damage syndromes, slow learner, emotionally disturbed (moderate). *Instruction levels:* kindergarten through 8th grade. *Curriculum:* full day—full curriculum, annual basis, and a 6 weeks summer school program. *Waiting period for enrollment:* none—new program. *Average annual enrollment:* figures unavailable—school less than a year old. *Individual tutoring:* included automatically in students curriculum.

TESTING FACILITIES: Strong testing program available with off-campus referral.

FACULTY: School is oriented to inter-discipline cooperation. *Professional services available to faculty:* neurology, psychology, audiometry, pediatric, ophthalmology, visual training, optometry, psychiatric, endocrinology. *Faculty-student ratio:* 1:8. *Faculty qualifications:* 75% of staff have had specialized training in remedial reading; graduate level training has been had by 75% of staff in reading, by 50% of staff in speech, by 50% of staff in learning disabilities; Masters Degrees are held by one-third of staff for reading, speech, and learning disabilities; and include certified speech therapists.

SPECIAL INFORMATION: School has parent association, and offers individual counseling to both parents and students.

Moore School
700 Peninsula Avenue
Burlingane, California
Director: Philip Walrod

EDUCATIONAL FACILITIES: *Remedial/developmental programs offered:* slow learner. *Instruction levels:* primary, elementary, junior and senior high. *Curriculum:* full day—full curriculum; annual basis. *Waiting period for enrollment:* September—none; January—none; Summer program—none. *Average annual enrollment:* 120 students. *Individual tutoring:* presented as an adjunct to the curriculum.

TESTING FACILITIES: Testing program available and referrals made.

FACULTY: School is oriented to inter-discipline cooperation. *Professional services available to faculty:* psychology, audiometry, visual training. *Faculty-student ratio:* 1:10. *Faculty qualifications:* 20% of the staff have had specialized training in remedial reading; graduate level training has been had by 10% of the staff in reading and by 10% of the staff in speech.

The Neuropsychiatric Institute School
760 Westwood Plaza
Los Angeles, California 90024

DIAGNOSTIC FACILITIES: *Diagnostic facilities offered:* the aphasias, dyslexia (genetic or developmental), speech (developmental), minimal brain damage syndromes, slow learner, psychiatric disorders. *Referral sources:* pediatrician, psychiatrist. *Ages accepted:* all ages. *Waiting period for first appointment:* emergency—immediate, other—2 weeks. *Staff and orientation:* a total child, multi-discipline team approach; with emphasis in the psychiatric area. *Professional services available:* neurology, psychology, (audiometry in 1969), pediatric, ophthalmology, optometry, psychiatric, endocrinology, and any others available in U.C.L.A.'s medical center. *Average annual case load:* varies.

TESTING FACILITIES: Testing program available.

EDUCATIONAL FACILITIES: *Remedial/developmental facilities:* the aphasias, dyslexia (genetic or developmental), speech (developmental), minimal brain damage syndromes, slow learner, emotionally disturbed (moderate and severe). *Instruction levels:* all ages.

Curriculum: tutorial, half day, full day—full curriculum. *Waiting period for enrollment:* emergency—immediate, other—2 or more weeks. *Average annual enrollment:* varies—majority in the emotionally disturbed (moderate and severe) category. *Program limits:* length of schooling determined by psychiatric progress (2 weeks to 2 years). *Staff:* majority of staff have had 2 or more years practical experience and have completed pertinent graduate courses.

SPECIAL INFORMATION: All patients admitted are automatically candidates for schooling, regardless of need. All levels of mentally retarded (2 years to 16 years) will be admitted beginning 1969. Training and research are major goal of institute, specializing in psychiatry, psychology, social work and education.

Occidatal College
Department of Speech
Speech and Reading Clinics
1600 Campus Road
Los Angeles, California 90041
Director: N. W. Freestone, Ph.D.

DIAGNOSTIC FACILITIES: *Diagnostic facilities offered:* the aphasias, dyslexia (genetic or developmental), speech (developmental). *Referral sources:* pediatrician, school—public and private, psychiatrist, psychologist, parent. *Ages accepted:* all ages. *Waiting period for first appointment:* Autumn—2 weeks; Spring—2 weeks; Summer—2 weeks. *Staff and orientation:* emphasis in the psychological and educational areas. *Professional services available:* psychology, audiometry. *Average annual case load:* 170—majority in the dyslexia category.

TESTING FACILITIES: Testing program available.

EDUCATIONAL FACILITIES: *Remedial/developmental facilities:* the aphasias, dyslexia (genetic or developmental), speech (developmental). *Instruction levels:* elementary, junior and senior high. *Curriculum:* annual basis. *Waiting period for enrollment:* none. *Average annual enrollment:* 170 students—majority in the dyslexia category. *Program limits:* no maximum time a student may be enrolled for a remedial program. *Staff:* majority of staff have completed pertinent graduate courses and have had 2 or more years practical experience.

San Diego Speech and Hearing Center
Department of Speech
8001 Frost Street
San Diego, California 92123
Executive Director: Donald F. Krebs.
Director: Frederieka Zink

DIAGNOSTIC FACILITIES: *Diagnostic facilities are offered for:* the aphasias, speech (developmental), minimal brain damage syndromes, slow learners. *Referral sources:* pediatrician, school—public and private, psychiatrist, psychologist, parent, physician, Public Health nurse. *Ages accepted:* 3 years to over 20 years. *Waiting period for first appointment:* Autumn, Spring, Summer—2 weeks to 1 month. *Staff and orientation:* a total child, multidiscipline team approach. *Professional services available:* neurology, psychology, audiometry, psychiatric, social service. *Average annual case load:* 300—majority in speech (developmental) and minimal brain damage syndromes categories.

TESTING FACILITIES: Testing program available.

EDUCATIONAL FACILITIES: *Remedial/developmental programs offered for:* the aphasias, speech (developmental), minimal brain damage syndromes, slow learner. *Instruction levels:* pre-school, primary, elementary, junior high, senior high, adult rehabilitation. *Curriculum:* tutorial only; annual basis. *Waiting time for enrollment:* no waiting period for enrollment. *Average annual enrollment:* 230—majority in speech (developmental) and minimal brain damage syndromes categories. *Program limits:* no maximum time a student may be enrolled for a remedial program. *Staff:* majority of staff members have had less than two years practical experience.

SPECIAL REQUIREMENTS: A case history is taken by Social Service as part of initial visit.

SPECIAL INFORMATION: School serves as a facility where recent Master graduates in speech pathology can serve their 9 months internship.

San Diego State College
Clinical Training Center
5402 College Avenue
San Diego, California
Director: Ramon Ross

DIAGNOSTIC FACILITIES: *Diagnostic facilities offered:* the aphasias, speech (developmental), minimal brain damage syndromes, slow learner. *Referral sources:* pediatrician, school—public and private, psychiatrist, psychologist, parent, community agencies. *Ages accepted:* 6 years to over 20 years. *Waiting period for first appointment:* varies—usually not more than 1 semester. *Staff and orientation:* a total child, multi-discipline team approach; with emphasis in the psychological, educational, speech and hearing pathology categories. *Professional services available:* psychology, audiometry, visual training, speech pathology, learning and reading difficulties. *Average annual case load:* varies with enrollment of students in training—approximately 500 per semester.

TESTING FACILITIES: Strong testing program available.

EDUCATIONAL FACILITIES: *Remedial/developmental facilities:* the aphasias, speech (developmental), slow learner, emotionally disturbed (moderate). *Instruction levels:* preschool, primary, elementary, junior and senior high. *Curriculum:* tutorial only; annual basis. *Waiting period for enrollment:* varies. *Average enrollment:* 500 per semester. *Program limits:* no maximum time a student may be enrolled for a remedial program. *Staff:* majority of staff members are currently enrolled in graduate school.

San Francisco State College
School of Education
Learning Clinic
1600 Holloway Avenue
San Francisco, California
Director: Dr. Louis H. Falik

DIAGNOSTIC FACILITIES: *Diagnostic facilities offered:* the aphasias,dyslexia (genetic or developmental), minimal brain damage syndromes, slow learner. *Referral sources:* pediatrician, school—public and private, psychiatrist, psychologist, parent. *Ages accepted:* 6 years to 16 years. *Waiting period for first appointment:* Autumn—4 weeks; Spring—2 weeks; Summer—8 weeks. *Staff and orientation:* a total child, multi-discipline team approach. *Professional services available:* neurology, psychology, audiometry, visual training, optometry, psychiatric, educationa!. *Average annual case load:* 80 cases.

TESTING FACILITIES: Testing program available.

EDUCATIONAL FACILITIES: *Remedial/developmental facilities:* the aphasias, dyslexia (genetic or developmental), minimal brain damage syndromes, slow learner, emotionally disturbed (moderate and severe). *Instruction levels:* primary, elementary, junior and senior high. *Curriculum:* tutorial only; annual basis. *Waiting period for enrollment:* 1 month. *Average annual enrollment:* 90 students—evenly divided in the categories. *Program limits:* no maximum time a student may be enrolled for a remedial program. *Staff:* majority of staff have completed pertinent graduate courses and have had 2 or more years practical experience.

Scherich's South Bay School
1108 S. Prospect
Redondo Beach, California
Director: Warren H. Scherich

EDUCATIONAL FACILITIES: *Remedial/developmental programs offered for:* the aphasias, dyslexia (genetic or developmental), speech (developmental), minimal brain damage syndromes, slow learner and emotionally disturbed (moderate). *Instruction levels:* pre-school through senior high. *Curriculum:* full day–full curriculum; annual basis. *Waiting period for enrollment:* about 3 weeks for the September semester, the January semester, and the Summer program. *Average annual enrollment:* 27 students–majority in the minimal brain damaged category. *Individual tutoring:* included automatically in students curriculum.

TESTING FACILITIES: Testing program available.

FACULTY: School oriented to inter-discipline cooperation. *Professional services available to the faculty:* neurology, psychology, audiometry, pediatric, ophthalmology, visual training, optometry, psychiatric, endocrinology. *Faculty-student ratio:* 1:6. *Faculty qualifications:* entire staff has had specialized training in remedial reading (trained at the school); graduate level training has been had by 25% of the staff in reading, by 25% of the staff in speech, and by 25% of the staff in learning disabilities; 25% of staff hold Masters Degrees in learning disabilities.

South Bay Center for Educational Therapy
1093 Pier Avenue
Hermosa Beach, California
Director: Janet Switzer, Ph.D.

EDUCATIONAL FACILITIES: *Remedial/developmental programs offered:* the aphasias, dyslexia (genetic or developmental), speech (developmental), minimal brain damage syndromes, slow learner, emotionally disturbed (moderate and severe). *Instruction levels:* pre-school, primary, elementary, junior high. *Curriculum:* tutorial only; annual basis. *Waiting time for enrollment:* September–6 weeks, January–6 weeks, Summer program–6 weeks. *Average annual enrollment:* 75. *Individual tutoring:* presented as an adjunct to the curriculum.

TESTING FACILITIES: Strong testing program available with off-campus referrals.

FACULTY: School is oriented to inter-discipline cooperation. *Professional services available to faculty:* neurology, psychology, audiometry, pediatric, ophthalmology, visual training, psychiatric, sensory-motor. *Faculty-student ratio:* 1:1 or 1:2. *Faculty qualifications:* teaching staff of 11; 72% have had specialized training in remedial reading; 81% have had graduate level training in reading and learning disabilities; 9% hold Masters Degrees in learning disabilities (majority of staff trained at Marianne Frostig Center).

SPECIAL REQUIREMENTS: Intake and follow-up interview with parents included in program. Center offers major program in motor training; also available, psycho-therapy as an adjunct to child educational therapy.

Stanford University
School of Medicine
Department of Speech Pathology and Audiology
Institute for Childhood Aphasias
1691 ElCamino Road
Palo Alto, California
Director: Jon Eisenson

DIAGNOSTIC FACILITIES: *Diagnostic facilities are offered for:* the aphasias, dyslexia (genetic or developmental), speech (developmental), minimal brain damage syndromes, slow learner, psychiatric. *Referral sources:* pediatrician, school–public and private, psychiatrist, psychologist, parent. *Ages accepted:* 3 years to 12 years. *Waiting period for first appointment:* 4-6 months. *Staff and orientation:* A total child, multi-discipline team approach; with emphasis on neurological, psychological, pediatric, educational. *Professional services available:* neurology, psychology, audiometry, pediatric. *Average annual case load:* 100.

TESTING FACILITIES: Strong testing program.

EDUCATIONAL FACILITIES: *Remedial/developmental programs offered:* the aphasias. *Instruction levels:* pre-school and primary. *Curriculum:* tutorial only; annual basis. *Waiting time for enrollment:* No waiting period mentioned. *Average annual enrollment:* 20-25 students. *Program limits:* No maximum time a student may be enrolled for a remedial program. *Staff:* majority of staff members have completed pertinent graduate courses and have had two or more years practical experience.

University of California
Psychology Clinic School
405 Hilgard Avenue
Los Angeles, California 90024
Assistant Director: Howard Adelman, Ph.D.

DIAGNOSTIC FACILITIES: *Diagnostic facilities offered:* wide range of diagnostic facilities available. *Referral sources:* any interested person. *Ages accepted:* all ages. *Waiting period for first appointment:* no waiting period given. *Staff and orientation:* a multi-disciplinary team approach. *Professional services available:* education, psychology, social work, and other related disciplines actively involved. *Average annual case load:* figures not given.

TESTING FACILITIES: Intensive diagnosis in intelligence, achievement and development-testing program available.

EDUCATIONAL FACILITIES: *Remedial/developmental facilities:* for those with average or superior intelligence, but are seriously retarded in basic school skills. *Instruction levels:* children, adolescents, and adults. *Curriculum:* remedial program designed for each student's specific needs. *Waiting period for enrollment:* varies—as to the openings available in the services needed. *Average annual enrollment:* no figure given. *Program limits:* it is expected by the Clinic School that each student will continue in the program until correct grade level is attained, and the student can return to and function satisfactorily in regular school classes. *Staff:* in addition to the professional staff of teachers, psychologists, and social workers—school has graduate and undergraduate student trainees.

SPECIAL INFORMATION: Summer school program offers a developmental program as well as the remedial school program. Individual and small-group tutoring is provided in remedial, developmental, as well as enrichment for the gifted. Athletic instruction is also available.

AUTHOR'S NOTE: Above information was collated from the facility's correspondence rather than the *questionnaire;* it would have been the Directory's loss if this fine unit were omitted and it is hoped that we have been accurate in our translation of their statements to us.

University of California
Speech and Hearing Center
Santa Barbara, California
Director: J. C. Snidecor

DIAGNOSTIC FACILITIES: *Diagnostic facilities offered:* the aphasias, speech (developmental), *Referral sources:* pediatrician, school—public and private, psychiatrist, psychologist, parent, speech pathologist, audiologist, otolaryngologist, neurologist. *Ages accepted:* all ages. *Waiting period for first appointment:* Autumn—2 weeks; Spring—4 weeks; Summer—no evaluations done. *Staff and orientation:* emphasis in the speech and hearing areas. *Professional services available:* psychology, audiometry. *Average annual case load:* 45—majority in the speech category.

TESTING FACILITIES: Testing program available.

Educational Facilities: *Remedial/developmental facilities:* the aphasias, speech (developmental). *Instruction levels:* all ages. *Curriculum:* tutorial only; annual basis. *Waiting period for enrollment:* none given. *Average annual enrollment:* no figures given. *Program limits:* no maximum time a student may be enrolled for a remedial program. *Staff:* majority of staff have completed pertinent graduate courses and have had 2 or more years practical experience.

White Memorial Hospital
Pediatric Clinic
1720 Brooklyn Avenue
Los Angeles, California
Director: W. F. Taylor

Diagnostic Facilities: *Diagnostic facilities are offered for:* the aphasias, dyslexia (genetic or developmental), speech (developmental), minimal brain damage syndromes, slow learner. *Referral sources:* pediatrician, school—public and private, psychiatrist, psychologist, parent. *Ages accepted:* 3 years to 16 years. *Waiting period for first appointment:* Autumn—1 month, Spring—1 month, Summer—2 weeks. *Staff and orientation:* a total child, multi-discipline team approach, with emphasis in the neurological and pediatric areas. *Professional services available:* neurology, psychology, audiometry, pediatric, ophthalmology, visual training, endocrinology, social service, speech pathology, physical medicine. *Average annual case load:* not given.

Testing Facilities: Testing program individualized by problem and age.

Educational Facilities: None available.

White Memorial Medical Center
Department of Speech and Audiology
304 N. Boyle
Los Angeles, California 90033
Director: Kenneth R. Lutz, Ph.D.

Diagnostic Facilities: *Diagnostic facilities offered:* the aphasias, speech (developmental), minimal brain damage syndromes, psychiatric disorders. *Referral sources:* pediatrician, school—public and private, psychiatrist, psychologist, parent, physician. *Ages accepted:* all ages. *Waiting period for first enrollment:* Autumn—3 weeks, Spring—3 weeks, Summer—3 weeks. *Staff and orientation:* a total child, multi-discipline team approach; with emphasis in the neurological and psychological areas. *Professional services available:* neurology, psychology, audiometry, pediatric, psychiatric. *Average annual case load:* 145—majority in the aphasias category.

Testing Facilities: Strong testing program available.

Educational Facilities: *Remedial/developmental facilities:* the aphasias, speech (developmental), minimal brain damage syndromes, slow learner. *Instruction levels:* preschool, primary, elementary, junior and senior high, adult rehabilitation. *Curriculum:* tutorial only; annual basis. *Waiting period for enrollment:* Autumn—4 weeks, Spring—4 weeks, Summer—4 weeks. *Average annual enrollment:* 90 students. *Program limits:* no maximum time a student may be enrolled for a remedial program. *Staff:* majority of staff have completed pertinent graduate courses.

Whittier College
Department of Education
Reading Clinic
13425 E. Philadelphia
Whittier, California 90608
Director: Lola B. Hoffman

Diagnostic Facilities: *Diagnostic facilities offered for:* dyslexia (genetic or developmental), minimal brain damage syndromes, slow learner. *Referral sources:* school—public and private, psychiatrist, psychologist, parent. *Ages accepted:* 6 years to 20 years. *Waiting period for first appointment:* none. *Average annual case load:* not given. *Staff and orientation:* emphasis in the educational area. *Professional services available:* audiometry.

TESTING FACILITIES: Testing program available.

EDUCATIONAL FACILITIES: *Remedial/developmental facilities for:* dyslexia (genetic or developmental), minimal brain damage syndromes, slow learner, emotionally disturbed (moderate). *Instruction levels:* primary, elementary, junior and senior high. *Curriculum:* tutorial only; annual (fall and spring semesters) basis, and a summer program. *Waiting period for enrollment:* Autumn—up to 4 months, Spring—0-4 months, Summer—0-4 months. *Average annual enrollment:* not given. *Program limits:* no maximum time a student may be enrolled for a remedial program. *Staff:* Staff members are college students working toward degrees in education.

SPECIAL INFORMATION: Clinic is a training institution for student teachers.

CONNECTICUT

Foster School Inc.
315 St. Ronan Street
New Haven, Connecticut 06511
Director: Mrs. Larraine Foster

EDUCATIONAL FACILITIES: *Remedial/developmental programs offered:* dyslexia (genetic or developmental), minimal brain damage syndromes, slow learner, emotionally disturbed (moderate). *Instruction level:* 1st through 8th grade. *Curriculum:* full day—full curriculum; annual basis (no summer program available). *Waiting period for enrollment:* none. *Average annual enrollment:* 47 students—majority in the moderately disturbed category. *Individual tutoring:* included automatically in students curriculum.

TESTING FACILITIES: Stanford Achievement testing program available in May of every year.

FACULTY: School is oriented to inter-discipline cooperation. *Professional services available to faculty:* neurology, psychology, audiometry, pediatric, ophthalmology, visual training, optometry, psychiatric, endocrinology. *Faculty-student ratio:* 1:4. *Faculty qualifications:* no information given.

SPECIAL INFORMATION: No diagnostic services available, educational facilities offered after clinical work-up by off-campus facilities—referrals made. School is an elementary day school committed to the proposition that many children along the continuum of central nervous dysfunction—moderately severe emotional disturbances—can function to age grade equivalency in an academic class of five where immediate attention can be given to the learning needs.

The Foundation School, Inc.
Post Office Box 719
Orange, Connecticut 06477
Director: Walter J. Bell

EDUCATIONAL FACILITIES: *Remedial/developmental programs offered:* the aphasias, minimal brain damage syndromes, emotionally disturbed (moderate). *Instruction levels:* primary, elementary. *Curriculum:* full day—full curriculum; annual basis. *Waiting period for enrollment:* September—6 months, January—6 months, Summer program—60 days. *Average annual enrollment:* 24 students. *Individual tutoring:* included automatically in students curriculum.

TESTING FACILITIES: Testing program available with referral.

FACULTY: School is oriented to inter-discipline cooperation. *Professional services available to faculty:* neurology, psychology, audiometry, pediatric, visual training, optometry, psychiatric. *Faculty-student ratio:* 1:3. *Faculty qualifications:* graduate level training in reading by 25% of staff; in speech by 25% of staff, in learning disabilities by 50% of staff; Master Degrees are held by 25% of staff in speech, by 50% of staff in learning disabilities.

SPECIAL INFORMATION: Diagnostic teaching used extensively. Program is non-graded team approach with completely individualized prescriptions utilizing language, science/math, perceptual/motor training areas. Individual appointment basis varies day-to-day with study carrels and audio-visual aids used extensively.

Grove School
Madison, Connecticut
Director: Dr. J. Sanford Davis

EDUCATIONAL FACILITIES: *Remedial/developmental programs:* minimal brain damage syndromes, emotionally disturbed (moderate and severe). *Instruction levels:* junior and senior high. *Curriculum:* full day-full curriculum; annual basis. *Waiting period for enrollment:* no waiting beyond a few months – referrals to other programs. *Average annual enrollment:* 37 students. *Individual tutoring:* included automatically in students curriculum.

TESTING FACILITIES: No diagnostic work-ups – all educational instruments for determining educational achievement.

FACULTY: School oriented to inter-discipline cooperation. *Professional services available to faculty:* neurology, psychology, pediatric, ophthalmology, optometry, psychiatric, endocrinology. *Faculty-student ratio:* 1:3. *Faculty qualifications:* 2 of the staff have had specialized training in remedial reading; graduate level training has been had by 3 of the staff in reading, by 1 of the staff in speech, by 4 staff members in learning disabilities; Masters Degrees are held by 1 staff member in reading, by 2 staff members in learning disabilities.

SPECIAL REQUIREMENTS: Boys boarding school – therapy sessions twice weekly.

The Ives School For Special Children
185 Cold Spring Street
New Haven, Connecticut 06517
Co-Directors: Mrs. Virginia Sperry, Mrs. Margaretta Hoadley

EDUCATIONAL FACILITIES: *Remedial/developmental programs offered:* the aphasias, dyslexia (genetic or developmental), speech (developmental), minimal brain damage syndromes, slow learner, emotionally disturbed (moderate). *Instruction levels:* pre-school. *Curriculum:* half day; annual basis. *Waiting period for enrollment:* child enrolled upon completion of evaluation at Yale child study center (2-3 months). *Average annual enrollment:* not given. *Individual tutoring:* included automatically in students curriculum.

TESTING FACILITIES: All testing done by Yale Child Development Unit, plus off-campus referral.

FACULTY: School is oriented to inter-discipline cooperation. *Professional services available to faculty:* neurology, psychology, audiometry, pediatric, ophthalmology, psychiatric. *Faculty-student ratio:* 1:2. *Faculty qualifications:* 1% of staff have had specialized training in remedial reading. Graduate level training has been had by 1% of staff in reading, 2% of staff in learning disabilities, 1% of staff has Masters in early childhood education.

Persons Reading School, Inc.
10 Arch Street
Norwalk, Connecticut 06850
Director: Mary Howard Grumbly

EDUCATIONAL FACILITIES: *Remedial/developmental programs offered:* the aphasias, dyslexia (genetic or developmental), speech (developmental), minimal brain damage syndromes, slow learner, emotionally disturbed (moderate). *Instruction levels:* primary, elementary, junior and senior high, above 18 (college preparatory). *Curriculum:* full day-basic curriculum; annual basis and summer program. *Waiting period for enrollment:* no waiting period given. *Average annual enrollment:* 55 students—majority in the dyslexia, slow learner, and minimal brain damaged categories. *Individual tutoring:* no information given.

TESTING FACILITIES: Testing program available and referrals made.

FACULTY: School is oriented to inter-discipline cooperation. *Professional services available to faculty:* neurology, psychology, pediatric, ophthalmology, visual training, psychiatric. *Faculty-student ratio:* 1:8. *Faculty qualifications:* entire staff has had specialized training in remedial reading; graduate level training has been had by 30% of the staff in reading, by 15% of the staff in speech and by 10% of the staff in learning disabilities; a portion of the staff hold Masters Degrees in psychology; a portion of the staff hold Masters Degrees in guidance, psychology, and English.

The Rectory School
Pomfret, Connecticut 06258
Headmaster: John B. Bigelow
Assistant: J. R. Jackman, Jr.

EDUCATIONAL FACILITIES: *Remedial/developmental programs offered:* dyslexia (genetic or developmental), slow learner, emotionally disturbed (moderate). *Instruction levels:* junior high. *Curriculum:* full day-full curriculum; annual basis. *Waiting time for enrollment:* none. *Average annual enrollment:* 70-80 combined in dyslexia (genetic or developmental) and slow learner categories; a few in the emotionally disturbed (moderate) category, total enrollment 147. *Individual tutoring:* presented as an adjunct to the curriculum.

TESTING FACILITIES: Testing program included in curriculum; strong testing program by arrangement.

FACULTY: School oriented to inter-discipline cooperation. *Professional services available to faculty:* psychology, pediatric, ophthalmology, optometry. *Faculty-student ratio:* 1:4. *Faculty qualifications:* entire staff is doing in-service training, which is oriented to Orton-Gillingham methods for language re-training; 20% of the staff has had graduate level training in reading.

SPECIAL REQUIREMENTS: All students get SRA Developmental Reading Course unless too disabled to benefit.

SPECIAL INFORMATION: Individual counseling on a regular basis is available.

Whitby School
969 Lake Avenue
Greenwich, Connecticut 06830
Headmaster: John P. Blessington

EDUCATIONAL FACILITIES: *Remedial/developmental programs offered:* dyslexia (genetic or developmental), minimal brain damage syndromes, slow learner, emotionally disturbed (moderate). *Instruction levels:* pre-school, primary, elementary, junior high. *Curriculum:* tutorial only, half day, and full day-full curriculum; annual basis, summer program. *Waiting time for enrollment:* waiting time varies from months to years—students accepted as space permits. *Average annual enrollment:* 55—majorities in the minimal brain damage syndrome and slow learner categories. *Individual tutoring:* included automatically in students curriculum, and presented as an adjunct to the curriculum.

TESTING FACILITIES: Testing program available.

FACULTY: School is oriented to inter-discipline cooperation. *Professional services available to faculty:* neurology, psychology, audiometry, pediatric, ophthalmology, visual training, optometry, psychiatric, endocrinology. *Faculty-student ratio:* 1:16. *Faculty qualifications:* 10% of staff had specialized training in remedial reading; 20% of the staff has had graduate level training in reading. 10% in speech, and 25% in learning disabilities. Team teaching specializing in the Montessori Method.

SPECIAL INFORMATION: School is a non-graded facility, and searches diligently to meet each student's specific need(s).

COLORADO

Adams State College
Department of Education
Speech & Hearing Clinic
Alamosa, Colorado
Director: Leo A. Cary

DIAGNOSTIC FACILITIES: *Diagnostic facilities are offered for:* the aphasias, speech (developmental). *Referral sources:* school – public and private, psychiatrist, psychologist, parent, general practicioner. *Ages accepted:* all ages. *Waiting period for first appointment:* Autumn – 1 week, Spring – 1 week, Summer – 1 week. *Staff and orientation:* emphasis on education. *Professional services available:* audiometry, speech disorders. *Average annual case load:* 69 – majority in the speech category.

TESTING FACILITIES: Testing program available.

EDUCATIONAL FACILITIES: *Remedial/developmental programs offered:* the aphasias, dyslexia (genetic or developmental), speech (developmental). *Instruction levels:* all ages. *Curriculum:* tutorial only; annual basis. *Waiting time for enrollment:* Autumn – 1 week, Spring – 1 week, Summer – 1 week. *Average annual enrollment:* 89 students – majority in the speech category. *Program limits:* no maximum time a student may be enrolled for a remedial program. *Staff:* majority of staff members have completed pertinent graduate courses and have had less than 2 years practical experience.

Children's Hospital
Department of Audiology and Speech Pathology
1056 E. 19th Street
Denver, Colorado
Director: B. D. Kimball, Ph.D.

DIAGNOSTIC FACILITIES: *Diagnostic facilities offered:* the aphasias, dyslexia (genetic or developmental), speech (developmental), minimal brain damage syndromes, slow learner, psychiatric disorders. *Referral sources:* pediatrician, psychiatrist, public health agencies. *Ages accepted:* 3 years to 20 years. *Waiting period for first appointment:* Autumn – 2 weeks; Spring – 2 weeks; Summer – 3 weeks. *Staff and orientation:* a total child, multi-discipline team approach. *Professional services available:* neurology, psychology, audiometry, pediatric, ophthalmology, visual training, psychiatric, endocrinology. *Average annual case load:* 60 – majority in the speech category.

TESTING FACILITIES: Testing program available.

EDUCATIONAL FACILITIES: *Remedial/developmental facilities:* the aphasias, dyslexia (genetic or developmental), speech (developmental), minimal brain damage syndromes, slow learner, emotionally disturbed (moderate). *Instruction levels:* pre-school, primary, elementary, junior and senior high. *Curriculum:* half day; annual basis. *Waiting period for enrollment:* Autumn – 2 weeks; Spring – 2 weeks; Summer – 2 weeks. *Average annual enrollment:* 135-155 students – majority in the speech category. *Program limits:* No maximum time a student may be enrolled for a remedial program. *Staff:* Masters Degree required – majority of staff have had 2 or more years practical experience.

SPECIAL INFORMATION: School age children seen for clinical training on a supplemental basis to public school program.

Colorado State University
Department of Hearing and Speech Science
Speech And Hearing Clinic
Fort Collins, Colorado

DIAGNOSTIC FACILITIES: *Diagnostic facilities offered:* the aphasias, speech (developmental), minimal brain damage syndromes, slow learner. *Referral sources;* pediatrician, school—public and private, psychiatrist, psychologist, parent. *Ages accepted:* all ages. *Waiting period for first appointment:* 3 months. *Staff and orientation:* emphasis in the educational area. *Professional services available:* psychology, audiometry, pediatric, psychiatric. *Average annual case load:* no figures given.

TESTING FACILITIES: None listed.

EDUCATIONAL FACILITIES: *Remedial/developmental facilities:* the aphasias, speech (developmental), minimal brain damage syndromes, slow learner, emotionally disturbed (moderate). *Instruction levels:* pre-school, primary, elementary, adult rehabilitation. *Curriculum:* tutorial only; annual basis. *Waiting period for enrollment:* none given. *Average annual enrollment:* no figures given. *Program limits:* no maximum time a student may be enrolled for a remedial program. *Staff:* majority of staff members are currently enrolled in graduate school.

Randell School of Denver
2160 South Cook Street
Denver, Colorado
Director: A. A. Brown

EDUCATIONAL FACILITIES: *Remedial/developmental programs offered:* speech (developmental), minimal brain damage syndromes, slow learner, emotionally disturbed (moderate). *Instruction levels;* elementary, junior and senior high. *Curriculum:* full day—full curriculum; annual basis. *Waiting period for enrollment:* no waiting. *Average annual enrollment:* 35—majority in the slow learner category. *Individual tutoring:* presented as an adjunct to the curriculum.

TESTING FACILITIES: No information given.

FACULTY: School is not oriented to inter-discipline cooperation. *Professional services available to faculty:* psychology, psychiatric. *Faculty-student ratio:* 1:10. *Faculty qualification:* 30% of staff have had specialized training in remedial reading; graduate level training has been had by 10% of staff in reading and speech, and by 5% of staff in learning disabilities.

The Reading Clinic
1245 Toedtli
Boulder, Colorado
Director: Mrs. Grace Klug

DIAGNOSTIC FACILITIES: *Diagnostic facilities are offered for:* the aphasias, dyslexia (genetic or developmental), minimal brain damage syndromes. *Referral sources:* pediatrician, school—public and private, psychiatrist, psychologist, parent. *Ages accepted:* all ages. *Waiting period for first appointment:* 2 week waiting period for the Autumn, Spring, and Summer sessions. *Staff and orientation:* emphasis in the psychological and educational areas. *Professional services available:* psychology, audiometry; others by referral. *Average annual case load:* 75—majority in the dyslexia category plus approximately 50 cases during Summer.

TESTING FACILITIES: Strong testing program available.

EDUCATIONAL FACILITIES: *Remedial/developmental facilities offered for:* the aphasias, dyslexia (genetic or developmental), minimal brain damage syndromes, emotionally disturbed (moderate). *Instruction levels:* primary through above 18—attending college (developmental reading). *Curriculum:* tutorial only; annual basis. *Waiting period for enrollment:* 8 week waiting period for the Autumn session. *Average annual enrollment:* 75 total students, plus 50 students for the Summer program. *Program limits:* no maximum time a student may be enrolled for a remedial program. *Staff:* majority of staff members have completed pertinent graduate courses and have had 2 or more years practical experience. Tutors have graduate training in psychology, social work, and remedial techniques; plus experience in teaching all levels, and doing social work or school psychology.

University of Colorado
Speech and Hearing Clinic
934 Broadway
Boulder, Colorado
Director: Ned W. Bowler

DIAGNOSTIC FACILITIES: *Diagnostic facilities are offered for:* the aphasias, dyslexia (genetic or developmental), speech (developmental), minimal brain damage syndromes. *Referral sources:* pediatrician, school – public and private, psychiatrist, psychologist, parent. *Ages accepted:* all ages. *Waiting period for first appointment:* Autumn – 2 weeks, Spring – 3 weeks, Summer – 3 weeks. *Staff and orientation:* Not given. *Professional services available:* neurology, psychology, audiometry, pediatric, ophthalmology, visual training, optometry, psychiatric. *Average annual case load:* 71 – majority in the speech category.

TESTING FACILITIES: Testing program available.

EDUCATIONAL FACILITIES: *Remedial/developmental programs offered:* the aphasias, speech (developmental), minimal brain damage syndromes. *Instruction levels:* all ages. *Curriculum:* tutorial only; annual basis. *Waiting time for enrollment:* Autumn – 1 week, Spring – 3 weeks, Summer – 1 week. *Average annual enrollment:* 71 students – majority in the speech category. *Program limits:* no maximum time a student may be enrolled for a remedial program. *Staff:* majority of staff are student trainees and are currently enrolled in graduate school, with less than 2 years practical experience.

University of Denver
Department of Speech Pathology and Audiology
Speech and Hearing Center
University Park Campus
Denver, Colorado 80210
Director: Jerome G. Alpiner, Ph.D.

DIAGNOSTIC FACILITIES: *Diagnostic facilities offered:* the aphasias, dyslexia (genetic or developmental), speech (developmental), minimal brain damage syndromes, slow learner. *Referral sources:* pediatrician, school – public, psychiatrist, psychologist. *Ages accepted:* all ages. *Waiting period for first appointment:* Autumn – 6 weeks, Spring – 6 weeks, Summer – 8 weeks. *Staff and orientation:* emphasis in the educational area. *Professional services available:* psychology, audiometry, speech pathology. *Average annual case load:* 46 – majority in the speech category.

TESTING FACILITIES: Strong testing program available.

SPECIAL INFORMATION: Further testing and therapy arranged as indicated.

EDUCATIONAL FACILITIES: *Remedial/developmental facilities offered:* the aphasias, speech (developmental), minimal brain damage syndromes, slow learner. *Instruction levels:* all ages – pre-school through adult rehabilitation. *Curriculum:* tutorial and half day; annual basis. *Waiting period for enrollment:* Autumn – 6 weeks, Spring – 6 weeks, Summer – 8 weeks. *Average annual enrollment:* Not given. *Program limits:* no maximum time a student may be enrolled for a remedial program. *Staff:* majority of staff members have had 2 or more years practical experience.

Western State College
Department of Education
Gunnison, Colorado 81230
Director: Kenneth R. Parsons

DIAGNOSTIC FACILITIES: *Diagnostic facilities offered:* speech (developmental), minimal brain damage syndromes, slow learner. *Referral sources:* pediatrician, school—public, psychologist, parent. *Ages accepted:* 3 years to 20 years. *Waiting period for first appointment:* none. *Average annual case load:* 50-70—majority in the minimal brain damaged and slow learner categories. *Staff and orientation:* psychological, educational. *Professional services available:* psychology, psychiatric, varies.

TESTING FACILITIES: Testing program available.

EDUCATIONAL FACILITIES: *Remedial/developmental facilities:* dyslexia (genetic or developmental), speech (developmental), minimal brain damage syndromes, slow learner, emotionally disturbed (moderate). *Instruction levels:* primary, elementary, junior and senior high. *Curriculum:* full day-full curriculum; annual basis. *Waiting period for enrollment:* none. *Average annual enrollment:* 92 students—majority in the slow learner category. *Program limits:* no maximum time a student may be enrolled for a remedial program. *Staff:* majority have had 2 or more years practical experience.

DELAWARE

University of Delaware
Department of Education
Reading Study Center
Newark, Delaware
Director: Russell G. Stouffer

DIAGNOSTIC FACILITIES: *Diagnostic facilities offered:* the aphasias, dyslexia (genetic or developmental), minimal brain damage syndromes, slow learner, psychiatric disorders. *Referral sources:* pediatrician, school—public and private, psychiatrist, psychologist, parent. *Ages accepted:* 6 years to 20 years. *Waiting period for first appointment;* Autumn—1-3 months, Spring—1-3 months, Summer—1-3 months. *Staff and orientation:* emphasis in the educational area. *Professional services available:* screening only—referral made for professional services when indicated. *Average annual case load:* 35-Winter, 130-Summer.

TESTING FACILITIES: Testing program available.

EDUCATIONAL FACILITIES: *Remedial/developmental facilities:* the aphasias, dyslexia (genetic or developmental), minimal brain damage syndromes, slow learner, emotionally disturbed (moderate). *Instruction levels:* primary, elementary, junior and senior high, above 18—attending college. *Curriculum:* tutorial only; annual basis. *Waiting period for enrollment:* Autumn (with full analysis)—1 week, Spring—1 week, Summer—1-3 months. *Average annual enrollment:* 35-40 students. *Program limits;* no maximum time a student may be enrolled for a remedial program. *Staff:* majority of staff are currently enrolled in graduate school.

DISTRICT OF COLUMBIA

The American University Clinic for Learning Disabilities
Department of Education
Washington, D.C. 20016
Director: Edith H. Grotberg, Ph.D.

DIAGNOSTIC FACILITIES: *Diagnostic facilities are offered for:* dyslexia (genetic or developmental), minimal brain damage syndromes. *Referral sources:* school—public and private, psychologist, parent. *Ages accepted:* 6 years to 20 years. *Waiting period for first appoint-*

ment: 1-2 weeks for interview to admit child to Summer clinic. *Staff and orientation:* emphasis in the psychological and educational areas. *Professional services available:* neurology, psychology, audiometry. *Average annual case load:* 75 – evenly divided.

TESTING FACILITIES: Strong testing program available with referrals.

EDUCATIONAL FACILITIES: *Remedial/developmental programs offered:* dyslexia (genetic or developmental), minimal brain damage syndromes, slow learner, and emotionally disturbed (moderate). *Instruction levels:* primary, elementary, junior high and senior high. *Curriculum:* half day; summer session only. *Waiting time for enrollment:* written acceptance on first come basis. *Average annual enrollment:* 100 students – evenly divided. *Program limits:* Remedial program limited to 1 summer only. *Staff:* majority of staff members have had 2 or more years practical experience.

SPECIAL INFORMATION: Clinic holds Fellowship, from U.S. Office of Education, to train personnel in learning disabilities.

Georgetown University
Psychological & Educational Service Bureau
35th and N Streets
Washington, D.C.
Director: William L. Kelly, S.J., Ph.D

DIAGNOSTIC FACILITIES: *Diagnostic facilities are offered for:* the aphasias, dyslexia (genetic or developmental), speech (developmental), slow learner. *Referral sources:* pediatrician, school – public and private, psychiatrist, psychologist, parent. *Ages accepted:* 6 years to over 20 years. *Waiting period for first appointment:* Autumn – 2 weeks, Spring – 2 weeks, Summer – 3-4 weeks. *Staff and orientation:* emphasis in the psychological and educational areas. *Professional services available:* psychology, visual training, reading and study skills. *Average annual case load:* 144 – majority in slow learner category.

TESTING FACILITIES: Strong testing program available.

SPECIAL REQUIREMENTS: Parent interview pre and post testing period, with psychologist and tester.

EDUCATIONAL FACILITIES: *Remedial/developmental programs offered:* the aphasias, dyslexia (genetic or developmental), speech (developmental), slow learner, emotionally disturbed (moderate). *Instruction levels:* elementary, junior high, senior high, above 18 – attending college (developmental reading). *Curriculum:* tutorial only; annual basis. *Waiting time for enrollment:* courses begin 3 times a year, possible to wait a few weeks. *Average annual enrollment:* not given. *Program limits:* 30 hours for course; additional if desired. *Staff:* majority of staff members have completed pertinent graduate courses and have had two or more years practical experience.

George Washington University
Psychological Clinic
718 21st Street, N.W.
Washington, D.C. 20006
Director: Dr. E. L. Phillips

DIAGNOSTIC FACILITIES: Information not given.

EDUCATIONAL FACILITIES: *Remedial/developmental facilities:* minimal brain damage syndromes, slow learner. *Instruction levels:* primary, elementary, junior and senior high, above 18 (attending college). *Curriculum:* tutorial only; annual basis. *Waiting period for enrollment:* none given. *Average annual enrollment:* no figures given. *Program limits:* no maximum time a student may be enrolled for a remedial program. *Staff:* majority of staff have had 2 or more years practical experience.

SPECIAL INFORMATION: Psychological Clinic takes only university students on campus; Reading clinic takes all ages, but deals with essentially uncomplicated reading problems.

The Kingsbury Center for Remedial Education
2138 Bancroft Place, N.W.
Washington, D.C. 20008
Director: Kenneth R. Oldman

EDUCATIONAL FACILITIES: *Remedial/developmental programs offered:* minimal brain damage syndromes, emotionally disturbed (moderate). *Instruction levels:* primary, elementary, junior and senior high, and above 18-college preparatory. *Curriculum:* tutorial only; semester and summer. *Waiting period for enrollment:* September – 1 month, January – 2 months, Summer program – none. *Average annual enrollment:* 175-200 students. *Individual tutoring:* included automatically in students curriculum.

TESTING FACILITIES: Strong testing program available.

FACULTY: School oriented to inter-discipline cooperation. *Professional services available to faculty:* neurology, psychology, audiometry, pediatric, ophthalmology, visual training, psychiatric. *Faculty-student ratio:* mostly 1:1; group tutoring 1:3 and 1:4; study skill 1:8 and 1:10. *Faculty qualifications:* entire staff has had specialized training in remedial reading; graduate level training has been had by entire staff in reading, by 75% of staff in speech, by 25% of staff in learning disabilities; Master Degrees are held by 40% of staff for reading and by 10% of staff for learning disabilities.

SPECIAL INFORMATION: Center is 29 years old, formerly the Remedial Education Center. Center trains all own tutors, requires college degrees, and at least 2 years classroom experience. Publishes various games and pamphlets.

Washington Hospital Center
Department of Hearing and Speech
110 Irving Street, N.W.
Washington, D.C.
Director: David M. Resnick, Ph.D.

DIAGNOSTIC FACILITIES: *Diagnostic facilities offered:* the aphasias, dyslexia (genetic or developmental), speech (developmental). *Referral sources;* pediatrician, school – public and private, parent, otolaryngologist. *Ages accepted:* all ages. *Waiting period for first appointment:* Autumn – none, Spring – none, Summer – 2 weeks. *Staff and orientation:* a total child, multi-discipline team approach. *Professional services available:* neurology, audiometry, ophthalmology, visual training. *Average annual case load:* 230-majority in the speech category.

TESTING FACILITIES: Testing program available.

EDUCATIONAL FACILITIES: *Remedial/developmental facilities:* the aphasias, speech (developmental). *Instruction levels;* pre-school, primary, elementary. *Curriculum:* not given. *Waiting period for enrollment:* varies. *Average annual enrollment:* 60-70 – majority in the speech category. *Program limits:* at the discretion of faculty. *Staff:* majority of staff have completed pertinent graduate courses and have had 2 or more years practical experience.

SPECIAL INFORMATION: Multi-disciplinary approach achieved with off-campus referral.

FLORIDA

Deerborne School
311 Sevilla Avenue
Coral Gables, Florida
Director: Marvin S. Cone

EDUCATIONAL FACILITIES: *Remedial/developmental programs offered for:* the Aphasias, dyslexia (genetic or developmental), speech (developmental), minimal brain damage syndromes, slow learner, emotionally disturbed (moderate). *Instruction levels:* pre-school, primary, elementary, junior high, senior high. *Curriculum:* full day—full curriculum. *Waiting time for enrollment:* none. *Individual tutoring:* presented as an adjunct to the curriculum.

TESTING FACILITIES: Testing program available.

FACULTY: School is oriented to inter-discipline cooperation. *Professional services available to faculty:* neurology, psychology, audiometry, pediatric, ophthalmology, visual training, optometry, psychiatric, endocrinology, clinical reading evaluation. *Faculty student ratio:* not given. *Faculty qualifications:* 70% of staff have had specialized training in remedial reading; graduate level training in reading—70%, speech—20%, learning disabilities—50%; Masters Degrees are held by 20% in reading, 5% in speech, 10% in learning disabilities.

SPECIAL INFORMATION: Facility is private school which has an over-all enrollment of approximately 300 students, of which approximately 10% fall in the atypical category. For these students, facility offers individual tutoring and testing, learning laboratories and a Montessori program. Facility is accredited by the State of Florida.

Diagnostic and Evaluation Clinic
2350 Lakeview Avenue, South
St. Petersburg, Florida 33712
Director: Ray C. Wunderlich, M.D.

DIAGNOSTIC FACILITIES: *Diagnostic facilities offered:* the aphasias, dyslexia (genetic or developmental), speech (developmental), minimal brain damage syndromes, slow learner, psychiatric disorders. *Referral sources:* psychiatrist, psychologist, parent, Health Department. *Ages accepted:* 3 years to 16 years. *Waiting period for first appointment:* Autumn—3 months, Spring—3 months, Summer—3 months. *Staff and orientation:* a total child, multi-discipline team approach. *Professional services available:* neurology, psychology, audiometry, pediatric, ophthalmology, visual training, optometry, psychiatric, endocrinology. *Average annual case load:* 48.

TESTING FACILITIES: No information given.

SPECIAL INFORMATION: Clinic is a Federal Pilot program, operating 1 day per month.

EDUCATIONAL FACILITIES: None available.

Green Valley School
at the Monastery
Orange City, Florida 32763
Director: Rev. George von Hilsheimer

EDUCATIONAL FACILITIES: *Remedial/developmental programs offered:* the aphasias, dyslexia (genetic or developmental), speech (developmental), minimal brain damage syndromes, slow learner, emotionally disturbed (moderate and severe). *Instruction levels:* elementary, junior and senior high, above 18 (college preparatory). *Curriculum:* full day—full curriculum; annual basis. *Waiting period for enrollment:* September—none; January—none; Summer program—none. *Average annual enrollment:* 280-410 students—majority in the slow learner category. *Individual tutoring:* included automatically in students curriculum.

TESTING FACILITIES: 34-session sequence of tests used on each admission, plus allergic, neurologic, endocrine and physical (internal) evaluations.

FACULTY: School is oriented to inter-discipline cooperation. *Professional services available to faculty:* neurology, psychology, audiometry, pediatric, ophthalmology, visual training, optometry, psychiatric, endocrinology, internal medicine, allergist. *Faculty-student ratio::* 1:4. *Faculty qualifications:* entire staff has had specialized training in remedial reading; graduate level training has been had by 25% of the staff in reading, by 25% of the staff in speech, and by 25% of the staff in learning disabilities.

SPECIAL INFORMATION: School refunds fees if, after 3 years, the child cannot function adequately in public school or college.

Howey Academy
South Palm Avenue
Howey-in-the-Hills, Florida 32737
Director: Dr. C. A. Vaughn, Jr.

EDUCATIONAL FACILITIES: *Remedial/developmental program for:* slow learner. *Instruction levels:* elementary (5 and 6-year-olds only), junior and senior high. *Curriculum:* half day; summer only. *Waiting period for enrollment:* Summer—none. *Average annual enrollment:* 30 students. *Individual tutoring:* information not given.

TESTING FACILITIES: Testing program available with referral.

FACULTY: School oriented to inter-discipline cooperation. *Professional services available to faculty:* neurology, psychology, audiometry, pediatric, ophthalmology, optometry, psychiatric, endocrinology. *Faculty-student ratio:* 1:10. *Faculty qualifications:* 10% of staff have had specialized training in remedial reading; graduate level training has been had by 10% of staff in reading; by 20% of staff in learning disabilities; Masters Degrees are held by 10% of staff in reading and by 20% of staff in learning disabilities.

SPECIAL INFORMATION: Programs are also offered in study skills, art therapy, spelling and penmanship.

Learning Disability School
Exceptional Child Center
425 S.W. 28th Street
Fort Lauderdale, Florida
Director: Dr. Robert Weiland

EDUCATIONAL FACILITIES: *Remedial/developmental programs offered:* the aphasias, dyslexia (genetic or developmental), minimal brain damage syndromes, emotionally disturbed (moderate and severe). *Instruction levels:* primary, elementary, junior high, senior high. *Curriculum:* tutorial, half day sessions, and full day—full curriculum. *Waiting time for enrollment:* depends upon age and educational level of applicant. *Average annual enrollment:* 200 students—majority in the dyslexia and emotionally disturbed (moderate) categories. *Individual tutoring:* included automatically in students curriculum.

TESTING FACILITIES: Testing program available.

FACULTY: School is oriented to inter-discipline cooperation. *Professional services available to faculty:* psychology, audiometry, pediatric, ophthalmology, visual training, optometry. *Faculty-student ratio:* 1:8. *Faculty qualifications:* entire staff had specialized training in remedial reading; entire staff has had graduate level training in reading; 60% in speech, and 50% in learning disabilities; 20% of staff members hold Masters Degrees in reading.

SPECIAL INFORMATION: The diagnostic center staff (part of regular school system) is located with the Learning Disability School.

The McGlannan School a Language Arts Center
5950 North Kendall Drive
Miami, Florida 33156
Director: Frances K. McGlannan

EDUCATIONAL FACILITIES: *Remedial/developmental programs offered:* genetic dyslexia (developmental and complex). *Instruction levels:* primary, elementary. *Curriculum:* full day—full curriculum: annual basis. *Waiting time for enrollment:* applications taken in Spring for September enrollment, January—limited admissions accepted. *Average annual enrollment:* 96 students. *Individual tutoring:* included automatically in students curriculum.

TESTING FACILITIES: Strong testing program available.

FACULTY: School is oriented to inter-discipline cooperation. *Professional services available to faculty:* neurology, psychology, audiometry, pediatric, ophthalmology, visual training, optometry, psychiatric, endocrinology, dental, genetic, genetic research. *Faculty-student ratio:* 1:4. *Faculty qualifications:* entire staff has had specialized training in remedial reading; graduate level training has been had by 20% of the staff in speech, by 75% of the staff in learning disabilities; Masters Degrees are held by 30% of the staff in reading, by 10% of the staff in speech, and 5% of the staff are doctoral candidates.

SPECIAL REQUIREMENTS: To be enrolled, students must conform to following criteria—average or above I.Q., a specific protocol, and demonstrable hereditary pattern.

SPECIAL INFORMATION: Facility uses clinical and perceptual development techniques in routine classroom environment on a research basis. A special staff is engaged in investigations regarding medical, hereditary factors (three generations), and protocol patterning of the student body. Facility also maintains a small population of children with other forms of learning disabilities.

The Mills School
1512 East Broward Boulevard
Fort Lauderdale, Florida
Director: Dr. Robert E. Mills

EDUCATIONAL FACILITIES: *Remedial/developmental programs:* the aphasias, dyslexia (genetic or developmental), speech (developmental), minimal brain damage syndromes, slow learner, emotionally disturbed (moderate). *Instruction levels:* primary, elementary, junior and senior high. *Curriculum:* full day—full curriculum; annual basis. *Waiting period for enrollment:* none. *Average annual enrollment:* 50-70 students. *Individual tutoring:* included automatically in students curriculum.

TESTING FACILITIES: Strong testing program available.

FACULTY: School oriented to inter-discipline cooperation. *Professional services available to faculty:* neurology, psychology, audiometry, pediatric, ophthalmology, visual training, optometry, psychiatric, endocrinology. *Faculty-student ratio:* 1:6. *Faculty qualifications:* entire staff has had specialized training in remedial reading; graduate level training by 10% of staff in reading, and 25% of staff in speech.

Reading Education and Development Clinic
330 West Platt Street
Tampa, Florida 33606
Director: Mrs J. Carvelli, M. Ed.

EDUCATIONAL FACILITIES: *Remedial/developmental programs offered for:* dyslexia (genetic or developmental), speech (developmental), minimal brain damage syndromes, slow learner, emotionally disturbed (moderate and severe). *Instruction levels:* pre-school through senior high. *Curriculum:* tutorial and full day—full curriculum; annual basis and summer program. *Waiting period for enrollment:* no waiting period. *Average annual enrollment:* 117 students—majority in the emotionally disturbed (moderate) category. *Individual tutoring:* included automatically in students curriculum.

TESTING FACILITIES: Testing program available with off-campus referral.

FACULTY: School is oriented to inter-discipline cooperation. *Professional services available to faculty:* neurology, psychology, audiometry, pediatric, ophthalmology, visual training, optometry, psychiatric, endocrinology. *Faculty-student ratio:* 1:8 *Faculty qualifications:* entire staff has had specialized training in remedial reading; graduate level training has been had by 8% of the staff in reading, by 8% of the staff in speech, and by 8% of the staff in learning disabilities; Masters degrees are held by 8% of the staff in reading, and by 8% of the staff in speech.

University of Florida
College of Education
Personnel Services Department
Children's Learning Center
Gainesville, Florida
Director: G. S. Hasterok

DIAGNOSTIC FACILITIES: *Diagnostic facilities are offered for:* dyslexia (genetic or developmental), minimal brain damage syndromes. *Referral sources:* pediatrician, school—public and private, psychiatrist, psychologist. *Ages accepted:* 3 years to 12 years. *Waiting period for first appointment:* none. *Staff and orientation:* psychological, educational. *Professional services available:* neurology, psychology, audiometry, pediatric, ophthalmology, visual training, psychiatric, endocrinology. *Average annual case load:* not available.

TESTING FACILITIES: Testing program available.

SPECIAL INFORMATION: Diagnostic facility is new; and is primarily a teaching, training, and research facility associated with the College of Education.

EDUCATIONAL FACILITIES: *Remedial/developmental programs offered:* dyslexia (genetic or developmental), minimal brain damage syndromes, emotionally disturbed (moderate). *Instruction levels:* pre-school, primary, elementary. *Curriculum:* tutorial only; annual basis. *Waiting time for enrollment:* none. *Average annual enrollment:* no figures available. *Program limits:* no maximum time a student may be enrolled for a remedial program. *Staff:* majority of staff members have completed pertinent graduate courses and have had two or more years practical experience. Graduate students and selected undergraduate students will carry out the remedial services, as part of their clinical experiences in Special Education curricula.

University of Florida
Department of Comprehensive English
Reading Laboratory and Clinic
310 Anderson Hall
Gainesville, Florida
Director: George Spache, Ph.D.

DIAGNOSTIC FACILITIES: *Diagnostic facilities offered;* minimal brain damage syndromes, slow learner, psychiatric disorders. *Referral sources:* pediatrician, school—public and private, psychiatrist, psychologist, parent. *Ages accepted:* all ages. *Waiting period for first appointment:* about 6-9 months each term. *Staff and orientation:* a total child, multi-discipline team approach; with emphasis in the psychological and educational areas. *Professional services available:* psychology, audiometry, ophthalmology, visual training. *Average annual case load:* about 100 (thorough 3 hours evaluation) remedial cases; and about 800 group tested college students.

TESTING FACILITIES: Testing program available.

EDUCATIONAL FACILITIES: *Remedial/developmental facilities:* dyslexia (genetic or developmental), slow learner, emotionally disturbed (moderate). *Instruction levels:* primary, elementary, junior and senior high, above 18-attending college. *Curriculum:* developmental individualized program during academic year; individual tutoring during the summer. *Waiting period for enrollment:* 6-9 months. *Average annual enrollment:* 800 students (college) during the year; 60 children (tutorial) for 6 weeks during the summer. *Program limits:* 6 weeks is maximum time for enrollment for a remedial program during the summer. *Staff;* portion of staff are currently enrolled in graduate school; majority of staff have completed pertinent graduate courses and have had 2 or more years practical experience.

University of Florida
Department of Speech
Speech and Hearing Clinic
321 Tigert Hall
Gainesville, Florida
Director: Dr. T. B. Abbott

DIAGNOSTIC FACILITIES: *Diagnostic facilities offered:* the aphasias and speech (developmental). *Referral sources:* pediatrician, school—public and private, psychiatrist, psychologist, parent. *Ages accepted:* all ages. *Waiting period for first appointment:* varies. *Staff and orientation:* emphasis in the educational area. *Professional services available:* neurology, psychology, audiometry, pediatric. *Average annual case load:* 35 – majority in the speech category.

TESTING FACILITIES: Not given.

EDUCATIONAL FACILITIES: *Remedial/developmental facilities offered:* the aphasias, and speech (developmental). *Instruction levels:* all ages – from pre-school through adult rehabilitation. *Curriculum:* tutorial only, annual basis. *Waiting period for enrollment:* varies. *Average annual enrollment:* not given. *Program limits:* no maximum time a student may be enrolled for a remedial program. *Staff:* majority of staff members have completed pertinent graduate courses and have had 2 or more years practical experience.

University of Miami
Department of Special Education
Child Development Center
Coral Gables, Florida 33124
Director: DeForest L. Strunk, Ed.D.

DIAGNOSTIC FACILITIES: *Diagnostic facilities are offered for:* the aphasias, dyslexia (genetic or developmental), speech (developmental), minimal brain damage syndromes, slow learner, psychiatric disorders. *Referral sources:* pediatrician, school – public and private, psychiatrist, psychologist, parent. *Ages accepted:* infancy to 16 years. *Waiting period for first appointment:* varies greatly. *Staff and orientation:* a total child, multidiscipline team approach. *Professional services available:* neurology, psychology, audiometry, pediatric, ophthalmology, psychiatric, endocrinology, education evaluation, social service, visiting nurse. *Average annual case load:* 250 new cases, 200 review cases.

TESTING FACILITIES: Testing available – thorough evaluation in all needed areas.

EDUCATIONAL FACILITIES: None available.

SPECIAL INFORMATION: The Special Education Department in cooperation with the Crippled Children's Society of Miami is establishing a program for children with learning disabilities to begin in September of 1967.

University of Miami
Guidance Center
Reading Clinic
Coral Gables, Florida
Director: Dr. Richard L. Carner

DIAGNOSTIC FACILITIES: *Diagnostic facilities offered:* dyslexia (genetic or developmental), minimal brain damage syndromes, slow learner. *Referral sources:* pediatrician, school – public and private, psychiatrist, psychologist, parent, neurologist. *Ages accepted:* 6 years to over 20 years. *Waiting period for first appointment:* Autumn – 3-4 weeks, Spring – 4-6 weeks, Summer – 2-3 weeks. *Staff and orientation:* emphasis in the psychological and educational areas. *Professional services available:* neurology, psychology, audiometry, pediatric, ophthalmology, visual training, optometry, psychiatric. *Average annual case load:* not given.

TESTING FACILITIES: Strong testing program available with referral when needed.

EDUCATIONAL FACILITIES: *Remedial/developmental facilities:* dyslexia (genetic or developmental), minimal brain damage syndromes, slow learner, emotionally disturbed (moderate). *Instruction levels:* all ages. *Curriculum:* tutorial only; annual basis. *Waiting period for enrollment:* 2 months. *Average annual enrollment:* 115-130 students. *Program limits:* no maximum time a student may be enrolled for a remedial program. *Staff:* majority of staff have completed pertinent graduate courses and have had 2 or more years practical experience.

SPECIAL INFORMATION: Clinic specializes in learning disabilities; Reading Specialists training; Masters and Doctoral programs.

The Vanguard School
Post Office Box 928
Lake Wales, Florida
Director: Harry E. Nelson

EDUCATIONAL FACILITIES: *Remedial/developmental programs offered:* the aphasias, dyslexia (genetic or developmental), speech (developmental), minimal brain damage syndromes, slow learner, emotionally disturbed (moderate). *Instruction levels:* pre-school, primary, elementary, junior and senior high. *Curriculum;* full day—full curriculum; annual basis. *Waiting period for enrollment:* September—6 months. *Average annual enrollment:* 96 students—majority in the minimal brain damaged syndromes category. *Individual tutoring:* presented as an adjunct to the curriculum.

TESTING FACILITIES: Strong testing program available with off-campus referral.

FACULTY: School is oriented to inter-discipline cooperation. *Professional services available to faculty:* neurology, psychology, audiometry, pediatric, ophthalmology, visual training, optometry, endocrinology. *Faculty-student ratio:* 1:4. *Faculty qualifications:* one third of staff have had specialized training in remedial reading; graduate level training has been had by one-third in reading, 5% in speech, 75% in learning disabilities; Masters Degrees are held by 10% of the staff in reading, 5% in speech, and one-third in learning disabilities.

GEORGIA

Brandon Hall School
2500 Spalding Drive
Dunwoody, Georgia
Director: Theodore Hecht

EDUCATIONAL FACILITIES: *Remedial/developmental programs offered for:* dyslexia (genetic or developmental). *Instruction levels:* junior high school, senior high, above 18—college preparatory. *Curriculum:* tutorial only and full day—full curriculum; annual basis. *Waiting time for enrollment:* no waiting time for the September session, the January session, nor the Summer program. *Average annual enrollment:* 30 students. *Individual tutoring:* included automatically in students curriculum.

TESTING FACILITIES: No testing program listed, off-campus referral given.

FACULTY: School is oriented to inter-discipline cooperation. *Professional services availabe to faculty:* neurology, psychology, audiometry, ophthalmology, visual training, psychiatric. *Faculty-student ratio:* 1:1. *Faculty qualification:* 10% of staff have had specialized training in remedial reading; graduate level training has been had by 25% of the staff in reading, 7% of the staff in speech, and by 20% of the staff in learning disabilities.

Emory University
Division of Teacher Education
Atlanta Speech School
2020 Peachtree Road, N.W.
Atlanta, Georgia 30309
Director: Robert L. McCroskey, Ph.D.

DIAGNOSTIC FACILITIES: *Diagnostic facilities offered:* the aphasias, dyslexia (genetic or developmental), speech (developmental), minimal brain damage syndromes, psychiatric disorders. *Referral sources:* pediatrician, school—public and private, psychiatrist, psychologist, parent. *Ages accepted:* all ages; including hearing screening procedures for newborns and infants. *Waiting period for first appointment:* Autumn—5 weeks; Spring—5 weeks; Summer—5 weeks. *Staff and orientation:* a total child, multi-discipline team approach; with emphasis in the neurological, psychological, educational areas. *Professional services available:* neurology, psychology, audiometry, pediatric, ophthalmology, visual training, psychiatric, otology, language pathology. *Average annual case load:* 620 (psychiatric disorders conducted in another department)—majority in the speech category.

TESTING FACILITIES: Strong testing program available.

EDUCATIONAL FACILITIES: *Remedial/developmental facilities:* the aphasias, dyslexia (genetic or developmental), speech (developmental), minimal brain damage syndromes. *Instruction levels:* pre-school, primary, elementary, above 18 (attending college), adult rehabilitation. *Curriculum:* tutorial only, half day program, and full day—full curriculum; annual basis. (Programs range from bi-monthly visits to the home of parents with deaf infants to the full day—full curriculum—depending upon the age, the type, and the severity of the child's problem.) *Waiting time for enrollment:* Autumn—6-12 months; Spring—6-12 months; Summer—1 month (summer sessions run independently). The waiting period will vary depending upon which department the child's program is assigned. *Average annual enrollment:* 285 students—majority in the speech category. *Program limits:* no maximum time a student may be enrolled for a remedial program. *Staff:* majority of staff have completed pertinent graduate courses and have had 2 or more years practical experience.

SPECIAL INFORMATION: Facility's program allows the possibility of longitudinal observation of children who are difficult to diagnose. Where it is indicated, these children are regularly observed by a variety of specialists while an on-going educational program is carried out and then, the teaching clinician and the auxiliary staff members 'staff' the child in order to arrive at an identification of the various kinds of disorders which contribute to the overall problem. The school offers programs for auditorially and language disordered children; pre-school program for auditorially and language disordered children; elementary programs (independent) for both auditorially and linguistically handicapped. Cooperative evaluations are conducted in conjunction with the Emory Reading Clinic, the Emory Psychiatric Clinic, and the Child Guidance Clinic. Facility will acquire (during the 1967-68 school year) a new building, which will enable it to increase its enrollment.

University of Georgia
Department of Educational Reading
Reading Clinic
Baldwin Hall
Athens, Georgia
Director: Byron Callaway

DIAGNOSTIC FACILITIES: *Diagnostic facilities offered:* educationally handicapped. *Referral sources:* school—public and private, psychologist. *Ages accepted;* 3 years to 6 years (occasionally), 6 years to 20 years (usually), over 20 years (occasionally). *Waiting period for first appointment:* Autumn—1-3 months; Spring—1-3 months; Summer—1-3 months. *Staff and orientation;* emphasis in the psychological and educational areas. *Professional services available:* audiometry. *Average annual case load:* not given.

TESTING FACILITIES: Testing program available.

EDUCATIONAL FACILITIES: *Remedial/developmental facilities:* speech (developmental), slow learner, emotionally disturbed (moderate). *Instruction levels:* elementary, junior and senior high, above 18-attending college. *Curriculum:* tutorial only; annual basis. *Waiting period for enrollment:* varies. *Average annual enrollment:* not given. *Program limits:* no maximum time student may be enrolled for a remedial program. *Staff:* majority of staff have completed pertinent graduate courses.

HAWAII

The Reading Clinic
1611 Keeaumoku Street
Room 209
Honolulu, Hawaii
Director: Mrs. Merrie C. Crumly

EDUCATIONAL FACILITIES: *Remedial/developmental programs offered for:* the aphasias, dyslexia (genetic or developmental), minimal brain damage syndromes, slow learner, emotionally disturbed (moderate). *Instruction levels:* pre-school, primary, elementary, junior high, senior high, adult rehabilitation. *Curriculum:* tutorial only; annual basis. *Waiting time for enrollment:* none. *Average annual enrollment:* 65 students. *Individual tutoring:* no information given.

TESTING FACILITIES: No information given.

FACULTY: No information given. *Professional services available to faculty:* not given. *Faculty-student ratio:* 1:5. *Faculty qualifications:* majority of faculty have completed pertinent graduate courses and have had two or more years practical experience.

SPECIAL REQUIREMENTS: Complete diagnosis (educational) required before acceptance.

SPECIAL INFORMATION: Classes limited to 5 pupils; all classes on an hourly basis.

Variety Club School
1212 University Avenue
Honolulu, Hawaii 96814
Director: Mrs. Rose Y. Lee

DIAGNOSTIC FACILITIES: No information given.

EDUCATIONAL FACILITIES: *Remedial/developmental facilities:* the aphasias, dyslexia (genetic or developmental), speech (developmental), minimal brain damage syndromes, slow learner. *Instruction levels:* pre-school and primary. *Curriculum:* tutorial only, half day, and full day—full curriculum; annual basis and summer program. *Waiting period for enrollment:* Autumn—usually none; Spring—usually none; Summer—usually none. *Average annual enrollment:* 24 students. *Program limits:* no maximum time a student may be enrolled for a remedial program. *Staff:* majority of staff have completed pertinent graduate courses and have had 2 or more years practical experience.

SPECIAL REQUIREMENTS: Private school for children with learning disabilities—3 years to 9 years old.

SPECIAL INFORMATION: Classes limited to 6 pupils.

Waialae Catholic Center
4449 Malia Street
Honolulu, Hawaii
Director: Sister Agnes Jerome

EDUCATIONAL FACILITIES: *Remedial/developmental programs offered:* the aphasias, dyslexia (genetic or developmental), speech (developmental), minimal brain damage syndromes, slow learner, emotionally disturbed, (moderate). *Instruction levels:* pre-school, primary, elementary, junior high. *Curriculum:* full day—full curriculum; annual basis. *Waiting time for enrollment:* not given, about 45 children on waiting list now. *Average annual enrollment:* not given. *Individual tutoring:* presented as an adjunct to the curriculum.

TESTING FACILITIES: Testing program available.

FACULTY: School is oriented to inter-discipline cooperation. *Professional services available to faculty:* in process of acquiring off-campus psychological referrals. *Faculty-student ratio:* 1:10. *Faculty qualifications:* 80% of staff have had specialized training in remedial reading; entire staff has had graduate level training in reading and learning disabilities, 25% in speech. The director holds a Masters Degree in Special Education with training beyond in reading, speech, and learning disabilities.

SPECIAL INFORMATION: Facility offers two types of classes—for the trainable and for learning disabilities.

IDAHO

Idaho State University
College of Education
Pocatello, Idaho

DIAGNOSTIC FACILITIES: *Diagnostic facilities offered:* speech (developmental), slow learner, psychiatric disorders. *Referral sources:* school – public, psychologist, parent. *Ages accepted:* 6 years to over 20 years. *Waiting period for first appointment:* not given. *Staff and orientation:* emphasis in the psychological and educational areas. *Professional services available:* psychology, audiometry, pediatric, ophthalmology, optometry, psychiatric. *Average annual case load:* not given.

TESTING FACILITIES: Testing program not given.

EDUCATIONAL FACILITIES: None available.

Idaho State University
Department of Speech Pathology and Audiology
Speech and Hearing Center
Box 116
Pocatello, Idaho
Director: R. Grange

DIAGNOSTIC FACILITIES: *Diagnostic facilities offered:* the aphasias, dyslexia (genetic or developmental), speech (developmental), minimal brain damage syndromes, slow learner. *Referral sources:* pediatrician, school – public and private, psychiatrist, psychologist, parent. *Ages accepted:* all ages. *Waiting period for first appointment:* Autumn – 1 week, Spring – 1 week, Summer – 1 week. *Staff and orientation:* a total child, multi-discipline team approach. *Professional services available:* psychology, audiometry, speech-language. *Average annual case load:* 90 – majority in the aphasias, dyslexia and speech categories.

TESTING FACILITIES: Testing program available.

EDUCATIONAL FACILITIES: *Remedial/developmental facilities:* the aphasias, dyslexia (genetic or developmental), speech (developmental), minimal brain damage syndromes, slow learner. *Instruction levels:* all ages. *Curriculum:* tutorial only and half day; annual basis. *Waiting period for enrollment:* none. *Average annual enrollment:* 35 students – majority in the aphasias and speech categories. *Program limits:* no maximum time a student may be enrolled for a remedial program. *Staff:* majority of staff have completed pertinent graduate courses and have had 2 or more years practical experience.

ILLINOIS

Bradley University
School of Speech Therapy
Peoria, Illinois 61606
Director: Dr. Andrew Paesani, Jr.

DIAGNOSTIC FACILITIES: *Diagnostic facilities are offered for:* the aphasias, speech (developmental), minimal brain damage syndromes, slow learner. *Referral sources:* pediatrician, school – public, psychiatrist, psychologist, parent. *Ages accepted:* all ages. *Waiting period for first appointment:* Autumn – 6 weeks, Spring – 8 weeks, Summer – 8 weeks. *Staff and orientation:* a total child, multi-discipline team approach. *Professional services available:* psychology, audiometry, pediatric, speech pathology. *Average annual case load:* 76 – majority in the speech category.

TESTING FACILITIES: Not given.

EDUCATIONAL FACILITIES: *Remedial/developmental facilities:* the aphasias, speech (developmental), minimal brain damage syndromes, slow learner, emotionally disturbed (moderate). *Instruction levels:* all ages. *Curriculum:* tutorial only; annual basis. *Waiting period for enrollment:* Autumn—4-8 weeks, Spring—6-8 weeks, Summer—4 weeks. *Average annual enrollment:* 79 students—majority in the speech category. *Program limits:* no maximum time a student may be enrolled for a remedial program. *Staff:* majority of staff members have completed pertinent graduate courses and have had two or more years practical experience.

Cook County Hospital
Department of Pediatrics
1825 West Harrison Street
Chicago, Illinois 60612
Director: Dr. Joseph Greengard,
Administrator: W. M. McCoy

DIAGNOSTIC FACILITIES: *Diagnostic facilities offered:* the aphasias, dyslexia (genetic or developmental), speech (developmental), minimal brain damage syndromes, slow learner, psychiatric disorders. *Referral sources:* pediatrician, school—public, psychologist, parent. *Ages accepted:* 3 years to 16 years. *Waiting period for first appointment:* Autumn—6 months; Spring—6 months; Summer—6 months. *Staff and orientation:* a total child, multi-discipline team approach; with emphasis in the neurological, psychological, pediatric, educational and psychiatric areas. *Professional services available:* neurology, psychology, audiometry, pediatric, ophthalmology, visual training, endocrinology. *Average annual case load:* not given.

TESTING FACILITIES: Primarily a medical evaluation program available with referral to hospital's Pediatric Neurology Clinic.

EDUCATIONAL FACILITIES: None available.

SPECIAL INFORMATION: Hospital does offer bedside teaching for hospitalized children (grade school and high school).

The Day School
800 Buena Avenue
Chicago, Illinois 60613
Director: Elizabeth B. Andrews

EDUCATIONAL FACILITIES: *Remedial/developmental programs:* speech (developmental), dyslexia (genetic or developmental), minimal brain damage syndromes. *Instruction levels:* primary, elementary, junior high (grades 9 and 10 only). *Curriculum:* full day—full curriculum; annual basis. *Waiting period for enrollment:* available as space permits. *Average annual enrollment:* 70-75 students. *Individual tutoring:* information not given.

TESTING FACILITIES: Psychological study, plus psychiatric interview (parent and child), with referral.

FACULTY: School is oriented to inter-discipline cooperation. *Professional services available to faculty:* psychology, psychiatric, special education. *Faculty-student ratio:* 1:3. *Faculty qualifications:* 50% of staff have had specialized training in remedial reading; 25% of staff hold Masters Degrees for learning disabilities.

SPECIAL REQUIREMENT: 11 months program participation required.

SPECIAL INFORMATION: 8 weeks residential camp program (includes academics) available where recommended.

Illinois College of Optometry
Clinic Department
3241 South Michigan Avenue
Chicago, Illinois
Director: Dr. Walter Yasko

DIAGNOSTIC FACILITIES: *Diagnostic facilities are offered for:* minimal brain damage syndromes, slow learner. *Referral sources:* pediatrician, school – public and private, psychiatrist, psychologist, optometrist, parent, remedial reading teachers. *Ages accepted:* 3 years to over 20 years. *Waiting period for first appointment:* 10 days to 2 weeks. *Staff and orientation:* optometric staff. *Professional services available:* visual training, optometry, teachers report. *Average annual case load:* approximately 800 per year; majority in slow learner catagory.

TESTING FACILITIES: Optometric testing program available.

EDUCATIONAL FACILITIES: *Remedial/developmental programs offered:* minimal brain damage syndromes, slow learners. *Instruction levels:* pre-school, primary, elementary, junior high, senior high, above 18-attending college (developmental reading). *Curriculum:* annual basis. *Waiting time for enrollment:* Autumn – 10 to 14 days. *Average annual enrollment:* approximately 400 students per year; majority in the slow learner category. *Program limits:* no maximum time a student may be enrolled for a remedial program. *Staff:* majority of staff members have completed pertinent graduate courses and have had two or more years practical experience.

SPECIAL INFORMATION: During Autumn and Spring the Vision Testing Department operates 4 days per week; seminar 3 mornings per week.

Keith Country Day School
1715 North Second Street
Rockford, Illinois 61108
Director: C. E. McDermaid

EDUCATIONAL FACILITIES: *Remedial/developmental programs offered:* dyslexia (genetic or developmental), minimal brain damage syndromes. *Instruction levels:* pre-school, primary, elementary, and junior high. *Curriculum:* full day – full curriculum; annual basis. *Waiting period for enrollment:* September – 0-1 year; January – no enrollment taken; Summer program – immediate if possible. *Average annual enrollment:* 35 students – majority in the dyslexia category. *Individual tutoring:* presented as an adjunct to the curriculum (tutoring and small groups of 2-6 students available).

TESTING FACILITIES: Testing program available.

FACULTY: School oriented to inter-discipline cooperation. *Professional services available to faculty:* neurology, psychology, audiometry, pediatric, ophthalmology, psychiatric. *Faculty-student ratio:* 1:10. *Faculty qualifications:* 2 staff members have had specialized training in remedial reading; graduate level training has been had by 2 staff members in reading, and by 1 staff member in learning disabilities.

Little Company of Mary Hospital
Department of Speech and Hearing Services
2800 W. 95th Street
Evergreen Park, Illinois
Director: Eric Fors

DIAGNOSTIC FACILITIES: *Diagnostic facilities offered:* the aphasias, speech (developmental), minimal brain damage syndromes. *Referral sources:* pediatrician, school – public and private, psychiatrist, psychologist, parent, social agencies. *Ages accepted:* all ages. *Waiting period for first appointment:* Autumn – 1 week; Spring – 1 week; Summer – 1 week. *Staff and orientation:* a total child, multi-discipline team approach; with emphasis in the neurological, psychological, pediatric and psychiatric areas. *Professional services available:* neurology, psychology, audiometry, pediatric, ophthalmology, psychiatric, endocrinology, EEG, EMG, brain scan. *Average annual case load:* 1,280 treatments – 160 patients.

TESTING FACILITIES: Testing program available.

EDUCATIONAL FACILITIES: *Remedial/developmental facilities:* the aphasias, speech (developmental), minimal brain damage syndromes. *Instruction levels:* pre-school, primary, elementary, junior and senior high, adult rehabilitation. *Curriculum:* tutorial only; annual basis. *Waiting period for enrollment:* Autumn – 1 week; Spring – 1 week; Summer – 1 week. *Average annual enrollment:* 160 students – majority in the aphasias category/1,280 treatments. *Program limits:* no maximum time a student may be enrolled for a remedial program. *Staff:* majority of staff have completed pertinent graduate courses and have had 2 or more years practical experience.

SPECIAL INFORMATION: This facility is a department within the Rehabilitation Unit of the general hospital, operating in conjunction with Physical Therapy, Occupational Therapy, Recreational Therapy, as well as operating independently.

Loyola University Guidance Center
820 N. Michigan Avenue
Chicago, Illinois
Director: T. M. Kennedy, Ph.D.

DIAGNOSTIC FACILITIES: *Diagnostic facilities offered:* the aphasias, dyslexia (genetic or developmental), speech (developmental), minimal brain damage syndromes, slow learner, psychiatric disorders. *Referral sources:* parent – with supporting material from relevant specialists. *Ages accepted:* 3 years to 15 years. *Waiting period for first appointment:* Autumn – 0-5 months, Spring – 0-5 months, Summer – 0-5 months. *Staff and orientation:* a total child, multi-discipline team approach. *Professional services available:* psychology, psychiatric, speech pathology. *Average annual case load:* not given.

TESTING FACILITIES: Testing program available.

EDUCATIONAL FACILITIES: Individual and group methods of intervention for outpatients. *Instruction levels:* pre-school, primary, elementary, junior high. *Curriculum:* annual basis. *Waiting period for enrollment:* Autumn – 0-6 months, Spring – 0-6 months, Summer – 0-6 months. *Average annual enrollment:* not given. *Program limits:* student may be enrolled for a remedial program until the age of 15 years. *Staff:* all full-time staff members have completed graduate degrees (M.D., Ph.D., M.S.W); clinical trainees have completed sufficient course work to be prepared for level of assignment.

Michael Reese Hospital
Henner Hearing and Speech Center
Department of Hearing and Speech-Otolaryngology
2929 S. Ellis Avenue
Chicago, Illinois
Director: Dr. Laszlo Stein

DIAGNOSTIC FACILITIES: *Diagnostic facilities offered:* the aphasias, dyslexia (genetic or developmental), speech (developmental), minimal brain damage syndromes, slow learner, psychiatric disorders. *Referral sources:* pediatrician, school – public and private, psychiatrist, psychologist. *Ages accepted:* all ages. *Waiting period for first appointment:* Autumn – 3-6 weeks, Spring – 3-6 weeks, Summer – 3-6 weeks. *Staff and orientation:* a total child, multi-discipline team approach. *Professional services available:* neurology, psychology, audiometry, pediatric, ophthalmology, psychiatric, endocrinology. *Average annual case load:* 450.

TESTING FACILITIES: Strong testing program available.

EDUCATIONAL FACILITIES: *Remedial/developmental facilities:* the aphasias, dyslexia, (genetic or developmental), speech (developmental), minimal brain damage syndromes, emotionally disturbed (moderate and severe). *Instruction levels:* pre-school, primary, elementary, adult rehabilitation. *Curriculum:* tutorial only; annual basis. *Waiting period for enrollment:* Autumn – 6 months, Spring – 6 months, Summer – 6 months. *Average annual enrollment:* 220 students. *Program limits:* no maximum time a student may be enrolled for a remedial program. *Staff qualifications:* majority of staff have completed pertinent graduate courses and have had 2 or more years practical experience.

National College of Education
Guidance Center
2840 Sheridan Road
Evanston, Illinois 60201
Director: Mrs. Bertha K. Stavrianos, Ph.D.

DIAGNOSTIC FACILITIES: *Diagnostic facilities offered:* dyslexia (genetic or developmental), minimal brain damage syndromes, slow learner. *Referral sources:* pediatrician, school—public and private, psychiatrist, psychologist, parent. *Ages accepted:* 6 years to 14 years. *Waiting period for first appointment:* Autumn—2-3 weeks; Spring—3-4 weeks, Summer—no facilities. *Staff and orientation:* emphasis in the psychological and educational areas. *Professional services available:* psychology, audiometry, optometry. *Average annual case load:* 100-110.

TESTING FACILITIES: Strong testing program available, with referral made.

EDUCATIONAL FACILITIES: *Remedial/developmental facilities:* dyslexia (genetic or developmental), minimal brain damage syndromes, slow learner, emotionally disturbed (moderate). *Instruction levels:* primary. *Curriculum:* annual basis. *Waiting period for enrollment:* varies, testing appointments and remedial programs operating at capacity by November and April. *Average annual enrollment:* 70-75 students. *Program limits:* none given. *Staff:* majority of staff members have completed pertinent graduate courses.

Northern Illinois University
College of Education
Reading Clinic
Graham Hall
DeKalb, Illinois
Director: Dr. Eugene B. Grant

DIAGNOSTIC FACILITIES: *Diagnostic facilities offered for:* dyslexia (genetic or developmental). *Referral sources:* school—public and private, parent. *Ages accepted:* 6 years to over 20 years. *Waiting period for first appointment:* Autumn—6-8 weeks, Spring—6-8 weeks, Summer—6-8 weeks. *Staff and orientation:* emphasis in the educational area. *Professional services available:* audiometry, all others through referral. *Average annual case load:* 120.

TESTING FACILITIES: Testing program available. with referral.

EDUCATIONAL FACILITIES: *Remedial/developmental facilities:* dyslexia (genetic or developmental). *Instruction levels:* primary, elementary, junior and senior high, and adult rehabilitation. *Curriculum:* tutorial only; annual basis. *Waiting period for enrollment:* not given. *Average annual enrollment:* 60-80 students. *Program limits:* no maximum time a student may be enrolled for a remedial program. *Staff:* 3 permanent staff members have doctoral level degrees; and much of the testing and instruction is done by students in a Masters Degree level program, under the supervision of the permanent staff.

SPECIAL INFORMATION: Educational facilities available for the above 18 age group, attending college, in another facility of the Northern Illinois University campus.

Northern Illinois University
Department of Speech
DeKalb, Illinois
Director: Louis Lerea

DIAGNOSTIC FACILITIES: *Diagnostic facilities offered for:* the aphasias, dyslexia (genetic or developmental), speech (developmental). *Referral sources:* pediatrician, school—public and private, psychiatrist, psychologist, parent, state agencies. *Ages accepted:* all ages. *Waiting period for first appointment:* Autumn—6 months, Spring—6 months. *Staff and orientation:* a total child, multi-discipline team approach. *Professional services available:* neurology, psychology, audiometry, pediatric, ophthalmology, optometry, psychiatric. *Average annual case load:* 50—majority in the speech category.

TESTING FACILITIES: Testing program available.

EDUCATIONAL FACILITIES: *Remedial/developmental facilities:* the aphasias, dyslexia (genetic or developmental), speech (developmental). *Instruction levels:* all ages. *Curriculum:* tutorial only (pre-school through senior high), full day—full curriculum (adult rehabilitation); annual basis. *Waiting period for enrollment:* Autumn—6 months, Spring—6 months. *Average annual enrollment:* 50 students—majority in the speech category. *Program limits:* no maximum time a student may be enrolled for a remedial program. *Staff:* majority of staff have completed pertinent graduate courses and have had 2 or more years practical experience.

Northwestern University
Department of Communicative Disorders
1831 Harrison
Evanston, Illinios
Director: David Rutherford

DIAGNOSTIC FACILITIES: *Diagnostic facilities offered:* the aphasias, dyslexia (genetic or developmental), speech (developmental), minimal brain damage syndromes, slow learner, *Referral sources:* pediatrician, school—public and private, psychiatrist, psychologist, parent. *Ages accepted:* all ages. *Waiting period for first appointment:* varies. *Staff and orientation:* to communicative disorders. *Professional services available:* psychology, audiometry, speech—language as a part of learning disabilities. *Average annual case load:* not given.

TESTING FACILITIES: Varies from one facility to another within the department.

EDUCATIONAL FACILITIES: *Remedial/developmental facilities:* the aphasias, dyslexia (genetic or developmental), speech (developmental), minimal brain damage syndromes, slow learner and emotionally disturbed (moderate)—only related to speech, learning and language problems. *Instruction levels:* all ages. *Curriculum:* clinic schedule—1 to 5 hours per week; annual basis. *Waiting period for enrollment:* varies. *Average annual enrollment:* not given. *Program limits:* no maximum time a student may be enrolled for a remedial program. *Staff:* portion of staff are currently enrolled in graduate school and have had less than 2 years practical experience; portion of staff have completed pertinent graduate courses; all are supervised by full-time staff and faculty.

Presbyterian-St. Luke's Hospital
Department of Pediatrics
1753 W. Congress Parkway
Chicago, Illinios
Director: Dr. J. Christian

DIAGNOSTIC FACILITIES: *Diagnostic facilities offered:* the aphasias, dyslexia (genetic or developmental), speech (developmental), minimal brain damage syndromes, slow learner, psychiatric disorders. *Referral sources:* pediatrician, school—public and private, psychiatrist, psychologist. *Ages accepted:* 3 years to 21 years. *Waiting period for first appointment:* depending on need—2-10 days. *Staff and orientation:* a total child, multi-discipline team approach; with emphasis in the neurological, psychological, pediatric, educational and psychiatric areas. *Professional services available:* neurology, psychology, audiometry, pediatric, ophthalmology, visual training, optometry, psychiatric, endocrinology. *Average annual case load:* for Health Center-2,880—majority in the psychiatric category; figures for private patients not available.

TESTING FACILITIES: All types of testing facilities available.

EDUCATIONAL FACILITIES: *Remedial/developmental facilities:* the aphasias, dyslexia, speech (developmental), minimal brain damage syndromes, slow learner, emotionally disturbed (moderate and severe). *Instruction levels:* all ages. *Curriculum:* tutorial, half day program, full day-full curriculum; annual basis at day hospital. *Waiting period for enrollment:* up to 6 months waiting (because of volume). *Average annual enrollment:* 10-15 students from each related category. *Program limits:* no maximum time a student may be enrolled for a remedial program. *Staff:* majority of staff have had 2 or more years practical experience.

Ravinia Reading and Educational Clinic, Inc.
580 Roger Williams Avenue
Highland Park, Illinois
Director: Robert W. Bell, Ph.D.

EDUCATIONAL FACILITIES: *Remedial/developmental programs offered:* the aphasias, dyslexia (genetic or developmental), minimal brain damage syndromes, emotionally disturbed (moderate and severe). *Instruction levels:* all ages – from pre-school through over 18 years-college preparatory. *Curriculum:* tutorial only; annual basis. *Waiting period for enrollment:* 30 days. *Average annual enrollment:* (clinic organized winter of 1966-67) figures not available. *Individual tutoring:* included automatically in students curriculum.

TESTING FACILITIES: Testing program available.

FACULTY: School oriented to inter-discipline cooperation. *Professional services available to faculty:* neurology, psychology, visual training, optometry, psychiatric. *Faculty-student ratio:* 1:1, 1:2, and 1:3. *Faculty qualifications:* 25% of staff have had specialized training in remedial reading; 25% of staff have had graduate level training in reading and learning disabilities; 25% of staff hold Masters Degrees in learning disabilities.

SPECIAL INFORMATION: Clinical work is of therapeutic nature, not a school curriculum. Current staff of Psychologist, language Therapist, Optometrist, Psychiatrist, and part-time reading Teacher will be augmented by additional language Therapist and speech Therapist as soon as possible.

Rockford College
Department of Education Evening College
Reading Clinic
5050 East State Street
Rockford, Illinois 61101
Director: Mrs. Shelton Richmond

DIAGNOSTIC FACILITIES: *Diagnostic facilities offered:* dyslexia (genetic or developmental). *Referral sources:* pediatrician, school – public and private, psychiatrist, psychologist, parent, optometrist. *Ages accepted:* 8 years to over 20 years. *Waiting period for first appointment:* Autumn – no waiting. Spring – 1-2 weeks, Summer – no waiting. *Staff and orientation:* emphasis in the educational area. *Professional services available:* community referral. *Average annual case load:* 200-250.

TESTING FACILITIES: Testing program available.

EDUCATIONAL FACILITIES: *Remedial/developmental facilities:* dyslexia (genetic or developmental), minimal brain damage syndromes (on referral of psychiatrist or psychologist). *Instruction levels:* 3rd and 4th grades, junior and senior high, above 18-attending college (developmental reading), adult rehabilitation. *Curriculum:* tutorial only; annual basis. *Waiting period for enrollment:* none. *Average annual enrollment:* 205-260 – majority in the dyslexia category. *Program limits:* no maximum time a student may be enrolled for a remedial program. *Staff:* majority of staff have completed pertinent graduate courses and have had 2 or more years practical experience.

Schwab Hospital
Department of Psychology, Speech, and Audiology
1401 S. California
Chicago, Illinois
Director: William G. Fischer

EDUCATIONAL FACILITIES: *Remedial/developmental programs offered:* the aphasias, dyslexia (genetic or developmental), speech (developmental), minimal brain damage syndromes, slow learner. *Instruction levels:* pre-school, primary, elementary, junior high, senior high, above 18 years attending college (developmental reading), adult rehabilitation. *Curriculum:* tutorial only; annual basis. *Waiting time for enrollment:* Autumn—30 days, Spring—30 days, Summer—30 days. *Individual tutoring:* basis for individual tutoring not given. *Average annual enrollment:* 15 students.

TESTING FACILITIES: Not given.

FACULTY: Not given. *Professional services available to faculty:* not given. *Faculty-student ratio:* not given. *Faculty qualifications:* not given.

University of Chicago
Department of Education
Speech and Language Clinic
950 E. 59th Street
Chicago, Illinois 60637
Director: Joseph M. Wepman, Ph.D.

DIAGNOSTIC FACILITIES: *Diagnostic facilities are offered for:* the aphasias, dyslexia (genetic or developmental), speech (developmental), minimal brain damage syndromes, slow learner, and psychiatric disorders. *Referral sources:* all referrals accepted. *Ages accepted:* all ages. *Waiting period for first appointment:* Autumn—2-3 weeks, Spring—2-3 weeks, Summer—2-3 weeks. *Staff and orientation:* psychological area. *Professional services available:* all services. *Average annual case load:* figures not given.

TESTING FACILITIES: Strong testing program available.

EDUCATIONAL FACILITIES: *Remedial/developmental programs offered:* the aphasias, dyslexia (genetic or developmental), speech (developmental), minimal brain damage syndromes, slow learner, emotionally disturbed (moderate and severe). *Instruction levels:* all ages. *Curriculum:* annual basis. *Waiting time for enrollment:* Autumn—2-3 weeks. *Average annual enrollment:* not given. *Program limits:* no maximum time a student may be enrolled for a remedial program. *Staff:* portion of staff members are currently enrolled in graduate school; majority of staff members have had two or more years practical experience.

SPECIAL INFORMATION: Clinic is a diagnostic and resource finding clinic with experimental therapy and occasional regular therapy.

University of Illinois—Medical Center
Center for Handicapped Children
840 S. Wood Street
Chicago, Illinois 60612
Director: Edward F. Lis, M.D.
Clinic Coordinator: Henrietta Schatland

DIAGNOSTIC FACILITIES: *Diagnostic facilities offered:* the aphasias, speech (developmental), minimal brain damage syndromes. *Referral sources:* medical referral must supplement referral from other sources; pediatrician, agencies. *Ages accepted:* 3 years to 12 years. *Waiting period for first appointment:* Autumn—3-5 months; Spring—3-5 months; Summer—3-5 months. *Staff and orientation:* a total child, multi-discipline team approach. *Professional services available:* psychology, pediatric, ophthalmology, and others. *Consultation services available*—neurology, audiometry, psychiatric, endocrinology. *Average annual case load:* 55-110—majority in the minimal brain damaged category (speech problem and minimal brain damage syndromes usually not the sole problem of the child).

TESTING FACILITIES: Strong testing program available.

EDUCATIONAL FACILITIES: *Remedial/developmental facilities:* the aphasias, speech (developmental), minimal brain damage syndromes. *Instruction levels:* 3 years to 12 years. *Curriculum:* no information given. *Waiting period for enrollment:* waiting period not given. *Average annual enrollment:* 55-110 students—majority in the minimal brain damaged category (speech not sole problem, brain damage may be one of several problems in the child).

Program limits: none given. *Staff:* no information given.

SPECIAL INFORMATION: Center handles *multiply handicapped* children—evaluate, plan and make referrals and suggestions for therapy.

INDIANA

Butler University
College of Education
Bureau of Clinical Services
Indianapolis, Indiana
Directors: Dr. R. W. Coulson, P. R. Coleman

DIAGNOSTIC FACILITIES: *Diagnostic facilities offered:* slow learner. *Referral sources:* pediatrician, school—public and private, psychiatrist, psychologist, parent. *Ages accepted:* 6 years to over 20 years. *Waiting period for first appointment:* Autumn—1-2 weeks; Spring—1-2 weeks; Summer—1-2 weeks. *Staff and orientation:* emphasis in the psychological and educational areas. *Professional services available:* psychology, educational. *Average annual case load:* not given.

TESTING FACILITIES: Testing program available.

EDUCATIONAL FACILITIES: None available.

SPECIAL INFORMATION: Clinic essentially serves children who have school-related difficulties, mostly emotional in nature. Clinic is developing facilities for the minimal brain damaged problems.

The Guidance Center of Saint Mary's College
State Theatre Building
214 South Michigan Street
South Bend, Indiana 46601
Director: Arthur E. Smith, Ph.D.

DIAGNOSTIC FACILITIES: *Diagnostic facilities offered:* minimal brain damage syndromes, slow learner. *Referral sources:* pediatrician, school—public and private, psychiatrist, psychologist, parent. *Ages accepted:* 6 years to over 20 years. *Waiting period for first appointment:* none. *Staff and orientation:* emphasis in the psychological and educational areas. *Professional services available:* psychology. *Average annual case load:* figures unavailable—new program.

TESTING FACILITIES: Testing program available.

EDUCATIONAL FACILITIES: *Remedial/developmental facilities:* slow learner. *Instruction levels:* elementary, junior and senior high, above 18-attending college, and adult rehabilitation. *Curriculum:* tutorial only; annual basis. *Average annual enrollment:* figures unavailable—new program. *Program limits:* no maximum time a student may be enrolled for a remedial program. *Staff:* majority of staff have completed pertinent graduate courses and have had 2 or more years practical experience.

Indiana State University
Department of Special Education
Speech & Hearing Clinic
Terre Haute, Indiana 47809
Director: Rutherford Porter
Clinic Director: Margaret Rowe

DIAGNOSTIC FACILITIES: *Diagnostic facilities are offered for:* the aphasias, dyslexia (genetic or developmental), speech (developmental), minimal brain damage syndromes, slow learner, psychiatric disorders. *Referral sources:* pediatrician, school—public, psychiatrist, psychologist, parent. *Ages accepted:* 6 years to over 20 years. *Waiting period for first appointment:* Autumn – 1 month, Spring – 1 month, Summer – 1 month. *Staff and orientation:* emphasis in the educational, speech, and hearing therapy areas. *Professional services available:* neurology, psychology, audiometry, pediatric, ophthalmology, optometry, psychiatric. *Average annual case load:* 15 (clinic sees cases after neurological examination).

TESTING FACILITIES: Testing program available.

EDUCATIONAL FACILITIES: *Remedial/developmental programs offered:* the aphasias, dyslexia (genetic or developmental), speech (developmental), minimal brain damage syndromes, slow learner, emotionally disturbed (moderate and severe). *Instruction levels:* all ages. *Curriculum:* private lessons; annual basis and summer session. *Waiting time for enrollment:* Autumn – 1 month, Spring – 1 month, Summer – 1 month. *Average annual enrollment:* 15-20 (individual lessons). *Program limits:* no maximum time a student may be enrolled for a remedial program. *Staff:* portion of staff members are currently enrolled in graduate school and have had less than 2 years practical experience, and a portion have had 2 or more years practical experience.

SPECIAL INFORMATION: Primarily a teacher training facility in the areas of speech, hearing therapy, mentally retarded, physically handicapped, emotionally disturbed, and psychometrics.

Indiana University Medical Center
Department of Pediatric Neurology
1100 W. Michigan
Indianapolis, Indiana
Director: Arthur L. Dren, M.D.

DIAGNOSTIC FACILITIES: *Diagnostic facilities offered:* the aphasias, dyslexia (genetic or developmental), speech (developmental), minimal brain damage syndromes, slow learner. *Referral sources:* pediatrician, school – public and private, psychiatrist, psychologist, public health nurse. *Ages accepted:* all ages. *Waiting period for first appointment:* Autumn – 2-3 weeks, Spring – 2-3 weeks, Summer – 2-3 weeks. *Staff and orientation:* a total child, multi-discipline team approach; with emphasis in the neurological, psychological, pediatric, educational, and psychiatric areas. *Professional services available:* neurology, psychology, audiometry, pediatric, ophthalmology, visual training, psychiatric, endocrinology, all medical, social services, nursing, O.T., P.T. *Average annual case load:* approximately 500.

TESTING FACILITIES: Testing program available.

EDUCATIONAL FACILITIES: None available.

Manchester College
Department of Psychology
North Manchester, Indiana
Director: Dr. Donald Colburn

DIAGNOSTIC FACILITIES: *Diagnostic facilities offered:* the aphasias, *Referral sources:* psychiatrist, psychologist, parent, physician, teacher. *Ages accepted:* 3 years to 16 years. *Waiting period for first appointment:* Autumn – 3-4 weeks. *Staff and orientation:* emphasis in the psychological, educational, psychiatric areas; limited to college students. *Professional services available:* audiometry, psychiatric, evaluation of speech disorders, evaluation of some learning problems. *Average annual case load:* not given.

TESTING FACILITIES: Strong testing program available.

EDUCATIONAL FACILITIES: *Remedial/developmental facilities:* the aphasias, speech (developmental). *Instruction levels:* pre-school, primary, elementary, junior high, and a non-credited course offered each quarter to the above 18-attending college group. *Curriculum:* tutorial only; annual basis. *Waiting period for enrollment:* Autumn – 2-4 weeks; Spring – 2-4 weeks; Summer – 2-4 weeks. *Average annual enrollment:* not given. *Program limits:* 1 quarter of college year is maximum time a student may be enrolled for remedial program. *Staff:* majority of staff have had 2 or more years practical experience.

SPECIAL INFORMATION: Program limited because of shortage of qualified staff.

IOWA

Iowa College of Education
Children's Reading Clinic
Iowa City, Iowa 52240
Director: Siegmar Muehl

DIAGNOSTIC FACILITIES: *Diagnostic facilities offered:* dyslexia (genetic or developmental), minimal brain damage syndromes, psychiatric disorders. *Referral sources:* pediatrician, school—public and private, psychiatrist, psychologist, parent. *Ages accepted:* 6 years to 16 years, very few in the 16 years to 20 years level. *Waiting period for first appointment:* 2-6 months waiting. *Staff and orientation:* emphasis in the psychological and educational areas. *Professional services available:* neurology, psychology, audiometry, pediatric, ophthalmology, psychiatric, endocrinology, all major medical services. *Average annual case load:* 35 cases with average I.Q. and reading problems.

TESTING FACILITIES: Testing program available—1 case a week during academic semester.

EDUCATIONAL FACILITIES: *Remedial/developmental facilities:* dyslexia (genetic or developmental), minimal brain damage syndromes. *Instruction levels:* primary, elementary, junior and senior high. *Curriculum:* tutorial only; annual basis. *Waiting period for enrollment:* generally 6 months. *Average annual enrollment:* 55 students. *Program limits:* no maximum time a student may be enrolled for a remedial program. *Staff:* portion of staff members are currently enrolled in graduate school; majority of staff members have completed pertinent graduate courses and have had 2 or more years practical experience.

SPECIAL REQUIREMENTS: Upon admission, child stays with program.

SPECIAL INFORMATION: Limited summer residential facilities. Major purpose of clinic is teacher training; courses offered in teaching retarded readers, diagnosis and supervision.

State College of Iowa
Educational Clinic
Speech Clinic
Cedar Falls, Iowa 50613
Educational Director: Dr. Ralph Scott,
Speech Clinical Director: Dr. Roy Eblen

DIAGNOSTIC FACILITIES: *Diagnostic facilities offered:* the aphasias, dyslexia (genetic or developmental), speech (developmental), minimal brain damage syndromes, slow learner. *Referral sources:* pediatrician, school—public and private, psychiatrist, psychologist, parent. *Ages accepted:* all ages. *Waiting period for first appointment:* waiting period varies from 2 weeks to 4 months. *Staff and orientation:* a total child, multi-discipline team approach; with emphasis in the education area. *Professional services available:* audiometry. *Average annual case load:* 250-280 cases.

TESTING FACILITIES: Testing program available.

EDUCATIONAL FACILITIES: *Remedial/developmental facilities:* the aphasias, dyslexia (genetic or developmental), speech (developmental), minimal brain damage syndromes, slow learner, emotionally disturbed (moderate). *Instruction levels:* all ages. *Curriculum:* tutorial only; annual basis. *Waiting period for enrollment:* Autumn—4-7 months. *Average annual enrollment:* 45 students—majority in the slow learner category (the children with other difficulties also tend to have emotional disturbances). *Program limits:* no maximum time a student may be enrolled for a remedial program. *Staff:* permanent college staff have completed pertinent graduate courses and have had 2 or more years practical experience; much tutorial and some diagnostic work done by college students in training. Educational and Speech Clinics are primarily to provide learning and clinical experiences for students preparing to work in speech correction and/or special education, and secondly to help referrals.

University Hospital School
Department of Pediatrics
Child Development Clinic
Iowa City, Iowa
Director: Gerald Solomons, M.D.

DIAGNOSTIC FACILITIES: *Diagnostic facilities are offered for:* the aphasias, dyslexia (genetic or developmental), speech (developmental), minimal brain damage syndromes, slow learner. *Referral sources:* pediatrician, psychiatrist, physician. *Ages accepted:* infant – 17 years. *Waiting period for first appointment:* Autumn – 3 months, Spring – 3 months, Summer – 3 months. *Staff and orientation:* a total child, multi-discipline team approach. *Professional services available:* neurology, psychology, audiometry, pediatric, ophthalmology, visual training, psychiatric, endocrinology. *Average annual case load:* average of 220; majority in minimal brain damage syndromes, slow learner; with 3-5% in dyslexia.

TESTING FACILITIES: Strong testing program.

EDUCATIONAL FACILITIES: None available, referrals made.

SPECIAL INFORMATION: Follow-ups made when possible, and return visits recommended for further evaluation, when necessary.

University of Dubuque
Department of Psychology
Student Counseling Bureau
Dubuque, Iowa
Director: D. E. Williams

DIAGNOSTIC FACILITIES: *Diagnostic facilities are offered for:* psychiatric disorders. *Referral sources:* school – public and private, psychiatrist, psychologist, parent, faculty, administration. *Ages accepted:* 12 years to over 20 years. *Waiting period for first appointment:* Autumn – 1 week, Spring – 1 week, Summer – 1 week. *Staff and orientation:* emphasis in the psychological and educational areas. *Professional services available:* psychology. *Average annual case load:* 20.

TESTING FACILITIES: Testing program available.

SPECIAL INFORMATION: Diagnostic facilities beginning 1967.

EDUCATIONAL FACILITIES: *Remedial/developmental facilities:* part of the regular curriculum of the university. *Instruction levels:* above 18-attending college (developmental reading). *Curriculum:* tutorial only; annual basis. *Waiting period for enrollment:* Autumn – 1 semester, Spring – 1 semester, Summer – 1 semester. *Average annual enrollment:* not given. *Program limits:* no maximum time a student may be enrolled for a remedial program. *Staff:* majority of staff members have had 2 or more years practical experience.

Kansas

Fort Hays Kansas State College
Division of Education and Psychology
Psychological Service Center
Hays, Kansas 67601
Director: John D. King,
Divisional Director: Dr. Calvin Hargin

DIAGNOSTIC FACILITIES: *Diagnostic facilities offered:* the aphasias, speech (developmental), minimal brain damage syndromes, slow learner, psychiatric disorders. *Referral sources:* pediatrician, school – public and private, psychiatrist, psychologist, parent. *Ages accepted:* 3 years to 16 years. *Waiting period for first appointment:* Autumn – 1 month; Spring – 1 month; Summer – 1 month. *Staff and orientation:* emphasis in the psychological, educational and psychiatric areas. *Professional services available:* psychology, audiometry, pediatric, ophthalmology, psychiatric. *Average annual case load:* 55—majority in the minimal brain damage syndromes and psychiatric disorders categories.

TESTING FACILITIES: Strong testing program available.

EDUCATIONAL FACILITIES: *Remedial/developmental facilities:* speech (developmental). *Instruction levels:* primary and elementary (summer only), above 18-attending college (annual). *Curriculum:* half day. *Waiting period for enrollment:* Autumn—brief; Spring—brief; Summer—brief. *Average annual enrollment:* 15 students. *Program limits:* no maximum time a student may be enrolled for a remedial program. *Staff:* majority of staff have completed pertinent graduate courses and have had 2 or more years practical experience.

Institute of Logopedics
2400 Jardine Drive
Wichita, Kansas 67219
Director: Charles W. Wurth

EDUCATIONAL FACILITIES: *Remedial/developmental programs for:* the aphasias, dyslexia (genetic or developmental), speech (developmental), minimal brain damage syndromes, slow learner, emotionally disturbed (moderate). *Instruction levels:* pre-school, primary, elementary, junior high. *Curriculum:* half day and full day—full curriculum; annual basis. *Waiting period for enrollment:* September—3 months. *Average annual enrollment:* 1500 students. *Individual tutoring:* presented as an adjunct to the curriculum.

TESTING FACILITIES: Strong testing evaluation program available.

FACULTY: School is oriented to inter-discipline cooperation. *Professional services available to faculty:* neurology, psychology, audiometry, pediatric, ophthalmology, visual training, psychiatric, endocrinology. *Faculty-student ratio:* 1:8 in special education; 1:1 in speech. *Faculty qualifications:* 10-15% of staff have had specialized training in remedial reading; graduate level training has been had by 10% of staff in reading. 40% of staff in speech, and 75% of staff in learning disabilities; Masters Degrees are held by 5% of staff in reading, by 30% of staff in speech, and by 50% of staff in learning disabilities.

Kansas State Teachers College
Department of Counseling Services
Emporia, Kansas
Director: Dr. D. F. Hetlinger

DIAGNOSTIC FACILITIES: *Diagnostic facilities offered:* dyslexia (genetic or developmental), minimal brain damage syndromes, slow learner. *Referral sources:* pediatrician, school—public and private, psychiatrist, psychologist, parent. *Ages accepted:* all ages. *Waiting period for first appointment;* Autumn—1-2 weeks, Spring—1-2 weeks. Summer—none. *Staff and orientation:* emphasis in the psychological and educational areas. *Professional services available:* psychology. *Average annual case load:* not given.

TESTING FACILITIES: Strong testing program available.

EDUCATIONAL FACILITIES: None available.

University of Kansas
Department of Psychology
Psychological Clinics
307 Fraser Hall
Lawrence, Kansas 66044
Director: M. Erik Wright, M.D.

DIAGNOSTIC FACILITIES: *Diagnostic facilities offered:* the aphasias, dyslexia (genetic or developmental), speech (developmental), minimal brain damage syndromes, slow learner. *Referral sources:* pediatrician, school—public and private, psychiatrist, psychologist, parent, social agencies. *Ages accepted:* all ages. *Waiting period for first appointment:* Autumn—1-3 weeks, Spring—2 weeks, Summer—3 weeks. *Staff and orientation:* a total child, multi-discipline team approach with emphasis in the psychological area. *Professional services available:* psychology, audiometry, speech pathology. *Average annual case load:* 99-124—majority in the minimal brain damaged category.

TESTING FACILITIES: Testing program available.

EDUCATIONAL FACILITIES: Remedial clinics and educational facilities available on campus.

SPECIAL INFORMATION: Plans for having, in 1968-69, a Mental Retardation Clinical Center, coordinating psychology, pediatrics, neurology, education, and speech pathology—with diagnosis and remedial facilities of significant scope.

University of Kansas Medical Center
Children's Rehabilitation Unit
Rainbow at 39th Street
Kansas City, Kansas
Director: Herbert C. Miller, M.D.

DIAGNOSTIC FACILITIES: *Diagnostic facilities offered:* the aphasias, dyslexia (genetic or developmental), speech (developmental), minimal brain damage syndromes, slow learner, and psychiatric disorders. *Referral sources:* pediatrician, school—public and private, psychiatrist, psychologist. *Ages accepted:* 3 years to 16 years. *Waiting period for first appointment:* 1-2 months. *Staff and orientation:* a total child, multi-discipline team approach; with emphasis in the neurological, psychological, pediatric, educational, and psychiatric areas. *Professional services available:* neurology, psychology, audiometry, pediatric, ophthalmology, visual training, psychiatric, endocrinology, and complete medical services. *Average annual case load:* 310-410—majority in the speech category.

TESTING FACILITIES: Strong testing program available.

EDUCATIONAL FACILITIES: *Remedial/developmental facilities:* the aphasias, dyslexia (genetic or developmental), speech (developmental), minimal brain damage syndromes, slow learner, emotionally disturbed (moderate and severe). *Instruction levels:* pre-school, primary, elementary, junior high, and adult rehabilitation. *Curriculum:* full day—full curriculum; annual basis. *Waiting period for enrollment:* varies. *Average annual enrollment:* 86-121 students—majority in the speech, slow learner, and moderately disturbed categories. *Program limits:* constant evaluation of a child's treatment status determines length of time spent in the program. *Staff:* majority of staff have completed pertinent graduate courses and have had 2 or more years practical experience.

KENTUCKY

Louisville General Hospital
Department of Pediatrics
Child Evaluation Center
323 E. Chestnut Street
Louisville, Kentucky 40202
Director: Dr. Bernard Weisskopf

DIAGNOSTIC FACILITIES: *Diagnostic facilities are offered for:* the aphasias, dyslexia (genetic or developmental), speech (developmental), minimal brain damage syndromes, slow learner. *Referral sources:* pediatrician, school—public and private, psychologist, health agency. *Ages accepted:* 3 years to 16 years. *Waiting period for first appointment:* Autumn—1 month, Spring—1 month, Summer—1 month. *Staff and orientation:* a total child, multi-discipline team approach; emphasis on neurology, psychology, pediatrics. *Professional services available:* neurology, psychology, audiometry, pediatric, ophthalmology, visual training, optometry, psychiatric, endocrinology. *Average annual case load:* 40; majority in minimal brain damage syndromes.

TESTING FACILITIES: Not given.

EDUCATIONAL FACILITIES: None available.

Morehead State University
Department of Psychology
Morehead, Kentucky
Director: L. Bradley Clough, Ph.D.

DIAGNOSTIC FACILITIES: *Diagnostic facilities offered:* the aphasias, dyslexia (genetic or developmental), speech (developmental), minimal brain damage syndromes, slow learner, psychiatric disorders. *Referral sources:* pediatrician, school—public and private, psychiatrist, psychologist, parent. *Ages accepted:* all ages. *Waiting period for first appointment:* Autumn—1-4 weeks; Spring—1-4 weeks; Summer—1-4 weeks. *Staff and orientation:* emphasis in the psychological and educational areas. *Professional services available:* psychology, audiometry, pediatric, ophthalmology, visual training, psychiatric. *Average annual case load:* 135—majority in the speech and slow learner categories.

TESTING FACILITIES: Strong testing program available.

EDUCATIONAL FACILITIES: *Remedial/developmental facilities:* the aphasias, dyslexia (genetic or developmental), speech (developmental), minimal brain damage syndromes, slow learner, emotionally disturbed (moderate and severe). *Instruction levels:* all ages. *Curriculum:* full day—full curriculum; annual basis. *Waiting period for enrollment:* Autumn—1 month; Spring—1 month; Summer—1 month. *Average annual enrollment:* 41 students—majority in the speech, minimal brain damaged syndromes, and slow learner category. *Program limits:* no maximum time a student may be enrolled for a remedial program, except the educational and remedial services are offered only through the college level. *Staff:* majority of staff have had 2 or more years practical experience.

Norton Psychiatric Clinic
Department of Psychiatry
231 West Oak Street
Louisville, Kentucky
Director: E. E. Landis, M.D.

DIAGNOSTIC FACILITIES: *Diagnostic facilities are offered for:* the aphasias, dyslexia (genetic or developmental), speech (developmental), minimal brain damage syndromes, slow learner, psychiatric. *Referral sources:* pediatrician, psychiatrist, psychologist, parent, physician. *Ages accepted:* 6 years to over 20 years. *Waiting period for first appointment:* variable. *Staff and orientation:* a total child, multi-discipline team approach, with emphasis on neurological, psychological, educational, and psychiatric areas. *Professional services available:* neurology, psychology, audiometry, pediatric, ophthalmology, optometry, psychiatric, endocrinology. *Average annual case load:* figures not kept.

TESTING FACILITIES: Testing program available.

EDUCATIONAL FACILITIES: None available.

SPECIAL INFORMATION: Clinic is a graduate division, fully university affiliated, in a private general hospital. As such, it is oriented primarily toward broad psychiatric education, diagnostic, and treatment work, generally from the age of 10 years and up. All voluntary.

LOUISIANA

Cerebral Palsy Center of Greater Baton Rouge
1805 College Drive
Baton Rouge, Louisiana 70808
Director: Paula F. Egel

EDUCATIONAL FACILITIES: *Treatment program offered for:* the aphasias, dyslexia (genetic or developmental), speech (developmental), minimal brain damage syndromes. *Instruction levels:* pre-school, primary, elementary, junior high. *Curriculum:* tutorial only; annual basis. *Waiting period for enrollment:* none given. *Average annual enrollment:* not given. *Individual tutoring:* corrective treatment.

TESTING FACILITIES: Complete except for projective testing. Strong testing program available for the minimally brain injured.

FACULTY: Staff is oriented to inter-discipline cooperation. *Professional services available to faculty:* neurology, psychology, audiometry, pediatric, ophthalmology, psychiatric, others-as needed. *Faculty-student ratio:* 1:1. *Faculty qualifications:* graduate level training has been had by 2 speech therapists; and 1 educational therapist (in learning disabilities); 1 speech therapist holds a Masters Degree.

Grambling College
Special Education Center
Grambling, Louisiana
Director: Famore J. Carter, Ph.D.

DIAGNOSTIC FACILITIES: *Diagnostic facilities are offered for:* speech (developmental), minimal brain damage syndromes, slow learner. *Referral sources:* pediatrician, school—public, psycholigist, Department of Public Welfare. *Ages accepted:* 6 years to 16 years. *Waiting period for first appointment:* Autumn—1 month, Spring—1½ months, Summer—3 months. *Staff and orientation:* a total child, multi-discipline team approach with emphasis on education. *Professional services available:* neurology, psychology, audiometry, optometry, psychiatric. *Average annual case load:* 850—majority in the slow learner and speech (developmental) categories.

TESTING FACILITIES: Strong testing program.

EDUCATIONAL FACILITIES: *Remedial/developmental programs offered:* speech (developmental), slow learner. *Instruction levels:* primary, elementary. *Curriculum:* full day-full curriculum; annual basis. *Waiting time for enrollment:* Autumn—1 month. *Average annual enrollment:* 50—majority in slow learner category. *Program limits:* no maximum time a student may be enrolled. *Staff:* majority of staff members have completed pertinent graduate courses.

The Hew School
Post Office Box 26093
4018 Downman Road
New Orleans, Louisiana
Director: Eldon B. Bonnet, A.C.S.W.

EDUCATIONAL FACILITIES: *Remedial/developmental programs offered:* minimal brain damage syndromes, slow learner, emotionally disturbed (moderate). *Instruction levels:* pre-school, primary, and elementary. *Curriculum:* full day-full curriculum; annual basis. *Waiting period for enrollment:* not given. *Average annual enrollment:* not given. *Individual tutoring:* presented as an adjunct to the curriculum.

TESTING FACILITIES: Testing program available.

FACULTY: School is oriented to inter-discipline cooperation. *Professional services available to faculty:* psychology, social service. *Faculty-student ratio:* 1:10. *Faculty qualifications:* entire staff had specialized training in remedial reading; 50% of staff have had graduate level training in learning disabilities.

SPECIAL INFORMATION: School indicates majority of enrollment is in the slow learner category.

Louisiana Polytechnic Institute
Department of Special Education
Post Office Box 1857, Tech Station
Ruston, Louisiana
Director: Ralph L. Wooldridge

DIAGNOSTIC FACILITIES: *Diagnostic facilities offered:* the aphasias, dyslexia (genetic or developmental), speech (developmental), minimal brain damage syndromes, slow learner, psychiatric disorders. *Referral sources:* pediatrician, school—public and private, psychiatrist, psychologist, parent. *Ages accepted:* 3 years to 21 years. *Waiting period for first appointment:* Autumn—6 weeks, Spring—2 months, Summer—6 weeks. *Staff and orientation;* a total child, multi-discipline team approach. *Professional services available:* neurology, psychology, audiometry, pediatric, ophthalmology, visual training, optometry, psychiatric, endocrinology, social service. *Average annual case load:* 223.

TESTING FACILITIES: Strong testing program available.

EDUCATIONAL FACILITIES: None available at this time—plans for developing an educational facility are contingent upon completion of a new facility by 1969.

Louisiana State University
Department of Education
Special Education Center
Room 45 Field House
Baton Rouge, Louisiana
Director: Merle F. Warren

DIAGNOSTIC FACILITIES: *Diagnostic facilities offered:* the aphasias, dyslexia (genetic or developmental), speech (developmental), minimal brain damage syndromes, slow learner. *Referral sources:* pediatrician, school—public and private, psychiatrist, psychologist,*Ages accepted:* 3 years to 20 years. *Waiting period for first appointment:* none given. *Staff and orientation:* emphasis in the psychological and educational areas. *Professional services available:* psychology, audiometry. *Average annual case load:* not given.

TESTING FACILITIES: Strong testing program available.

EDUCATIONAL FACILITIES: None available—referral for off-campus schooling.

Louisiana State University
Department of Speech
Speech and Hearing Clinic
Baton Rouge, Louisiana 70803
Director: Stuart I. Gilmore

DIAGNOSTIC FACILITIES: *Diagnostic facilities offered:* the aphasias, dyslexia (genetic or developmental), speech (developmental), minimal brain damage syndromes, slow learner, psychiatric disorders. *Referral sources:* pediatrician, school—public and private, psychiatrist, psychologist, parent, teachers. *Ages accepted:* all ages. *Waiting period for first appointment:* Autumn—1-8 weeks; Spring—1-8 weeks; Summer—1-5 weeks. *Staff and orientation:* a total child, multi-discipline team approach. *Professional services available:* neurology, psychology, audiometry, pediatric, language, speech. *Average annual case load:* 78-87—majority in the speech category.

TESTING FACILITIES: Strong testing program available.

EDUCATIONAL FACILITIES: *Remedial/developmental facilities:* the aphasias, speech (developmental), minimal brain damage syndromes, emotionally disturbed (moderate). *Instruction levels:* pre-school, primary, elementary, junior and senior high, adult rehabilitation. *Curriculum:* tutorial only; annual basis. *Waiting period for enrollment:* Autumn—1-18 weeks; Spring—1-18 weeks; Summer—1-6 weeks. *Average annual enrollment:* 76-83 students—majority in the speech category. *Program limits:* no maximum time a student may be enrolled for a remedial program. *Staff:* majority of staff have had 2 or more years practical experience, with graduate students used on diagnostic and therapeutic teams.

SPECIAL INFORMATION: Primarily oriented to training speech and hearing personnel, and research—case load dependent upon clinical needs.

Louisiana State University in New Orleans
Special Education Center
Lakefront
New Orleans 22, Louisiana
Director: Dr. Alfred Stern, Ph.D.

DIAGNOSTIC FACILITIES: *Diagnostic facilities are offered for:* dyslexia (genetic or developmental), speech (developmental), minimal brain damage syndromes, slow learner. *Referral sources:* public school only. *Ages accepted:* 6 years to 20 years. *Waiting period for first appointment:* 9-month waiting period for the Autumn, Spring and Summer sessions. *Staff and orientation:* a total child, multi-discipline team approach; with emphasis in the psychological and educational areas. *Professional services available:* psychology, audiometry. *Average annual case load:* 156 – majority in the slow learner category.

TESTING FACILITIES: Strong testing program available with referral.

EDUCATIONAL FACILITES: *Remedial/developmental programs offered for:* slow learner, and moderate/emotionally disturbed. *Instruction levels:* elementary and junior high. *Curriculum:* tutorial only; annual basis. *Waiting period for enrollment:* none given. *Average annual enrollment:* approximately 100 students. *Program limits:* 1 semester is the limit a student may be enrolled for a remedial program. *Staff:* no information given.

SPECIAL INFORMATION: Supervised tutorial program in connection with undergraduate and graduate courses in reading.

The Magnolia School, Inc.
100 Central Avenue
New Orleans, Louisiana
Director: Daniel F. Graham

EDUCATIONAL FACILITIES: *Remedial/developmental programs offered:* the aphasias, speech (developmental), minimal brain damage syndromes, slow learner, emotionally disturbed (moderate). *Instruction levels:* primary and elementary. *Curriculum:* half day and full day – full curriculum; annual basis. *Waiting period for enrollment:* none. *Average annual enrollment:* not given. *Individual tutoring:* presented as an adjunct to the curriculum.

TESTING FACILITIES: Not listed – referral given.

FACULTY: School is oriented to inter-discipline cooperation. *Professional services available to faculty:* neurology, psychology, audiometry, pediatric, psychiatric, endocrinology, *Faculty-student ratio:* 1:10. *Faculty qualifications:* information not given.

SPECIAL INFORMATION: Local public and trade schools used for placement of children who have reached the level of community placement prior to disenrollment. School works closely with the following services: 1) Tulane Medical School; 2) Ochsner Foundation; 3) Louisiana State Medical School.

Northeast Louisiana State College
Department of Special Education
Special Education Center
Monroe, Louisiana
Director: Dr. Levelle Haynes

DIAGNOSTIC FACILITIES: *Diagnostic facilities offered:* the aphasias, dyslexia (genetic or developmental), speech (developmental), minimal brain damage syndromes, slow learner. *Referral sources:* public school only. *Ages accepted:* 3 years to 20 years. *Waiting period for first appointment:* no waiting list kept. *Staff and orientation:* a total child, multi-discipline team approach; emphasis in the psychological and educational areas. *Professional services available:* psychology, audiometry. *Average annual case load:* not given.

TESTING FACILITIES: Strong testing program available.

SPECIAL INFORMATION: The above service is exclusively for the public school systems served.

EDUCATIONAL FACILITIES: None available—although some are in the special classes for the mentally retarded on temporary basis.

SPECIAL INFORMATION: Entire staff holds Masters Degrees—and many working toward Doctorates.

Northwestern State College
Department of Special Education
Special Education Center
Natchitoches, Louisiana
Director: M. J. Cousins, Ph.D.

DIAGNOSTIC FACILITIES: *Diagnostic facilities offered:* the aphasias, dyslexia (genetic or developmental), speech (developmental), minimal brain damage syndromes, slow learner. *Referral sources:* public school only. *Ages accepted:* 6 years to 16 years. *Waiting period for first appointment:* Autumn—1 month; Spring—1 month; Summer—1 month. *Staff and orientation:* a total child, multi-discipline team approach; emphasis in the educational area. *Professional services available:* psychology, audiometry, education, social service. *Average annual case load:* 110—majority in the slow learner category.

TESTING FACILITIES: Testing program available.

EDUCATIONAL FACILITIES: *Remedial/developmental facilities:* the aphasias, dyslexia (genetic or developmental), speech (developmental), slow learner. *Instruction levels:* primary, elementary, junior high. *Curriculum:* full day—full curriculum; annual basis. *Waiting period for enrollment:* none. *Average annual enrollment:* 48 students—majority in the slow learner category. *Program limits:* no maximum time a student may be enrolled for a remedial program. *Staff:* majority of staff have had 2 or more years practical experience.

University of Southwestern Louisiana
Department of Special Education
Special Education Center
Box 515 N.S.L.
Lafayette, Louisiana
Director: Dr. Charles J. Faulk

DIAGNOSTIC FACILITIES: *Diagnostic facilities are offered for:* speech (developmental), minimal brain damage syndromes, slow learner. *Referral sources:* pediatrician, school—public and private, psychiatrist, psychologist, parent, community agencies. *Ages accepted:* 3 years to 20 years. *Waiting period for first appointment:* Autumn—2 months, Spring—2 months, Summer—2 months. *Staff and orientation:* a total child, multi-discipline team approach. *Professional services available:* psychology, audiometry, visual training; also neurology, pediatric, ophthalmology, optometry, psychiatric, endocrinology when indicated. *Average annual case load:* evaluate approximately 1,000 students yearly.

TESTING FACILITIES: Strong testing program available.

EDUCATIONAL FACILITIES: None available, except for Summer classes for the gifted, mentally retarded and educationally retarded in reading and mathmatics. *Staff:* majority of staff members have had two or more years practical experience.

MAINE

Farmington State College
Speech and Hearing Clinic
Farmington, Maine
Director: Richard W. Holmes

DIAGNOSTIC FACILITIES: *Diagnostic facilities offered:* speech (developmental). *Referral sources:* pediatrician, school—public, psychiatrist. *Ages accepted:* 3 years to 16 years. *Waiting period for first appointment:* Autumn—45 days, Spring—45 days, Summer—30 days. *Staff and orientation:* emphasis in the educational area. *Professional services available to faculty:* audiometry. *Average annual case load:* 20.

TESTING FACILITIES: Testing program available.

EDUCATIONAL FACILITIES: None available.

SPECIAL INFORMATION: This is a Speech and Hearing Clinic with strong emphasis on the aphasias.

Winter Harbor Reading School
Winter Harbor, Maine
Director: Dr. Howard H. Flierl

EDUCATIONAL FACILITIES: *Remedial/developmental programs offered:* the aphasias, dyslexia (genetic or developmental), minimal brain damage syndromes. *Instruction levels:* junior and senior high. *Curriculum:* full day—full curriculum; boarding—summer only. *Waiting period for enrollment:* no waiting period given—enrollment from January through May only. *Average annual enrollment:* 50 students—majority in dyslexia, mostly developmental. *Individual tutoring:* included automatically in students curriculum.

TESTING FACILITIES: All students acquired through referral with completed testing. On campus curriculum diagnostic testing available.

FACULTY: School is oriented to inter-discipline cooperation. *Professional services available to faculty:* not given. *Faculty-student ratio:* 1:4. *Faculty qualifications:* 50% of staff have had specialized training in remedial reading; one-third of staff have had graduate level training in reading and learning disabilities; Masters Degrees are held by one-third of the staff in reading and by 10% of the staff in learning disabilities.

SPECIAL REQUIREMENTS: Summer boarding school (enrollment from January through May) for boys.

SPECIAL INFORMATION: School offers a reading and study skills program—staff, with graduate training in history, English, and math, is oriented to remedial and study skill approach.

MASSACHUSETTS

Boston School for the Deaf
Aphasic Department
800 North Main Street
Randolph, Massachusetts
Director: Sister M. Laurand, CSJ

EDUCATIONAL FACILITIES: *Remedial/developmental programs are offered for:* the aphasias, speech (developmental), minimal brain damage syndromes. *Instruction levels:* pre-school (diagnostic), primary, elementary. *Curriculum:* (pre-school) tutorial only; (primary and elementary) full day—full curriculum—annual basis. *Waiting period for enrollment:* September—2-year waiting period. *Average annual enrollment:* 75 students—majority in the aphasias category. *Individual tutoring:* included automatically in students curriculum.

TESTING FACILITIES: Testing program available.

FACULTY: School is oriented to inter-discipline cooperation. *Professional services available to faculty:* psychology, audiometry. *Faculty-student ratio:* 1:8. *Faculty qualifications:* 50% of staff have had specialized training in remedial reading; graduate level training of staff—50% in reading. 100% in speech and learning disabilities; entire staff holds Masters Degrees in Speech.

SPECIAL INFORMATION: Many other professional services available through off-campus referral. Individual tutoring is done by graduate students in the teacher-training program (affiliated with Boston University).

Boston University
School of Education
Educational Clinic
765 Commonwealth Avenue
Boston, Massachusetts
Directors: J. Richard Chambers, Thomas E. Culliton, Jr.

DIAGNOSTIC FACILITIES: *Diagnostic facilities are offered for:* dyslexia (genetic or developmental). *Referral sources:* school—public and private, parent. *Ages accepted:* 6 years to 20 years. *Waiting period for first appointment:* Autumn—1 month, Spring—2 months, Summer—no services (June to September). *Staff and orientation:* a total child, multi-discipline team approach; with emphasis in the educational area. *Professional services available:* audiometry, ophthalmology, visual training. *Average annual case load:* 112.

TESTING FACILITIES: Testing program available.

EDUCATIONAL FACILITIES: *Remedial/developmental programs offered:* the aphasias, dyslexia (genetic or developmental), emotionally disturbed (moderate and severe). *Instruction levels:* primary, elementary, junior high, senior high. *Curriculum:* half day; annual basis. *Waiting time for enrollment:* enrollment closed for year when the restricted figure of 30 is reached (15 elementary and 15 secondary). *Average annual enrollment:* 30. *Program limits:* no maximum time a student may be enrolled for a remedial program, but rarely will a student be enrolled for longer than 1 academic year. *Staff:* majority of staff members are currently enrolled in graduate school, and have had two or more years practical experience.

SPECIAL INFORMATION: The remedial/developmental facilities for the aphasias and dyslexia are in connection with University Hospital, and for the emotionally disturbed in connection with the Department of Special Education. Instruction for the above 18-attending college level is handled at the College Reading Center.

Boston University
Department of Special Education
Psycho-Educational Clinic
765 Commonwealth Avenue
Boston, Massachusetts 02115
Director: Albert T. Murphy

DIAGNOSTIC FACILITIES: *Diagnostic facilities offered:* the aphasias, dyslexia (genetic or developmental), speech (developmental), minimal brain damage syndromes, slow learner, psychiatric disorders. *Referral sources:* pediatrician, school—public and private, psychiatrist, psychologist, parent, service organizations. *Ages accepted:* all ages. *Waiting period for first appointment:* Autumn—3-6 months; Spring—3-6 months; Summer—3-6 months. *Staff and orientation:* a total child, multi-discipline team approach; with emphasis in the psychological and educational areas. *Professional services available:* neurology, psychology, audiometry, pediatric, ophthalmology, psychiatric, endocrinology. *Average annual case load:* 100-200—majority in the speech and slow learner categories.

TESTING FACILITIES: Strong testing program available.

SPECIAL INFORMATION: The speech and hearing teams have specialized batteries for testing. Clinic offers diagnostic classes to see child in non-testing situations.

EDUCATIONAL FACILITIES: *Remedial/developmental facilities:* the aphasias, dyslexia (genetic or developmental), speech (developmental), minimal brain damage syndromes, slow learner, emotionally disturbed (moderate and severe). *Instruction levels:* all ages. *Curriculum:* tutorial, half day class, full day—full curriculum; annual basis. *Waiting period for enrollment:* Autumn—3-6 months; Spring—3-6 months; Summer—3-6 months. *Average annual enrollment:* 100-200 students. *Program limits:* no maximum time a student may be enrolled for a remedial program. *Staff:* faculty consists of 7 full-time administrators, supervisors, consultants, and senior clinicians; as well as 7 Professors (Ph.D. level), 6 post Masters, Doctoral students, advanced graduate students, junior clinicians, and underclassmen.

Brooks School
North Andover, Massachusetts 01845
Director: Frank D. Ashburn

EDUCATIONAL FACILITIES: *Remedial/developmental programs offered:* emotionally disturbed (moderate). *Instruction levels:* junior and senior high. *Curriculum:* full day—full curriculum; annual basis. *Waiting period for enrollment:* tests are given and previous records received by February—enrollment completed by March 15, for following year. *Average annual enrollment:* 225 students. *Individual tutoring:* presented as an adjunct to the curriculum.

TESTING FACILITIES: Testing program available with referral.

FACULTY: School oriented to inter-discipline cooperation. *Professional services available to faculty:* neurology, psychology, audiometry, pediatric, ophthalmology, optometry, psychiatric, endocrinology. *Faculty-student ratio:* 1:8. *Faculty qualifications:* specialized training in remedial reading has been had by 1 in 33 of the staff; 1 staff member has had graduate level training in reading.

Brookvale School
Windsor, Massachusetts 01226
Director: David G. Lynes

EDUCATIONAL FACILITIES: *Remedial/developmental programs offered:* slow learner, emotionally disturbed (moderate). *Instruction levels:* senior high and above 18-college preparatory. *Curriculum:* full day—full curriculum; annual basis. *Waiting period for enrollment:* September—none; January—sometimes; Summer program—none. *Average annual enrollment:* not given. *Individual tutoring:* included automatically in students curriculum.

TESTING FACILITIES: Testing program available with referral.

FACULTY: School is oriented to inter-discipline cooperation. *Professional services available to faculty:* neurology, psychology, audiometry, visual training. *Faculty-student ratio:* 1:4 and 1:8. *Faculty qualifications:* entire staff has had specialized training in remedial reading; 1 member of staff has had graduate level training in learning disabilities.

SPECIAL REQUIREMENTS: Residential school for boys only.

SPECIAL INFORMATION: School specializes in high school drop-outs or potentials.

Children's Hospital Medical Center
The Adolescents Unit
300 Longwood Avenue
Boston, Massachusetts 02115
Director: J. R. Gallagher, M.D.

DIAGNOSTIC FACILITIES: *Diagnostic facilities are offered for:* the aphasias, dyslexia (genetic or developmental), minimal brain damage syndromes, and slow learner. *Referral sources:* pediatrician, school—public and private, psychiatrist, psychologist, parent, physician. *Ages accepted:* 12 years to 20 years. *Waiting period for first appointment:* Autumn—3 weeks, Spring—3 weeks, Summer—3 weeks. *Staff and orientation:* a total child, multidiscipline team approach. *Professional services available:* neurology, psychology, audiometry, pediatric, ophthalmology, psychiatric, endocrinology, all medical specialties. *Average annual case load:* varies.

TESTING FACILITIES: Strong testing program available.

EDUCATIONAL FACILITIES: None available.

Eagle Hill School
Mardwick, Massachusetts
Medical Director: Dr. James Cavanaugh,
Educational Director: Charles Drake

EDUCATIONAL FACILITIES: *Remedial/developmental programs:* dyslexia (genetic or developmental), minimal brain damage syndromes. *Instruction levels:* primary, elementary. *Curriculum:* full day—full curriculum; annual basis. *Waiting period for enrollment:* none at present. *Average annual enrollment:* 30 boys. *Individual tutoring:* included automatically in students curriculum.

TESTING FACILITIES: Testing program available—full educational, some medical; with off-campus referral.

FACULTY: School is oriented to inter-discipline cooperation. *Professional services available to faculty:* psychology, audiometry, pediatric, visual training, optometry. *Faculty-student ratio:* 1:3. *Faculty qualifications:* 50% of staff have had specialized training in remedial reading; graduate level training has been had by 20% of staff in reading, by 10% of staff in speech and learning disabilities.

SPECIAL INFORMATION: Non-graded; perceptual-motor training basic to curriculum.

Hillcrest School
20 Amory Street
Brookline, Massachusetts
Director: J.F.M. Fitzgerald

EDUCATIONAL FACILITIES: *Remedial/developmental programs:* dyslexia (genetic or developmental), emotionally disturbed (moderate). *Instruction levels:* junior and senior high. *Curriculum:* full day—full curriculum; annual basis. *Waiting period for enrollment:* enrollment taken at any time. *Average annual enrollment:* not given. *Individual tutoring:* included automatically in students curriculum.

TESTING FACILITIES: In severe cases, testing done prior to referral.

FACULTY: School is oriented to inter-discipline cooperation. *Professional services available to faculty:* neurology, psychology, audiometry, pediatric, ophthalmology, visual training, optometry, psychiatric, endocrinology. *Faculty-student ratio:* 1:4. *Faculty qualifications:* 50% of staff have had specialized training in remedial reading; 50% of staff have had graduate level training in reading; one-third of staff hold Masters Degrees in reading.

The Kingsley School
397 Marlborough Street
Boston, Massachusetts
Director: Lowell V. Kingsley

EDUCATIONAL FACILITIES: *Remedial/developmental programs offered:* dyslexia (genetic or developmental) minimal brain damage syndromes, slow learner. *Instruction levels:* primary, elementary, junior high. *Curriculum:* tutorial only; summer only. Full day—full curriculum; annual basis. *Waiting period for enrollment:* September—completed in Spring, January—none taken. Summer program—1 month. *Average annual enrollment:* 80 students. *Individual tutoring:* presented as an adjunct to the curriculum in Summer.

TESTING FACILITIES: Strong testing program is automatically included in students curriculum.

FACULTY: School is oriented to inter-discipline cooperation. *Professional services available to faculty:* neurology, psychology, audiometry, pediatric, ophthalmology, visual training, optometry, psychiatric, endocrinology, speech therapy. *Faculty-student ratio:* 1:8. *Faculty qualifications:* 50% of staff have had specialized training in remedial reading; one-third of staff have had graduate level training in reading and learning disabilities.

SPECIAL REQUIREMENTS: Each child gets intensive help in reading or other basic skill, each day, in the hands of a specially trained remedial teacher.

SPECIAL INFORMATION. Program is remedial for children of normal intelligence. School considers itself "remedial academic" rather than remedial-therapeutic.

Lee Academy
Post Office Box 250
Lee, Massachusetts
Assistant to the Head-Master: Edgar A. McCoy

EDUCATIONAL FACILITIES: *Remedial/developmental programs offered:* slow learner and emotionally disturbed (moderate). *Instruction levels:* senior high and above 18 (college preparatory). *Curriculum:* full day—full curriculum. *Waiting period for enrollment:* September—1 month, January—2 weeks (if space is available), Summer program—2 weeks. *Average annual enrollment:* 130 students. *Individual tutoring:* included automatically in students curriculum.

TESTING FACILITIES: Testing program available.

FACULTY: School is oriented to inter-discipline cooperation. *Professional services available to faculty:* psychology, psychiatric. *Faculty-student ratio:* 1:4. *Faculty qualifications:* not given.

SPECIAL INFORMATION: Academy deals with educational rather than emotional problems, and has a liberal arts faculty, sensitive to learning problems and necessary adjustment to peers.

Massachusetts General Hospital
Language Clinic
Fruit Street
Boston, Massachusetts
Director: Vincent Perlo, M.D.

EDUCATIONAL FACILITIES: *Remedial/developmental programs:* the aphasias, dyslexia (genetic or developmental), speech (developmental), minimal brain damage syndromes. *Instruction levels:* all ages. *Curriculum:* tutorial only; annual basis. *Waiting period for enrollment:* September—3-12 months; January—no enrollments taken; Summer program—3-12 months. *Average annual enrollment:* 140-165 students—majority in the dyslexia category. *Individual tutoring:* included automatically in students curriculum.

TESTING FACILITIES: Testing program available.

FACULTY: School is oriented to inter-discipline cooperation. *Professional services available to faculty:* neurology, psychology, audiometry, pediatric, ophthalmology, psychiatric, endocrinology. *Faculty-student ratio:* 1:1 to small group for speech; 1:1 in reading. *Faculty qualifications.* 100% of reading teachers have had specialized training in remedial reading; graduate level training has been had by 60% of staff in reading, and by entire staff in speech; Masters Degrees are held by 50% of staff in reading, and by 75% in speech.

SPECIAL INFORMATION: Clinic offers: a training course in reading, a practicum: and clinical practice in speech for graduate students.

New England Medical Center Hospitals
Speech, Hearing and Language Center
171-185 Harrison Avenue
Boston, Massachusetts 02111
Clinical Director: Hubert L. Gerstman, D.Ed.

DIAGNOSTIC FACILITIES: *Diagnostic facilities are offered for:* the aphasias, dyslexia-genetic or developmental (when in multi-handicapped cases), speech (developmental), minimal brain damage syndromes, slow learner, psychiatric. *Referral sources:* pediatrician, school—public and private, psychiatrist, psychologist, parent, physician, dentist. *Ages accepted:* 3 years to over 20 years. *Waiting period for first appointment:* 2-4 weeks. *Staff and orientation:* a total child, multi-discipline team approach. *Professional services available:* neurology, psychology, audiometry, pediatric, ophthalmology, visual training, psychiatric, endocrinology, dental. *Average annual case load:* 715-815; majority in the aphasias and speech categories.

TESTING FACILITIES: Testing program available.

EDUCATIONAL FACILITIES: *Remedial/developmental programs offered:* the aphasias, dyslexia-genetic or developmental (only when associated with other conditions), speech (developmental), minimal brain damage syndromes, slow learner, emotionally disturbed (moderate and severe). *Instruction levels:* pre-school, primary, elementary, junior high, senior high, and adult rehabilitation. *Curriculum:* tutorial, therapy, and counseling; annual basis. *Waiting period for enrollment:* 2-6 weeks—Autumn, 2-6 weeks—Spring, Summer—2-6 weeks. *Average annual enrollment:* 175-490 students; majority in the aphasias, speech and minimal brain damaged syndromes categories. *Program limits:* No maximum time a student may be enrolled for a remedial program. *Staff:* majority of staff members have completed pertinent graduate courses and have had two or more years practical experience.

SPECIAL REQUIREMENTS: Remediational stress is on family training and counseling. Frequent evaluation follow-ups.

Perceptual Education and Research Center (PERC)
57 Grove Street
Wellesley, Massachusetts
Director: Charles Drake

EDUCATIONAL FACILITIES: *Remedial/developmental programs:* dyslexia (genetic or developmental), minimal brain damage syndromes. *Instruction levels:* primary, elementary, junior and senior high, above 18-college preparatory. *Curriculum:* tutorial only; annual basis. *Waiting period for enrollment:* 3 months for testing; 2 weeks for tutoring. *Average annual enrollment:* testing-300; tutoring-100 students. *Individual tutoring:* included automatically in students curriculum.

TESTING FACILITIES: Strong testing program available.

FACULTY: School is oriented to inter-discipline cooperation. *Professional services available to faculty:* neurology, psychology, audiometry, pediatric, ophthalmology, visual training, optometry, psychiatric. *Faculty-student ratio:* 1:3. *Faculty qualifications:* 20% of staff have had specialized training in remedial reading; graduate level training has been had by 20% of staff in reading, by 10% of staff in speech, by 10% of staff in learning disabilities; Masters Degrees are held by 10% of staff in reading, speech, and learning disabilities.

SPECIAL INFORMATION: Center is a teacher training facility. Center refers to the Reading Research Institute for Summer programs.

The Reading Institute of Boston
116 Newbury Street
Boston, Massachusetts 02116
Director: Samuel Joslow

EDUCATIONAL FACILITIES: *Remedial/developmental programs offered:* the aphasias, dyslexia (genetic or developmental), minimal brain damage syndromes, slow learner, emotionally disturbed (moderate). *Instruction levels:* primary, elementary, junior and senior high, above 18 (college preparatory). *Curriculum:* tutorial only; annual basis. *Waiting period for enrollment:* none. *Average annual enrollment:* 1,500 students. *Individual tutoring:* included automatically in students curriculum.

TESTING FACILITIES: Testing program available with referrals when necessary.

FACULTY: School is oriented to inter-discipline cooperation. *Professional services available to faculty:* neurology, psychology, audiometry, pediatric, ophthalmology, visual training, optometry, psychiatric, hospital services (for physical and some above mentioned services). *Faculty-student ratio:* 1:8. *Faculty qualifications:* entire staff has had specialized training in remedial reading; entire staff has had graduate level training in reading; entire staff holds Masters Degrees for reading.

SPECIAL INFORMATION: Institute's thesis is: to reach the student, and then to teach him; this is predicated on psycho-educational principles.

Reading Research Institute
32 Locust Avenue
Lexington, Massachusetts
Director: Charles Drake

EDUCATIONAL FACILITIES: *Remedial/developmental programs:* dyslexia (genetic or developmental), minimal brain damage syndromes. *Instruction levels:* primary, elementary, junior and senior high, above 18-college preparatory. *Curriculum:* full day—full curriculum; summer only. *Waiting period for enrollment:* none given. *Average annual enrollment:* 130 (summer program). *Individual tutoring:* included automatically in students curriculum.

TESTING FACILITIES: All testing for the summer program done at Perceptual Education and Research Center, except for referrals from hospitals and clinics in other areas.

FACULTY: School is oriented to inter-discipline cooperation. *Professional services available to faculty:* psychology, audiometry, pediatric, visual training, optometry. *Faculty-student ratio:* 1:3. *Faculty qualifications:* entire staff has had specialized training in remedial reading; graduate level training has been had by 30% of staff in reading, by 10% of staff in speech and learning disabilities; 10% of staff holds Masters Degrees in reading.

SPECIAL INFORMATION: Facility refers to the Perceptual Education and Research Center for academic educational programs.

State College
Department of Special Education
Fitchburg, Massachusetts
Director: William J. Goldman

DIAGNOSTIC FACILITIES: *Diagnostic facilities offered:* speech (developmental), minimal brain damage syndromes, slow learner. *Referral sources:* pediatrician, school—public and private, psychiatrist, psychologist. *Ages accepted:* 3 years to 20 years. *Waiting period for first appointment:* 1-16 weeks. *Staff and orientation:* a total child, multi-discipline team approach; with emphasis in the psychological, pediatric, educational and psychiatric areas. *Professional services available:* psychology, audiometry, pediatric, ophthalmology, visual training, optometry, psychiatric. *Average annual case load:* not given.

TESTING FACILITIES: Testing program available.

EDUCATIONAL FACILITIES (UNDER CONSTRUCTION): *Remedial/developmental facilities:* the aphasias, dyslexia (genetic or developmental), speech (developmental), minimal brain damage syndromes, slow learner, emotionally disturbed (moderate and severe). *Instruction levels:* pre-school, primary, elementary, junior and senior high. *Curriculum:* full day—full curriculum; annual basis. *Waiting period for enrollment:* unknown at this time. *Average annual enrollment:* figures unavailable at this time. *Program limits:* 2 years limit for a student remedial program. *Staff:* majority of staff have had 2 or more years practical experience.

University of Massachusetts
Department of Education
Amherst, Massachusetts
Director: Arnold Zaeske

DIAGNOSTIC FACILITIES: *Diagnostic facilities offered:* dyslexia (genetic or developmental), minimal brain damage syndromes, slow learner. *Referral sources:* pediatrician, school—public and private, psychiatrist, psychologist. *Ages accepted:* 6 years to over 20 years. *Waiting period for first appointment:* Autumn—3 months; Spring—3 months; Summer—

3 months. *Staff and orientation:* emphasis in the educational area. *Professional services available:* (by referral)—audiometry, ophthalmology, visual training, optometry, psychiatric. *Average annual case load:* 70—majority in the slow learner category.

TESTING FACILITIES: Testing program available.

EDUCATIONAL FACILITIES: None available.

Worcester Youth Guidance Center
Department of Psychology
Belmont Street
Worcester, Massachusetts

DIAGNOSTIC FACILITIES: *Diagnostic facilities are offered for:* minimal brain damage syndromes, slow learner, and psychiatric disorders. *Referral sources:* pediatrician, school—public and private, psychiatrist, psychologist, parent. *Ages accepted:* 3 years to 16 years. *Waiting period for first appointment:* Autumn—3 months, Spring—3 months, Summer—3 months. *Staff and orientation:* a total child, multi-discipline team approach. *Professional services available:* neurology, psychology, audiometry, pediatric, visual training, psychiatric, endocrinology. *Average annual case load:* not given.

TESTING FACILITIES: Testing program available.

EDUCATIONAL FACILITIES: *Remedial/developmental programs offered for:* minimal brain damage syndromes, emotionally disturbed (moderate and severe). *Instruction levels:* pre-school. *Curriculum:* full day-full curriculum; annual basis. *Waiting period for enrollment:* Autumn—4 months, Spring—4 months, Summer—4 months. *Average annual enrollment:* 40 students—majority in the minimal brain damaged category. *Program limits:* no maximum time a student may be enrolled for a remedial program. *Staff:* majority of staff members have completed pertinent graduate courses and have had 2 or more years practical experience.

MARYLAND

Coppin State College
Department of Special Education
2500 W. North Avenue
Baltimore, Maryland
Director: Dr. Peter Valletutti

DIAGNOSTIC FACILITIES: (Under construction—to be completed February 1968) *Diagnostic facilities will be offered for:* the aphasias, dyslexia (genetic or developmental), speech (developmental), minimal brain damage syndromes, slow learner. *Referral sources:* pediatrician, school—public and private, psychiatrist, psychologist, parent. *Ages to be accepted:* 3 years to 20 years. *Waiting period for first appointment:* unknown. *Staff and orientation:* emphasis will be on education. *Professional services will be available:* neurology, psychology, audiometry, pediatric, ophthalmology, psychiatric. *Average annual case load:* unknown.

TESTING FACILITIES: To be determined.

EDUCATIONAL FACILITIES: (Under construction—to be completed February 1968) *Remedial/developmental programs will be offered:* the aphasias, dyslexia (genetic or developmental), speech (developmental), minimal brain damage syndromes, slow learner, and emotionally disturbed (moderate). *Instruction levels will be:* pre-school, primary, elementary, junior high, senior high. *Curriculum will be:* tutorial only; annual basis. *Waiting time for enrollment:* unknown. *Average annual enrollment:* unknown. *Program limits:* there will be no maximum time a student may be enrolled for a remedial program. *Staff:* majority of staff members will have completed pertinent graduate courses and have two or more years practical experience.

Easter Seal Treatment Center of the Montgomery County Society for Crippled Children and Adults, Inc.
1000 Twinbrook Parkway
Rockville, Maryland 20851
Director: Rear Admiral K. M. McManes

EDUCATIONAL FACILITIES: *Remedial/developmental programs:* the aphasias, dyslexia (genetic or developmental), speech (developmental), minimal brain damage syndromes, emotionally disturbed (moderate). *Instruction levels:* pre-school. *Curriculum:* half day; annual basis. *Waiting period for enrollment:* September – 6 weeks, January, – none, Summer program – none. *Average annual enrollment:* 90-100 students – majority in the minimal brain damaged category. *Individual tutoring:* included automatically in students curriculum.

TESTING FACILITIES: Testing program available.

FACULTY: School is oriented to inter-discipline cooperation. *Professional services available to faculty:* neurology, psychology, audiometry, pediatric, opthalmology, psychiatric. *Faculty-student ratio:* 1:1, 1:4, 1:10. *Faculty qualifications:* one-third of staff have had specialized training in remedial reading; graduate level training has been had by 50% of staff in speech, by 25% of staff in learning disabilities; 50% of staff hold Masters Degrees in speech.

Johns Hopkins Hospital
Division of Audiology and Speech
Hearing and Speech Center
Baltimore, Maryland 21205
Director: Dr. W. G. Hardy

DIAGNOSTIC FACILITIES: *Diagnostic facilities are offered for:* the aphasias, speech (developmental), minimal brain damage syndromes, slow learner. *Referral sources:* pediatrician, school – public and private, psychiatrist, psychologist, parent, otologist. *Ages accepted:* all ages (large patient-load in the 0-3 year range). *Waiting period for first appointment:* Autumn – 2-4 months, Spring – 2-4 months, Summer – 2-4 months. *Staff and orientation:* a total child, multi-discipline team approach. *Professional services available:* neurology, psychology, audiometry, pediatric, ophthalmology, visual training, optometry, psychiatric, endocrinology, and all services needed. *Average annual case load:* 1,050-1,450 – majority in the minimal brain damaged category.

TESTING FACILITIES: Strong testing program available – concerned primarily with hearing, language, and speech disorders or development lags.

EDUCATIONAL FACILITIES: None available.

SPECIAL INFORMATION: Facility carefully considers the medical history, the observations of referral source, and all pertinent data acquired from their own services – when evaluating a child.

Homewood School Reading Clinic
4906 Roland Avenue
Baltimore, Maryland 21210
Director: Dr. Will J. Massey

EDUCATIONAL FACILITIES: *Remedial/developmental programs offered:* the aphasias, dyslexia (genetic or developmental), speech (developmental), minimal brain damage syndromes, emotionally disturbed (moderate). *Instruction levels:* all ages. *Curriculum:* tutorial only; annual basis and summer program. *Waiting period for enrollment:* none. *Average annual enrollment:* not given. *Individual tutoring:* presented as an adjunct to the curriculum.

TESTING FACILITIES: Testing program available.

FACULTY: School oriented to inter-discipline cooperation. *Professional services available to faculty:* neurology, psychology, audiometry, pediatric, ophthalmology, visual training, optometry, psychiatric, endocrinology. *Faculty-student ratio:* 1:1. *Faculty qualifications:*

Talmudical Academy of Baltimore
Cottage and Springhill Avenues
Baltimore, Maryland
Vice-Principal: Rabbi Ephraim Shapiro

EDUCATIONAL FACILITIES: *Remedial/developmental program offered:* slow learner. *Instruction levels:* primary, elementary. *Curriculum:* tutorial only; annual basis. *Waiting time for enrollment:* none. *Average annual enrollment:* not given. *Individual tutoring:* presented as an adjunct to the curriculum.

TESTING FACILITIES: No information given.

FACULTY: Faculty orientation not indicated. *Professional services available to faculty:* psychology, pediatric. *Faculty-student ratio:* 1:16. *Faculty qualifications:* 2 staff members have had specialized training in remedial reading.

University of Maryland Hospital
Department of Pediatrics
Clinic for the Exceptional Child
Redwood and Greene Streets
Baltimore, Maryland
Director: Ruth W. Baldwin, M.D.

DIAGNOSTIC FACILITIES: *Diagnostic facilities offered:* minimal brain damage syndromes, slow learner. *Referral sources:* pediatrician, school—public and private, psychiatrist, psychologist, parent, clinics (prefer all to be screened by physician prior to being seen). *Ages accepted:* 3 years to 20 years. *Waiting period for first appointment:* 2-3 months, except emergencies. *Staff and orientation:* emphasis in the pediatric area. *Professional services available:* neurology, psychology, audiometry, pediatric, ophthalmology, visual training, psychiatric, endocrinology. *Average annual case load:* not given.

TESTING FACILITIES: Testing program as to the need indicated.

EDUCATIONAL FACILITIES: None available.

SPECIAL INFORMATION: Specialty clinics and research laboratories for polysaccharide and amino acid tests are available for clinical evaluation of patients.

University of Maryland
Department of Education
Reading Center
College Park, Maryland
Director: Dr. Robert M. Wilson

DIAGNOSTIC FACILITIES: *Diagnostic facilities offered:* dyslexia (genetic or developmental), minimal brain damage syndromes. *Referral sources:* pediatrician, school—public and private, psychiatrist, psychologist, parent. *Ages accepted;* 6 years to 16 years. *Waiting period for first appointment:* 2 months. *Staff and orientation:* emphasis in the educational area. *Professional services available:* psychology; others by referral. *Average annual case load:* 14-17—majority in the minimal brain damaged category.

TESTING FACILITIES: Strong testing program available.

EDUCATIONAL FACILITIES: *Remedial/developmental facilities:* dyslexia (genetic or developmental), minimal brain damage syndromes. *Instruction levels:* primary, elementary, junior and senior high. *Curriculum:* tutorial only; annual basis. *Waiting period for enrollment:* 2 months. *Average annual enrollment:* 14-17—majority in the minimal brain damaged category. *Program limits:* no maximum time a student may be enrolled for a remedial program. *Staff:* majority of staff have completed pertinent graduate courses and have had 2 or more years practical experience.

MICHIGAN

Calvin Psychological Institute
Psychological Department
752 Giddings, S.E.
Grand Rapids, Michigan
Director: R. J. Bijkerk

DIAGNOSTIC FACILITIES: *Diagnostic facilities offered:* the aphasias, dyslexia (genetic or developmental), minimal brain damage syndromes, slow learner, psychiatric disorders. *Referral sources:* pediatrician, school – public and private, psychiatrist, psychologist, psychiatric institutions, ministers. *Ages accepted:* all ages. *Waiting period for first appointment:* 1-2 weeks (if urgent). *Staff and orientation:* a total child, multi-discipline team approach; with emphasis in the psychological and educational areas. *Professional services available:* psychology, audiometry, visual training, optometry. *Average annual case load:* 225 – majority in the slow learner category.

TESTING FACILITIES: Strong testing program available.

EDUCATIONAL FACILITIES: *Remedial/developmental facilities:* the aphasias, dyslexia (genetic or developmental), minimal brain damage syndromes, slow learner, emotionally disturbed (moderate). *Instruction levels:* all ages. *Curriculum:* tutorial only, half day; annual basis. *Waiting period for enrollment:* 1-2 weeks (if urgent), or 3-4 weeks. *Average annual enrollment:* 225 – majority in the slow learner category. *Program limits:* no maximum time a student may be enrolled for a remedial program. *Staff:* majority of staff have had 2 or more years practical experience.

SPECIAL REQUIREMENTS: The individual testing program includes parent interview, review of school records, family and medical history, and peer group compatibility.

Central Michigan University
Department of Education
Psycho-Educational Clinic
Mt. Pleasant, Michigan 48858
Director: Dr. John Weiser

DIAGNOSTIC FACILITIES: *Diagnostic facilities are offered for:* speech (developmental), minimal brain damage syndromes, slow learner, and psychiatric disorders. *Referral sources:* school – public and private, parent, neighborhood youth corps. *Ages accepted:* all ages. *Waiting period for first appointment:* unknown – new clinic. *Staff and orientation:* emphasis in the psychological and educational areas. *Professional services available:* psychology, audiometry. *Average annual case load:* no figures available at this time.

TESTING FACILITIES: Testing program will be available.

EDUCATIONAL FACILITIES: None available at this time.

SPECIAL INFORMATION: Remedial/developmental programs planned to begin within the next 2 years.

Central Michigan University
Department of Speech and Drama
Speech & Hearing Clinic
Mt. Pleasant, Michigan
Director: Keith L. Maxwell, Ph.D.

DIAGNOSTIC FACILITIES: *Diagnostic facilities are offered for:* the aphasias, dyslexia (genetic or developmental), speech (developmental), slow learner. *Referral sources:*

neurologist, pediatrician, school—public and private, psychiatrist, psychologist, parent. *Ages accepted:* all ages. *Waiting period for first appointment:* Autumn—1-2 weeks, Spring—1 month, Summer—3 months. *Staff and orientation:* emphasis in the educational area. *Professional services available:* neurology, psychology, audiometry, pediatric, ophthalmology. *Average annual case load:* 36-63; majority in the dyslexia category.

TESTING FACILITIES: Testing program available.

EDUCATIONAL FACILITIES: *Remedial/developmental programs offered:* the aphasias, dyslexia (genetic or developmental), speech (developmental), minimal brain damage syndromes, slow learner. *Instruction levels:* all ages. *Curriculum:* tutorial only on an annual basis, and full day—full curriculum on a summer-only basis. *Waiting period for enrollment:* Autumn—1-2 months, Spring—1-3 months, Summer (six weeks program only). *Average annual enrollment:* 38-80 students; majority in the speech category. *Program limits:* no maximum time a student may be enrolled for a remedial program; Summer clinic limited to 6-week program. *Staff:* portion of staff members are currently enrolled in graduate school and have had less than 2 years practical experience; majority of supervisory staff members have completed pertinent graduate courses and have had 2 or more years practical experience.

Childrens Orthogenic School
10235 W. 7 Mile Road
Detroit, Michigan 48221
Director: Sidney W. Graber

EDUCATIONAL FACILITIES: *Remedial/developmental programs offered for:* the aphasias, dyslexia (genetic or developmental), speech (developmental), minimal brain damage syndromes, slow learner, emotionally disturbed (moderate and severe). *Instruction levels:* pre-school, primary, elementary, junior high. *Curriculum:* full day—full curriculum; annual basis. *Waiting period for enrollment:* none given. *Average annual enrollment:* 50 students. *Individual tutoring:* included automatically in students curriculum.

TESTING FACILITIES: Testing program available with referral.

FACULTY: School is oriented to inter-discipline cooperation. *Professional services available to faculty:* neurology, psychology, audiometry, pediatric, visual training, optometry, psychiatric. *Faculty-student ratio:* 1:4. *Faculty qualifications:* graduate level training has been had by 10% of staff in reading, by 10% in speech, and by 25% in learning disabilities; Masters Degrees are held by 10% of the staff in reading, and 20% in learning disabilities.

Marygrove College Speech and Hearing Clinic
8425 W. McNichols
Detroit, Michigan 48221
Director: Sister Mary Solanus, Ph.D.

EDUCATIONAL FACILITIES: *Remedial/developmental programs offered:* the aphasias, dyslexia (genetic or developmental), speech (developmental), minimal brain damage syndromes, slow learner, emotionally disturbed (moderate). *Instruction levels:* pre-school to above 18—college preparatory. *Curriculum:* tutorial only; annual basis. *Waiting period for enrollment:* 6 months waiting period for the September and January sessions. *Average annual enrollment:* not given. *Individual tutoring:* included automatically in students curriculum.

TESTING FACILITIES: Testing program available.

FACULTY: School is oriented to inter-discipline cooperation. *Professional services available to faculty:* neurology, psychology, audiometry, pediatric, ophthalmology, visual training, optometry, psychiatric, endocrinology. *Faculty-student ratio:* 1:4. *Faculty qualifications:* 50% of staff have had specialized training in remedial reading; 50% of staff have had graduate level training in reading and speech, entire staff has had graduate training in learning disabilities; 50% of staff hold Masters Degrees in reading and learning disabilities, and 10% in speech. and 40% have Doctorates in speech.

University of Michigan
Division of Reading Improvement Services
Bureau of Psychological Services
1610 Washtenaw
Ann Arbor, Michigan
Director: Donald E. P. Smith

DIAGNOSTIC FACILITIES: *Diagnostic facilities offered:* dyslexia (genetic or developmental), minimal brain damage syndromes, slow learner. *Referral sources:* school—public and private. *Ages accepted:* 6 years to over 20 years. *Waiting period for first appointment:* Autumn—2 weeks; Spring—2 weeks; Summer—2 weeks. *Staff and orientation:* a total child, multi-discipline team approach; with emphasis in the psychological and educational areas. *Professional services available:* neurology, psychology, audiometry, pediatric, ophthalmology, visual training, psychiatric, endocrinology. *Average annual case load:* 100.

TESTING FACILITIES: Testing program available.

EDUCATIONAL FACILITIES: *Remedial/developmental facilities:* dyslexia (genetic or developmental), minimal brain damage syndromes, slow learner. *Instruction levels:* primary, elementary, junior and senior high, above 18—attending college, adult rehabilitation. *Curriculum:* half day (small group, 1 hour a day or evening); annual basis. *Waiting period for enrollment:* Autumn—2 weeks; Spring—2 weeks; Summer—2 weeks. *Average annual enrollment:* 100 students. *Program limits:* no maximum time a student may be enrolled for a remedial program. *Staff:* majority of staff have had 2 or more years practical experience.

SPECIAL INFORMATION: Facility treats learning problems as learning problems with pedagogical treatment the preferred mode. All clients participate in experiments.

Wayne State University
Department of Educational Psychology
Learning Abilities Laboratory
341 Education Building
Detroit, Michigan
Director: Dr. Walter J. Ambinder

DIAGNOSTIC FACILITIES: *Diagnostic facilities are offered for:* dyslexia (genetic or developmental), minimal brain damage syndromes. *Referral sources:* pediatrician, school—public and private, psychiatrist, psychologist, parent, child guidance centers, social services. *Ages accepted:* 3 years to 20 years. *Waiting period for first appointment:* 3 weeks waiting period for Autumn, Spring, Summer sessions. *Staff and orientation:* emphasis in the psychological and educational areas; neurological pediatric consultation available as necessary. *Professional services available:* psychology, audiometry, pediatric, psychiatric. *Average annual case load:* not given.

TESTING FACILITIES: Testing program available.

EDUCATIONAL FACILITIES: *Remedial/developmental facilities:* dyslexia (genetic or developmental), minimal brain damage syndromes, emotionally disturbed (moderate). *Instruction levels:* primary, elementary, junior and senior high. *Curriculum:* tutorial only; annual basis. *Waiting period for enrollment:* 10 weeks maximum. *Average annual enrollment:* not given. *Program limits:* no maximum time a student may be enrolled for a remedial program. *Staff:* majority of staff members have completed pertinent graduate courses and have had 2 or more years practical experience.

SPECIAL INFORMATION: Primary function is teacher training. Co-ordination with child's school is carried on to the extent of quarterly written reports, interpretation of diagnostic information and on-going programs to teachers and administrators. Limited work with parent groups is also available.

Wayne State University
Department of Speech and Special Education
Speech and Hearing Center
5900 Second Avenue
Detroit, Michigan 48202
Director: George A. Kopp, Ph.D.

DIAGNOSTIC FACILITIES: *Diagnostic facilities offered:* the aphasias, dyslexia (genetic or developmental), speech (developmental), minimal brain damage syndromes, slow learner. *Referral sources:* pediatrician, school—public and private, psychiatrist, psychologist, parent, hospitals, other agencies. *Ages accepted:* all ages. *Waiting period for first appointment:* Autumn—6-8 months, Spring—6-8 months, Summer—6-8 months. *Staff and orientation:* a total child, multi-discipline team approach; with emphasis in the educational area. *Professional services available:* neurology, psychology, audiometry, pediatric. *Average annual case load:* 250—majority in the speech category.

TESTING FACILITIES: Strong testing program available.

EDUCATIONAL FACILITIES: *Remedial/developmental facilities:* the aphasias, dyslexia (genetic or developmental), speech (developmental), minimal brain damage syndromes, slow learner, emotionally disturbed (moderate and severe). *Instruction levels:* all ages. *Curriculum:* tutorial only; annual basis. *Waiting period for enrollment:* Autumn—3-4 weeks, Spring—3-4 weeks, Summer—3-4 weeks. *Average annual enrollment:* 420 students—majority in the speech category. *Program limits:* no maximum time a student may be enrolled in a remedial program. *Staff:* majority of staff members have completed pertinent graduate courses and have had 2 or more years practical experience. 4 staff members hold full Ph.D. degrees; 1 holds D.D.S. degree; 2 junior staff members hold Masters Degrees.

SPECIAL INFORMATION: Center comments on its excellent physical plant and equipment.

MINNESOTA

Gillette State Hospital for Crippled Children
Department of Schooling
1003 East Ivy Avenue
St. Paul, Minnesota 55106
Director: Phyllis Moran

DIAGNOSTIC FACILITIES: *Diagnostic facilities offered:* the aphasias, dyslexia (genetic or developmental), speech (developmental), minimal brain damage syndromes, slow learner, psychiatric disorders. *Referral sources:* pediatrician, school—public, psychiatrist, psychologist, parent. *Ages accepted:* 3 years to 20 years. *Waiting period for first appointment:* varies with type of request. *Staff and orientation:* a total child, multi-discipline team approach; with emphasis in the pediatric and orthopedic areas. *Professional services available:* neurology, psychology, audiometry, pediatric, ophthalmology, psychiatric, endocrinology. *Average annual case load:* not given.

TESTING FACILITIES: Strong testing program available.

EDUCATIONAL FACILITIES: *Remedial/developmental facilities:* speech (developmental), minimal brain damage syndromes, slow learner, emotionally disturbed (moderate). *Instruction levels:* primary, elementary, junior and senior high. *Curriculum:* tutorial only, full day—full curriculum; annual basis. *Waiting period for enrollment:* Autumn—1-2 weeks, Spring—1-2 weeks, Summer—1-2 weeks. *Average annual enrollment:* not given. *Program limits:* no maximum time a student may be enrolled for a remedial program. *Staff:* entire staff of teachers hold B.S. Degrees, several hold Masters Degrees.

Moorhead State College
Special Education
Moorhead, Minnesota
Director: Dr. Martin Tonn

DIAGNOSTIC FACILITIES: *Diagnostic facilities offered:* the aphasias, speech (developmental). *Referral sources:* pediatrician, school—public and private, psychiatrist, psychologist, parent. *Ages accepted:* all ages. *Waiting period for first appointment:* Autumn—2-3 weeks; Spring—2-3 weeks; Summer—2-3 weeks. *Staff and orientation:* emphasis in the psychological and educational areas. *Professional services available:* psychology, audiometry. *Average annual case load:* 25—majority in the speech category.

TESTING FACILITIES: No information given.

EDUCATIONAL FACILITIES: *Remedial/developmental facilities:* the aphasias, speech (developmental). *Instruction levels:* pre-school, primary, elementary, junior and senior high, adult rehabilitation. *Curriculum:* tutorial only; annual basis. *Waiting period for enrollment:* Autumn—2-3 weeks; Spring—2-3 weeks, Summer—2-3 weeks. *Average annual enrollment:* 25 students—majority in the speech category. *Program limits:* no maximum time a student may be enrolled for a remedial program. *Staff:* majority of staff have completed pertinent graduate courses and have had 2 or more years practical experience.

St. Cloud State College
Department of Special Education
St. Cloud, Minnesota
Director: Stanley Knox

DIAGNOSTIC FACILITIES: *Diagnostic facilities offered:* the aphasias, dyslexia (genetic or developmental), speech (developmental), minimal brain damage syndromes, slow learner. *Referral sources:* pediatrician, school—public and private, psychiatrist, psychologist. *Ages accepted:* 3 years to 16 years. *Waiting period for first appointment:* Autumn—2 months; Spring—2 months, Summer—2 months. *Staff and orientation:* emphasis in the psychological and educational areas. *Professional services available:* psychology, audiometry. *Average annual case load:* 75-95—majority in the slow learner category.

TESTING FACILITIES: Depends on staff.

EDUCATIONAL FACILITIES: *Remedial/developmental facilities:* the aphasias, speech (developmental), slow learner, emotionally disturbed (moderate). *Instruction levels:* pre-school, primary, elementary, junior high. *Curriculum:* tutorial only; annual basis. *Waiting period for first appointment:* none. *Average annual enrollment:* not given. *Program limits:* no maximum time a student may be enrolled for a remedial program. *Staff:* majority of staff have completed pertinent graduate courses and have had 2 or more years practical experience.

University of Minnesota
Department of Speech
Duluth, Minnesota
Director: Robert F. Pierce

DIAGNOSTIC FACILITIES: *Diagnostic facilities offered:* the aphasias, speech (developmental). *Referral sources:* pediatrician, school—public and private, psychiatrist, psychologist, parent. *Ages accepted:* 3 years to 6 years. *Waiting period for first appointment:* approximately 6 months. *Staff and orientation:* emphasis in the educational area. *Professional services available:* neurology, psychology, audiometry, pediatric, ophthalmology, visual training, optometry, psychiatric, endocrinology. *Average annual case load:* 15-20 (aphasia cases limited to 5-10 annually).

TESTING FACILITIES: Testing program available.

EDUCATIONAL FACILITIES: *Remedial/developmental facilities:* the aphasias, speech (developmental), minimal brain damage syndromes. *Instruction levels:* pre-school, primary, elementary, adult rehabilitation. *Curriculum:* tutorial only; annual basis. *Waiting period for enrollment:* none. *Average annual enrollment:* not given. *Program limits:* no maximum time a student may be enrolled for a remedial program. *Staff:* majority of staff have had 2 or more years practical experience.

Special Information: Clinic offers differential diagnostic services and pre-school training for acoustically handicapped and language disturbed children – preparing them for school placement.

MISSISSIPPI

The Mississippi State College for Women
Department of Education
Post Office Drawer 280
Columbus, Mississippi 39701
Director: Roy L. Cox

Diagnostic Facilities: *Diagnostic facilities offered:* dyslexia (genetic or developmental), speech (developmental), slow learner. *Referral sources:* School – public and private, parent. *Ages accepted:* 6 years to 20 years. *Waiting period for first appointment:* Autumn – 2 weeks; Spring – 2 weeks; Summer – 2 weeks. *Staff and orientation:* emphasis in the educational area. *Professional services available:* audiometry, visual training. *Average annual case load:* not given.

Testing Facilities: None given.

Educational Facilities: *Remedial/developmental facilities:* speech (developmental), slow learner. *Instruction levels:* primary, elementary, junior and senior high. *Curriculum:* full day – full curriculum (retarded only); annual basis. *Waiting period for enrollment:* none given. *Average annual enrollment:* not given. *Program limits:* no maximum time a student may be enrolled for a remedial program. *Staff:* majority of staff have completed pertinent graduate courses and have had 2 or more years practical experience.

Mississippi State University
Department of Special Education
Post Office Box 81
State College, Mississippi
Director: Ladean Ebersole

Diagnostic Facilities: *Diagnostic facilities are offered for:* dyslexia (genetic or developmental), slow learner. *Referral sources:* pediatrician, school – public and private, psychologist, parent. *Ages accepted:* 3 years to 20 years. *Waiting period for first appointment:* 3-4 week waiting period for Autumn, Spring, and Summer. *Staff and orientation:* a total child, multi-discipline team approach; with emphasis in the educational area. *Professional services available:* psychology. *Average annual case load:* 80 per semester.

Testing Facilities: Testing program available.

Educational Facilities: *Remedial/developmental facilities are offered for:* dyslexia (genetic or developmental), slow learner. *Instruction levels:* primary, elementary, junior and senior high. *Curriculum:* annual basis and summer program available. *Waiting period for enrollment:* 3-4 weeks waiting period for Autumn, Spring, and Summer sessions. *Average annual enrollment:* 80 students per semester, majority in the slow learner category. *Program limits:* remedial program limits are – semester – 16 weeks; Summer – 6 weeks. *Staff:* majority of staff members have completed pertinent graduate courses and have had 2 or more years practical experience.

Special Requirements: Case history on each student enrolled – by the teacher, supervising teacher, psychologist, physician.

Special Information: Reading Clinic considers diagnosis and treatment.

University of Mississippi
University Medical Center
School of Medicine
Department of Pediatrics
Child Development Clinic
Jackson, Mississippi
Director: Margaret Bailly Batson, M.D., Ph.D.

DIAGNOSTIC FACILITIES: *Diagnostic facilities are offered for:* the aphasias, dyslexia (genetic or developmental), speech (developmental), minimal brain damage syndromes, slow learner, psychiatric. *Referral sources:* pediatrician, school—public and private, psychiatrist, psychologist, parent, pediatric out-patient department, State Health and Welfare departments. *Ages accepted:* 6 years to 14 years. *Waiting period for first appointment:* not given. *Staff and orientation:* a total child, multi-discipline team approach. *Professional services available:* neurology, psychology, audiometry, pediatric, ophthalmology, visual training, optometry, psychiatric, endocrinology. *Average annual case load:* 200.

TESTING FACILITIES: Not given.

EDUCATIONAL FACILITIES: No information given.

SPECIAL INFORMATION: Guidance facility for learning disorders from minimal brain damage.

University of Mississippi
Division of Speech Correction
Speech and Hearing Clinic
University, Mississippi 38677
Director: Ralph E. Frybarger

DIAGNOSTIC FACILITIES: *Diagnostic facilities offered:* the aphasias, speech (developmental). *Referral sources:* pediatrician, school—public and private, psychiatrist, psychologist, parent. *Ages accepted:* all ages. *Waiting period for first appointment:* Autumn—none; Spring—none; Summer—3-4 months. *Staff and orientation:* emphasis in the educational area. *Professional services available:* audiometry, any service available at the medical school. *Average annual case load:* 30—majority in the speech category.

TESTING FACILITIES: Testing program available.

EDUCATIONAL FACILITIES: None available—outpatient clinic only.

SPECIAL INFORMATION: This University Clinic offers teaching and clinician training, as well as community service. Clinic work is done with College of Liberal Arts, School of Education, and School of Medicine.

University of Southern Mississippi
Department of Speech and Hearing Sciences
Special Education and Psychological Clinic
Southern Station
Hattiesburg, Mississippi
Executive Director: Dr. Erl Mehearg
Department Director: Dr. Robert Peters

DIAGNOSTIC FACILITIES: *Diagnostic facilities are offered for:* the aphasias, dyslexia (genetic or developmental), speech (developmental), minimal brain damage syndromes, slow learner. *Referral sources:* pediatrician, school—public and private, psychiatrist, psychologist, parent. *Ages accepted:* 3 years to over 20 years. *Waiting period for first appointment:* Autumn—4 weeks, Spring—4 weeks, Summer—4 weeks. *Staff and orientation:* psychological, educational, for a total child, multi-discipline team approach. *Professional services available:* psychology, audiometry, visual training, speech pathology. *Average annual case load:* 70.

Testing Facilities: Testing program available.

Educational Facilities: *Remedial/developmental programs offered for:* the aphasias, dyslexia (genetic or developmental), speech (developmental), emotionally disturbed (moderate). *Instruction levels:* pre-school, primary, elementary, adult rehabilitation. *Curriculum:* tutorial only, full day—full curriculum; annual basis. *Waiting time for enrollment:* Autumn—4 weeks, Spring—4 weeks, Summer—4 weeks. *Average annual enrollment:* 60 students. *Program limits:* no maximum time a student may be enrolled for a remedial program. *Staff:* majority of staff have had two or more years practical experience.

MISSOURI

Central Institute for Deaf
Department of Outpatient Clinics and School
818 South Euclid
St. Louis, Missouri
Director: S. Richard Silverman

Diagnostic Facilities: *Diagnostic facilities offered:* the aphasias, speech (developmental), minimal brain damage syndromes, slow learner. *Referral sources:* pediatrician, school—public and private, psychiatrist, psychologist, parent. *Ages accepted:* all ages. *Waiting period for first appointment:* waiting period for Autumn, Spring, and Summer—for adults less than 1 week—for children (to 15 years) 3-5 weeks. *Staff and orientation:* emphasis in the educational area. *Professional services available:* psychology, audiometry, educational. *Average annual case load:* not given.

Testing Facilities: Testing program available.

Educational Facilities: *Remedial/developmental facilities:* the aphasias, speech (developmental), minimal brain damage syndromes, slow learner. *Instruction levels:* pre-school, primary, elementary, and adult rehabilitation. *Curriculum:* tutorial, half day, and full day—full curriculum; annual basis. *Waiting period for enrollment:* waiting period for full time school is dependent upon type of program needed, it can range from no waiting period to a wait of 2-3 years. *Average annual enrollment:* not given. *Program limits:* no maximum time a student may be enrolled for a remedial program. *Staff:* majority of staff members have completed pertinent graduate courses and have had 2 or more years practical experience.

Fontbonne College Clinic
Department of Speech, Division of Speech Correction
6800 Wydown Boulevard
St. Louis, Missouri 63105
Director: Sister Dorothea Marie Buchanan, CSJ

Diagnostic Facilities: *Diagnostic facilities offered:* the aphasias, dyslexia (genetic or developmental), speech (developmental). *Referral sources:* pediatrician, school—private, psychologist, parent. *Ages accepted:* all ages. *Waiting period for first appointment:* Autumn—1 month; Spring—1 month; Summer—1 month. *Staff and orientation:* a total child, multi-discipline team approach; with emphasis in the pediatric and educational areas. *Professional services available:* audiometry. *Average annual case load:* 85-120.

Testing Facilities: Testing program available with referral.

Educational Facilities: *Remedial/developmental facilities:* the aphasias, dyslexia (genetic or developmental), speech (developmental), emotionally disturbed (moderate). *Instruction levels:* all ages. *Curriculum:* tutorial only, and half day (language development); annual basis. *Waiting period for enrollment:* Autumn—1 month; Spring—1 month; Summer—1 month. *Average annual enrollment:* 67-77 students—majority in the dyslexia category. *Program limits:* no maximum time a student may be enrolled for a remedial program. *Staff:* majority of staff have completed pertinent graduate courses and have had 2 or more years practical experience.

Special Information: Clinic offers a pre-school diagnostic-teaching program for children ages 3½ years to 5 years, who manifest language and speech delay with no significant history or etiology; the testing is psychological and for hearing—the child can not be accepted if there is a gross hearing deficit or mental deficiency. Clinic's program consists of language and speech stimulation, perceptual-auditory and visual training; motor coordination tasks, and behavior modifications—with a goal of conditioning the child for more formal training and to channel him into the program best suited for his needs.

Menorah Medical Center
Hearing and Speech Center
4949 Rockhill Road
Kansas City, Missouri
Director: Dr. Jack Katz

Diagnostic Facilities: *Diagnostic facilities offered:* the aphasias, speech (developmental), minimal brain damage syndromes. *Referral sources:* pediatrician, school—public and private, psychiatrist, psychologist, parent. *Ages accepted:* all ages. *Waiting period for first appointment:* Autumn, Spring, and Summer the waiting period is—1-2 days (hospital inpatient) or 1-4 weeks (outpatient). *Staff and orientation:* a total child, multi-discipline team approach; with emphasis in the educational area. *Professional services available:* neurology, psychology, audiometry, pediatric, ophthalmology, psychiatric, endocrinology. *Average annual case load:* 90-100—majority in the speech category.

Testing Facilities: Testing program available.

Edcuational Facilities: *Remedial/developmental facilities:* the aphasias, speech (developmental). *Instruction levels:* pre-school, primary, elementary, junior and senior high, and adult rehabilitation. *Curriculum:* tutorial only; annual basis. *Waiting period for enrollment:* Autumn, Spring, Summer—1-2 days (hospital inpatient) or 1-4 weeks (outpatient). *Average annual enrollment;* 70-80 students—majority in the speech category. *Program limits:* no maximum time a student may be enrolled for a remedial program. *Staff:* majority of staff have had 2 or more years practical experience.

Special Information: Facility engaged in minimal brain damaged research project.

Miriam School
524 Bismarck Avenue
Webster Groves, Missouri 63119
Director: Eleanore T. Kenney, Ph.D.

Educational Facilities: *Remedial/developmental programs:* the aphasias, dyslexia (genetic or developmental), speech (developmental), minimal brain damage syndromes, slow learner, emotionally disturbed (moderate). *Instruction levels:* pre-school, primary, elementary. *Curriculum:* half day (for pre-school age) and full day—full curriculum; annual basis. *Waiting period for enrollment:* not given. *Average annual enrollment:* not given. *Individual tutoring:* included automatically in students curriculum.

Testing Facilities: Strong testing program available after admission.

Faculty: School is oriented to inter-discipline cooperation. *Professional services available to faculty:* psychology, audiometry, psychiatric, speech. *Faculty-student ratio::* 1:7—full day students, 1:6—pre-school students. *Faculty qualifications:* 50% of staff have had specialized training in remedial reading; 10% of staff have had graduate level training in learning disabilities.

Special Information: After educational diagnosis, individual program planned for each child to work with both strengths and weaknesses—individual work carried on with particular weaknesses in sensory motor areas. Regular mothers discussion meetings with social worker—active Parents Association.

Missouri State Teachers College
Department of Special Programs
Reading Clinic
Speech and Hearing Clinic
Violette Hall
Kirksville, Missouri 63501
Director: William Hall, M.D.
Reading Department Head: Mrs. Viola Martin

DIAGNOSTIC FACILITIES: *Diagnostic facilities are offered for:* the aphasias, dyslexia (genetic or developmental), speech (developmental), minimal brain damage syndromes, slow learner. *Referral sources:* pediatrician, school—public and private, psychologist, parent. *Ages accepted:* 6 years to over 20 years (3 years to over 20 years, in speech). *Waiting period for first appointment:* Autumn—1-4 weeks, Spring—1-4 weeks, Summer—1-4 weeks. *Staff and orientation:* emphasis in the psychological, and educational areas. *Professional services available:* psychology, audiometry, visual training. *Average annual case load:* 340.

TESTING FACILITIES: Testing program available.

EDUCATIONAL FACILITIES: *Remedial/developmental programs offered for:* the aphasias, dyslexia (genetic or developmental), speech (developmental), minimal brain damage syndromes, slow learner. *Instruction levels:* pre-school, primary, elementary, junior high, senior high, above 18 years—attending college (developmental), adult rehabilitation. *Curriculum:* tutorial only, annual basis; full day—full curriculum, summer only. *Waiting time for enrollment:* Autumn—2-8 weeks; Spring—2-8 weeks; Summer—2-8 weeks. *Average annual enrollment:* 80 students. *Program limits:* student may be enrolled until sufficient progress is shown; or no progress shown. *Staff:* majority of staff members have completed pertinent graduate courses and have had 2 or more years practical experience.

Psychological Associates
8220 Delmar
St. Louis, Missouri 63124
Director: Marshall Rosenberg

EDUCATIONAL FACILITIES: *Remedial/developmental programs offered:* the aphasias, dyslexia (genetic or developmental), speech (developmental), minimal brain damage syndromes, slow learner, emotionally disturbed (moderate and severe). *Instruction levels:* pre-school, primary, elementary, junior and senior high. *Curriculum:* tutorial only; annual basis. *Waiting period for enrollment:* 1 week. *Average annual enrollment:* 227 students—majority in the minimal brain damaged, slow learner, and moderately disturbed categories. *Individual tutoring:* included automatically in students curriculum.

TESTING FACILITIES: Strong testing program available.

FACULTY: School oriented to inter-discipline cooperation. *Professional services available to faculty:* neurology, psychology, audiometry, pediatric, ophthalmology, visual training, optometry, psychiatric. *Faculty-student ratio:* 1:1. *Faculty qualifications:* 80% of the staff have had specialized training in remedial reading; graduate level training has been had by 80% of the staff in reading, and by 15% of the staff in learning disabilities.

The Rehabilitation Institute
Department of Speech
3600 Troost Avenue
Kansas City, Missouri
Director: Miss Jane Loehr

DIAGNOSTIC FACILITIES: *Diagnostic facilities are offered for:* the aphasias, dyslexia (genetic or developmental), speech (developmental). *Referral sources:* pediatrician, school—public and private, psychiatrist, psychologist, parent. *Ages accepted:* all ages. *Waiting period for first appointment:* Autumn—2 weeks, Spring—2 weeks, Summer—2 weeks. *Staff and orientation:* a total child, multi-discipline team approach. *Professional services available:* psychology, audiometry, speech pathology. *Average annual case load:* 85 – majority in the speech category.

TESTING FACILITIES: Testing program available.

EDUCATIONAL FACILITIES: *Remedial/developmental programs offered:* the aphasias, speech (developmental). *Instruction levels:* all ages. *Curriculum:* tutorial only; annual basis. *Waiting time for enrollment:* usually none. *Average annual enrollment:* 70 students – majority in the speech category. *Program limits:* no maximum time a student may be enrolled for a remedial program. *Staff:* majority of staff members have completed pertinent graduate courses and have had 2 or more years practical experience.

SPECIAL INFORMATION: Facility is a United Fund Agency, offering physical therapy, occupational therapy, speech therapy, psychological services, vocational training, and placement.

St. Louis University
Department of Speech
Speech and Hearing Clinics
15 N. Grand Boulevard
St. Louis, Missouri
Director: Barbara J. Seelye, Ph.D.

DIAGNOSTIC FACILITIES: *Diagnostic facilities offered:* the aphasias, dyslexia (genetic or developmental), speech (developmental), minimal brain damage syndromes, slow learner, psychiatric disorders (on consultation). *Referral sources:* pediatrician, school – public and private, psychiatrist, psychologist, parent. *Ages accepted:* all ages. *Waiting period for first appointment:* Autumn – 2 weeks; Spring – 8 weeks; Summer – 6 weeks. *Staff and orientation:* a total child, multi-discipline team approach; with emphasis in the educational area. *Professional services available:* neurology, psychology, audiometry, pediatric, psychiatric – all by referral. *Average annual case load;* 89 – majority in the speech category.

TESTING FACILITIES: Testing program available.

EDUCATIONAL FACILITIES: *Remedial/developmental facilities:* the aphasias, dyslexia (genetic or developmental), speech (developmental), minimal brain damage syndromes, slow learner. *Instruction levels:* pre-school. *Curriculum:* all ages on out-patient tutorial basis; annual basis. *Waiting period for enrollment:* Autumn – 2 weeks; Spring – 8 weeks; Summer – 6 weeks. *Average annual enrollment:* 100 students. *Program limits:* no maximum time a student may be enrolled for a remedial program. *Staff:* majority of staff have completed pertinent graduate courses and have had 2 or more years practical experience.

University of Missouri Medical Center
Multiple Handicap Clinic
Building TD-4
Columbia, Missouri
Director: Bob Briggs, Administration

DIAGNOSTIC FACILITIES: *Diagnostic facilities are offered:* the aphasias, dyslexia (genetic or developmental), speech (developmental), minimal brain damage syndromes, slow learner. *Referral sources:* pediatrician, school – public and private, psychiatrist, psychologist, parent, agencies. *Ages accepted:* 3 years to 21 years. *Waiting period for first appointment:* approximately 6 months. *Staff and orientation:* a total child, multi-discipline team approach, with emphasis on neurological, psychological, pediatric, and educational areas. *Professional services available:* neurology, psychology, audiometry, pediatric, ophthalmology, visual training, psychiatric, endocrinology, education, speech, physical medicine. *Average annual case load:* 170 – majority in the slow learner and minimal brain damaged categories.

TESTING FACILITIES: Strong testing program available.

EDUCATIONAL FACILITIES: None available.

University of Missouri
Speech and Hearing Clinic
Area of Speech Pathology-Audiology
Department of Speech and Dramatic Art
Parker Hall
Columbia, Missouri 65201
Director: Charlotte G. Wells, Ph.D.

DIAGNOSTIC FACILITIES: *Diagnostic facilities offered:* the aphasias, speech (developmental). *Referral sources:* pediatrician, school—public and private, psychiatrist, psychologist, parent. *Ages accepted:* all ages. *Waiting period for first appointment:* Autumn—2 weeks, Spring—2 weeks, Summer—1 week. *Staff and orientation:* emphasis in the educational area. *Professional services available:* neurology, psychology, audiometry, pediatric, psychiatric. *Average annual case load:* not given.

TESTING FACILITIES: Testing program available.

EDUCATIONAL FACILITIES: *Remedial/developmental facilities:* the aphasias, speech (developmental). *Instruction levels:* all ages. *Curriculum:* tutorial only; annual basis. *Waiting period for enrollment:* Autumn—1-2 weeks, Spring—1-2 weeks, Summer—1 week, *Average annual enrollment:* 65-75 students—majority in the speech category. *Program limits:* no maximum time a student may be enrolled for a remedial program. *Staff:* majority of staff have had 2 or more years practical experience.

University of Missouri
University Testing and Counseling Service
Department of Extra-Divisional Administration
220 Parker Hall
Columbia, Missouri 65201
Director: Dr. Paul T. King

DIAGNOSTIC FACILITIES: *Diagnostic facilities are offered for:* slow learner. *Referral sources:* pediatrician, school—public and private, psychiatrist, psychologist, vocational rehabilitation, employment service, welfare. *Ages accepted:* 16 years to over 20 years. *Waiting period for first appointment:* Autumn—1 week, Spring—1 week, Summer—1 week. *Staff and orientation:* emphasis in the psychological and educational areas. *Professional services available:* none listed. *Average annual case load:* 15.

TESTING FACILITIES: Testing program available.

EDUCATIONAL FACILITIES: None available.

MONTANA

Eastern Montana College
Center for Handicapped Children
1500 N. 30th Street
Billings, Montana
Director: Everett D. Peery, D. Ed.

EDUCATIONAL FACILITIES: *Remedial/developmental programs offered for:* speech (developmental), minimal brain damage syndromes. *Instruction levels:* pre-school through junior high. *Curriculum:* full day—full curriculum; annual basis. *Waiting period for enrollment:* September—6 months to 1 year. *Average annual enrollment:* 8-16 students and occasionally others with multiple problems. *Individual tutoring:* included automatically in students curriculum—as required.

TESTING FACILITIES: Testing program available.

FACULTY: School is oriented to inter-discipline cooperation. *Professional services available to faculty:* neurology, psychology, audiometry, pediatric, ophthalmology, psychiatric, endocrinology. *Faculty-student ratio:* 1:3. *Faculty qualifications:* 30% of staff have had specialized training in remedial reading; graduate level training has been had by 30% of staff in reading, 40% of staff in speech, and 10% of staff in learning disabilities; 40% of staff hold Masters Degrees in speech.

SPECIAL INFORMATION: Center's program includes: *diagnostic and evaluation services for:* physically, orthopedically, speech, hearing, mentally and multiply handicapped. *Special clinics for:* mental retardation evaluation, speech, hearing, and cleft palate. *Medical clinics for:* orthopedically and multiply handicapped. *Professional services available:* coordinator-director, public health nurse, psychologist, speech pathologist, audiologist, physical therapist, occupational therapist, special education teachers. Medical specialists participate on a part-time basis in all evaluation clinics and all medical specialties are available as required.

Eastern Montana College
Reading Clinic
Billings, Montana
Director: Dr. Hap Gilliland

DIAGNOSTIC FACILITIES: *Diagnostic facilities are offered for:* dyslexia (genetic or developmental), minimal brain damage syndromes, slow learner. *Referral sources:* pediatrician, school—public and private, psychiatrist, psychologist, parent. *Ages accepted:* 6 years to over 20 years. *Waiting period for first appointment:* Autumn—30 days, Spring—15 days, Summer—30 days. *Staff and orientation:* emphasis on education. *Professional services available:* psychology, audiometry, ophthalmology, and others on referral. *Average annual case load:* 105—majority in the dyslexia category.

TESTING FACILITIES: Testing program available.

EDUCATIONAL FACILITIES: *Remedial/developmental programs offered:* dyslexia (genetic or developmental), minimal brain damage syndromes, emotionally disturbed (moderate). *Instruction levels:* junior high, senior high, above 18—attending college (developmental reading), and adult rehabilitation. *Curriculum:* tutorial only; annual basis (January through August). *Waiting time for enrollment:* Autumn—3 months, Spring—30 days, Summer—30 days. *Average annual enrollment:* 120—majority in the dyslexia category. *Program limits:* no maximum time a student may be enrolled for a remedial program. *Staff:* 50% of staff members are currently enrolled in graduate school and have had less than 2 years practical experience, while 50% have completed pertinent graduate courses and have had 2 or more years practical experience.

SPECIAL REQUIREMENTS: Student enrolls for an 8-week period, and re-enrolls when justified.

NEBRASKA

Creighton Memorial Saint Joseph's Hospital
Department of Speech and Hearing
2305 South Tenth Street
Omaha, Nebraska
Director: Mrs. Martha Bryans

DIAGNOSTIC FACILITIES: *Diagnostic facilities are offered for:* the aphasias, dyslexia (genetic or developmental), speech (developmental), minimal brain damage syndromes, slow learner. *Referral source:* pediatrician, school—public and private, psychiatrist, psychologist. *Ages accepted:* all ages. *Waiting period for first appointment:* Autumn—2 to 3 weeks, Spring—2 weeks, Summer—1 week. *Staff and orientation:* emphasis in the neurological and pediatric, and psychiatric areas. *Professional services available:* no information given. *Average annual case load:* 77—majority in the aphasias (including C.V.A.'s), dyslexia, and speech categories.

TESTING FACILITIES: Testing program available.

EDUCATIONAL FACILITIES: *Remedial/developmental facilities* (speech therapy only): the aphasias, dyslexia (genetic or developmental), speech (developmental), minimal brain damage syndromes, slow learner. *Instruction levels:* pre-school, primary, adult rehabilitation. *Curriculum:* tutorial only; annual basis. *Waiting time for enrollment:* Autumn—2 to 3 weeks, Spring—2 weeks, Summer—1 week. *Average annual enrollment:* 50—majority in the aphasias, dyslexia, and speech categories. *Program limits:* no maximum time a student may be enrolled for a remedial program. *Staff:* no information given other than limited staff at this time.

Kearney State College
Department of Speech Pathology
Kearney, Nebraska 68847
Director: Emmett L. O'Leary, M.A.

DIAGNOSTIC FACILITIES: *Diagnostic facilities offered:* speech (developmental), slow learner. *Referral sources:* pediatrician, school—public and private, psychologist, parent. *Ages accepted:* 3 years to 6 years. *Waiting period for first appointment:* Autumn—1 month; Spring—2 months; Summer—3 months. *Staff and orientation:* emphasis in the psychological and educational areas. *Professional services available:* psychology, audiometry, ophthalmology. *Average annual case load:* 70—majority in the speech category.

TESTING FACILITIES: Testing program available.

EDUCATIONAL FACILITIES: *Remedial/developmental facilities:* speech (developmental), slow learner. *Instruction levels:* all ages. *Curriculum:* hourly sessions; annual basis. *Waiting period for enrollment:* Autumn—1 month; Spring—2 months; Summer—3 months. *Average annual enrollment:* 70 students—majority in the speech category. *Program limits:* no maximum time a student may be enrolled for a remedial program. *Staff:* majority of staff have had 2 or more years practical experience.

Union College
Department of Education & Psychology
3800 South 48th Street
Lincoln, Nebraska
Director: George P. Stone

DIAGNOSTIC FACILITIES: *Diagnostic facilities are offered for:* speech (developmental), minimal brain damage syndromes, slow learner. *Referral sources:* pediatrician, school—public and private, psychiatrist, psychologist, parent. *Ages accepted:* all ages. *Waiting period for first appointment:* not more than 5 days waiting period for Autumn, Spring, or Summer. *Staff and orientation:* emphasis in the psychological and educational areas. *Professional services available:* psychology, audiometry; all others on referral. *Average annual case load:* not given.

TESTING FACILITIES: Testing program available.

EDUCATIONAL FACILITIES: *Remedial/developmental facilities offered:* speech (developmental), slow learner. *Instruction levels:* pre-school, primary, elementary, junior and senior high, above 18-attending college (developmental reading). *Curriculum:* half day, and full day—full curriculum; annual basis. *Waiting period for enrollment:* not more than 5-day *limits:* no maximum time a student may be enrolled for a remedial program. *Staff:* majority of staff members have completed pertinent graduate courses and have had 2 years or more practical experience.

University of Nebraska
College of Medicine
Department of Pediatrics
Evaluation and Counseling Clinic
Omaha, Nebraska
Director: Robert B. Kugel, M.D.

DIAGNOSTIC FACILITIES: *Diagnostic facilities are offered for:* the aphasias, dyslexia (genetic or developmental), speech (developmental), minimal brain damage syndromes, slow learner, psychiatric. *Referral sources:* any source. *Ages accepted:* 3 years – 16 years. *Waiting period for first appointment:* none. *Staff and orientation:* a total child, multi-discipline team approach. *Professional services available:* neurology, psychology, audiometry, pediatric, ophthalmology, psychiatric, endocrinology. *Average annual case load:* not available.

TESTING FACILITIES: None given.

EDUCATIONAL FACILITIES: No information given on educational facilities. *Staff:* majority of staff have completed pertinent graduate courses and have had 2 or more years practical experience.

University of Nebraska
Department of Speech and Dramatic Art
Speech and Hearing Laboratory
12th and R Streets
Lincoln, Nebraska
Director: Dr. Herbert F. Schliesser

DIAGNOSTIC FACILITIES: *Diagnostic facilities offered:* the aphasias, dyslexia (genetic or developmental), speech (developmental). *Referral sources:* pediatrician, school – public and private, psychiatrist, psychologist, parent. *Ages accepted:* all ages. *Waiting period for first appointment:* Autumn – 4 weeks, Spring – 2 weeks, Summer – 2 weeks. *Staff and orientation:* a total child, multi-discipline team approach. *Professional services available:* neurology, psychology, audiometry, pediatric, psychiatric, otolaryngology. *Average annual case load:* 115-150 – majority in the speech category.

TESTING FACILITIES: Testing program available.

EDUCATIONAL FACILITIES: *Remedial/developmental facilities:* the aphasias, dyslexia (genetic or developmental), speech (developmental), minimal brain damage syndromes, slow learner, emotionally disturbed (moderate). *Instruction levels:* pre-school. *Curriculum:* annual basis. *Waiting period for enrollment:* Autumn – 4 weeks, Spring – 2 weeks, Summer – 2 weeks. *Average annual enrollment:* 98-155 students – majority in the speech category. *Program limits:* no maximum time a student may be enrolled for a remedial program. *Staff:* majority of staff have completed pertinent graduate courses and have had 2 or more years practical experience.

SPECIAL INFORMATION: All children and adults are seen for therapy for oral communication problems. Concomitant difficulties in other areas are not treated here directly, but facility is in close communication with such efforts.

NEW HAMPSHIRE

Cardigan Mountain School
on Canaan Street Lake
Canaan, New Hampshire
Headmaster: Norman Wakely

EDUCATIONAL FACILITIES: *Remedial/developmental programs offered:* dyslexia (genetic or developmental). *Instruction level:* junior high. *Curriculum:* half day (Summer), and full day – full curriculum; annual basis, and Summer program (half day). *Waiting period for enrollment:* September – enrollment usually filled by June; January – normally do not accept enrollment; Summer program – usually filled by mid-May. *Average annual enrollment:* 25 students. *Individual tutoring:* presented as an adjunct to the curriculum.

TESTING FACILITIES: Testing program available with off-campus referrals.

FACULTY: School is oriented to inter-discipline cooperation. *Professional services available to faculty:* neurology, psychology, audiometry, pediatric, ophthalmology, visual training, optometry, psychiatric, endocrinology. *Faculty-student ratio:* 1:10. *Faculty qualifications:* 16% of staff have had specialized training in remedial reading; graduate level training has been had by 10% of the staff in reading, by 10% of the staff in speech, and by 5% of the staff in learning disabilities.

SPECIAL INFORMATION: Only about 20% of students admitted to the school have language or reading disabilities. These students are tutored or have 2 or 3 in a class. All classes are small (10-14 students) and have special conference periods to assist those having difficulty.

Dartmouth Medical School
Child Psychiatry Division
Hanover, New Hampshire
Director: Raymond Sobel

DIAGNOSTIC FACILITIES: *Diagnostic facilities offered:* the aphasias, dyslexia (genetic or developmental), minimal brain damage syndromes, slow learner, psychiatric disorders. *Referral sources:* pediatrician, school—public and private, psychiatrist, psychologist, parent. *Ages accepted:* all ages. *Waiting period for first appointment:* none. *Staff and orientation:* a total child, multi-discipline team approach; with emphasis in the neurological, psychological, pediatric, educational and psychiatric areas. *Professional services available:* neurology, psychology, audiometry, pediatric, ophthalmology, optometry, psychiatric, endocrinology. *Average annual case load:* not given.

TESTING FACILITIES: Not listed.

EDUCATIONAL FACILITIES: None available.

NEW JERSEY

Center for Child and Adolescent Development
16 Grove Avenue,
Verona, New Jersey
Director: Dr. S. Lesser

EDUCATIONAL FACILITIES: *Remedial/developmental programs offered for:* dyslexia (genetic or developmental), minimal brain damage syndromes. *Instruction levels:* not given. *Curriculum:* (supplementary to school program during year, after school programs once or twice weekly) 8 weeks—full time; summer only. *Waiting period for enrollment:* not given. *Average annual enrollment:* 75 students (on supplementary basis only). *Individual tutoring:* presented as an adjunct to the curriculum.

TESTING FACILITIES: Testing program available.

FACULTY: School oriented to inter-discipline cooperation. *Professional services available to faculty:* psychology, visual training, optometry, psychiatric. *Faculty-student ratio:* 1:4. *Faculty qualifications:* 50% of staff have had graduate level training in learning disabilities; 50% of staff hold Masters Degrees in learning disabilities.

SPECIAL INFORMATION: The center is not a school, but offers training in basic learning skills; including visual and auditory perception, visual-motor coordination, conceptual.

Glassboro State College
Department of Education
Diagnostic and Consultation Center
Glassboro, New Jersey 08028
Director: Horace T. Keller

DIAGNOSTIC FACILITIES: *Diagnostic facilities offered:* speech (developmental), minimal brain damage syndromes, slow learner. *Referral sources:* pediatrician, school—public and private, psychiatrist, psychologist, parent. *Ages accepted:* 6 years to 20 years. *Waiting period for first appointment:* Autumn—2 weeks; Spring—2 weeks; Summer—no service offered. *Staff and orientation:* emphasis in the psychological and educational areas. *Professional services available:* psychology, audiometry. *Average annual case load:* 225—majority in the slow learner category.

TESTING FACILITIES: Testing program available.

EDUCATIONAL FACILITIES: *Remedial/developmental facilities:* speech (developmental), minimal brain damage syndromes, slow learner. *Instruction levels:* primary, elementary, junior and senior high, above 18-attending college. *Curriculum:* tutorial only; annual basis. *Waiting period for enrollment:* not given—programs begin in September, February, and June. *Average annual enrollment:* 60 students—20 per category. *Program limits:* no maximum time a student may be enrolled for a remedial program. *Staff:* majority of staff have completed pertinent graduate courses and have had 2 or more years practical experience.

Lord Stirling Schools Inc.
Lord Stirling Road
Basking Ridge, New Jersey
Director: John L. Aylward

EDUCATIONAL FACILITIES: *Remedial/developmental programs offered:* speech (developmental), minimal brain damage syndromes, slow learner, emotionally disturbed (moderate and severe). *Instruction levels:* pre-school, primary, elementary, junior high. *Curriculum:* full day—full curriculum; annual basis. *Waiting period for enrollment:* September—none; January—none. *Average annual enrollment:* 45 students—majority in the moderately disturbed and slow learner categories. *Individual tutoring:* included automatically in students curriculum.

TESTING FACILITIES: Testing program available with off-campus referral.

FACULTY: School is oriented to inter-discipline cooperation. *Professional services available to faculty:* psychology, psychiatric, social service, learning disabilities specialist. *Faculty-student ratio:* 1:8. *Faculty qualifications:* 50% of staff have had specialized training in remedial reading; graduate level training has been had by 10% of the staff in speech, and by 30% of the staff in learning disabilities; Masters Degrees are held by 10% of the staff for reading and by 10% of the staff for learning disabilities.

SPECIAL INFORMATION: School offers 2 (State approved) classes for the socially and emotionally maladjusted, used by the public schools in this area for their special educational problems.

Newark State College
Department of Special Education
Child Study Center: Evaluation, Psychological, Speech, Hearing, Reading, Orthodontic Clinics
Union, New Jersey 07083
Director: Edward L. LaCrosse, Ed.D.

DIAGNOSTIC FACILITIES: *Diagnostic facilities are offered for:* the aphasias, dyslexia (genetic or developmental), speech (developmental), minimal brain damage syndromes, slow and retarded learners, psychiatric, psychological. *Referral sources:* pediatrician, school—public and private, psychiatrist, psychologist, parent, VRA, welfare agencies, health agencies, hospitals, parent associations. *Ages accepted:* infant to adult. *Waiting period for first appointment:* no waiting period. *Staff and orientation:* a total child, multidiscipline team approach, with emphasis on education. *Professional services available:* neurology, psychology, audiometry, pediatric, ophthalmology, optometry, psychiatric, endocrinology, genetic. *Average annual case load:* 780.

TESTING FACILITIES: Strong testing program available.

Educational Facilities: *Remedial/developmental programs offered:* the aphasias, dyslexia (genetic or developmental), speech (developmental). *Instruction levels:* pre-school (deaf); primary, elementary, junior high, senior high (speech and remedial reading); above 18-attending college (developmental reading); and adult rehabilitation. *Curriculum:* annual basis. *Waiting time for enrollment:* not given, students are selected at the beginning of the Autumn semester, Spring semester, and the Summer session. *Average annual enrollment:* 290 students – no emotional problems. *Program Limits:* the maximum time a student may be enrolled for a remedial program is 2 semesters. *Staff:* majority of student-staff members are currently enrolled in graduate school; majority of faculty members have had 2 or more years practical experience (work by student-staff under faculty supervision).

Special Information: Faculty provides multi-disciplinary evaluations, working under a U.S. Public Health Service grant.

State College
Department of Education
Reading Clinic – Child Study Center
Union, New Jersey
Director: Dr. Sam Laurie

Diagnostic Facilities: *Diagnostic facilities offered:* the aphasias, dyslexia (genetic or developmental), speech (developmental), minimal brain damage syndromes, slow learner, psychiatric disorders. *Referral sources:* pediatrician, school – public and private, psychiatrist, psychologist, parent. *Ages accepted:* 6 years to 20 years. *Waiting period for first appointment:* Autumn – 2 months, Spring – 2 months, Summer – no program. *Staff and orientation:* a total child, multi-discipline team approach. *Professional services available:* neurology, psychology, audiometry, pediatric, ophthalmology, visual training, optometry, psychiatric. *Average annual case load:* 97.

Testing Facilities: Testing program available.

Educational Facilities: *Remedial/developmental facilities:* dyslexia (genetic or developmental), speech (developmental), minimal brain damage syndromes, slow learner, emotionally disturbed (moderate). *Instruction levels:* primary, elementary, junior high. *Curriculum:* tutorial only; annual basis. *Waiting period for enrollment:* Autumn – 2 months, Spring – 1 week, Summer – 2 weeks. *Average annual enrollment:* 160 – majority in the dyslexia and slow learner categories. *Program limits:* no maximum time a student may be enrolled for a remedial program. *Staff:* majority of staff have completed pertinent graduate courses and have had 2 or more years practical experience.

Trenton State College
Child Study and Demonstration Center
Trenton, New Jersey
Director: Dr. Robert Micali

Diagnostic Facilities: *Diagnostic facilities are offered for:* the aphasias, dyslexia (genetic or developmental), speech (developmental), minimal brain damage syndromes, slow learner, psychiatric disorders. *Referral sources:* school – public and private. *Ages accepted:* 6 years to 20 years. *Waiting period for first appointment:* none given. *Staff and orientation:* a total child, multi-discipline team approach; with emphasis in the psychological, educational and psychiatric areas. *Professional services available:* psychology, audiometry, ophthalmology, visual training, psychiatric. *Average annual case load:* 50-75.

Testing Facilities: Strong testing program available.

Educational Facilities: No information given.

Special Information: Program is primarily for pre-service and in-service training of teachers, supported under the Title III funds.

NEW MEXICO

Eastern New Mexico University
Child Study Clinic & Speech and Hearing Clinic
Portales, New Mexico 88130
Director: John R. Cochran, Ph.D.

EDUCATIONAL FACILITIES: *Remedial/developmental programs offered:* the aphasias, speech (developmental), minimal brain damage syndromes, emotionally disturbed (moderate). *Instruction levels:* all ages. *Curriculum:* tutorial only; annual basis. *Waiting time for enrollment:* September – 2 months, January – 1 month, Summer program – 1 week. *Average annual enrollment:* not given. *Individual tutoring:* included automatically in students curriculum.

TESTING FACILITIES: Strong testing program available.

FACULTY: School is oriented to inter-discipline cooperation. *Professional services available to faculty:* psychology, audiometry, pediatric, optometry, psychiatric, speech pathology and reading clinic. *Faculty-student ratio::* 1:16. *Faculty qualifications:* 50% of staff has had graduate level training in reading; entire staff has had graduate level training in speech and learning disabilities; 75% of staff hold Masters Degrees in speech.

SPECIAL INFORMATION: Re: remedial reading – referred to on-campus Reading Clinic, which deals with college and public school students.

Eastern New Mexico University
Department of Speech Pathology-Audiology-Teaching of Deaf
Speech and Hearing Clinic
Portales, New Mexico 88130
Director: John R. Cochran, Ph.D.

DIAGNOSTIC FACILITIES: *Diagnostic facilities offered:* the aphasias, dyslexia (genetic or developmental), speech (developmental), minimal brain damage syndromes, slow learner. *Referral sources:* pediatrician, school – public and private, psychiatrist, psychologist, parent. *Ages accepted:* all ages. *Waiting period for first appointment:* Autumn – 1-2 weeks; Spring – 1-2 weeks; Summer – 1-2 weeks. *Staff and orientation:* a total child, multi-discipline team approach. *Professional services available:* psychology, audiometry. *Average annual case load:* not given.

TESTING FACILITIES: Strong testing program available.

EDUCATIONAL FACILITIES: *Remedial/developmental facilities:* the aphasias, dyslexia (genetic or developmental), speech (developmental). *Instruction levels:* not given. *Curriculum:* not given. *Waiting period for enrollment:* 0-1 semester. *Average annual enrollment:* not given. *Program limits:* no maximum time a student may be enrolled for a remedial program. *Staff:* majority of staff have completed pertinent graduate courses and have had 2 or more years practical experience.

Special Education Center
722 Silver Avenue, S.E.
Albuquerque, New Mexico
Director: Mrs. Jeannette P. Reed

EDUCATIONAL FACILITIES: *Remedial/developmental programs offered:* the aphasias, dyslexia (genetic or developmental), speech (developmental), minimal brain damage syndromes, slow learner, emotionally disturbed (moderate and severe). *Instruction levels:* pre-school, primary, elementary, junior and senior high. *Curriculum:* tutorial only – for preschool children only; half day, and full day is offered according to the need of each individual child; regular school year basis, plus 6 weeks of summer school. *Waiting period for enrollment:* none. *Average annual enrollment:* not given. *Individual tutoring:* presented as an adjunct to the curriculum.

TESTING FACILITIES: Strong testing program available.

FACULTY: School is oriented to inter-discipline cooperation. *Professional services available to faculty:* neurology, psychology, audiometry, pediatric, ophthalmology, visual training, psychiatric, endocrinology. *Faculty-student ratio:* 1:3. *Faculty qualifications:* 75% of staff have had specialized training in remedial reading; entire staff has had graduate level training in reading, speech, and learning disabilities; entire staff holds Masters Degrees in reading, speech, and learning disabilities.

University of New Mexico
College of Education
Department of Education, Guidance and Counseling
Manzanita Center
Albuquerque, New Mexico
Director: George L. Keppers

DIAGNOSTIC FACILITIES: *Diagnostic facilities offered:* the aphasias, dyslexia (genetic or developmental), speech (developmental), minimal brain damage syndromes, slow learner, psychiatric disorders (limited). *Referral sources:* pediatrician, school—public and private, psychiatrist, psychologist, parent, self-referred. *Ages accepted:* all ages. *Waiting period for first appointment:* Autumn—2 months. *Staff and orientation:* emphasis in the educational area. *Professional services available:* neurology, psychology, pediatric, ophthalmology, visual training, optometry, psychiatric, endocrinology. *Average annual case load:* 66—majority in the slow learner category.

TESTING FACILITIES: Testing program available.

EDUCATIONAL FACILITIES: *Remedial/developmental facilities:* the aphasias, dyslexia (genetic or developmental), speech (developmental), minimal brain damage syndromes, slow learner, emotionally disturbed (moderate). *Instruction levels:* all ages. *Curriculum:* full day—full curriculum, on basis of 1 hour per week; annual basis. *Waiting period for enrollment:* 2 months. *Average annual enrollment:* 138—majority in the slow learner and emotionally disturbed categories. *Program limits:* no maximum time a student may be enrolled for a remedial program—except, the age limit for remedial reading is 7 years to 17 years. *Staff:* majority of staff have completed pertinent graduate courses and have had 2 or more years practical experience.

SPECIAL INFORMATION: Primary purpose of Center is training for graduate students in counseling, guidance, and special education. Counselors are students working on Masters Degrees and graduate assistants working on their Doctoral Degrees.

Western New Mexico University
Teacher Education Center
Department of Research
Silver City, New Mexico 19088
Director: Dr. David M. Dennis

DIAGNOSTIC FACILITIES: *Diagnostic facilities offered:* the aphasias, dyslexia (genetic or developmental), speech (developmental), minimal brain damage syndromes, slow learner. *Referral sources:* school—public and private, psychologist, parent, State. *Ages accepted:* 3 years to 16 years. *Waiting period for first appointment:* Autumn—2-3 weeks; Spring—2-3 weeks; Summer—no program. *Staff and orientation:* a total child, multi-discipline team approach; with emphasis in the educational area. *Professional services available:* neurology, psychology, audiometry, pediatric, ophthalmology, visual training, psychiatric, endocrinology. *Average annual case load:* 250—majority in the slow learner category (expecting 640 cases in 1968—majority same).

TESTING FACILITIES: Testing program available.

EDUCATIONAL FACILITIES: *Remedial/developmental facilities offered:* speech, slow learner. *Instruction levels:* elementary. *Curriculum:* full day—full curriculum; annual basis. *Waiting period for enrollment:* Autumn—no waiting for upper grades, 4-8 weeks for lower grades;

Spring—no waiting for upper grades, 4-8 weeks for lower grades; Summer—none. *Average annual enrollment:* 20 students. *Program limits:* 8 years is the maximum time a student may be enrolled for a remedial program. *Staff:* majority of staff have completed pertinent graduate courses and have had 2 or more years practical experience.

SPECIAL INFORMATION: Facility is primarily engaged in research.

NEW YORK

The Adams School
(lower school) 110 East 35th Street
New York City, New York 10016
(upper school) 248 East 31st Street
New York City, New York 10016
Director: Dr. I. H. Wexner

EDUCATIONAL FACILITIES: *Remedial/developmental programs offered:* speech (developmental), minimal brain damage syndromes, emotionally disturbed (moderate). *Instruction levels:* (lower school)—primary, and elementary. (upper school)—junior and senior high, above 18 (college preparatory), and vocational preparatory. *Curriculum:* full day—full curriculum; annual basis and summer program (day camp/skills program). *Waiting period for enrollment:* lower school—1 year waiting; upper school—no waiting. *Average annual enrollment:* 250 students—majority in the minimal brain damaged and moderately disturbed categories. *Individual tutoring:* included automatically in students curriculum.

TESTING FACILITIES: Testing program available.

FACULTY: Schools are oriented to inter-discipline cooperation. *Professional services available to faculty:* neurology, psychology, audiometry, pediatric, ophthalmology, visual training, optometry, psychiatric. *Faculty—student ratio:* 1:4. *Faculty qualifications:* entire staff has had specialized training in remedial reading; graduate level training has been had by 50% of the staff in reading, by 20% of the staff in speech, and by 80% of the staff in learning disabilities; Masters Degrees are held by 40% of the staff in reading, by 10% of the staff in speech, and by 20% of the staff in learning disabilities.

SPECIAL INFORMATION: School is chartered by the New York State Board of Regents, specifically for the exceptional child, who is neurologically impaired or emotionally disturbed.

Brooklyn College
Department of Education
Educational Clinic
Brooklyn, New York 11210
Director: Professor Samuel Goldberg, Ph. D.

DIAGNOSTIC FACILITIES: *Diagnostic facilities are offered:* the aphasias, dyslexia (genetic or developmental), speech (developmental), minimal brain damage syndromes, slow learner, and psychiatric disorders. *Referral sources:* pediatrician, school—public and private, psychiatrist, psychologist, parent. *Ages accepted:* 3 years to 18 years. *Waiting period for first appointment:* approximately a 3-month waiting period for Autumn, Spring, and Summer. *Staff and orientation:* a total child, multi-discipline team approach. *Professional services available:* neurology, psychology, pediatric, psychiatric, social work. *Average annual case load:* 75-100.

TESTING FACILITIES: Strong testing program available.

EDUCATIONAL FACILITIES: *Remedial/developmental facilities:* for dyslexia (genetic or developmental), slow learner, emotionally disturbed (moderate). *Instruction levels:* grades 1 through 9. *Curriculum:* tutorial only; annual basis. *Waiting period for enrollment:* no waiting period—child taken upon decision of staff after clinic evaluation. *Average annual enrollment:* 10-18 students. *Program limits:* student may be enrolled until clinic it determined they have done all it can. *Staff:* majority of staff have had 2 or more years practical experience.

SPECIAL REQUIREMENTS: Complete clinical study—then help is offered on an individual basis and parents are included in the remedial program.

SPECIAL INFORMATION: Graduate students in education and psychology do remediation under supervision of staff psychologists.

Gilbert School
341 Bridge Street
Brooklyn, New York
Director: Harold J. Gilbert

EDUCATIONAL FACILITIES: *Remedial/developmental facilities:* dyslexia (genetic or developmental), slow learner. *Instruction levels:* primary, elementary, junior and senior high, above 18-college preparatory. *Curriculum:* half day, full day—full curriculum; annual basis. *Waiting period for enrollment:* none. *Average annual enrollment:* not given. *Individual tutoring:* included automatically in students curriculum.

TESTING FACILITIES: No information given.

FACULTY: School oriented to inter-discipline cooperation. *Professional services available to faculty:* none listed. *Faculty-student ratio:* 1:10. *Faculty qualifications:* one-third of staff have had specialized training in remedial reading and graduate level training in reading.

The Gow School
South Wales, New York 14139
Head Master: Norman W. Howard

EDUCATIONAL FACILITIES: *Remedial/developmental programs offered:* for dyslexia (genetic or developmental). *Instruction levels:* junior and senior high, above 18-college preparatory. *Curriculum:* entirely boarding school type; annual basis—no summer school program. *Waiting period for enrollment:* September—none (testing throughout year for entrance following September—usually filled by April 15th for following September). *Average annual enrollment:* 110 boarding students. *Individual tutoring:* not usually, for classes are 2-6 boys.

TESTING FACILITIES: Testing program available.

FACULTY: School is oriented to inter-discipline cooperation. *Professional services available to faculty:* none listed. *Faculty-student ratio:* 1:8. *Faculty qualifications:* 4 staff members have had specialized training in remedial reading, including in-service training staff. Head master is Orton-trained.

Green Chimneys School
Putnam Lake Road
Brewster, New York 10509
Director: Samuel B. Ross, Jr.

EDUCATIONAL FACILITIES: *Remedial/developmental programs offered:* the aphasias, dyslexia (genetic or developmental), minimal brain damage syndromes, slow learner, emotionally disturbed (moderate). *Instruction levels:* pre-school, primary, elementary, junior and senior high. *Curriculum:* full day—full curriculum; annual basis. *Waiting period for enrollment:* no waiting period for the September, January, or Summer sessions. *Average annual enrollment:* not given.

TESTING FACILITIES: Testing program available.

FACULTY: School is oriented to inter-discipline cooperation. *Professional services available to faculty:* neurology, psychology, audiometry, pediatric, ophthalmology, visual training, optometry, psychiatric, endocrinology, orthopedic. *Faculty-student ratio:* 1:8. *Faculty qualifications:* 20% of staff have had specialized training in remedial reading; 20% of staff have had graduate level training in reading and learning disabilities; 1% of staff holds

Masters Degrees in reading and learning disabilities. 2 psychiatrists spend two days per week each at school—group and individual therapy is made available. Staff includes resident physician, nurse, and consultant in learning disabilities.

SPECIAL INFORMATION: September-June is regular school; July-August session is half day academics—half day camp.

Harlem Hospital Center
Department of Psychiatry, Division of Child Psychiatry
136th Street and Lenox Avenue
New York, New York 10021
Directors: Elizabeth B. Davis, M.D., Virginia N. Wiling, M.D.

DIAGNOSTIC FACILITIES: *Diagnostic facilities offered:* the aphasias, speech (developmental) dyslexia (genetic or developmental), minimal brain damage syndromes, slow learner, psychiatric disorders. *Referral sources:* pediatrician, school—public and private, psychiatrist, psychologist, parent, court. *Ages accepted:* 3 years to 16 years. *Waiting period for first appointment:* Autumn—1 week, Spring—3 weeks, Summer—2-3 weeks. *Staff and orientation:* a total child, multi-discipline team approach, with emphasis in the neurological, pediatric, and educational areas. *Professional services available:* neurology, psychology, audiometry, pediatric, ophthalmology, psychiatric, endocrinology, general hospital facilities, and department of psychiatry. *Average annual case load:* not given.

TESTING FACILITIES: Clinical evaluation plus full psychological testing programs available.

EDUCATIONAL FACILITIES: None available.

Hofstra University
The Reading Center
Hempstead, New York 11550
Director: Dr. Miriam Schleich

DIAGNOSTIC FACILITIES: *Diagnostic facilities offered:* dyslexia (genetic or developmental), minimal brain damage syndromes. slow learner, psychiatric disorders, general educational disabilities (reading). *Referral sources:* pediatrician, school—public and private, psychiatrist, psychologist, parent. *Ages accepted:* 6 years to over 20 years. *Waiting period for first appointment:* Autumn, Spring and Summer—approximately 1-6 weeks. *Staff and orientation:* emphasis in the educational area. *Professional services available:* psychology, audiometry, visual training, optometry, psychiatric. *Average annual case load:* 57—majority in the psychiatric disorders category.

TESTING FACILITIES: Testing program available.

EDUCATIONAL FACILITIES: *Remedial/developmental facilities;* dyslexia (genetic or developmental), minimal brain damage syndromes, slow learner, emotionally disturbed (moderate), general educational disability. *Instruction levels:* primary, elementary, junior and senior high, above 18-attending college, and adult rehabilitation. *Curriculum:* tutorial only; annual basis and summer program. *Waiting period for enrollment:* Autumn, Spring, Summer —1-6 weeks. *Average annual enrollment:* 57—majority in the moderately disturbed category. *Program limits:* no maximum time a student may be enrolled for a remedial program. *Staff:* majority have completed pertinent graduate courses and have had 2 or more years practical experience.

Ithaca College
Department of Speech Pathology and Audiology
Sir Alexander Ewing Speech and Hearing Clinic
Ithaca, New York
Director: T. Walter Carlin, Ph.D.

DIAGNOSTIC FACILITIES: *Diagnostic facilities offered:* the aphasias, dyslexia (genetic or developmental), speech (developmental), minimal brain damage syndromes, slow learner. *Referral sources:* pediatrician, school—public and private, psychiatrist, psychologist, parent. *Ages accepted:* all ages. *Waiting period for first appointment:* not given. *Staff and orientation:* a total child, multi-discipline team approach; with emphasis in the educational area. *Professional services available:* neurology, psychology, audiometry, pediatric, ophthalmology, visual training, otologist, orthodontist. *Average annual case load:* 71—majority in the speech category.

TESTING FACILITIES: Testing program available.

EDUCATIONAL FACILITIES: *Remedial/developmental facilities:* the aphasias, speech (developmental), minimal brain damage syndromes, emotionally disturbed (moderate). *Instruction levels:* all ages. *Curriculum:* tutorial only; annual basis. *Waiting period for enrollment:* Autumn—no waiting. *Average annual enrollment:* 55 students—majority in the speech category. *Program limits:* no maximum time a student may be enrolled for a remedial program. *Staff:* majority of staff have had 2 or more years practical experience.

The Karafin Educational Center
153 Main Street
Mt. Kisco, New York
Director: Dr. Albert I. Karafin

EDUCATIONAL FACILITIES: *Remedial/developmental programs offered:* dyslexia (genetic or developmental), minimal brain damage syndromes, slow learner, emotionally disturbed (moderate). *Instruction levels:* primary, elementary, junior high, senior high, above 18-college preparatory. *Curriculum:* tutorial, half-day, full day; annual and summer basis. *Waiting time for enrollment:* students may be enrolled at any time. *Average annual enrollment:* not given. *Individual tutoring:* included automatically in students curriculum.

TESTING FACILITIES: Testing program, with off-campus referral.

FACULTY: School oriented to inter-discipline cooperation. *Professional services available to faculty:* neurology, psychology, audiometry, pediatric, ophthalmology, visual training, optometry, psychiatric, endocrinology. *Faculty-student ratio:* 1:3. *Faculty qualifications:* 10% of faculty have had specialized training in remedial reading; 10% of faculty have had graduate level training in reading, 2% in speech, 20% in learning disabilities; 5% of faculty hold Masters Degrees in reading, 1% in speech, 10% in learning disabilities.

SPECIAL INFORMATION: Educational approach varies to meet each individual student's specific needs.

Lake Grove School
Moriches Road
Lake Grove, New York
Director: A. A. Brayson

EDUCATIONAL FACILITIES: *Remedial/developmental programs:* minimal brain damage syndromes, slow learner, emotionally disturbed (moderate). *Instruction levels:* primary, elementary, junior and senior high. *Curriculum:* full day—full curriculum; annual basis. *Waiting period for enrollment:* none. *Average annual enrollment:* 100 students. *Individual tutoring:* included automatically in students curriculum.

TESTING FACILITIES: Testing program available.

FACULTY: School oriented to inter-discipline cooperation. *Professional services available to faculty:* neurology, psychology, audiometry, pediatric, ophthalmology, visual training, optometry, psychiatric, endocrinology. *Faculty-student ratio:* 1:8. *Faculty qualifications:* specialized training in remedial reading—by 25% of staff; graduate level training in reading by 10% of staff, in learning disabilities by 30% of staff; Masters Degree held by 1 staff member in reading and learning disabilities.

The Lorge School
301 East 52nd Street
New York, New York
Director: Irving Gold

EDUCATIONAL FACILITIES: *Remedial/developmental programs:* minimal brain damage syndromes, slow learner, emotionally disturbed (moderate). *Instruction levels:* junior and senior high. *Curriculum:* full day–full curriculum; annual basis. *Waiting period for enrollment:* September–none, January–2 months. *Average annual enrollment:* 60 students–majority in the slow learner category. *Individual tutoring:* included automatically in students curriculum.

TESTING FACILITIES: Testing program available.

FACULTY: School is oriented to inter-discipline cooperation. *Professional services available to faculty:* neurology, psychology, visual training, psychiatric, social work. *Faculty-student ratio:* 1:8. *Faculty qualifications:* 1 staff member has had specialized training in remedial reading; graduate level training has been had by 1 staff member in reading, and by 2 members in learning disabilities; 1 staff member holds a Masters Degree in reading.

Maimonides Medical Center
Community Mental Health Center
Department of Child Psychiatry
4802 10th Avenue
Brooklyn, New York
Director: Norman Sher, M.D.

DIAGNOSTIC FACILITIES: *Diagnostic facilities offered:* the aphasias, dyslexia (genetic or developmental), minimal brain damage syndromes, slow learner, psychiatric disorders. *Referral sources:* pediatrician, school–public and private, psychiatrist, psychologist, parent, religious. *Ages accepted:* 3 years to 12 years. *Waiting period for first appointment;* Autumn–2-3 weeks, Spring–3-4 weeks, Summer–0-2 weeks. *Staff and orientation:* a total child, multi-discipline team approach; with emphasis in the neurological, psychological, pediatric, educational and psychiatric areas. *Professional services available:* neurology, psychology, audiometry, pediatric, ophthalmology, visual training, psychiatric, endocrinology. *Average annual case load:* 253–majority in the psychiatric category.

TESTING FACILITIES: Strong testing program available.

EDUCATIONAL FACILITIES: See Maimonides Medical Center, Department of Services and Learning.

Maimonides Medical Center
Community Mental Health Center
Department of Child Psychiatry Services and Learning
4802 10th Avenue
Brooklyn, New York 11219
Director: C. Pollack, Ph.D.

DIAGNOSTIC FACILITIES: See Maimonides Medical Center, Department of Psychiatry.

EDUCATIONAL FACILITIES: *Remedial/developmental facilities offered for:* dyslexia (genetic or developmental), minimal brain damage syndromes, emotionally disturbed (moderate). *Instruction levels:* not given. *Curriculum:* tutorial only. *Waiting period for enrollment:* no waiting. *Average annual enrollment:* 65 students–majority in the dyslexia category–all in the emotionally disturbed category. *Program limits:* no maximum time a student may be enrolled for a remedial program. *Staff:* majority of staff have completed pertinent graduate courses and have had 2 or more years practical experience.

SPECIAL INFORMATION: Majority of tutorial work re: reading is done by volunteer parent-tutors trained by staff psychologist. Parent-tutors work with children on 1:1 basis in the schools of Community Mental Health Catchment area.

Maimonides School
34-01 Mott Avenue
Far Rockaway, New York
Director: H. M. Stiskin

EDUCATIONAL FACILITIES: *Remedial/developmental programs offered:* the aphasias, speech (developmental), minimal brain damage syndromes, slow learner, emotionally disturbed (moderate). *Instruction levels:* pre-school, primary, and elementary. *Curriculum:* full day—full curriculum; annual basis. *Waiting period for enrollment:* September—5 months, January—5 months, Summer program—none. *Average annual enrollment:* 75 students—majority in the minimal brain damaged category. *Individual tutoring:* included automatically in students curriculum.

TESTING FACILITIES: Strong testing program available.

FACULTY: School is oriented to inter-discipline cooperation. *Professional services available to faculty:* neurology, psychology, audiometry, pediatric, ophthalmology, visual training, optometry, psychiatric. *Faculty-student ratio:* 1:3. *Faculty qualifications:* 10% of staff have had specialized training in remedial reading; graduate level training has been had by 20% of the staff in reading and speech, and 40% in learning disabilities; 20% of staff hold Masters Degrees in learning disabilities.

Methodist Hospital of Brooklyn
Department of Speech and Hearing
506 Sixth Street
Brooklyn, New York
Therapist: George Ford

DIAGNOSTIC FACILITIES: *Diagnostic facilities offered:* the aphasias, speech (developmental). *Referral sources:* pediatrician, school—public and private, psychiatrist, psychologist. *Ages accepted:* all ages. *Waiting period for first appointment:* none. *Staff and orientation:* a total child, multi-discipline team approach. *Professional services available:* audiometry, pediatric, otolaryngology, rehabilitation. *Average annual case load:* figures not available—new program.

TESTING FACILITIES: Testing program available.

EDUCATIONAL FACILITIES: *Remedial/developmental facilities:* the aphasias, speech (developmental). *Instruction levels:* adult rehabilitation. *Curriculum:* not given. *Waiting period for enrollment:* not given. *Average annual enrollment:* figures not available—new program. *Program limits:* no maximum time a student may be enrolled for a remedial program. *Staff:* majority of staff have completed pertinent graduate courses and have had 2 or more years practical experience.

SPECIAL INFORMATION: Program is in process of being implemented. At present time one speech therapist is available. Department will be expanded as the need is indicated.

New York Medical College
Center for Mental Retardation
1249 5th Avenue
New York City, New York 10029
Director: Margaret Joan Giannini, M.D.

DIAGNOSTIC FACILITIES: *Diagnostic facilities offered for:* the aphasias, dyslexia (genetic or developmental), speech (developmental), minimal brain damage syndromes, slow learner, psychiatric disorders. *Referral sources:* pediatrician, school—public and private, psychiatrist, psychologist, parent, all social services, religious, legal. *Ages accepted:* 3 years to 20 years. *Staff and orientation:* a total child, multi-discipline team approach; with emphasis in the neurological, psychological, pediatric, educational, psychiatric areas. *Professional services available:* neurology, psychology, audiometry, pediatric, ophthalmology, visual training, optometry, psychiatric, endocrinology, all medical and para-medical. *Average annual case load:* 750-950—majority in the minimal brain damaged category. *Waiting period for first appointment:* Autumn—1-3 months, Spring—2-4 months, Summer—1 month.

TESTING FACILITIES: Testing program available.

EDUCATIONAL FACILITIES: *Remedial/developmental facilities:* speech (developmental), minimal brain damage syndromes, slow learner, emotionally disturbed (moderate). *Instruction levels:* pre-school and primary. *Curriculum:* type not given; annual basis. *Waiting period for enrollment:* Autumn – 1-3 months, Spring – 2-4 months, Summer – 1 month. *Average annual enrollment:* 300 students – majority in the speech and minimal brain damaged categories. *Program limits:* no maximum time a student may be enrolled for a remedial program. *Staff:* Staff has had 2 or more years practical experience.

SPECIAL INFORMATION: Only complete multi-disciplined evaluation given with primary focus on mental retardation.

New York University
Bellevue Medical Center
Department of Neurology and Psychiatry
Language Research Unit
550 First Avenue
New York City, New York
Director: S. B. Wortis, Chairman

DIAGNOSTIC FACILITIES: *Diagnostic facilities offered:* the aphasias, dyslexia (genetic or developmental), speech (developmental), minimal brain damage syndromes, slow learner, psychiatric disorders. *Referral sources:* pediatrician, school – public and private, psychiatrist, psychologist, parent. *Ages accepted:* 3 years to 12 years. *Waiting period for first appointment:* unknown. *Staff and orientation:* a total child, multi-discipline team approach. *Professional services available:* neurology, psychology, audiometry, pediatric, ophthalmology, visual training, optometry, psychiatric, endocrinology. *Average annual case load:* not given.

TESTING FACILITIES: Testing program available.

EDUCATIONAL FACILITIES: *Remedial/developmental facilities:* the aphasias, dyslexia (genetic or developmental), speech (developmental), minimal brain damage syndromes, slow learner, emotionally disturbed (moderate and severe). *Instruction levels:* pre-school, primary, elementary, junior and senior high. *Curriculum:* tutorial only. *Waiting period for enrollment:* unknown. *Average annual enrollment:* not given. *Program limits;* no maximum time a student may be enrolled for a remedial program. *Staff:* majority of staff have had 2 or more years practical experience.

SPECIAL INFORMATION: This unit is part of the Department of Psychiatry of a large medical center. Complete diagnostic facilities are available. Treatment is given to selected cases for research purposes.

New York University
Bellevue Medical Center
Department of Psychiatry
Language Research Unit
550 First Avenue
New York City, New York 10016
Director: Archie A. Silver, M.D.

DIAGNOSTIC FACILITIES: *Diagnostic facilities offered:* the aphasias, dyslexia (genetic or developmental), speech (developmental), minimal brain damage syndromes, slow learner, psychiatric disorders. *Referral sources:* pediatrician, school – public and private, psychiatrist, psychologist, parent. *Ages accepted:* 3 years to 12 years. *Waiting period for first appointment:* none given. *Staff and orientation:* a total child, multi-discipline team approach. *Professional services available:* neurology, psychology, audiometry, pediatric, ophthalmology, psychiatric, endocrinology, educational. *Average annual case load:* not given.

TESTING FACILITIES: Not given.

EDUCATIONAL FACILITIES: No information given.

New York University Medical Center
Institute of Rehabilitation Medicine
Department of Speech Pathology Services; Pediatric Division
400 East 34th Street
New York City, New York 10016
Director: Martha Taylor Sarno

DIAGNOSTIC FACILITIES: *Diagnostic facilities offered:* the aphasias (including acquired), dyslexia (genetic or developmental), speech (developmental), minimal brain damage syndromes. *Referral sources:* medical accepted only. *Ages accepted:* 3 years to 20 years. *Waiting period for first appointment:* usually not more than 2 weeks. *Staff and orientation:* a total child, multi-discipline team approach; with emphasis in the neurological, psychological, pediatric, educational, psychiatric areas. *Professional services available:* neurology, psychology, audiometry, pediatric, ophthalmology, visual training, optometry, psychiatric, endocrinology, all other medical and para-medical specialties. *Average annual case load:* 265—majority in the speech category.

TESTING FACILITIES: Strong testing program available.

EDUCATIONAL FACILITIES: None available.

SPECIAL INFORMATION: Children with language and speech disorders treated on in-patient basis (average length of residence is 2 months) or out-patient basis—bi-weekly (treatment approximately 80 children per year).

Psychological Consultation Center
Department of Psychology
525 W. 120th Street
New York, New York
Director: Sheldon R. Roen, Ph.D.

DIAGNOSTIC FACILITIES: *Diagnostic facilities are offered for:* minimal brain damage syndromes, slow learner and psychiatric disorders. *Referral sources:* pediatrician, school—public and private, psychiatrist, psychologist, parent. *Ages accepted:* all ages. *Waiting period for first appointment:* Autumn—2 weeks, Spring—2 weeks, no Summer service. *Staff and orientation:* psychological and educational. *Professional services available:* psychology, audiometry, psychiatric. *Average annual case load:* Not given.

TESTING FACILITIES: Not given.

EDUCATIONAL FACILITIES: *Remedial/developmental programs offered for:* slow learner and emotionally disturbed (moderate). *Instruction levels:* not given. *Curriculum:* not given. *Waiting period for enrollment:* not given. *Average annual enrollment:* not given. *Program limits:* no maximum time a student may be enrolled for a remedial program. *Staff:* portion of the staff are currently enrolled in graduate school; portion of the staff have completed pertinent graduate courses.

Queens College
Department of Education
Educational Clinic
Kissetta Boulevard
Flushing, New York 11367
Diagnostic Director: A. Angrilli
Educational Director: J. Roberts

DIAGNOSTIC FACILITIES: *Diagnostic facilities offered:* minimal brain damage syndromes, slow learner, psychiatric disorders. *Referral sources:* school—public and private. *Ages accepted:* 3 years to 20 years. *Waiting period for first appointment:* Autumn—1 month; Spring—1 month; Summer—2 months. *Staff and orientation:* a total child, multi-discipline team approach. *Professional services available:* neurology, psychology, audiometry, pediatric, psychiatric. *Average annual case load:* 60.

TESTING FACILITIES: Testing program available.

EDUCATIONAL FACILITIES: *Remedial/developmental facilities:* slow learner. *Instruction level:* elementary. *Curriculum:* tutorial only; annual basis. *Waiting period for enrollment:* Autumn – 1 semester; Spring – 1 semester; Summer – 1 semester. *Average annual enrollment:* 25 students. *Program limits:* no maximum time a student may be enrolled for a remedial program. *Staff:* majority of staff are currently enrolled in graduate school and have had less than 2 years practical experience.

Rochester Institute of Technology
Counseling Center
Post Office Box 3405
Rochester, New York 14614
Director: Laurence Lipsett, Ed.D.

DIAGNOSTIC FACILITIES: *Diagnostic facilities offered:* dyslexia (genetic or developmental), minimal brain damage syndromes, slow learner. *Referral sources:* pediatrician, school – public and private, psychiatrist, psychologist, parent. *Ages accepted:* all ages. *Waiting period for first appointment:* Autumn – 10 days; Spring – 10 days; Summer – 10 days. *Staff and orientation:* emphasis in the psychological and educational areas. *Professional services available:* psychology. *Average annual case load:* 36-50 – majority in the slow learner category.

TESTING FACILITIES: Testing program available.

SPECIAL INFORMATION: Community facilities available for referral.

EDUCATIONAL FACILITIES: Referred to the Reading and Study Clinic of Rochester Institute of Technology.

Rochester Institute of Technology
Reading and Study Clinic
Post Office Box 3405
Rochester, New York 14614
Director: A. B. Herr

DIAGNOSTIC FACILITIES: Referred to the Counseling Center of Rochester Institute of Technology.

EDUCATIONAL FACILITIES: *Remedial/developmental facilities:* dyslexia (genetic or developmental), speech (developmental), minimal brain damage syndromes, slow learner, emotionally disturbed (moderate). *Instruction levels:* primary (limited), elementary, junior and senior high, above 18 – attending college, adult rehabilitation. *Curriculum:* tutorial, half day (30-90 hours duration, with possibility of re-enrollment); annual basis, and Summer program (6 weeks). *Waiting period for enrollment:* waiting for tutorial program is approximately 2 weeks. Waiting for instruction program depends on date of application and completion of preliminary testing. *Average annual enrollment:* varies. *Individual tutoring:* included automatically in students curriculum. *Program limits:* no maximum time a student may be enrolled for a remedial program. *Faculty:* clinic is oriented to inter-discipline cooperation. *Professional services available to faculty:* psychology, pediatric, ophthalmology, optometry, psychiatric, endocrinology. *Faculty-student ratio:* varies with level and severity – 1:3, 1:4, 1:8, 1:10. *Faculty qualifications:* 75% of the staff have had specialized training in remedial reading; 75% of the staff have had graduate level training and hold Masters Degrees (or equivalent) in reading; majority of staff have had 5 or more years practical experience.

SPECIAL INFORMATION: Small group instruction offered three times a year. Major focus is on corrective, developmental, and remedial reading. Facility offers all improvement in review courses – non credit – with on-campus testing required for most courses.

St. Agnes Hospital
Children's Rehabilitation Center
North Street
White Plains, New York
Medical Director: Angeles Badell Ribera

DIAGNOSTIC FACILITIES: *Diagnostic facilities offered:* the aphasias, dyslexia (genetic or developmental), speech (developmental), minimal brain damage syndromes, slow learner. *Referral sources:* pediatrician, school—public and private, psychiatrist, psychologist, physiatric. *Ages accepted:* 3 years to 16 years. *Approximate waiting period for first appointment:* Autumn—1 month, Spring—1 month, Summer—1 month. *Staff and orientation:* a total child, multi-discipline team approach. *Professional services available:* neurology, psychology, audiometry, pediatric, ophthalmology, physiatric. *Average annual case load:* 50-60.

TESTING FACILITIES: Testing program available.

EDUCATIONAL FACILITIES: *Remedial/developmental facilities:* speech (developmental). *Instruction levels:* pre-school, primary, elementary, junior high. *Curriculum:* tutorial only, half day, and full day—full curriculum; annual basis. *Approximate waiting period for enrollment:* Autumn—1 month, Spring—1 month, Summer—1 month. *Average annual enrollment:* 50-60 students. *Program limits:* student may be enrolled for a remedial program until the age of 14 years. *Staff:* majority of staff have completed pertinent graduate courses and have had 2 or more years practical experience.

St. Vincent's Hospital and Medical Center of New York
Department of Rehabilitation Medicine
153 West 11th Street
New York, New York
Director: Samuel Sverdlik, M.D.

DIAGNOSTIC FACILITIES: *Diagnostic facilities offered for:* the aphasias, speech (developmental), minimal brain damage syndromes. *Referral sources:* pediatrician, school—public and private, psychiatrist, psychologist, parent, Catholic Charities. *Ages accepted:* all ages. *Waiting period for first appointment:* Autumn—2-3 months, Spring—3-4 weeks, Summer—2-4 weeks. *Staff and orientation:* a total child, multi-discipline team approach. *Professional services available:* neurology, psychology, audiometry, pediatric, ophthalmology, psychiatric, endocrinology. *Average annual case load:* not given.

TESTING FACILITIES: Testing program available.

EDUCATIONAL FACILITIES: *Remedial/developmental facilities offered:* the aphasias, speech (developmental), minimal brain damage syndromes. *Instruction levels:* all ages—from preschool through adult rehabilitation. *Curriculum:* tutorial only; annual basis. *Waiting period for enrollment:* 1-2 week waiting period for Autumn, Spring and Summer. *Average annual enrollment:* not given. *Program limits:* no maximum time a student may be enrolled for a remedial program. *Staff:* majority of staff members have completed pertinent graduate courses and have had 2 or more years practical experience.

SPECIAL INFORMATION: All staff members have or are completing professional experience requirements needed for the Certificate of Clinical Competency issued by the American Speech and Health Association.

State University College
Department of Education
Reading Center
Fredonia, New York
Director: John E. Connelly

DIAGNOSTIC FACILITIES: *Diagnostic Facilities offered:* the aphasias, dyslexia (genetic or developmental), minimal brain damage syndromes, slow learner. *Referral sources:* pediatrician, school—public and private, psychologist, parent. *Ages accepted:* 6 years to over 20 years. *Waiting period for first appointment:* Autumn—3 to 4 weeks, Spring—4 to 6 weeks, Summer—2 weeks. *Staff and orientation:* a total child, multi-discipline team approach; with emphasis on education. *Professional services available:* psychology, audiometry, visual training. *Average annual case load:* 100-150.

TESTING FACILITIES: Strong testing program available.

EDUCATIONAL FACILITIES: *Remedial/developmental programs offered:* the aphasias, dyslexia (genetic or developmental), speech (developmental). *Instruction levels:* primary, elementary, junior high, senior high, above 18—attending college (developmental reading). *Curriculum:* tutorial only, half day; annual basis. *Waiting time for enrollment:* Autumn—3 to 4 weeks, Spring—5 weeks, Summer—2 weeks. *Average annual enrollment:* 100-150 students. *Program limits:* no maximum time a student may be enrolled for a remedial program. *Staff:* majority of staff members have completed pertinent graduate courses and have had 2 or more years practical experience.

SPECIAL INFORMATION: A Graduate Degree in Reading is offered.

State University College
Department of Education
Speech and Hearing Center
Fredonia, New York
Director: Dr. Henry C. Youngerman

DIAGNOSTIC FACILITIES: *Diagnostic facilities offered:* the aphasias, dyslexia (genetic or developmental), speech (developmental), minimal brain damage syndromes. *Referral sources:* pediatrician, school—public and private. *Ages accepted:* all ages. *Waiting period for first appointment:* none. *Staff and orientation:* emphasis in the educational area. *Professional services available:* neurology, psychology, audiometry, pediatric, otolaryngology. *Average annual case load:* 85—majority in the speech category.

TESTING FACILITIES: Testing program available.

EDUCATIONAL FACILITIES: *Remedial/developmental facilities:* the aphasias, dyslexia (genetic or developmental), speech (developmental), minimal brain damage syndromes, emotionally disturbed (moderate). *Instruction levels:* pre-school, primary, elementary, junior and senior high, adult rehabilitation. *Curriculum:* tutorial only. *Waiting period for enrollment:* none. *Average annual enrollment:* 97 students—majority in the speech category. *Program limits:* no maximum time a student may be enrolled for a remedial program. *Staff:* majority of staff have completed pertinent graduate courses and have had 2 or more years practical experience.

State University New York College at Cortland
Department of Speech and Theatre Arts
Cortland, New York
Director: Morris Bogard, Ph.D.

DIAGNOSTIC FACILITIES: *Diagnostic facilities are offered:* speech (developmental). *Referral sources:* school—private. *Ages accepted:* 3 years to 12 years, and 16 years to 20 years. *Waiting period for first appointment:* none given. *Staff and orientation:* emphasis in the educational area. *Professional services available:* psychology, audiometry, pediatric, dental facilities. *Average annual case load:* not given.

TESTING FACILITIES: No information given.

EDUCATIONAL FACILITIES: *Remedial/developmental program offered:* for speech (developmental). *Instruction levels:* above 18—attending college (developmental reading). *Curriculum:* tutorial only; annual basis. *Waiting period for enrollment:* not given. *Average annual enrollment:* limited—children at campus school. *Program limits:* no maximum time a student may be enrolled for a remedial program. *Staff:* majority of staff members have completed pertinent graduate courses and have had 2 or more years practical experience.

SPECIAL REQUIREMENTS: Speech services are offered to students attending the college and pupils at the campus school.

SPECIAL INFORMATION: Program is in developmental stages—expansion is planned.

Stephen Gaynor School
22 West 74th Street,
New York, New York 10023
Director: Dr. M. Michael

EDUCATIONAL FACILITIES: *Remedial/developmental programs:* dyslexia (genetic or developmental), speech (developmental), minimal brain damage syndromes, slow learner, emotionally disturbed (moderate). *Instruction levels:* pre-school, primary, elementary. *Curriculum:* full day—full curriculum. *Waiting period for enrollment:* September—open; January—4 months; Summer program—none. *Average annual enrollment:* not given. *Individual tutoring:* included automatically in students curriculum.

TESTING FACILITIES: Strong testing program available with off-campus referral.

FACULTY: School oriented to inter-discipline cooperation. *Professional services available to faculty:* neurology, psychology, audiometry, pediatric, ophthalmology, visual training, optometry, psychiatric, endocrinology. *Faculty-student ratio:* 1:4. *Staff qualifications:* specialized training in remedial reading—90% of staff; graduate level training in reading—70% of staff, speech—20% of staff, learning disabilities—90% of staff; Masters Degrees held by 50% of staff for reading, 10% of staff for speech, 50% of staff for learning disabilities.

Student Skills Centers, Inc.
New York City Center—248 East 31st Street
New York City, New York
Rockville Center —72 N. Village Avenue
Long Island, New York
Director: Joseph Baron

EDUCATIONAL FACILITIES: *Remedial/developmental programs offered:* speech (developmental), minimal brain damage syndromes, slow learner, emotionally disturbed (moderate), acceleration, reading, tutorial problems. *Instruction levels:* elementary, junior and senior high, above 18 (college preparatory). *Curriculum:* tutorial only; course or annual basis, and summer program. *Waiting period for enrollment:* no waiting. *Average annual enrollment:* 425 students. *Individual tutoring:* included automatically in students curriculum.

TESTING FACILITIES: Testing program available.

FACULTY: School is oriented to inter-discipline cooperation. *Professional services available to faculty:* psychology, audiometry, visual training, psychiatric. *Faculty-student ratio:* 1:4. *Faculty qualifications:* entire staff has had specialized training in remedial reading; graduate level training has been had by 80% of the staff in reading, by 10% of the staff in speech, and by 70% of the staff in learning disabilities; Masters Degrees are held by 50% of the staff for reading, by 10% of the staff for speech, and by 10% of the staff for learning disabilities.

Study Center for Learning Disabilities
135 Wester Avenue
Albany, New York
Director: N. Dale Bryant

DIAGNOSTIC FACILITIES: *Diagnostic facilities offered:* dyslexia (genetic or developmental), minimal brain damage syndromes, slow learner. *Referral sources:* pediatrician, school—public and private, psychiatrist, psychologist, parent. *Ages accepted:* 6 years to 16 years. *Waiting period for first appointment:* 2-3 month waiting period for Autumn, Spring, and Summer. *Staff and orientation:* a total child, multi-discipline team approach. *Professional services available:* neurology, psychology, audiometry, pediatric, ophthalmology, visual training, optometry, psychiatric, endocrinology. *Average annual case load:* 90-110—majority in the minimal brain damaged category.

TESTING FACILITIES: Strong testing program available.

EDUCATIONAL FACILITIES: *Remedial/developmental facilities:* minimal brain damage syndromes, slow learner, emotionally disturbed (moderate). *Instruction levels:* primary, elementary, junior high. *Curriculum:* tutorial only; annual basis. *Waiting period for enrollment:* no waiting list kept; cases selected for research and training purposes. *Average annual enrollment:* 10-15 students: *Program limits:* no maximum time a student may be enrolled for a remedial program. *Staff:* majority of staff members have completed pertinent graduate courses and have had 2 or more years practical experience.

Syracuse University
School of Education
Syracuse, New York 13210
Director: Dean Krathwohl

DIAGNOSTIC FACILITIES: *Diagnostic facilities offered:* the aphasias, dyslexia (genetic or developmental), speech (developmental), minimal brain damage syndromes, slow learner, psychiatric disorders. *Referral sources:* pediatrician, school—public and private, psychiatrist, psychologist, parent. *Ages accepted:* all ages. *Waiting period for first appointment:* Autumn—30 days; Spring—30 days; Summer—30 days. *Staff and orientation:* a total child, multi-discipline team approach; with emphasis in the psychological and educational areas. *Professional services available:* neurology, psychology, audiometry, pediatric, ophthalmology, visual training, optometry, psychiatric, endocrinology. *Average annual case load:* not given.

TESTING FACILITIES: No listing given.

EDUCATIONAL FACILITIES: *Remedial/developmental facilities:* the aphasias, dyslexia (genetic or developmental), speech (developmental), minimal brain damage syndromes, slow learner, emotionally disturbed (moderate). *Instruction levels:* all ages. *Curriculum:* tutorial only, half day; annual basis. *Waiting period for enrollment:* Autumn—30 days; Spring—30 days; Summer—30 days. *Average annual enrollment:* not given. *Program limits:* no maximum time a student may be enrolled for a remedial program. *Staff:* majority of staff have completed pertinent graduate courses and have had 2 or more years practical experience.

Teachers College Reading Center
Department of Psychology
525 West 120th Street
New York City, New York
Director: Dr. Anna McKillop

DIAGNOSTIC FACILITIES: *Diagnostic facilities offered:* dyslexia (genetic or developmental), minimal brain damage syndromes. *Referral sources:* pediatrician, school—public and private, psychiatrist, psychologist, parent. *Ages accepted:* 6 years to 16 years. *Waiting period for first appointment:* Autumn—1 month; Spring—1 month; Summer—1 month. *Staff and orientation:* emphasis in the psychological and educational areas. *Professional services available:* psychology, audiometry. *Average annual case load:* 13—majority in the dyslexia category.

TESTING FACILITIES: Testing program available.

EDUCATIONAL FACILITIES: *Remedial/developmental facilities:* dyslexia (genetic or developmental), minimal brain damage syndromes, emotionally disturbed (moderate). *Instruction levels:* primary, elementary, junior and senior high. *Curriculum:* tutorial only; annual basis. *Waiting period for enrollment:* Autumn—6 months; Spring—6 months; Summer—6 months. *Average annual enrollment:* 23 students—majority in the dyslexia and moderately disturbed categories. *Program limits:* no maximum time a student may be enrolled for a remedial program—usually 5 semesters. *Staff:* majority of staff have completed pertinent graduate courses. Tutoring is done by graduate students. Supervision is on a 1:10 ratio.

SPECIAL REQUIREMENTS: Enrollment limited to numerical I.Q. of 90 or above.

SPECIAL INFORMATION: Facility is a training center for graduate students in psychology, remedial reading. About 20% of children enrolled are dyslexic.

NEVADA

College of Education
Teaching and Resource Center
Reading Clinic
10 Artemisia Way
Reno, Nevada 89507
Director: Dr. Paul M. Hollingsworth

DIAGNOSTIC FACILITIES: *Diagnostic facilities offered:* the aphasias, dyslexia (genetic or developmental). *Referral sources:* school—public and private, psychologist, parent. *Ages accepted:* 6 years to 12 years. *Waiting period for first appointment:* Autumn—2 weeks; Spring—2 months; Summer—2 months. *Staff and orientation:* a total child, multi-discipline team approach; with emphasis in the neurological, psychological, and educational areas. *Professional services available:* neurology, psychology, audiometry, ophthalmology, visual training, psychiatric, endocrinology, physician. *Average annual case load:* 6.

TESTING FACILITIES: Testing program available.

EDUCATIONAL FACILITIES: *Remedial/developmental facilities:* the aphasias, dyslexia (genetic or developmental), emotionally disturbed (moderate). *Instruction levels:* primary, elementary, junior high, above 18—attending college. *Curriculum:* tutorial only; annual basis. *Average annual enrollment:* 22 students. *Program limits:* no maximum time a student may be enrolled for a remedial program. *Staff:* majority of staff have completed pertinent graduate courses and have had 2 or more years practical experience.

NORTH CAROLINA

Duke University
Medical Center
Durham, North Carolina

DIAGNOSTIC FACILITIES: *Diagnostic facilities offered:* the aphasias, dylsexia (genetic or developmental), speech (developmental). *Referral sources:* pediatrician, school—public and private, psychiatrist, psychologist, parent, agencies. *Ages accepted:* all ages. *Waiting period for first appointment:* Autumn—2 weeks, Spring—2 weeks, Summer—2 weeks. *Staff and orientation:* emphasis in the neurological, pediatric, educational areas. *Professional services available:* neurology, psychology, audiometry, pediatric, ophthalmology, visual training, optometry, psychiatric, endocrinology, speech, hearing. *Average annual case load:* varies.

TESTING FACILITIES: Testing program available.

EDUCATIONAL FACILITIES: *Remedial/developmental facilities:* the aphasias, dyslexia (genetic or developmental), speech (developmental), minimal brain damage syndromes, slow learner, emotionally disturbed (moderate). *Instruction levels:* all ages. *Curriculum:* tutorial only, half day, full day—full curriculum. *Waiting period for enrollment:* Autumn—2 weeks, Spring—2 weeks, Summer—2 weeks. *Average annual enrollment:* varies. *Program limits:* no maximum time a student may be enrolled for a remedial program. *Staff:* information not given.

Duke University
Medical Center
Division of Medical Psychology
Department of Psychiatry
Durham, North Carolinia
Director: R. C. Carson

DIAGNOSTIC FACILITIES: *Diagnostic facilities offered:* dyslexia (genetic or developmental), minimal brain damage syndromes, slow learner, psychiatric disorders. *Referral sources:* pediatrician, school—public and private, psychiatrist, psychologist, parent. *Waiting period for first appointment:* Autumn—3 weeks, Spring—3 weeks, Summer—3 weeks. *Staff and orientation:* a total child, multi-discipline team approach; with emphasis in the psychological area. *Professional services available:* neurology, psychology, audiometry, pediatric, ophthalmology, psychiatric, endocrinology. *Average annual case load:* not given.

TESTING FACILITIES: Variable.

EDUCATIONAL FACILITIES: *Remedial/developmental facilities:* minimal brain damage syndromes, slow learner, emotionally disturbed (moderate and severe). *Instruction levels:* not given. *Curriculum:* no classes—annual basis. *Waiting period for enrollment:* not given. *Average annual enrollment:* not given. *Program limits:* no limits given. *Staff:* majority of staff members have completed pertinent graduate courses and have had 2 or more years practical experience.

North Carolina State University
Department of Psychology
Post Office Box 5096
Raleigh, North Carolina 27607
Director: Dr. H. M. Carter

DIAGNOSTIC FACILITIES: *Diagnostic facilities offered:* dyslexia (genetic or developmental), minimal brain damage syndromes, slow learner. *Referral sources:* pediatrician, school—public and private, psychiatrist, parent. *Ages accepted:* 3 years to 20 years. *Waiting period for first appointment:* Autumn—2 weeks, Spring—1 month, Summer—2 weeks. *Staff and orientation:* emphasis in the psychological and educational areas. *Professional services available:* psychology. *Average annual case load:* not given.

TESTING FACILITIES: Testing program available.

EDUCATIONAL FACILITIES: None available.

NORTH DAKOTA

Minot State College
Department of Special Education
Speech and Hearing Clinic
Minot, North Dakota 58701
Director: Edna Gelbert, Ph.D.

DIAGNOSTIC FACILITIES: *Diagnostic facilities offered:* the aphasias, dyslexia (genetic or developmental), speech (developmental), minimal brain damage syndromes, slow learner, (and although no psychiatrist on staff—work is done with and referrals made on autistic and disturbed cases.) *Referral sources:* pediatrician, school—public and private, psychiatrist, psychologist, parent, otologist, welfare. *Ages accepted:* all ages. *Waiting period for first appointment:* Autumn—4 weeks, Spring—6 weeks, Summer—6 weeks. *Staff and orientation:* a total child, multi-discipline team approach; with emphasis in the psychological and educational areas. *Professional services available:* psychology and audiometry. *Professional referrals available, with reports back to clinic:* neurology, pediatric, ophthalmology, visual training, optometry, psychiatric. *Average annual case load:* 2,890—majority in the hearing and speech categories.

TESTING FACILITIES: Strong testing program available.

EDUCATIONAL FACILITIES: *Remedial/developmental facilities:* the aphasias, dyslexia (genetic or developmental), speech (developmental), minimal brain damage syndromes, slow learner (Summer only), emotionally disturbed (moderate, if speech is involved), hearing. *Instruction levels:* all ages. *Curriculum:* tutorial only; half day nursery; annual basis and Summer session. *Waiting period for enrollment:* varies. *Average annual enrollment:* 222—

majority in the speech category. *Program limits:* no maximum time a student may be enrolled for a remedial program. *Staff:* majority of staff have completed pertinent graduate courses and have had 2 or more years practical experience.

SPECIAL INFORMATION: Programs begin: early September, December, March, and June.

University of North Dakota
Evaluation Center for Exceptional Children
Grand Forks, North Dakota
Director: Louis B. Silverman, M.D.

DIAGNOSTIC FACILITIES: *Diagnostic facilities are offered for:* the aphasias, dyslexia (genetic or developmental), speech (developmental), minimal brain damage syndromes, slow learner, psychiatric. *Referral sources:* pediatrician, school—public and private, psychiatrist, psychologist, parent, social service agency, any University Speech & Hearing Clinic. *Ages accepted:* 3 years to 20 years. *Waiting period for first appointment:* program just starting—unable to give a waiting period now. *Staff and orientation:* a total child, multi-discipline team approach. *Professional services available:* neurology, psychology, audiometry, pediatric, ophthalmology, optometry, psychiatric, speech pathology. *Average annual case load:* figure unavailable at this time.

TESTING FACILITIES: Strong testing program available.

SPECIAL INFORMATION: Funded by Children's Service.

OHIO

Antioch College
Department of Speech and Drama
Speech Clinic
Yellow Springs, Ohio 45387
Director: Arthur Solomon, Ph.D.

DIAGNOSTIC FACILITIES: *Diagnostic facilities offered:* speech (developmental). *Referral sources:* pediatrician, school—public, psychiatrist, psychologist, parent. *Ages accepted:* 3 years to 12 years. *Waiting period for first appointment:* Autumn—0-1 week; Spring—0-1 week; Summer—0-1 week. *Staff and orientation:* emphasis in the psychological and educational areas. *Professional services available:* psychology, pediatric. *Average annual case load:* 20 children.

TESTING FACILITIES: Speech testing program available.

SPECIAL INFORMATION: Functional defects of speech and language (articulatory), voice, developmental, and stuttering, plus behavior problems stemming from speech disorder are handled by clinic.

EDUCATIONAL FACILITIES: None available.

Barney Children's Medical Center
1735 Chapel Street
Dayton, Ohio 45404
Medical Director: John E. Allen, M.D.

DIAGNOSTIC FACILITIES: *Diagnostic facilities offered:* the aphasias, dyslexia (genetic or developmental), speech (developmental), minimal brain damage syndromes, slow learner, psychiatric disorders. *Referral sources:* pediatrician, school—public and private, psychiatrist, psychologist, health agencies. *Ages accepted:* 3 years to 20 years. *Waiting period for first appointment:* Autumn—1 month, Spring—1 month, Summer—1 month. *Staff and orientation:* a total child, multi-discipline team approach; with emphasis in the neurological, psychological, pediatric, and psychiatric areas. *Professional services available:* neurology, psychology, audiometry, pediatric, ophthalmology, visual training, psychiatric, endocrinology. *Average annual case load:* not given.

TESTING FACILITIES: No information given.

EDUCATIONAL FACILITIES: *Remedial/developmental facilities:* the aphasias, dyslexia (genetic or developmental), speech (developmental). *Instruction levels:* not given. *Curriculum:* not given. *Waiting period for enrollment:* not given. *Average annual enrollment:* not given. *Program limits:* no maximum time a student may be enrolled for a remedial program. *Staff:* majority of staff have had 2 or more years practical experience.

SPECIAL INFORMATION: Center is new – no pertinent statistical facts at this time.

Bowling Green State University
The Reading Center
301 Hanna Hall
Bowling Green, Ohio 43402
Director: Joseph S. Nemeth

EDUCATIONAL FACILITIES: *Remedial/developmental programs offered:* dyslexia (genetic or developmental), minimal brain damage syndromes, emotionally disturbed (moderate). *Instruction levels:* primary, elementary, junior and senior high. *Curriculum:* tutorial only annual basis and Summer session. *Waiting period for enrollment:* none given. *Average annual enrollment:* 150 students. *Individual tutoring:* included automatically in students curriculum.

TESTING FACILITIES: Testing program available.

FACULTY: School orientation not given. *Professional services available to faculty:* neurology, psychology, audiometry, pediatric, ophthalmology, visual training, optometry, psychiatric. *Faculty-student ratio:* 1:8. *Staff qualifications:* entire staff has had specialized training in remedial reading; graduate level training has been had by the entire staff in reading and speech, with 50% in learning disabilities; and 75% of staff hold Masters Degrees in reading.

Cleveland Hearing and Speech Center
11206 Euclid
Cleveland, Ohio
Director: I. Brown

DIAGNOSTIC FACILITIES: *Diagnostic facilities offered:* the aphasias, speech (developmental). *Referral sources:* pediatrician, school – public and private, psychiatrist, psychologist, parent. *Ages accepted:* all ages. *Waiting period for first appointment:* Autumn – 2 weeks, Spring – 2 weeks, Summer – 2 weeks. *Staff and orientation:* a total child, multi-discipline team approach. *Professional services available:* neurology, psychology, audiometry, pediatric, ophthalmology, visual training, optometry, psychiatric, endocrinology, all pertinent resources. *Average annual case load:* 1,300 – majority in speech (developmental).

TESTING FACILITIES: Testing program available.

EDUCATIONAL FACILITIES: *Remedial/developmental programs offered:* the aphasias, speech (developmental). *Instruction levels:* all ages. *Curriculum:* individual therapy; annual basis. *Waiting time for enrollment:* Autumn – 1 month, Spring – 1 month, Summer – 1 month. *Average annual enrollment:* 650 students – majority in speech (developmental). *Program limits:* no maximum time a student may be enrolled for a remedial program. *Staff:* majority of staff members have completed pertinent graduate courses and have had 2 or more years practical experience.

Cleveland Metropolitan General Hospital
Department of Pediatrics
3395 Scranton Road
Cleveland, Ohio
Director: Robert Schwartz, M.D.

DIAGNOSTIC FACILITIES: *Diagnostic facilities are offered for:* the aphasias, dyslexia (genetic or developmental), speech (developmental), minimal brain damage syndromes, and the slow learner. *Referral sources:* pediatrician, school—public and private, psychiatrist, psychologist, parent (only if family has no available physician), social agencies. *Ages accepted:* infant to 18 years. *Waiting period for first appointment:* Spring waiting period; no waiting in Autumn or Summer. *Staff and orientation:* a total child, multi-discipline team approach. *Professional services available:* neurology, psychology, audiometry, pediatric, ophthalmology, psychiatric, endocrinology, orology, orthopedics, general surgery, neurosurgery, social service, other. *Average annual case load:* 750-800.

TESTING FACILITIES: Strong testing program available.

EDUCATIONAL FACILITIES: *Remedial/developmental program offered:* the aphasias, dyslexia (genetic or developmental), speech (developmental), minimal brain damage syndromes, the slow learner, emotionally disturbed (moderate-related program). *Instruction levels:* pre-school, primary, elementary, junior high, senior high. *Curriculum:* tutorial only, half day, and full day—full curriculum; annual basis. *Waiting time for enrollment:* none given. *Average annual enrollment:* not given. *Program limits:* no maximum time a student may be enrolled for a remedial program. *Staff:* majority of staff members have completed pertinent graduate courses and have had 2 or more years practical experience.

SPECIAL INFORMATION: Facility is a complete medical, psychological and social serviced program in a medical school/community hospital.

Kent State University
College of Education
Educational Child Study Center
Kent, Ohio 44240
Director: Dr. Marjorie Snyder

DIAGNOSTIC FACILITIES: *Diagnostic facilities offered:* the aphasias, dyslexia (genetic or developmental), speech (developmental), minimal brain damage syndromes, slow learner. *Referral sources:* pediatrician, school—public and private, psychiatrist, psychologist, parent, pediatric neurologist. *Ages accepted:* all ages. *Waiting period for first appointment:* Autumn—4-6 months; Spring—4-6 months; Summer—4-6 months. *Staff and orientation:* a total child, multi-discipline team approach; with emphasis in the neurological, psychological, pediatric, educational, psychiatric areas. *Professional services available:* neurology, psychology, audiometry, pediatric, ophthalmology, visual training, optometry, psychiatric, endocrinology, social service. *Average annual case load:* 114—majority in the minimal brain damaged category.

TESTING FACILITIES: Strong testing program available.

EDUCATIONAL FACILITIES: *Remedial/developmental facilities:* the aphasias, dyslexia (genetic or developmental), speech (developmental), minimal brain damage syndromes, emotionally disturbed (moderate). *Instruction levels:* primary, elementary, junior and senior high, above 18-attending college, adult rehabilitation. *Curriculum:* tutorial only; annual basis and summer program. *Waiting period for enrollment:* not given. *Average annual enrollment:* 69 students—majority in the minimal brain damaged category. *Program limits:* no maximum time a student may be enrolled for a remedial program. *Staff:* majority of staff have completed pertinent graduate courses and have had 2 or more years practical experience with a portion of the staff currently enrolled in graduate school.

SPECIAL REQUIREMENTS: Only extreme cases which cannot be serviced within school accepted in the Autumn and Spring programs. The Summer program consists mainly of the tutorial work as a requirement for the practicum course.

SPECIAL INFORMATION: Purpose of center is training graduate students in reading specialization and school psychology, and research and service to children with learning difficulties.

Kent State University
Department of Psychology
Psychological Clinic
Kent, Ohio 44240
Director: Dr. Arvin I. Lubetkin

DIAGNOSTIC FACILITIES: *Diagnostic facilities offered:* the aphasias, dyslexia (genetic or developmental), speech developmental, minimal brain damage syndromes, slow learner, psychiatric disorders. *Referral sources:* pediatrician, school – public and private, psychiatrist, psychologist, parent. *Ages accepted:* 3 to 6 years. *Waiting period for first appointment:* Autumn – 3 months, Spring – 3 months, Summer – 1 month. *Staff and orientation:* emphasis in the psychological area. *Professional services available:* neurology, psychology, audiometry, pediatric, ophthalmology, psychiatric. *Average annual case load:* 335 – majority in the psychiatric disorders category.

TESTING FACILITIES: Testing program available.

EDUCATIONAL FACILITIES: None available – referrals made.

Kent State University
Department of Speech
Kent, Ohio
Director: John R. Montgomery

DIAGNOSTIC FACILITIES: *Diagnostic facilities are offered for:* the aphasias, dyslexia (genetic or developmental), speech (developmental). *Referral sources:* pediatrician, school – public and private, psychiatrist, psychologist, parent. *Ages accepted:* 3 years to over 20 years. *Waiting period for first appointment:* Autumn – 1 month, Spring – 1 month, Summer – 1 month. *Staff and orientation:* a total child, multi-discipline team approach. *Professional services available:* neurology, psychology, audiometry, pediatric, speech and language. *Average annual case load:* 45 – majority in the aphasias category.

TESTING FACILITIES: Testing program available.

EDUCATIONAL FACILITIES: *Remedial/developmental programs offered:* the aphasias, speech (developmental), slow learner. *Instruction levels:* pre-school, primary. *Curriculum:* not given. *Waiting time for enrollment:* not given. *Average annual enrollment:* not given. *Program limits:* none given. *Staff:* majority of staff members have completed pertinent graduate courses and have had 2 or more years practical experience.

Mary Manse College
Department of Psychology and Education
Toledo, Ohio 43620
Director: Sister M. Louise

DIAGNOSTIC FACILITIES: *Diagnostic facilities offered:* the aphasias, speech (developmental), slow learner. *Referral sources:* pediatrician, school – public and private, psychiatrist, psychologist. *Ages accepted:* 3 years to 16 years. *Waiting period for first appointment:* Autumn – 2 weeks, Spring – 2 weeks, Summer – 2 weeks. *Staff and orientation:* emphasis in the psychological and educational areas. *Professional services available:* psychology, audiometry, visual training. *Average annual case load:* 55 – majority in the slow learner category.

TESTING FACILITIES: Not given.

EDUCATIONAL FACILITIES: *Remedial/developmental facilities:* speech (developmental), slow learner, emotionally disturbed (moderate). *Instruction levels:* all ages. *Curriculum:* tutorial only (by appointment); annual basis. *Waiting period for enrollment:* not given. *Average annual enrollment:* not given. *Program limits:* no maximum time a student may be enrolled for a remedial program. *Staff:* majority of staff have completed pertinent graduate courses and have had 2 or more years practical experience.

SPECIAL INFORMATION: Diagnostic and educational facilities are of an individual nature and are extended to serve the blind, deaf, speech disorders; partially sighted, emotionally disturbed, bright children – low achievers. Diagnostic service only (no educational) for the mentally retarded.

Ohio State University
School of Optometry
Optometry Clinic
352 West Tenth Avenue
Columbus, Ohio 43210
Director: Bradford W. Wild, O.D., Ph.D.

DIAGNOSTIC FACILITIES: *Diagnostic facilities offered:* for minimal brain damage syndromes, slow learner. *Referral sources:* pediatrician, school – public and private, psychiatrist, psychologist, parent. *Ages accepted:* all ages. *Waiting period for first appointment:* Autumn – 4 weeks, Spring – 4 weeks, Summer – 4 weeks. *Staff and orientation:* emphasis in the psychological and educational areas. *Professional services available:* neurology, psychology, audiometry, pediatric, ophthalmology, visual training, optometry, psychiatric, endocrinology. *Average annual case load:* 60.

TESTING FACILITIES: Not given.

EDUCATIONAL FACILITIES: *Remedial/developmental facilities:* minimal brain damage syndromes, slow learner, emotionally disturbed (moderate). *Instruction levels:* all ages. *Curriculum:* tutorial only; annual basis. *Waiting period for enrollment:* Autumn – 4 weeks, Spring – 4 weeks, Summer – 4 weeks. *Average annual enrollment:* 90 students. *Program limits:* no maximum time a student may be enrolled for a remedial program. *Staff:* majority of staff have had 2 or more years practical experience.

Ohio State University
Department of Psychology
Child Study Center
65 South Oval Drive
Columbus, Ohio 43210
Coordinator: Donald C. Smith

DIAGNOSTIC FACILITIES: *Diagnostic facilities offered:* dyslexia (genetic or developmental) minimal brain damage syndromes. *Referral sources:* pediatrician, school – public and private, psychiatrist, psychologist, parent. *Ages accepted:* 3 years to 20 years. *Waiting period for first appointment:* Autumn – 6 months; Spring – 3 months; Summer – 9 months. *Staff and orientation:* emphasis in the psychological and educational areas. *Professional services available:* psychology, audiometry, optometry. *Average annual case load:* 75 – majority in the dyslexia category.

TESTING FACILITIES: Strong testing program available.

EDUCATIONAL FACILITIES: *Remedial/developmental facilities:* dyslexia (genetic or developmental), minimal brain damage syndromes. *Instruction levels:* pre-school, primary, elementary, junior high. *Curriculum:* tutorial only; annual basis. *Waiting period for enrollment:* Autumn – 9 months; Spring – 6 months; Summer – 12 months. *Average annual enrollment:* 43-50 students – majority in the dyslexia category. *Program limits:* no maximum time a student may be enrolled for a remedial program. *Staff:* majority of staff members are currently enrolled in graduate school and have had less than 2 years practical experience.

Ohio University
Center for Psychological Services
McKee House
Athens, Ohio
Director: Michael Havek

DIAGNOSTIC FACILITIES: *Diagnostic facilities offered:* minimal brain damage syndromes, and psychiatric disorders. *Referral sources:* psychiatrist, psychologist, parent, faculty, and staff. *Ages accepted:* 16 years to over 20 years. *Waiting period for first appointment:* Autumn – 2 days, Spring – 10 days, Summer – 2 days. *Staff and orientation:* emphasis in the psychological and educational areas. *Professional services available:* psychology, audiometry, psychiatric, physician. *Average annual case load:* less than 12 students in the minimal brain damaged category, while several hundred with psychiatric disorders.

TESTING FACILITIES: Testing program available.

SPECIAL REQUIREMENTS: Services are for students enrolled on full time basis at the university.

SPECIAL INFORMATION: Services also available for educational, career and personal/social problems (minor to severe).

Ohio University
Department of Speech Pathology, Audiology, and Speech Science
Speech and Hearing Clinic
Ewing Hall
Athens, Ohio 45701
Coordinator of Clinical Service: Ronald Williams

DIAGNOSTIC FACILITIES: No information given.

EDUCATIONAL FACILITIES: *Remedial/developmental facilities:* the aphasias, speech (developmental), minimal brain damage syndromes, slow learner, emotionally disturbed (moderate). *Instruction levels:* all ages. *Curriculum:* tutorial only; annual basis. *Waiting period for enrollment:* Autumn – 1-2 weeks, Spring – 1-2 weeks, Summer – none. *Average annual enrollment:* 135 students – majority in the speech category. *Program limits:* no limits given. *Staff:* majority of staff are currently enrolled in graduate school and have had less than 2 years practical experience.

SPECIAL INFORMATION: No remedial reading program offered.

Otterbein College
Educational Development Laboratory
Westerville, Ohio
Director: Dr. Benjamin Center

DIAGNOSTIC FACILITIES: *Diagnostic facilities offered:* the aphasias, dyslexia (genetic or developmental), speech (developmental), minimal brain damage syndromes, slow learner. *Referral sources:* pediatrician, school – public and private, psychiatrist, psychologist, parent. *Ages accepted:* all ages. *Waiting period for first appointment:* Autumn – 2 weeks, Spring – 2 weeks, Summer – 2 weeks. *Staff and orientation:* a total child, multi-discipline team approach; with emphasis on the psychological and educational areas. *Professional services available:* psychology, audiometry, visual training, optometry, and special education. *Average annual case load:* 350 – majority in dyslexia and slow learner categories.

TESTING FACILITIES: Strong testing program available.

EDUCATIONAL FACILITIES: *Remedial/developmental programs offered:* the aphasias, dyslexia (genetic or developmental), speech (developmental), minimal brain damage syndromes, slow learner, emotionally disturbed (moderate). *Instruction levels:* pre-school, primary, elementary, junior high, senior high, above 18-attending college (developmental reading), adult rehabilitation. *Curriculum:* tutorial, half day, full day – full curriculum; on an annual basis and Summer session. *Waiting period for enrollment:* Autumn – 2 weeks, Spring – 2 weeks, Summer – 2 weeks. *Average annual enrollment:* 360 – majority in dyslexia and slow learner categories. *Program limits:* no maximum time a student may be enrolled for a remedial program. *Staff:* majority of staff members have had 2 or more years practical experience.

The University of Akron
Department of Speech
Speech and Hearing Clinic
222 James Street
Akron, Ohio 44304
Director: Dr. E. J. Hittle

DIAGNOSTIC FACILITIES: *Diagnostic facilities are offered for:* the aphasias, dyslexia (genetic or developmental), speech (developmental), minimal brain damage syndromes, slow learner. *Referral sources:* pediatrician, school—public and private, psychiatrist, psychologist, parent, otologist. *Ages accepted:* 3 years through over 20 years. *Waiting period for first appointment:* Autumn—2 weeks, Spring—2 weeks, Summer—2 weeks. *Staff and orientation:* a total child, multi-discipline team approach, with emphasis on education. *Professional services available:* on campus—psychology, audiometry, social service; consulting disciplines—neurology, pediatric, ophthalmology, visual training, optometry, psychiatric. *Average annual case load:* 65-95—majority in speech (developmental).

TESTING FACILITIES: Testing program available.

EDUCATIONAL FACILITIES: *Remedial/developmental programs offered:* the aphasias, speech (developmental), minimal brain damage syndromes, slow learner. *Instruction levels:* pre-school, primary, elementary, junior high, senior high, adult rehabilitation. *Curriculum:* tutorial only; annual basis. *Waiting time for enrollment:* Autumn—2-4 weeks, Spring—2-4 weeks, Summer—none. *Average annual enrollment:* 48-67 students—majority in speech (developmental) category. *Program limits:* no maximum time a student may be enrolled for a remedial program. *Staff:* portion of staff members are currently enrolled in graduate school and have had less than 2 years practical experience, while the majority of staff members have completed pertinent graduate courses.

University Hospitals
Children's Unit—Hanna Pavilion
Department of Psychiatry
Cleveland, Ohio 44106
Director: Willard D. Boaz, M.D.

DIAGNOSTIC FACILITIES: *Diagnostic facilities are offered for:* the aphasias, dyslexia (genetic or developmental), speech (developmental), minimal brain damage syndromes, slow learner, psychiatric disorders. *Referral sources:* pediatrician, school—public and private, psychiatrist, psychologist, parent, general practitioner. *Ages accepted:* 3 years—12 years. *Waiting period for first appointment:* 1 to 3 months. *Staff and orientation:* neurological, psychological, pediatric, educational, psychiatric; with a total child, multi-discipline team approach. *Professional services available:* neurology, psychology, audiometry, pediatric, ophthalmology, psychiatric, endocrinology; including facilities of general hospital and university campus. *Average annual case load:* 35—majority in psychiatry.

TESTING FACILITIES: Strong testing program.

EDUCATIONAL FACILITIES: None given.

SPECIAL REQUIREMENTS: Physicians' approval required on all admissions.

OKLAHOMA

Central State College
Department of Education and Psychology
Speech and Hearing Clinic
Edmond, Oklahoma
Director: Mrs. Lillian Ivey

DIAGNOSTIC FACILITIES: *Diagnostic facilities are offered for:* the aphasias, dyslexia (genetic or developmental), speech (developmental). *Referral sources:* pediatrician, school—

public and private, psychologist, parent. *Ages accepted:* all ages. *Waiting period for first appointment:* Autumn—1 week, Spring—2 weeks, Summer—2 weeks. *Staff and orientation:* emphasis in the educational area. *Professional services available:* audiometry, speech evaluation. *Average annual case load:* 53—majority in speech (developmental) category.

TESTING FACILITIES: Testing program available.

EDUCATIONAL FACILITIES: *Remedial/developmental programs offered:* the aphasias, dyslexia (genetic or developmental), speech (developmental). *Instruction levels:* all ages. *Curriculum:* tutorial only; annual basis. *Waiting period for enrollment:* Autumn—1 week, Spring—2 weeks, Summer—2 weeks. *Average annual enrollment:* 53 students—majority in the speech category. *Program limits:* no maximum time a student may be enrolled for a remedial program. *Staff:* majority of staff members have completed pertinent graduate courses and have had 2 or more years practical experience.

Payne County Guidance Center
Payne County Health Department
701 South Walnut—Post Office Box 471
Stillwater, Oklahoma
Director: C. W. Moore, M.D.

DIAGNOSTIC FACILITIES: *Diagnostic facilites offered:* the aphasias, dyslexia (genetic or developmental), speech (developmental), minimal brain damage syndromes, slow learner, psychiatric disorders. *Referral sources:* pediatrician, school—public and private, psychiatrist, psychologist, parent. *Ages accepted:* 3 years to 12 years. *Waiting period for first appointment:* 2 weeks. *Staff and orientation:* a total child, multi-discipline team approach. *Professional services available:* neurology, psychology, audiometry, pediatric, ophthalmology, psychiatric. *Average annual case load:* not given.

TESTING FACILITIES: Testing program available.

EDUCATIONAL FACILITIES: *Remedial/developmental facilities:* speech (developmental), minimal brain damage syndromes, emotionally disturbed (moderate). *Instruction level:* primary. *Curriculum:* no information given. *Waiting period for enrollment:* not given. *Average annual enrollment:* not given. *Program limits:* students not accepted past 3rd grade level. *Staff:* majority of staff members have had 2 or more years practical experience.

Tulsa Education Foundation, Inc.
1516 South Quaker
Tulsa, Oklahoma
Director: Dr. George Truka

EDUCATIONAL FACILITIES: *Remedial/developmental programs offered:* minimal brain damage syndromes. *Instruction levels:* primary, elementary. *Curriculum:* full day—full curriculum; annual basis. *Waiting period for enrollment:* depends on need and facilities available. *Average annual enrollment:* 56 students. *Individual tutoring:* included automatically in students curriculum.

TESTING FACILITIES: Strong testing program available.

FACULTY: School is oriented to inter-discipline cooperation. *Professional services available to faculty:* neurology, psychology, audiometry, pediatric, ophthalmology, optometry, psychiatric. *Faculty-student ratio:* 1:8. *Faculty qualifications:* entire staff has had specialized training in remedial reading; graduate level training has been had by 80% of staff in reading, by 20% of the staff in speech, and by 25% of the staff in learning disabilities.

University of Oklahoma Medical Center
Department of Pediatrics
Child Study Center
601 N.E. 18th Street
Oklahoma City, Oklahoma
Director: Richard C. Gillartin, M.D.

DIAGNOSTIC FACILITIES: *Diagnostic facilities offered:* the aphasias, dyslexia (genetic or developmental), speech (developmental), minimal brain damage syndromes, slow learner. *Referral sources:* pediatrician, school—public and private, psychiatrist, psychologist. *Ages accepted:* 3 years to 16 years. *Waiting period for first appointment:* October—5 months. *Staff and orientation:* a total child, multi-discipline team approach. *Professional services available:* neurology, psychology, audiometry, pediatric, ophthalmology, visual training, optometry, psychiatric, endocrinology, social services. *Average annual case load:* 190-230—majority in the minimal brain damaged category.

TESTING FACILITIES: Testing program available.

EDUCATIONAL FACILITIES: *Remedial/developmental facilities:* dyslexia (genetic or developmental), minimal brain damage syndromes. *Instruction level:* primary. *Curriculum:* tutorial only; annual basis. *Waiting period for enrollment:* openings filled upon availabilities. *Average annual enrollment:* 15 students—majority in the dyslexia category. *Program limits:* no maximum time a student may be enrolled for a remedial program. *Staff:* portion of staff are currently enrolled in graduate school; majority of staff have completed pertinent graduate courses, and have had 2 or more years practical experience.

University of Oklahoma
Department of Special Education
Norman, Oklahoma
Director: P. T. Teska

DIAGNOSTIC FACILITIES: *Diagnostic facilities offered:* slow learner. *Referral sources:* pediatrician, school—public and private, psychiatrist, psychologist, parent. *Ages accepted:* all ages. *Waiting period for first appointment:* Autumn—2 weeks, Spring—1-2 weeks, Summer 2-weeks. *Staff and orientation:* emphasis in the psychological and educational areas. *Professional services available:* psychology. *Average annual case load:* not given.

TESTING FACILITIES: Testing program available.

EDUCATIONAL FACILITIES: *Remedial/developmental facilities:* slow learner. *Instruction levels:* primary, elementary, junior and senior high. *Curriculum:* full day—full curriculum; annual basis. *Waiting period for enrollment:* depends upon enrollment. *Average annual enrollment:* 10-12 students. *Program limits:* a student may be enrolled for a remedial program only through the 12th year. *Staff:* majority of staff have had 2 or more years practical experience.

Community Speech and Hearing Center
University Station
Box 2262
Enid, Oklahoma
Director: Thayne A. Hedges, Ph.D.

DIAGNOSTIC FACILITIES: *Diagnostic facilites are offered for:* the aphasias, speech (developmental), minimal brain damage syndromes. *Referral sources:* all sources. *Ages accepted:* 3 years to over 20 years. *Waiting period for first appointment:* 2 weeks. *Staff and orientation:* a total child, multi-discipline team approach. *Professional services available:* psychology, audiometry, pediatric, ophthalmology, speech pathology. *Average annual case load:* not given.

TESTING FACILITIES: No testing program listed.

EDUCATIONAL FACILITIES: *Remedial/developmental programs offered for:* the aphasias, speech (developmental), minimal brain damage syndromes. *Instruction levels:* pre-school, primary, elementary, junior high, senior high, above 18-attending college (developmental reading), adult rehabilitation. *Curriculum:* speech pathology; annual basis. *Waiting time for enrollment:* 2 months. *Average annual enrollment:* not given. *Program limits:* no maximum time a student may be enrolled for a remedial program. *Staff:* majority of staff members have had 2 or more years practical experience.

OREGON

Oregon College of Education
Department of Special Education and Rehabilitation
Education Evaluation Center
Monmouth, Oregon
Director: Dr. Donald H. Duncan

DIAGNOSTIC FACILITIES: *Diagnostic facilities offered:* the aphasias, dyslexia (genetic or developmental), speech (developmental), minimal brain damage syndromes, slow learner, psychiatric disorders. *Referral sources:* pediatrician, school – public and private, psychiatrist, psychologist, parent, mental health clinics. *Ages accepted:* 3 years to 21 years. *Waiting period for first appointment:* 1 month. *Staff and orientation:* a total child, multi-discipline team approach; with emphasis in the psychological, educational, speech, audiology, otology areas. *Professional service available:* psychology, audiometry, psychiatric, otology. *Average annual case load:* 223 – majority in the speech category.

TESTING FACILITIES: Strong testing program available.

EDUCATIONAL FACILITIES: *Remedial/developmental facilities:* speech (developmental), slow learner, reading and study skills. *Instruction levels:* pre-school, primary, elementary, junior and senior high. *Curriculum:* tutorial only; annual basis. *Waiting period for enrollment:* Autumn – 2 weeks, Spring – 2 weeks, Summer – 2 weeks. *Average annual enrollment:* 70 students. *Program limits:* no maximum time a student may be enrolled for a remedial program. *Staff:* majority of staff have completed pertinent graduate courses and have had 2 or more years practical experience.

Oregon State University
Department of Speech
Speech and Hearing Clinic
Corvallis, Oregon 97331
Director: Dr. C. N. Harris

DIAGNOSTIC FACILITIES: *Diagnostic facilities offered:* the aphasias, dyslexia (genetic or developmental), speech (developmental), minimal brain damage syndromes, slow learner. *Referral sources:* pediatrician, school – public and private, psychiatrist, psychologist, parent, medical school (University of Oregon). *Ages accepted:* all ages. *Waiting period for first appointment:* Autumn – 2 weeks, Spring – 2 weeks or less, Summer – no waiting. *Staff and orientation (clinic and hospital):* neurological, psychological, pediatric, educational, psychiatric emphasized for a total child, multi-discipline team approach. *Professional (hospital) services available:* neurology, psychology, audiometry, pediatric, ophthalmology, visual training, optometry, psychiatric. *Average annual case load:* 18-23 – majority in the speech category.

TESTING FACILITES: Testing program available at both – clinic and hospital.

EDUCATIONAL FACILITIES: None available.

SPECIAL INFORMATION: Facility works closely with the Crippled Children's Division of the University of Oregon Medical School, located at Good Samaritan Hospital.

University of Oregon
School of Education
DeBusk Memorial Center
Eugene, Oregon
Director: Ruth Waugh

DIAGNOSTIC FACILITIES: *Diagnostic facilities offered:* dyslexia (genetic or developmental), minimal brain damage syndromes, slow learner, psychiatric disorders. *Referral sources:*

pediatrician, school—public and private, psychiatrist, psychologist, parent. *Ages accepted:* all ages. *Waiting period for first appointment:* Autumn—3 weeks, Spring—3 weeks, Summer—1 week. *Staff and orientation:* a total child, multi-discipline team approach. *Professional services available:* neurology, psychology, audiometry, pediatric, ophthalmology, visual training, optometry, psychiatric. *Average annual case load:* 550-majority in the slow learner category.

TESTING FACILITIES: Strong testing program available.

EDUCATIONAL FACILITIES: *Remedial/developmental facilities:* dyslexia (genetic or developmental), minimal brain damage syndromes, slow learner, emotionally disturbed (moderate). *Instruction levels:* primary, elementary, junior high. *Curriculum:* tutorial only; annual basis. *Waiting period for enrollment:* Autumn—2 months, Spring—3 months, Summer—3 months. *Average annual enrollment:* 200 students—majority in the emotionally disturbed (moderate) category. *Program limits:* no maximum time a student may be enrolled for a remedial program. *Staff:* majority of staff have completed pertinent graduate courses and have had 2 or more years practical experience.

Southern Oregon College
Department of Speech
Speech and Hearing Center
Ashland, Oregon 97520
Director: Leon Mulling

DIAGNOSTIC FACILITIES: *Diagnostic facilities are offered for:* speech (developmental). *Referral sources:* pediatrician, school—public, psychiatrist, psychologist, parent. *Ages accepted:* 3 years to 12 years. *Waiting period for first appointment:* Autumn—2 weeks, Spring—2 weeks, Summer—2 weeks. *Staff and orientation:* emphasis on education. *Professional services available:* psychology, audiometry. *Average annual case load:* 95.

TESTING FACILITIES: Testing program available.

EDUCATIONAL FACILITIES: *Remedial/developmental program offered:* speech (developmental). *Instruction levels:* pre-school, primary, elementary. *Curriculum:* tutorial only; annual basis. *Waiting period for enrollment:* Autumn—2 weeks, Spring—2 weeks, Summer—2 weeks. *Average annual enrollment:* 95 students. *Program limits:* no maximum time a student may be enrolled for a remedial program. *Staff:* at present, staff members consist of: a Ph.D. in speech pathology and undergraduate students who are (in general) majors in elementary education.

SPECIAL INFORMATION: Facility at present is a State service.

Willamette University
Department of Psychology
Salem, Oregon
Director: C. H. Derthick

DIAGNOSTIC FACILITIES: *Diagnostic facilities offered:* minimal brain damage syndromes, psychiatric disorders. *Referral sources:* pediatrician, school—public and private, psychiatrist, psychologist. *Ages accepted:* 6 years to over 20 years. *Waiting period for first appointment:* Autumn—1-2 weeks, Spring—1-2 weeks, Summer—no program. *Staff and orientation:* emphasis in the psychological area. *Professional services available:* none listed. *Average annual case load:* not given.

TESTING FACILITIES: Strong testing program available.

EDUCATIONAL FACILITIES: None available.

SPECIAL INFORMATION: Most cases come from vocational rehabilitation, not by referral.

University of Oregon Medical School
Crippled Children's Division
Department of Speech and Hearing
3181 S.W. Sam Jackson Park Road
Portland, Oregon 97201
Director: Harold Lillywhite

DIAGNOSTIC FACILITIES: *Diagnostic facilities offered:* the aphasias, dyslexia (genetic or developmental), speech (developmental), minimal brain damage syndromes, slow learner. *Referral sources:* pediatrician, school—public and private, psychiatrist, psychologist, health agency, physician. *Ages accepted:* 3 years to 20 years. *Waiting period for first appointment:* Autumn—6 weeks; Spring—6 weeks; Summer—6 weeks. *Staff and orientation:* a total child, multi-discipline team approach. *Professional services available:* neurology, psychology, audiology, pediatric, ophthalmology, visual training, psychiatric, endocrinology, speech pathology. *Average annual case load:* 40.

TESTING FACILITIES: Not given.

EDUCATIONAL FACILITIES: *Remedial/developmental facilities:* the aphasias, dyslexia (genetic or developmental), speech (developmental), minimal brain damage syndromes, slow learner, emotionally disturbed (moderate and severe). *Instruction levels:* pre-school, primary, elementary, junior and senior high. *Curriculum:* tutorial only, half day; annual basis. *Waiting period for enrollment:* Autumn—6 months; Spring—6 months; Summer—6 months. *Average annual enrollment:* 15-20 students. *Program limits:* no maximum time a student may be enrolled for a remedial program. *Staff:* majority of staff have had 2 or more years practical experience.

PENNSYLVANIA

Albert Einstein Medical Center (Northern Division)
Department of Child Psychiatry
Tabor and Old York Roads
Philadelphia, Pennsylvania 19141
Director: Harold Kolansky, M.D.

DIAGNOSTIC FACILITIES: *Diagnostic facilities are offered for:* the aphasias, dyslexia (genetic or developmental), speech (developmental), minimal brain damage syndromes, slow learner, psychiatric. *Referral sources:* pediatrician, school—public and private, psychiatrist, psychologist, parent, physician. *Ages accepted:* 3 years—16 years. *Waiting period for first appointment:* Autumn—3 months; Spring—3 months; Summer—3 months. *Staff and orientation:* a total child, multi-discipline team approach. *Professional services available:* neurology, psychology, audiometry, pediatric, ophthalmology, psychiatric, endocrinology, genetic, biochemistry. *Average annual case load:* 112—majority in psychiatric, minimal brain damage syndromes, slow learner categories.

TESTING FACILITIES: Strong testing program.

EDUCATIONAL FACILITIES: None available.

SPECIAL INFORMATION: Facility puts emphasis on the 'total child'—his physical, neurological, and psychological development with an individual *prescription* written for each child to meet his individual needs. Parental counseling, supportive therapy, and regulation of medication for children, are offered. Referrals made on educational facilities.

Bloomsburg State College
Department of Speech Correction, Section on Communication Disorders
Bloomsburg, Pennsylvania
Coordinator of Speech and Hearing Services: Margaret C. Lefevre

DIAGNOSTIC FACILITIES: *Diagnostic facilities offered:* the aphasias, speech (developmental), minimal brain damage syndromes, slow learner. *Referral sources:* pediatrician, school—public and private, psychiatrist, psychologist, parent, college students. *Ages accepted:* all ages. *Waiting period for first appointment:* Autumn—2-4 weeks; Spring—1-6 weeks; Summer—1-4 weeks. *Staff and orientation:* emphasis in the psychological, speech, and hearing areas. *Professional services available:* psychology, audiometry, speech, language. *Average annual case load:* 68—majority in the speech and slow learner categories.

TESTING FACILITIES: Strong testing program available.

EDUCATIONAL FACILITIES: *Remedial/developmental facilities:* the aphasias, minimal brain damage syndromes, slow learner, with speech the focal point. *Instruction levels:* all ages. *Curriculum:* therapy only, full day—full curriculum: annual basis. BVR summer program only. *Waiting period for enrollment:* Autumn—1-6 weeks. *Average annual enrollment:* not given. *Program limits:* no maximum time a student may be enrolled for a remedial program. *Staff:* majority of staff have completed pertinent graduate courses and have had 2 or more years practical experience; a portion of staff are student clinicians working under supervision.

California State College
Department of Special Education
Speech and Hearing Clinic
California, Pennsylvania
Director: Dr. Arthur G. Henry

DIAGNOSTIC FACILITIES: *Diagnostic facilities offered:* the aphasias, speech (developmental). *Referral sources:* pediatrician, school—public and private, psychologist, parent. *Ages accepted:* all ages. *Waiting period for first appointment:* Autumn—2 weeks; Spring—2 weeks; Summer—2 weeks. *Staff and orientation:* emphasis in the psychological and educational areas. *Professional services available:* psychology, audiometry. *Average annual case load:* 45—majority in the speech category.

TESTING FACILITIES: Testing program available.

EDUCATIONAL FACILITIES: None available.

Children's Hospital of Philadelphia
Rehabilitation Department
1740 Bainbridge Street
Philadelphia, Pennsylvania 19146
Director: Mary D. Ames, M.D.

DIAGNOSTIC FACILITIES: *Diagnostic facilities offered:* the aphasias, dyslexia (genetic or developmental), speech (developmental), minimal brain damage syndromes, slow learner. *Referral sources:* pediatrician, psychiatrist, physician. *Ages accepted:* 3 years to 12 years. *Waiting period for first appointment:* Autumn—3-4 weeks, Spring—3-4 weeks, Summer—3-4 weeks. *Staff and orientation:* a total child, multi-discipline team approach. *Professional services available:* neurology, psychology, audiometry, pediatric, ophthalmology, visual training, complete hospital services. *Average annual case load:* 120-165, majority in speech (developmental).

TESTING FACILITIES: Testing program available.

EDUCATIONAL FACILITIES: *Remedial/developmental programs offered:* speech (developmental). *Instruction levels:* pre-school, *Curriculum:* tutorial only, and half day; annual basis. *Waiting time for enrollment:* Autumn—3-4 weeks, Spring—3-4 weeks, Summer—3-4 weeks. *Average annual enrollment:* 50-75 students. *Program limits:* no maximum time a student may be enrolled for a remedial program. *Staff:* majority of staff members have had 2 or more years practical experience.

SPECIAL INFORMATION: General program is mainly for children presenting chronic, multiple handicaps.

Children's Hospital of Pittsburgh
Speech Clinic
DeSoto Street
Pittsburgh 13, Pennsylvania
Director: Lawrence Bloom

DIAGNOSTIC FACILITIES: *Diagnostic facilities are offered for:* the aphasias, speech (developmental), minimal brain damage syndromes. *Referral sources:* pediatrician, school—public and private, psychiatrist, psychologist, parent (referrals from schools must have pediatric screening). *Ages accepted:* 3 years to 16 years. *Waiting period for first appointment:* Autumn—8 months to 1 year, Spring—8 months to 1 year, Summer—8 months to 1 year. *Staff and orientation:* a total child, multi-discipline team approach. *Professional services available:* neurology, psychology, audiometry, pediatric, ophthalmology, psychiatric, endocrinology, speech, language, social service. *Average annual case load:* 185—majority in the speech category.

TESTING FACILITIES: Testing program available.

EDUCATIONAL FACILITIES: *Remedial/developmental programs offered:* the aphasias, speech (developmental), minimal brain damage syndromes. *Instruction levels:* children under 16 years. *Curriculum:* tutorial only; annual basis. *Waiting period for enrollment:* 8 months to 1 year waiting period for the Autumn, Spring, and Summer sessions. *Average annual enrollment:* 185—majority in the speech category. *Program limits:* no maximum time a student may be enrolled for a remedial program. *Staff:* majority of staff members have completed pertinent graduate courses and have had 2 or more years practical experience.

SPECIAL INFORMATION: Facility deals with speech and language disorders of all types, including those which may be found with minimal brain damage syndromes.

The Devereux Foundation
19 South Waterloo Road
Devon, Pennsylvania 19333
Director: Edward L. French, Ph.D.

EDUCATIONAL FACILITIES: *Remedial/developmental programs offered:* the aphasias, dyslexia (genetic or developmental), speech (developmental), minimal brain damage syndromes, slow learner, emotionally disturbed (moderate and severe). *Instruction levels:* primary, elementary, junior and senior high, above 18-college preparatory. *Curriculum:* full day—full curriculum; annual basis. *Waiting period for enrollment:* no waiting. *Average annual enrollment:* not given. *Individual tutoring:* included automatically in students curriculum.

TESTING FACILITIES: Details not given, referrals made to their Department of Psychology.

FACULTY: Orientation not given. *Professional services available to faculty:* neurology, psychology, audiometry, pediatric, ophthalmology, visual training, optometry, psychiatric, endocrinology, educators, social service. *Faculty-student ratio:* 1:1 (including all residential treatment personnel). *Faculty qualifications:* 6% of staff have had specialized training in remedial reading; graduate level training of the staff—1% in reading, 3% in speech, 2% in learning disabilities; Masters Degrees are held by 2% of staff in reading, by 3% of the staff in speech, and by 2% of staff in learning disabilities.

Edinboro State College
Department of Psychology and Special Education
Leader Clinic
Edinboro, Pennsylvania 16412
Director: Dr. John S. Schell

DIAGNOSTIC FACILITIES: *Diagnostic facilities offered:* the aphasias, speech (developmental), minimal brain damage syndromes, slow learner. *Referral sources:* pediatrician, school – public and private, psychologist, parent, therapists, agencies. *Ages accepted:* all ages. *Waiting period for first appointment:* Autumn – 1 month; Spring – 1 month; Summer – 1 month. *Staff and orientation:* emphasis in the psychological and educational areas. *Professional services available:* psychology, audiometry. *Average annual case load:* 29 – majority in the speech category.

TESTING FACILITIES: Strong testing program available.

EDUCATIONAL FACILITIES: *Remedial/developmental facilities:* the aphasias, speech (developmental) minimal brain damage syndromes, slow learner. *Instruction levels:* all ages. *Curriculum:* tutorial only, half day program, full day – full curriculum; annual basis. *Waiting period for enrollment:* maximum waiting – 1 semester. *Average annual enrollment:* 29 students – majority in the speech category. *Program limits:* no maximum time a student may be enrolled for a remedial program. *Staff:* majority of staff have completed pertinent graduate courses and have had 2 or more years practical experience.

SPECIAL INFORMATION: Clinic is a student training center, and has a B.V.R. in-patient speech program.

Edinboro State College
Department of Psychology
Leader Clinic
Edinboro, Pennsylvania 16412
Director: Dr. John S. Schell

DIAGNOSTIC FACILITIES: *Diagnostic facilities are offered for:* minimal brain damage syndromes, slow learner, psychiatric disorders. *Referral sources:* pediatrician, school – public and private, psychiatrist, psychologist, parent. *Ages accepted:* 6 years to over 20 years. *Waiting period for first appointment:* Autumn – 2 weeks, Spring – 2 weeks, Summer – 2 weeks. *Staff and orientation:* emphasis in the psychological and educational areas. *Professional services available:* psychology, audiometry, speech therapy. *Average annual case load:* 85 – majority in the psychiatric disorders category.

TESTING FACILITIES: Testing program available.

EDUCATIONAL FACILITIES: This is an evaluation facility primarily, although some therapy is available – especially for emotionally disturbed and speech therapy.

Episcopal Hospital
Department of Physical Medicine and Rehabilitation
Front Street and Lehigh Avenue
Philadelphia, Pennsylvania
Director: K. C. Archibald, M.D.

DIAGNOSTIC FACILITIES: *Diagnostic facilities offered:* the aphasias, dyslexia (genetic or developmental), speech (developmental), minimal brain damage syndromes, slow learner, psychiatric disorders. *Referral sources:* pediatrician, school – public, psychiatrist, psychologist, parent, other hospitals. *Ages accepted:* all ages. *Waiting period for first appointment:* none given. *Staff and orientation:* emphasis in the neurological, psychological, pediatric, and psychiatric areas. *Professional services available:* neurology, psychology, audiometry, pediatric, ophthalmology, psychiatric, and endocrinology, *Average annual case load:* not given.

TESTING FACILITIES: Not given.

EDUCATIONAL FACILITIES: *Remedial/developmental facilities:* the aphasias, speech (developmental), emotionally disturbed (moderate). *Instruction levels:* pre-school and adult rehabilitation. *Curriculum:* annual basis. *Waiting period for enrollment:* not given. *Average annual enrollment:* not given. *Program limits:* no maximum time a student may be enrolled for a remedial program. *staff:* majority of staff members have completed pertinent graduate courses and have had 2 or more years practical experience.

SPECIAL INFORMATION: Educational facilities are unclassified on a school-grade level; they are conducted in clinic (hospital) usually on an individual basis.

Gettysburg College
Office of Guidance Services
Gettysburg, Pennsylvania
Director: William H. Jones

DIAGNOSTIC FACILITIES: *Diagnostic facilities offered:* slow learner, psychiatric disorders. *Referral sources:* pediatrician, psychiatrist, psychologist. *Ages accepted:* 16 years to over 20 years. *Waiting period for first appointment:* no waiting. *Staff and orientation:* emphasis in the psychological and educational areas. *Professional services available:* psychology, psychiatric, educational. *Average annual case load:* not given.

TESTING FACILITIES: Testing program available.

EDUCATIONAL FACILITIES: *Remedial/developmental facilities:* slow learner and emotionally disturbed (moderate). *Instruction levels:* adult rehabilitation. *Curriculum:* tutorial only and full day–full curriculum; annual basis. *Waiting period for enrollment:* no waiting. *Average annual enrollment:* 1,800 students. *Program limits:* no maximum time a student may be enrolled for a remedial program. *Staff:* majority of staff have completed pertinent graduate courses and have had 2 or more years practical experience.

SPECIAL INFORMATION: This is primarily an adult rehabilitation facility.

Greenbank School
RD #1
Glenmoore, Pennsylvania
Director: Thomas K. Porter

EDUCATIONAL FACILITIES: *Remedial/developmental programs:* slow learner, emotionally disturbed (moderate). *Instruction levels:* junior and senior high. *Curriculum:* no information given. *Waiting period for enrollment:* September–30-60 days; January–30-60 days; Summer program–10 days. *Average annual enrollment:* 40 boys. *Individual tutoring:* included automatically in students curriculum.

TESTING FACILITIES: No program listed–off-campus referrals made.

FACULTY: Orientation not given. *Professional services available to faculty:* psychology, optometry, psychiatric. *Faculty-student ratio:* 1:8. *Faculty qualifications:* 1 staff member has had specialized training in remedial reading: 1 staff member holds a Masters Degree in reading.

SPECIAL INFORMATION: The majority of the school's enrollment has minimum I.Q. of 100. Facility refers to majority of student body as passive-aggressive personalities.

Indiana University of Pennsylvania
Department of Special Education and Clinical Services
Campus Laboratory School
Indiana, Pennsylvania 15701
Chairman: Dr. Morton Morris, under the jurisdiction of: Dr. George A. W. Stougger, Jr., Dean of the School of Education

DIAGNOSTIC FACILITIES: Referral to on-campus clinic.

EDUCATIONAL FACILITIES: *Remedial/developmental facilities offered:* the aphasias, dyslexia (genetic or developmental), speech (developmental, therapy), minimal brain damage syndromes, slow learner. *Instruction levels:* pre-school, primary, elementary. *Curriculum:* full day–full curriculum; annual basis, Summer program. *Waiting period for enrollment:* to be determined. *Average annual enrollment:* 30-40 in the speech category–additional figures to be determined with the initiation of additional classes in September 1968. *Program limits:* no maximum time a student may be enrolled for a remedial program. *Staff:* majority of staff have completed pertinent graduate courses and have had 2 or more years practical experience.

Special Information: Two demonstration classes to be initiated September 1968 in Learning Research Center. One class to be for instruction and diagnosis of children with learning disabilities (ages 4 years to 6-7 years). The other class will demonstrate program for the mildly retarded (ages 10 years to 12 years).

Indiana University of Pennsylvania
Department of Special Education
Speech and Hearing Clinic
Indiana, Pennsylvania
Director: Maude O. Brungard

Diagnostic Facilities: *Diagnostic facilities offered:* the aphasias, dyslexia (genetic or developmental), speech (developmental), minimal brain damage syndromes, slow learner. *Referral sources:* pediatrician, school—public and private, psychiatrist, psychologist, parent. *Ages accepted:* all ages. *Waiting period for first appointment:* Autumn—4 weeks, Spring—4 weeks, Summer—6 weeks. *Staff and orientation:* emphasis in the educational area. *Professional services available:* psychology, audiometry. *Average annual case load:* 50—majority in the speech category.

Testing Facilities: Testing program available.

Educational Facilities: *Remedial/developmental facilities:* the aphasias, dyslexia (genetic or developmental), speech (developmental), minimal brain damage syndromes, slow learner, emotionally disturbed (moderate). *Instruction levels:* not given. *Curriculum:* not given. *Waiting period for enrollment:* not given. *Average annual enrollment:* 50 students—majority in the speech category. *Program limits:* no maximum time a student may be enrolled for a remedial program. *Staff:* majority have had 2 or more years practical experience.

Special Requirement: Correction for speech problems only.

Institute of the Pennsylvania Hospitals
Department of Psychology and Re-education
111 N. 49th Street
Philadelphia, Pennsylvania
Director: Cynthia S. Klinman

Diagnostic Facilities: *Diagnostic facilities:* the aphasias, dyslexia (genetic or developmental), speech (developmental), minimal brain damage syndromes, slow learner, psychiatric disorders. *Referral sources:* pediatrician, school—public and private, psychiatrist, psychologist, parent, self-referral. *Ages accepted:* all ages. *Waiting period for first appointment:* Autumn—1 week, Spring—1 week, Summer—1 week. *Staff and orientation:* emphasis in the psychological and educational areas. *Professional services available:* psychology. *Average annual case load:* 375—majority in the psychiatric category.

Testing Facilities: Testing program available.

Educational Facilities: *Remedial/developmental facilities:* dyslexia (genetic or developmental), slow learner, and emotionally disturbed (moderate). No further information given.

Laughlen Children's Center
Broad and Frederick Streets
Seweckley, Pennsylvania
Director: Elizabeth S. Lesquin

Educational Facilities: *Remedial/developmental programs:* the aphasias, dyslexia (genetic or developmental), speech (developmental), minimal brain damage syndromes, slow learner, emotionally disturbed (moderate). *Instruction levels:* pre-school, primary, elementary. *Curriculum:* tutorial only, annual basis. *Waiting period for enrollment:* September—2 months; January—6 months; Summer program—usually filled by April. *Average annual enrollment:* 78 students—majority in the speech category. *Individual tutoring:* included automatically in students curriculum.

TESTING FACILITIES: Strong testing program available.

FACULTY: School oriented to inter-discipline cooperation. *Professional services available to faculty:* neurology, psychology, audiometry, pediatric, ophthalmology, visual training, optometry, psychiatric. *Faculty-student ratio:* 1:1 (in most cases), 1:8 in groups. *Faculty qualifications:* entire staff has had specialized training in remedial reading; graduate level training has been had by 80% of staff in reading, entire staff in speech, 80% of staff in learning disabilities: Masters Degrees are held by 40% of staff for reading, by 67% of staff for speech, by 80% of staff for learning disabilities.

Main Line Day School (& Reading Center)
527 E. Lancaster Avenue
St. Davids, Pennsylvania
Director: Dr. B. Hershone

EDUCATIONAL FACILITIES: *Remedial/developmental programs offered:* dyslexia (genetic or developmental), minimal brain damage syndromes. *Instruction levels:* primary, elementary, junior high. *Curriculum:* full day—full curriculum; annual basis plus Summer program. *Waiting time for enrollment:* no waiting time. *Average annual enrollment:* none given. *Individual tutoring:* included automatically in students curriculum.

TESTING FACILITIES: Testing program marked as varied; no listing given; off-campus referrals made.

FACULTY: School is oriented to inter-discipline cooperation. *Professional services available to faculty:* neurology, psychology, audiometry, pediatric, visual training, optometry, psychiatric. *Faculty-student ratio:* 1:8. *Faculty qualifications:* entire staff has had specialized training in remedial reading; 75% of staff members have had graduate level training in reading, and 25% in learning disabilities; 75% of staff members hold Masters Degrees in reading, and 25% in learning disabilities.

SPECIAL INFORMATION: School operates a tutorial reading center also.

The Matthews School
2001 Pennsylvania Avenue
Fort Washington, Pennsylvania 19034
Director: Gerald Schatz

EDUCATION FACILITIES: *Remedial/developmental programs offered:* the aphasias, dyslexia (genetic or developmental), speech (developmental), minimal brain damage syndromes, emotionally disturbed (moderate). *Instruction levels:* primary, elementary, junior high, senior high. *Curriculum:* full day—full curriculum; annual basis. *Waiting time for enrollment:* September session—2 months; January session—1 month, Summer program—1 month. *Average annual enrollment:* 60 students (28 resident and 32 day); majority in dyslexia. *Individual tutoring:* included automatically in students curriculum.

TESTING FACILITIES: Testing program available.

FACULTY: School is oriented to inter-discipline cooperation. *Professional services available to faculty:* neurology, psychology, audiometry, pediatric, ophthalmology, visual training, psychiatric. *Faculty-student ratio:* 1:4. *Faculty qualifications:* 95% of staff have had specialized training in remedial reading; entire staff has had graduate level training in reading, and 30% in speech; 20% of staff hold Masters Degrees in reading.

SPECIAL INFORMATION: Facility's population consists of primary—moderate to severe learning disabilities, which are correctable with concomitant intelligence and appearance.

Mercy Hospital
Division of Psychology
Audiology, Speech, and Psychology Clinic
Locust Street
Pittsburgh, Pennsylvania
Director: Bernard Yadoff, Ph.D.

DIAGNOSTIC FACILITIES: *Diagnostic facilities offered for:* the aphasias, dyslexia (genetic or developmental), speech (developmental), minimal brain damage syndromes, slow learner, psychiatric disorders. *Referral sources:* pediatrician, school—public and private, psychiatrist, psychologist, parent. *Ages accepted:* all ages. *Waiting period for first appointment:* several months at any time of year. *Staff and orientation:* emphasis in the neurological, psychological, pediatric, and educational areas. *Professional services available:* neurology, psychology, audiometry, pediatric, ophthalmology. *Average annual case load:* program just beginning—figures unknown at this time.

TESTING FACILITIES: Strong testing program available, with emphasis on case history.

EDUCATIONAL FACILITIES: None available—referral made.

Mercy Hospital
Division of Psychology
Audiology, Speech, and Psychology Clinic
Locust Street
Pittsburgh, Pennsylvania
Director: Shirley J. Salmon, Ph.D.

DIAGNOSTIC FACILITIES: *Diagnostic facilities offered for:* the aphasias, speech (developmental), minimal brain damage syndromes. *Referral sources:* pediatrician, school—public, psychologist, parent, neurologist. *Ages accepted:* 3 years to 12 years; and over 20 years. *Waiting period for first appointment:* Autumn—1 month, Spring—2 months, Summer—2-3 months. *Staff and orientation:* a total child, multi-discipline team approach; with emphasis in the neurological, psychological, pediatric, educational, and psychiatric areas. *Professional services available:* neurology, psychology, audiometry, pediatric, ophthalmology, psychiatric, endocrinology. *Average annual case load:* 44—majority in the aphasias category.

TESTING FACILITIES: Testing program available.

EDUCATIONAL FACILITIES: *Remedial/developmental facilities:* the aphasias, speech (developmental), minimal brain damage syndromes. *Instruction levels:* above 18-attending college (developmental reading), and adult rehabilitation. *Curriculum:* tutorial only: *Waiting period for enrollment:* Autumn—1 month, Spring—2 months, Summer—2-3 months. *Average annual enrollment:* 5 students. *Program limits:* no maximum time a student may be enrolled for a remedial program. *Staff:* majority of staff members have had 2 or more years practical experience.

Millersville State College
Department of Education
Reading Clinic
Millersville, Pennsylvania 17551
Director: Joseph Torchia

DIAGNOSTIC FACILITIES: *Diagnostic facilities offered:* the aphasias, dyslexia (genetic or developmental), minimal brain damage syndromes, slow learner. *Referral sources:* pediatrician, school—public and private, psychologist, parent. *Ages accepted:* 3 years to 20 years. *Waiting period for first appointment:* Autumn—1-2 days, Spring 1-2 days, Summer—1-2 days. *Staff and orientation:* emphasis in the psychological and educational areas. *Professional services available:* neurology, psychology, audiometry, ophthalmology. *Average annual case load:* 24.

TESTING FACILITIES: Strong testing program available.

SPECIAL INFORMATION: Chief purpose of Reading Clinic is improvement of reading skills. Services listed are used to deal with problems and prescribe programs. Some teaching is done with students enrolled in reading course—all programs of instruction supervised by director of Reading Clinic.

EDUCATIONAL FACILITIES: Referral made to the on-campus Reading Clinic.

Muhlenberg College
Department of Psychology
Counseling and Guidance Clinic
Allentown, Pennsylvania
Director: Walter H. Brackin, Ph.D.

DIAGNOSTIC FACILITIES: *Diagnostic facilities offered:* minimal brain damage syndromes, slow learner. *Referral sources:* pediatrician, school—public and private, psychiatrist, psychologist, parent. *Ages accepted:* 6 years to over 20 years. *Waiting period for first appointment:* Autumn—1 week, Spring—1 week, Summer—1 week. *Staff and orientation:* emphasis in the psychological and educational areas. *Professional services available:* psychology. *Average annual case load:* not given.

TESTING FACILITIES: Strong testing program available.

EDUCATIONAL FACILITIES: *Remedial/developmental facilities:* reading clinic. *Instruction levels:* above 18-attending college. *Curriculum:* annual basis. *Waiting period for enrollment:* reading programs coincide with college semesters. *Average annual enrollment:* not given. *Program limits:* no maximum time a student may be enrolled for a remedial program. *Staff:* majority of staff have had 2 or more years practical experience.

The Pathway School
Box 181
Norristown, Pennsylvania 19404
Director: Sheldon R. Rappaport, Ph. D.

EDUCATIONAL FACILITIES: *Remedial/developmental programs offered:* minimal brain damage syndromes. *Instruction levels:* elementary. *Curriculum:* full-day, full-curriculum; annual basis. *Waiting time for enrollment:* September session—day program—1 month; residential program—6 months. *Average annual enrollment:* 76 students. *Individual tutoring:* presented as an adjunct to the curriculum.

TESTING FACILITIES: Full battery of tests available.

FACULTY: School oriented to inter-discipline cooperation. *Professional services available to faculty:* neurology, psychology, pediatric, ophthalmology, visual training, optometry, psychiatric, dental. *Faculty-student ratio:* 1.2:1. *Faculty qualifications:* 4 staff members have had special training in remedial reading; 3 staff members have had training at graduate level in reading, and 3 staff members have had training at graduate level in speech, with 25% having had graduate training in learning disabilities. 2 staff members hold Masters Degrees in Reading, 10% have Masters Degrees in learning disabilities.

SPECIAL INFORMATION: School's population consists of at least average intellectual potential coupled with cerebral dysfunction, which has interfered with child's achieving full potential.

Pennsylvania College of Optometry
Department of Clinics
6100 North 12th Street
Philadelphia, Pennsylvania
Director: Dr. William Walton

DIAGNOSTIC FACILITIES: *Diagnostic facilities offered:* dyslexia (genetic or developmental), minimal brain damage syndromes, slow learner. *Referral sources:* pediatrician, school—public and private, psychiatrist, psychologist, parent. *Ages accepted:* all ages. *Waiting period for first appointment:* 2 week waiting—Autumn, Spring, and Summer. *Staff and orientation:* a total child, multi-discipline team approach. *Professional services available:*

visual training, optometry. *Average annual case load:* not given.

TESTING FACILITIES: Vision testing program available.

EDUCATIONAL FACILITIES: None available – referred.

Pennsylvania Hospital Community Mental Health Center
Department of Medicine
8th and Spruce Streets
Philadelphia, Pennsylvania 19107
Director: James R. Harris, M.D.

DIAGNOSTIC FACILITIES: *Diagnostic facilities offered:* minimal brain damage syndromes. *Referral sources:* pediatrician, school – public and private, psychiatrist, psychologist, parent, any. *Ages accepted:* 3 years to 20 years. *Waiting period for first appointment:* none. *Staff and orientation:* emphasis in the neurological, psychological, and psychiatric areas. *Professsional services available:* neurology, psychology, audiometry, ophthalmology, psychiatric, endocrinology. *Average annual case load:* 20.

TESTING FACILITIES: Testing program available.

EDUCATIONAL FACILITIES: None available.

SPECIAL INFORMATION: Facility primarily funded by a research grant.

Pittsburgh Child Guidance Center
201 DeSoto Street
Pittsburgh 13, Pennsylvania
Director: Meyer Sonis, M.D.

EDUCATIONAL FACILITIES: *Remedial/developmental programs offered:* minimal brain damage syndromes, emotionally disturbed (moderate). *Instruction levels:* primary, elementary. *Curriculum:* tutorial only; annual basis. *Waiting time for enrollment:* unavailable at this time. *Average annual enrollment:* unavailable at this time. *Individual tutoring:* group and individual. *Program limits:* evaluation at 6-month periods for continuance.

TESTING FACILITIES: None given.

FACULTY: Information unavailable. *Professional services available to faculty:* information unavailable. *Faculty-student ratio:* information unavailable. *Faculty qualifications:* majority of staff members have completed pertinent graduate courses and have had 2 or more years practical experience.

SPECIAL INFORMATION: Clinic beginning as of April, 1967, with children having perceptual and emotional problems, along with learning difficulties. A three-year funded project with plans for flexible tutorial and consultative services – interim programs only. Facility is directed to those who require educational and psychological services in order to supplement or enroll into existing, regular, or special programs.

School Psychology Center
Department of Special Education
119 E. PC II
University Park, Pennsylvania
Director: Dr. Joseph L. French

DIAGNOSTIC FACILITIES: *Diagnostic facilities are offered for:* minimal brain damage syndromes and slow learner. *Referral sources:* pediatrician, school – public and private, psychiatrist, psychologist, parent. *Ages accepted:* 3 years to 16 years. *Waiting period for first appointment:* Autumn – 2-6 weeks, Spring – 2-6 weeks, Summer – 2-6 weeks. *Staff and orientation:* psychological and educational. *Professional services available:* psychology, audiometry, ophthalmology. *Average annual case load:* not given.

TESTING FACILITIES: Testing available, but no information given.

EDUCATIONAL FACILITIES: None available.

Shippensburg State College
Department of Education and Psychology, Clinical Services
Shippensburg, Pennsylvania 17257
Division Chairman: Dr. George Kaluger
Department Chairman: Dr. Chester Eastep

DIAGNOSTIC FACILITIES: *Diagnostic facilities offered:* aphasias, dyslexia (genetic or developmental), minimal brain damage syndromes, slow learner. *Referral sources:* pediatrician, school—public and private, psychiatrist, psychologist, parent,County Division of Special Services. *Ages accepted:* 6 years to 20 years. *Waiting period for first appointment:* Autumn —1-3 weeks; Spring—2-3 weeks; Summer—1-2 weeks. *Staff and orientation:* emphasis in the psychological and educational areas. *Professional services available:* psychology, analysis, remedial reading (professional services are available by off-campus referral). *Average annual case load:* 81-140—majority in the brain damage and slow learner categories. Depart is oriented to learning disabilities and *not* mental retardation.

TESTING FACILITIES: Testing program available.

SPECIAL INFORMATION: Diagnostic services not part of regular college function, but done privately by faculty working in the field of learning disabilities. Basic work being done with school children, referred by school psychologists, as having normal intelligence but not normal learning abilities—much of the work has been experimental and exploratory. Department is oriented to learning disorders, not mental retardation.

EDUCATIONAL FACILITIES: *Remedial/developmental facilities:* slow learner. *Instruction levels:* elementary. *Curriculum:* half day; Summer only. *Waiting period for enrollment:* none. *Average annual enrollment:* 25 students. *Program limits:* each Summer program requires a re-enrollment. *Staff:* majority of staff have had 2 or more years practical experience.

SPECIAL INFORMATION: Educational department provides an in-service training to interested school districts—to enable them to handle their own problems, as they arise. This service is not a college function, but done by interested members of staff.

Slippery Rock State College Experimental School for Exceptional Children
Department of Special Education
Slippery Rock State College
Slippery Rock, Pennsylvania 16057
Director: Dr. Jack C. Dinger

DIAGNOSTIC FACILITIES: *Diagnostic facilities offered:* the aphasias, dyslexia (genetic or developmental), speech (developmental), minimal brain damage syndromes, slow learner, psychiatric disorders. *Referral sources:* pediatrician, school—public and private, psychiatrist, psychologist, parent. *Ages accepted:* 3 years to 16 years. *Waiting period for first appointment:* Autumn—3 weeks, Spring—3 weeks, Summer—1 week. *Staff and orientation:* a total child, multi-discipline team approach; with emphasis in the psychological and educational areas. *Professional services available:* psychology, pediatric, psychiatric, speech therapist, developmental physical educator. *Average annual case load:* 85—majority in the brain damage and slow learner categories.

TESTING FACILITIES: Strong testing program available.

EDUCATIONAL FACILITIES: *Remedial/developmental facilities:* minimal brain damage syndromes, slow learner, emotionally disturbed (moderate and severe). *Instruction levels:* preschool, primary, elementary. *Curriculum:* full day—full curriculum; annual basis. *Waiting period for enrollment:* none. *Average annual enrollment:* 17 students—majority in the slow learner category. *Program limits:* no maximum time a student may be enrolled for a remedial program. *Staff:* majority of staff have had 2 or more years practical experience.

SPECIAL INFORMATION: Tutorial services provided in highly individualized program of instruction.

State College
Department of Guidance
Guidance Center
Millersville, Pennsylvania
Director: C. I. Kent

DIAGNOSTIC FACILITIES: *Diagnostic facilities offered:* speech (developmental), slow learner. *Referral sources:* pediatrician, school—public, psychiatrist, psychologist. *Ages accepted:* 6 years to 20 years. *Waiting period for first appointment:* limited to accommodations. *Staff and orientation:* a total child, multi-discipline team approach; with emphasis in the psychological and educational areas. *Professional services available:* neurology, psychology, audiometry, pediatric, psychiatric. *Average annual case load:* 30—college students, 25 referrals.

TESTING FACILITIES: Testing program available.

SPECIAL INFORMATION: This service is rendered largely for laboratory school children to the degree the staff can accommodate.

EDUCATIONAL FACILITIES: *Remedial/developmental facilities:* speech (developmental), emotionally disturbed (moderate). *Instruction levels:* elementary, junior and senior (occasionally) high, above 18-attending college. *Curriculum:* Summer only. *Waiting period for enrollment:* Autumn—1-2 weeks, Spring—1-2 weeks, Summer—1-2 weeks. *Average annual enrollment:* 40-45 students. *Program limits:* no maximum time a student may be enrolled for a remedial program. *Staff:* majority of staff have had 2 or more years practical experience.

SPECIAL INFORMATION: Majority of services are provided for the students enrolled at the college; however, as time permits, psychological, speech and hearing, and reading development are offered.

Temple University
Laboratory School of the Reading Clinic
Cheltenham and Sedgwick Avenues
Philadelphia, Pennsylvania 19150
Director: Dr. Paul Daniels

EDUCATIONAL FACILITIES: *Remedial/developmental programs:* dyslexia (genetic or developmental), minimal brain damage syndromes, slow learner, emotionally disturbed (moderate). *Instruction levels:* primary, elementary, junior and senior high, above 18—college preparatory. *Curriculum:* full day—full curriculum; annual basis. *Waiting period for enrollment:* September—16 weeks; January—16 weeks; Summer program—9 weeks. *Average annual enrollment:* 78 students—majority in the dyslexia category. *Individual enrollment:* presented as an adjunct to the curriculum.

TESTING FACILITIES: Testing program available with on-campus referral.

FACULTY: School is oriented to inter-discipline cooperation. *Professional services available to faculty:* neurology, psychology, audiometry, visual training, optometry, psychiatric. *Faculty-student ratio:* 1:4 and 1:8. *Faculty qualifications:* entire staff has had specialized training in remedial reading; graduate level training in reading by entire staff, in speech by 10% of staff, in learning disabilities by entire staff; 80% of staff hold Masters Degrees in reading.

Temple University
Department of Psychology
The Reading Clinic
Carnell Hall
Broad Street and Montgomery Avenue
Philadelphia, Pennsylvania 19122
Director: Dr. Roy A. Kress

DIAGNOSTIC FACILITIES: *Diagnostic facilities are offered for:* dyslexia (genetic or developmental), minimal brain damage syndromes, slow learners. *Referral sources:* pediatrician, school—public and private, psychiatrist, psychologist, parent. *Ages accepted:* 6 years to over 20 years. *Waiting period for first appointment:* Autumn—3-4 weeks, Spring—6-8 weeks, Summer—1-2 weeks. *Staff and orientation:* a total child, multi-discipline team approach, is clinic philosophy. Permanent staffing is basically psychological/educational. *Professional services available:* psychology, audiometry, optometry, psychiatric, speech, others through referral. *Average annual case load:* 1,000.

TESTING FACILITIES: Strong testing program available.

EDUCATIONAL FACILITIES: *Remedial/developmental programs offered:* dyslexia (genetic or developmental), speech (developmental), minimal brain damage syndromes, slow learner, emotionally disturbed (moderate). *Instruction levels:* primary, elementary, junior high, senior high, above 18-attending college (developmental reading), adult rehabilitation. *Curriculum:* tutorial, half day, and full day—full curriculum; annual basis and Summer sessions. *Waiting time for enrollment:* dependent on particular program involved. *Average annual enrollment:* 500 students, including all programs, all ages. *Program limits:* no maximum time a student may be enrolled for a remedial program. *Staff:* majority of staff members have completed pertinent graduate courses and have had 2 or more years practical experience.

Temple University
Department of Speech
Speech and Hearing Center
1908 N. Park Avenue
Philadelphia, Pennsylvania
Director: H. Goehl, Ph.D.

DIAGNOSTIC FACILITIES: *Diagnostic facilities offered:* the aphasias, speech (developmental). *Referral sources:* pediatrician, school—public and private, psychiatrist, psychologist, parent. *Ages accepted:* all ages. *Waiting period for first appointment:* Autumn—3 weeks, Spring—3 weeks, Summer—3 weeks. *Staff and orientation:* emphasis in the psychological area. *Professional services available:* neurology, psychology, audiometry, pediatric, ophthalmology, visual training, optometry, psychiatric, endocrinology. *Average annual case load:* 125—majority in the speech category.

TESTING FACILITIES: Strong testing program available.

SPECIAL REQUIREMENT: Patient must submit physician's report prior to diagnosis.

EDUCATIONAL FACILITIES: *Remedial/developmental facilities:* the aphasias, speech (developmental). *Instruction levels:* all ages. *Curriculum:* tutorial only; annual basis. *Waiting period for enrollment:* Autumn—2 weeks, Spring—2 weeks, Summer—2 weeks. *Average annual enrollment:* 100 students—majority in the speech category. *Program limits:* no maximum time a student may be enrolled for a remedial program. *Staff:* majority of staff are currently enrolled in graduate school.

University of Pennsylvania
Graduate School of Education
Reading Clinic
3700 Walnut street
Philadelphia, Pennsylvania 19104
Director: Ralph C. Preston, Ph.D.

DIAGNOSTIC FACILITIES: *Diagnostic facilities offered:* dyslexia (genetic or developmental), minimal brain damage syndromes, slow learner, reading difficulties. *Referral sources:* pediatrician, school—public and private, psychiatrist, psychologist, parent, ophthalmologist, self-referral. *Ages accepted:* all ages. *Waiting period for first appointment:* Autumn—1 month, Spring—8 months, Summer—none. *Staff and orientation:* a total child, multi-discipline team approach (research project); with emphasis in the educational area. *Professional services available:* neurology, psychology, audiometry, pediatric, ophthalmology, psychiatric, physical anthropology. *Average annual case load:* 117-122, majority in the reading disabilities category.

TESTING FACILITIES: Strong testing program available.

EDUCATIONAL FACILITIES: *Remedial/developmental facilities:* dyslexia (genetic or developmental), minimal brain damage syndromes, slow learner, emotionally disturbed (moderate). *Instruction levels:* primary, elementary, junior and senior high, above 18 – attending college, adult rehabilitation. *Curriculum:* for primary, elementary, junior high, and adult rehabilitation – tutorial only; for senior high – Summer only; for above 18 – 6 weeks course. *Waiting period for enrollment:* Autumn – no waiting, Spring – 5 months, Summer – no waiting. *Averate annual enrollment:* 19-24 students – majority in the dyslexia category. *Program limits:* no maximum time a student may be enrolled for a remedial program. *Staff:* majority of staff have completed pertinent graduate courses and have had 2 or more years practical experience.

Vanguard School
Box 277
Haverford, Pennsylvania 19041
Directors: H. D. Evans, Milton Brutten, Ph.D.

EDUCATIONAL FACILITIES: *Remedial/developmental programs offered for:* the aphasias, dyslexia (genetic or developmental), speech (developmental), minimal brain damage syndromes, slow learner, emotionally disturbed (moderate). *Instruction levels:* pre-school, primary, elementary, junior high, senior high, above 18 – college preparatory. *Curriculum:* full day – full curriculum; annual basis. *Waiting time for enrollment:* 6 months. *Average annual enrollment:* 475 students – majority in minimal brain damaged syndromes and dyslexia categories. *Individual tutoring:* presented as an adjunct to the curriculum.

TESTING FACILITIES: Strong testing program available.

FACULTY: School is oriented to inter-discipline cooperation. *Professional services available to faculty:* neurology, psychology, audiometry, pediatric, visual training, optometry, psychiatric. *Faculty-student ratio:* 1:4. *Faculty qualifications:* 10% of the staff have had specialized training in remedial reading; graduate level training has been had by 10% of the staff in reading, by 20% of the staff in speech, by 40% of the staff in learning disabilities; Masters Degrees are held by 10% of the staff for reading, by 20% of the staff for speech, by 30% of the staff for learning disabilities.

West Chester State College
Department of Speech and Theater
Speech and Hearing Clinic
620 S. High Street
Westchester, Pennsylvania
Director: Dr. Harold L. Hayes

DIAGNOSTIC FACILITIES: *Diagnostic facilities are offered for:* the aphasias, speech (developmental). *Referral sources:* pediatrician, school – public and private, psychiatrist, psychologist, otolaryngologist. *Ages accepted:* 3 years – over 20 years. *Waiting period for first appointment:* Autumn – 1 day to 2 months, Spring – 1 day to 2 months. *Staff and orientation:* educational with a total child multi-discipline team approach. *Professional services available:* audiometry, dental. *Professional services available, though referred:* neurology, psychology, pediatric, ophthalmology, visual training, optometry, psychiatric, endocrinology. *Average annual case load:* 42-60, majority in speech (developmental).

TESTING FACILITIES: Testing program available.

EDUCATIONAL FACILITIES: *Remedial/developmental programs offered:* the aphasias, speech (developmental), minimal brain damage syndromes, slow learner. *Instruction levels:* pre-school, primary, elementary, junior high, above 18 attending college. *Curriculum:* tutorial only, annual basis. *Waiting time for enrollment:* Autumn – 2 weeks to 4 months, Spring – 2 weeks to 4 months. *Average annual enrollment:* 31-36, majority in speech (developmental) category. *Program limit:* no maximum time a student may be enrolled for a remedial program. *Staff:* majority of staff members have completed pertinent graduate courses and have had 2 or more years practical experience.

SPECIAL INFORMATION: Program primarily aimed at developing and improving oral communication skills. Facility plans expansion in the near future.

RHODE ISLAND

Governor Center School
293 Governor Street
Providence, Rhode Island 02906
Director: Anne Hale

EDUCATIONAL FACILITIES: *Remedial/developmental programs offered:* the aphasias, dyslexia (genetic or developmental), speech (developmental), minimal brain damage syndromes, slow learner, emotionally disturbed (moderate). *Instruction levels:* pre-school, primary, elementary. *Curriculum:* half day classes; annual basis. *Waiting period for enrollment:* applications taken in Spring for September enrollment: *Average annual enrollment:* 64 students. *Individual tutoring:* presented as an adjunct to the curriculum.

TESTING FACILITIES: Intelligence, achievement, and learning testing programs available by referral (testing done at Governor Medical Center).

FACULTY: School is oriented to inter-discipline cooperation. *Professional services available to faculty:* neurology, psychology, audiometry, pediatric, visual training, optometry, psychiatric, endocrinology, speech and language therapy, occupational therapy, physical therapy. *Faculty-student ratio:* 1:6 for regular; 1:1 and 1:4 for tutorial. *Faculty qualifications:* entire staff has had graduate level training in learning disabilities; 1 staff member holds a Masters Degree in learning disabilities.

SPECIAL INFORMATION: Regular classes meet three hours a day – 5 days a week, this is considered a full school day. Majority of tutition is funded by cities in Rhode Island and/or the Commonwealth of Massachusetts, as this facility is a part of an over-all program designed to help children with minimal learning disorders.

University of Rhode Island
Department of Education
Reading Center
Kingston, Rhode Island 02881
Director: Dr. Leonard W. Joll

DIAGNOSTIC FACILITIES: *Diagnostic facilities offered:* dyslexia (genetic or developmental), minimal brain damage syndromes, slow learner. *Referral sources:* pediatrician, school – public and private, psychologist, parent. *Ages accepted:* 6 years to over 20 years. *Waiting period for first appointment:* Autumn – 3-8 weeks; Spring – 3-8 weeks; Summer – 3-8 weeks. *Staff and orientation:* emphasis in the psychological and educational areas. *Professional services available:* psychology, audiometry, ophthalmology, optometry. *Average annual case load:* 35-plus – majority in the slow learner category.

TESTING FACILITIES: Testing program available.

EDUCATIONAL FACILITIES: *Remedial/developmental facilities:* dyslexia, minimal brain damage syndromes, slow learner. *Instruction levels:* primary, elementary, junior and senior high. *Curriculum:* tutorial only; annual basis. *Waiting period for enrollment:* Autumn – 3-8 weeks; Spring – 3-8 weeks; Summer – 3-8 weeks. *Average annual enrollment:* 35-plus students – majority in the slow learner category. *Program limits:* no maximum time a student may be enrolled for a remedial program. *Staff:* majority of staff have completed pertinent graduate courses and have had 2 or more years practical experience.

Special Information: Re: personnel----this facility are unique in that they have a sum total of 88 years experience in the area of reading disabilities.

SOUTH CAROLINA

University of South Carolina
School of Education
Reading Clinic
Columbia, South Carolina 29208
Director: Paul C. Berg

Diagnostic Facilities: *Diagnostic facilities offered:* dyslexia (genetic or developmental). *Referral sources:* pediatrician, school—public and private, psychiatrist, psychologist, parent, health agencies. *Ages accepted:* 3 years to 6 years (rarely); 6 years to over 20 years. *Waiting period for first appointment:* 6-month waiting period for the Autumn, Spring, and Summer sessions. *Staff and orientation:* a total child, multi-discipline team approach; with emphasis in the educational area. *Professional services available:* psychology, and audiometry—occasionally; visual training and optometry—currently but not usually. *Average annual case load:* 120.

Testing Facilities: Strong testing program available.

Educational Facilities: *Remedial/developmental facilities:* for the aphasias, dyslexia (genetic or developmental), minimal brain damage syndromes, slow learner, emotionally disturbed (moderate). *Instruction levels:* primary, elementary, junior and senior high, adult rehabilitation. *Curriculum:* tutorial only; summer only. *Waiting period for enrollment:* Autumn—9 months, Spring—5 months, Summer—no waiting or 12 months. *Average annual enrollment:* 60 students. *Program limits:* no maximum time a student may be enrolled for a remedial program. (20 to 40 sessions is the usual amount—minimum enrollment is 20 sessions.) *Staff:* entire staff has completed pertinent graduate courses and the majority have had 2 or more years practical experience.

SOUTH DAKOTA

Augustana College
Crippled Children's Hospital and School
Department of Speech Education
Sioux Falls, South Dakota

Diagnostic Facilities: *Diagnostic facilities are offered for:* aphasias, dyslexia (genetic or developmental), speech (developmental), minimal brain damage syndromes, slow learner. *Referral sources:* pediatrician, school—public and private, psychiatrist, psychologist, parent, minister. *Ages accepted:* 3 years to 20 years. *Waiting period for first appointment:* short waiting period. *Staff and orientation:* neurological, psychological, pediatric, educational and psychiatric. *Professional services available:* neurology, psychology, audiometry, pediatric, ophthalmology, visual training, optometry, psychiatric, endocrinology. *Annual case load:* no figures given.

Testing Facilities: Testing program available with off-campus referrals made.

Educational Facilities: No information given.

University of South Dakota
Department of Speech
Speech and Hearing Clinic
Vermillion, South Dakota
Director: Sylvester Clifford

DIAGNOSTIC FACILITIES: *Diagnostic facilities offered:* the aphasias, speech (developmental), minimal brain damage syndromes, slow learner. *Referral sources:* pediatrician, school – public and private, psychiatrist, psychologist, parent, neurologist. *Ages accepted:* all ages. *Waiting period for first appointment:* 2 weeks. *Staff and orientation:* a total child, multi-discipline team approach. *Professional services available:* psychology, audiometry, consulting otologist, speech pathology, physical therapy, remedial reading,and arithmetic. *Average annual case load:* not given.

TESTING FACILITIES: Strong testing program available.

EDUCATIONAL FACILITIES: *Remedial/developmental facilities:* the aphasias, dyslexia (genetic or developmental), speech (developmental), minimal brain damage syndromes, slow learner, emotionally disturbed (moderate). *Instruction levels:* all ages. *Curriculum:* tutorial only, therapy only in most cases; year around. *Waiting period for enrollment:* 2 weeks. *Average annual enrollment:* 24-36 students. *Program limits:* no maximum time a student may be enrolled for a remedial program. *Staff:* majority of staff have had 2 or more years practical experience.

TENNESSEE

The Bill Wilkerson Hearing and Speech Center
1114 19th Avenue, South
Nashville, Tennessee
Director: Freeman McConnell, Ph.D.

DIAGNOSTIC FACILITIES: *Diagnostic facilities offered:* the aphasias, speech (developmental), minimal brain damage syndromes. *Referral sources:* pediatrician, school – public and private, psychiatrist, psychologist, parent, neurology, otolaryngology. *Ages accepted:* all ages. *Waiting period for first appointment:* Autumn – 3-12 weeks; Spring – 3-12 weeks; Summer – 3-12 weeks. *Staff and orientation:* a total child, multi-discipline team approach. *Professional services available:* audiology, language pathology, speech pathology. *Average annual case load:* 620 – majority in the speech category.

TESTING FACILITIES: Testing programs available.

EDUCATIONAL FACILITIES: *Remedial/developmental facilities:* the aphasias, speech (developmental), minimal brain damage syndromes. *Instruction levels:* all ages. *Curriculum:* tutorial only; annual basis. *Waiting period for enrollment:* Autumn – 3-12 weeks; Spring – 1-12 weeks; Summer – 3-12 weeks. *Average annual enrollment:* not given. *Program limits:* no limits. *Staff:* majority have completed pertinent graduate courses and have had 2 or more years practical experience.

East Tennessee State University
Department of Special Education
Johnson City, Tennessee 37601
Director: Sol Cedler, Ph.D.

DIAGNOSTIC FACILITIES: *Diagnostic facilities offered:* the aphasias, dyslexia (genetic or developmental), speech (developmental), minimal brain damage syndromes, slow learner. *Referral sources:* pediatrician, school – public and private, psychiatrist, psychologist, parent. *Ages accepted:* all ages. *Waiting period for first appointment:* Autumn – 1 month; Spring – 1 month; Summer – 1 month. *Staff and orientation:* emphasis in the psychological and educational areas. *Professional services available:* neurology, audiometry, pediatric, ophthalmology, optometry, psychiatric, endocrinology. *Average annual case load:* no figures given – varies.

TESTING FACILITIES: Testing program available.

EDUCATIONAL FACILITIES: *Remedial/developmental facilities:* the aphasias, speech (developmental), minimal brain damage syndromes, slow learner. *Instruction levels:* all ages. *Curriculum:* tutorial only; annual basis. *Waiting period for enrollment:* Autumn – 1 month;

Spring – 1 month; Summer – 1 month. *Average annual enrollment:* no figures given – varies. *Program limits:* no maximum time a student may be enrolled for a remedial program. *Staff:* majority of staff have had 2 or more years practical experience.

Memphis Speech and Hearing Center
807 Jefferson Avenue
Memphis, Tennessee 38105
Director: John A. Irwin

DIAGNOSTIC FACILITIES: *Diagnostic facilities are offered for:* the aphasias, dyslexia (genetic or developmental), speech (developmental), minimal brain damage syndromes, slow learner. *Referral sources:* pediatrician, school – public and private, psychiatrist, psychologist, parent, physician. *Ages accepted:* all ages. *Waiting period for first appointment:* Autumn – 1 month, Spring – 1 month, Summer – 1 month. *Staff and orientation:* neurological, psychological, pediatric – with speech and/or hearing problems involved. *Professional services available:* psychology, audiometry, speech, language. *Average annual case load:* 400 – majority in the speech category.

TESTING FACILITIES: Strong testing program available.

EDUCATIONAL FACILITIES: *Remedial/developmental facilities offered for:* the aphasias, dyslexia (genetic or developmental), speech (developmental), minimal brain damage syndromes, slow learner. *Instruction levels:* any age (if speech, language and/or hearing problems involved). *Curriculum:* tutorial only; annual basis. *Waiting period for enrollment:* Autumn – 1 month, Spring – 1 month, Summer – 1 month. *Average annual enrollment:* 400 students – majority in the speech category. *Program limits:* no maximum time a student may be enrolled for a remedial program. *Staff:* majority of staff have had 2 or more years practical experience.

Peabody College
Child Study Center
Box 158
Nashville, Tennessee
Director: Donald Neville

DIAGNOSTIC FACILITIES: *Diagnostic facilities are offered for:* dyslexia (genetic or developmental), minimal brain damage syndromes, slow learners, psychiatric. *Referral sources:* pediatrician, school – public and private, psychiatrist, psychologist, parent. *Ages accepted:* 3 years to 16 years. *Waiting period for first appointment:* Autumn – 4-6 weeks, Spring – 8-12 weeks, Summer – 6 weeks. *Staff and orientation:* neurology, psychology, education. *Professional services available:* psychology, pediatrics, psychiatrics. *Average annual case load:* no figure given.

TESTING FACILITIES: Testing program available.

EDUCATIONAL FACILITIES: *Remedial/developmental programs offered:* dyslexia (genetic or developmental), minimal brain damage syndromes, slow learner, emotionally disturbed (moderate and severe). *Instruction levels:* primary, elementary, junior high, senior high. *Curriculum:* tutorial only; annual basis. *Waiting time for enrollment:* Autumn – 4-6 weeks, Spring – 8-12 weeks, Summer – 6 weeks. *Average annual enrollment:* not given. *Program limits:* no maximum time a student may be enrolled for a remedial program. *Staff:* majority of staff members have had 2 or more years practical experience.

SPECIAL INFORMATION: Portion of tutoring is done by graduate students under supervision. Center is a teacher training facility.

Southern College of Optometry
Department of Vision Training
1245 Madison
Memphis, Tennessee 38104
Director; Harvey T. Brown, O.D.

Diagnostic Facilities: *Diagnostic facilities offered:* minimal brain damage syndromes, slow learner. *Referral sources:* pediatrician, school—public and private, psychiatrist, psychologist, parent, optometrist. *Ages accepted:* all ages. *Waiting period for first appointment:* 1 week waiting for Autumn, Spring, and Summer sessions. *Staff and orientation:* emphasis in the visual-motor pediatric area. *Professional services available:* visual training, optometry. *Average annual case load:* 300—majority in the slow learner category.

Testing Facilities: Visual testing program available.

Educational Facilities: *Remedial/developmental facilities:* minimal brain damage syndromes, slow learner. *Instruction levels:* pre-school, primary, elementary, junior and senior high. *Curriculum:* full day—full curriculum; annual basis. *Waiting period for enrollment:* 1 week waiting for the Autumn, Spring and Summer sessions. *Average annual enrollment:* 300 students—majority in the slow learner category. *Program limits:* no maximum time a student may be enrolled for a remedial program. *Staff:* majority of staff members have completed pertinent graduate courses and have had 2 or more years practical experience.

Tennessee Technological University
Department of Educational Psychology & Guidance
Counseling Center-Human Development Laboratory
Cookeville, Tennessee 38501
Directors: John Flanders, Sherwell K. Tolleson

Diagnostic Facilities: *Diagnostic facilities are offered for:* minimal brain damage syndromes, slow learner. *Referral sources:* school—private, psychologist, parent. *Ages accepted:* 6 years to 20 years. *Waiting period for first appointment:* Autumn—1 week, Spring—1 week, Summer—1 week. *Staff and orientation:* psychological, educational. *Professional services available:* psychology, audiometry. *Average annual case load:* 60—majority in the slow learner category.

Testing Facilities: Strong testing program.

Educational Facilities: *Remedial/developmental programs offered for:* slow learner, emotionally disturbed (moderate). *Instruction levels:* junior high, above 18 years—attending college (developmental reading). *Curriculum:* half day, summer only. *Waiting time for enrollment:* Autumn—1 month, Spring—1 month, Summer 1—month. *Average annual enrollment:* 300 in the slow learner category. *Program limits:* no maximum time a student may be enrolled. *Staff:* majority of staff members have completed pertinent graduate courses and have had 2 or more years practical experience.

University of Tennessee
Department of Curriculum and Instruction
College of Education
Reading Center
Knoxville, Tennessee
Director: W. C. Davies, Ph.D.

Diagnostic Facilities: *Diagnostic facilities offered:* the aphasias, dyslexia (genetic or developmental), speech (developmental), minimal brain damage syndromes, slow learner, psychiatric disorders. *Referral sources:* school—public and private, psychiatrist, psychologist, parent. *Ages accepted:* 6 years to 16 years. *Waiting period for enrollment:* Autumn—1 quarter, Spring—1 quarter, Summer—no Summer program. *Staff and orientation:* emphasis in the educational area. *Professional services available:* neurology, psychology, audiometry, psychiatric. *Average annual case load:* not given.

Testing Facilities: Testing program available.

Educational Facilities: None available in department—referrals made to on-campus facilities and other.

Webb School of Knoxville
Route 18
Knoxville, Tennessee
Director: Robert Webb

EDUCATIONAL FACILITIES: *Remedial/developmental program offered:* reading (developmental). *Instruction levels:* junior and senior high. *Curriculum:* full day—full curriculum; annual basis. *Waiting period for enrollment:* 9 months. *Average annual enrollment:* not given. *Individual tutoring:* included automatically in students curriculum.

TESTING FACILITIES: Developmental reading testing program available.

FACULTY: School is oriented to inter-discipline cooperation. *Professional services available to faculty:* none given. *Faculty-student ratio:* 1:10. *Faculty qualifications:* 1 staff member has had specialized training in remedial reading; and 1 staff member has had graduate level training in reading.

TEXAS

Abilene Christian College
Department of Speech
Station ACC
Abilene, Texas 79601
Director: Ima F. Clevenger, Ph.D.

DIAGNOSTIC FACILITIES: *Diagnostic facilities are offered for:* the aphasias, dyslexia (genetic or developmental), speech (developmental), minimal brain damage syndromes, slow learner. *Referral sources:* pediatrician, school—public and private, psychiatrist, psychologist. *Ages accepted:* infants to elderly. *Waiting period for first appointment:* depends upon the nature and severity of the patient. *Staff and orientation:* a total child, multi-discipline team approach, with emphasis on the neurological, psychological, pediatric, educational. *Professional services available:* neurology, psychology, audiometry, pediatric, ophthalmology, physical therapy, occupational therapy, speech therapy, orthopedics and language therapy. *Average annual case load:* 205—majority in the dyslexia category.

TESTING FACILITIES: Testing available, but no information given.

EDUCATIONAL FACILITIES: Information not given.

SPECIAL INFORMATION: West Texas Rehabilitation Center handles the clinical practicum.

Stephen F. Austin
Post Office Box 6160
Nacogdoches, Texas
Director: J. Lewis

DIAGNOSTIC FACILITIES: *Diagnostic facilities offered:* minimal brain damage syndromes, slow learner. *Referral sources:* pediatrician, school—public and private, psychiatrist, psychologist, parent. *Ages accepted:* all ages. *Waiting period for first appointment:* no waiting period. *Staff and orientation:* emphasis in the psychological area. *Professional services available:* psychology, audiometry. *Average annual case load:* 6.

TESTING FACILITIES: Testing program available.

EDUCATIONAL FACILITIES: None available.

Baylor University
Office of Testing
131 Burleson Hall
Waco, Texas
Director: Dr. J. V. West

DIAGNOSTIC FACILITIES: *Diagnostic facilities offered:* speech (developmental), minimal brain damage syndromes, slow learner. *Referral sources:* pediatrician, school – public and private, psychiatrist, psychologist, parent. *Ages accepted:* 3 years to 20 years. *Waiting period for first appointment:* Autumn – 1 week, Spring – 1 week, Summer – 1 week. *Staff and orientation:* emphasis in the psychological and educational areas. *Professional services available:* psychology, audiometry. *Average annual case load:* 75.

TESTING FACILITIES: Testing program available.

EDUCATIONAL FACILITIES: *Remedial/developmental facilities:* speech (developmental), minimal brain damage syndromes. *Instruction level:* pre-school, primary. *Curriculum:* annual basis. *Waiting period for enrollment:* Autumn – 1 week, Spring – 1 week, Summer – 1 week. *Average annual enrollment:* not given. *Program limits:* 1 year is the maximum time a student may be enrolled for a remedial program. *Staff:* majority of staff have had 2 or more years practical experience.

The Callier Hearing and Speech Center
Division of Audiology and Speech Pathology
3819 Maple Avenue
Dallas, Texas 75219
Director: Aram Glorig, M.D.
Divisional Director: John P. Moncur, Ph.D.

DIAGNOSTIC FACILITIES: *Diagnostic facilities offered for:* the aphasias, speech (developmental). *Referral sources:* pediatrician, school – public and private, psychiatrist, psychologist, parent, outpatient clinics of all local hospitals. *Ages accepted:* all ages. *Waiting period for first appointment:* 3 weeks or less. *Staff and orientation:* a total child, multi-discipline team approach; with emphasis in the psychological area. *Professional services available:* neurology, psychology, audiometry, pediatric, psychiatric. *Average annual case load:* 1,000 – majority in the speech category.

TESTING FACILITIES: Testing program available.

EDUCATIONAL FACILITIES: None available.

Edgemoor School
2711 Fountain View
Houston, Texas
Director; Mrs. Lee Crawford

EDUCATIONAL FACILITIES: *Remedial/developmental programs:* the aphasias, dyslexia (genetic or developmental), speech (developmental), minimal brain damage syndromes, slow learner, emotionally disturbed (moderate). *Instruction levels;* pre-school, primary, elementary, junior and senior high. *Curriculum:* all levels (3 years to 18 years) ungraded; annual basis. *Waiting period for enrollment:* none. *Average annual enrollment:* 65 students – majority in the minimal brain damaged category. *Individual tutoring:* depends on child's needs – included automatically in curriculum, or presented as an adjunct to the curriculum.

TESTING FACILITIES: Strong testing program available.

FACULTY: School is oriented to inter-discipline cooperation. *Professional services available to faculty:* neurology, psychology, audiometry, pediatric, ophthalmology, visual training, optometry, psychiatric. *Faculty-student ratio:* 1:5. *Faculty qualifications:* 75% of staff have had specialized training in remedial reading; graduate level training has been had by 75% of the staff in reading. 10% in speech, 50% in learning disabilities; 70% of staff hold Masters Degrees.

SPECIAL INFORMATION: School is transitional in that it offers – strengthening, remediation, and educational therapy in order to return the child to regular classes in public school.

Our Lady of the Lake College
Harry Jersig Speech and Hearing Center
411 S.W. 24th Street
San Antonio, Texas 78207
Director: Sister Mary Arthur Carrow

DIAGNOSTIC FACILITIES: *Diagnostic facilities are offered for:* the aphasias, dyslexia (genetic or developmental), speech (developmental), minimal brain damage syndromes. *Referral sources:* pediatrician, school – public and private, psychiatrist, psychologist, parent. *Ages accepted:* all ages. *Waiting period for first appointment:* Autumn – 3 weeks, Spring 3 – weeks, Summer – 3 weeks. *Staff and orientation:* a total child, multi-discipline team approach. *Professional services available:* psychology, audiometry, language, speech, and academic. *Average annual case load:* 508 – majority in the speech, the aphasias, and minimal brain damaged categories.

TESTING FACILITIES: Strong testing program available.

EDUCATIONAL FACILITIES: *Remedial/developmental programs offered:* the aphasias, dyslexia (genetic or developmental), speech (developmental), minimal brain damage syndromes. *Instruction levels:* pre-school, primary, elementary, junior high, adult rehabilitation. *Curriculum:* tutorial and half day; annual basis. *Waiting time for enrollment:* Autumn – 2 weeks, Spring – 2 weeks, Summer – none. *Average annual enrollment:* 125 students – majority in the speech (developmental) category. *Program limits:* no maximum time a student may be enrolled for a remedial program. *Staff:* majority of staff members have completed pertinent graduate courses and have had 2 or more years practical experience.

Houston Speech and Hearing Center
1343 Moursund
Houston, Texas 77025
Director: Jack L. Bangs

EDUCATIONAL FACILITIES: *Remedial/developmental programs offered:* the aphasias, dyslexia (genetic or developmental), speech (developmental), minimal brain damage syndromes, slow learner. *Instruction level:* pre-school. *Curriculum:* various daily classes available; annual basis. *Waiting period for enrollment:* September – 3 weeks; January – 6 weeks; Summer program – 3 weeks. *Average annual enrollment:* 190-200 students. *Individual tutoring:* presented as an adjunct to the curriculum.

TESTING FACILITIES: Testing program available.

FACULTY: School is oriented to inter-discipline cooperation. *Professional services available to faculty:* neurology, psychology, audiometry, pediatric, ophthalmology, visual training, optometry, psychiatric, endocrinology, physical therapy, occupational therapy. *Faculty-student ratio:* 1:8. *Faculty qualifications:* 20% of the staff have had specialized training in remedial reading; graduate level training has been had by 5% of the staff in reading, by 100% of the staff in speech, and by 20% of the staff in learning disabilities; Masters Degrees are held by 100% of the staff for speech, and by 20% of the staff for learning disabilities.

SPECIAL INFORMATION: Center functions in a multi-disciplinary environment, and concentrates on the assessment and training of pre-school children with language and learning disorders. Training follows a pre-academic curriculum guide devised at the center.

Southern Methodist University
Department of Education
Reading Clinic
Dallas, Texas 75222
Director: Dorothy Kendall Bracken

DIAGNOSTIC FACILITIES: *Diagnostic facilities offered:* aphasias, dyslexia (genetic or developmental), speech (developmental), minimal brain damage syndromes, slow learner,

Referral sources: pediatrician, school – public and private, psychiatrist, psychologist, parent, teachers, principal, nurses, social workers, friends, ophthalmologist. *Ages accepted:* 6 years to over 20 years. *Waiting period for first appointment:* Autumn – 3 months; Spring – 3 months; Summer – 5 months. *Staff and orientation:* a total child, multi-discipline team approach; with emphasis in the educational area. *Professional services available:* neurology, psychology, audiometry, pediatric, ophthalmology, visual training, optometry, psychiatric, endocrinology. *Average annual case load:* 293 – majority in the aphasias category.

TESTING FACILITIES: Strong testing program available.

EDUCATIONAL FACILITIES: *Remedial/developmental facilities:* aphasias, dyslexia, speech, minimal brain damage syndromes, emotionally disturbed (moderate). *Instruction levels:* all ages from primary grade on up. *Curriculum:* tutorial only; annual basis. *Program limits:* 2 years is the maximum time a student may be enrolled for a remedial program. *Staff:* majority of staff have had 2 or more years practical experience.

SPECIAL INFORMATION: Clinic is further oriented to the proposition that causes of disabilities are multiple and may also include factors which were not listed in questionnaire – such as visual, educational, social, environmental, etc. Facility has been in operation for over 20 years.

Southwest Texas State College
San Marcos, Texas 78666
Director: Empress Y. Zedler, Ph.D.

EDUCATIONAL FACILITIES: *Remedial/developmental programs offered:* the aphasias, dyslexia (genetic or developmental), speech (developmental), minimal brain damage syndromes, slow learner. *Instruction levels:* all ages. *Curriculum:* tutorial only, and half day; annual basis, and summer program. *Waiting period for enrollment:* none. *Average annual enrollment:* 20 students. *Individual tutoring:* included automatically in students curriculum.

TESTING FACILITIES: Testing program available.

FACULTY: School oriented to inter-discipline cooperation. *Professional services available to faculty:* neurology, psychology, audiometry, pediatric, ophthalmology, psychiatric. *Faculty-student ratio:* 1:20. *Faculty qualifications:* entire staff (4) has had specialized training in remedial reading; has had graduate level training in reading, speech, and learning disabilities; Masters Degrees are held by1 member of the staff for reading, by 4 members of the staff for speech and learning disabilities.

Texas Woman's University Institute for Mental and Physical Development
Drawer E TWU Station
Denton, Texas
Director: Ted. W. Booker, Ph.D.

DIAGNOSTIC FACILITIES: *Diagnostic facilities are offered for:* the aphasias, dyslexia (genetic or developmental), speech (developmental), minimal brain damage syndromes, slow learner. *Referral sources:* any source. *Ages accepted:* 3 years to 20 years. *Waiting period for first appointment:* 3-week waiting period for Autumn, Spring, and Summer sessions. *Staff and orientation:* a total child, multi-discipline team approach. *Professional services available:* psychology, audiometry, pediatric, psychiatric, special educators. The services of neurology, ophthalmology and optometry available on consultation. *Average annual case load:* 50 – majority in the aphasias category.

TESTING FACILITIES: Strong testing program available.

EDUCATIONAL FACILITIES: *Remedial/developmental facilities are offered for:* the aphasias, dyslexia (genetic or developmental), speech (developmental), minimal brain damage syndromes, slow learner, emotionally disturbed (moderate). *Instruction levels:* pre-school, primary, elementary, junior and senior high, and above 18 – attending college (developmental reading). *Curriculum:* annual basis. *Waiting period for enrollment:* 3-week waiting period for Autumn, Spring, and Summer. *Average annual enrollment:* 78 students – majority in the slow learner category. *Program limits:* no maximum time a student may be enrolled for a remedial program. *Staff:* majority of staff members have completed pertinent graduate courses and have had 2 or more years practical experience.

SPECIAL INFORMATION: The institute works with all types of individuals (although limited in number) with learning disorders or handicapping conditions by combining the medical, psychological and educational approach in a multi-disciplinary setting to the diagnosis, treatment and education; for the purpose of training university student in 14 disciplines to work with handicapped children.

Tyler Language Research and Training Center
1600 Boldt at 5th Street
Tyler, Texas
Director: Clifton W. Wolf, M.S.

EDUCATIONAL FACILITIES: *Remedial/developmental programs offered:* dyslexia (genetic or developmental). *Instruction levels:* primary, elementary, junior and senior high, above 18 – college preparatory. *Curriculum:* tutorial only; annual basis. *Waiting period for enrollment:* September – 2 months, January – 2 months, Summer program – none. *Average annual enrollment:* 11 students. *Individual tutoring:* included automatically in students curriculum.

TESTING FACILITIES: Strong testing program available.

FACULTY: School is oriented to inter-discipline cooperation. *Professional services available to faculty:* neurology, psychology, audiometry, pediatric, ophthalmology, optometry, psychiatric, endocrinology. *Faculty-student ratio:* 1:1. *Faculty qualifications:* entire staff has had specialized training in remedial reading; entire staff has had graduate level training in reading. All teachers (certified) have received 2 years of additional training in language therapy.

SPECIAL INFORMATION: Diagnostic services for children and adults with learning disorders and language re-training for those with specific dyslexia is offered.

University of Texas
Department of Pediatrics
Medical Branch
Child Development Clinic
Galveston, Texas 77550
Director: ArrNell Boelsche, M.D.

DIAGNOSTIC FACILITIES: *Diagnostic facilities are offered for:* the aphasias, dyslexia (genetic or developmental), speech (developmental), minimal brain damage syndromes, slow learner, psychiatric. *Referral sources:* pediatrician, psychiatrist, physician. *Ages accepted:* 3 years to 16 years. *Waiting period for first appointment:* 1-2 month waiting period. *Staff and orientation:* a total child, multi-discipline team approach; with emphasis on neurology, psychology, and pediatrics. *Professional services available:* neurology, psychology, audiometry, pediatrics, ophthalmology, psychiatrics, endocrinology, and any other services available in general medical school setting. *Average annual case load:* 307.

TESTING FACILITIES: Strong testing program offered.

EDUCATIONAL FACILITIES: None available.

SPECIAL REQUIREMENTS: Medical, social service, nursing and communication disorder evaluations done on each child.

SPECIAL INFORMATION: Testing battery depends on the child and his problems; projective techniques are also used.

University of Houston at Memorial Baptist Hospital
Speech Clinic
1100 Louisiana
Houston, Texas
Director: Donna R. Fox, Ph.D.

DIAGNOSTIC FACILITIES: *Diagnostic facilities are offered for:* the aphasias, speech (developmental). *Referral sources:* pediatrician, school—public and private, psychiatrist, psychologist, parent, speech and hearing agencies, vocational rehabilitation. *Ages accepted:* all ages. *Waiting period for first appointment:* Autumn—2 weeks. *Staff and orientation:* a total child, multi-discipline team approach. *Professional services available:* neurology, psychology, audiometry, pediatric, visual training, psychiatric. *Average annual case load:* 110—majority in the speech category.

TESTING FACILITIES: Strong testing program available.

EDUCATIONAL FACILITIES: *Remedial/developmental facilities offered:* for the aphasias and speech (developmental). *Instruction levels:* all ages—from pre-school through adult rehabilitation. *Curriculum:* tutorial only, annual basis. *Waiting period for enrollment:* Autumn—2 weeks; Spring—2 weeks; Summer—1 month. *Average annual enrollment:* 110 students—majority in the speech category. *Program limits:* no maximum time a student may be enrolled for a remedial program. *Staff:* majority of staff members are currently enrolled in graduate school and have had less than 2 years practical experience.

University of Texas
College of Education
Learning Disabilities Center
Austin, Texas 78712
Director: W. R. Harmer

DIAGNOSTIC FACILITIES: *Diagnostic facilities offered:* the aphasias, dyslexia (genetic or developmental), minimal brain damage syndromes, slow learner. *Referral sources:* pediatrician, school—public and private, psychiatrist, psychologist, parent. *Ages accepted:* 6 years to 20 years. *Waiting period for first appointment:* Autumn—1 month, Spring—1 month, Summer—1 month. *Staff and orientation:* emphasis in the psychological and educational areas. *Professional services available:* psychology, audiometry. *Average annual case load:* not given.

TESTING FACILITIES: Strong testing program available.

EDUCATIONAL FACILITIES: *Remedial/developmental facilities:* the aphasias, dyslexia (genetic or developmental), minimal brain damage syndromes. *Instruction levels:* primary, elementary, junior high. *Curriculum:* tutorial only; annual basis. *Waiting period for enrollment:* Autumn—6-9 months; Spring—6-9 months; Summer—6-9 months. *Average annual enrollment:* 38 students—majority in the dyslexia category. *Program limits:* no maximum time a student may be enrolled for a remedial program. *Staff:* majority of staff have completed pertinent graduate courses and have had 2 or more years practical experience.

University of Texas
Medical Branch
Department of Neurology and Psychiatry
Division of Child Psychiatry
Galveston, Texas
Director: Henry L. Burks, M.D.

DIAGNOSTIC FACILITIES: *Diagnostic facilities are offered for:* minimal brain damage syndromes, slow learner, psychiatric. *Referral sources:* pediatrician, school—public and private, psychiatrist, psychologist, parent, social agency. *Ages accepted:* 3 years to 16 years. *Waiting period for first appointment:* Autumn—1 month, Spring—1 month, Summer—2 weeks. *Staff and orientation:* psychiatric. *Professional services available:* neurology, psychology, audiometry, pediatric, ophthalmology, psychiatric, endocrinology, special education. *Average annual case load:* 350.

TESTING FACILITIES: Testing information not given.

EDUCATIONAL FACILITIES: *Remedial/developmental programs offered:* minimal brain damage syndromes, slow learner, emotionally disturbed (moderate and severe) *Instruction levels:* pre-school, primary, elementary, junior high, senior high. *Curriculum:* half day;

annual basis. *Waiting time for enrollment:* Autumn – 6 weeks, Spring – 6 weeks, Summer – 6 weeks. *Average annual enrollment:* unavailable. *Program limits:* no maximum time a student may be enrolled for a remedial program. *Staff:* majority of staff members are currently enrolled in graduate school and have had 2 or more years practical experience.

West Texas Rehabilitation Center
4601 Hartford
Abilene, Texas 79605
Director: Shelley V. Smith

EDUCATIONAL FACILITIES: *Remedial/developmental programs available:* the aphasias, dyslexia (genetic or developmental), speech (developmental). *Instruction levels:* all ages. *Curriculum:* tutorial only, half day classes, and full day – full curriculum; annual basis, and Summer only (for some). *Waiting period for enrollment:* no waiting after evaluations, for September, and January enrollment; no waiting for the Summer program. *Average annual enrollment:* 260 students – majority in the speech category. *Individual tutoring:* included automatically in students curriculum.

TESTING FACILITIES: Strong testing program available.

FACULTY: School oriented to inter-discipline cooperation. *Professional services available to faculty:* neurology, psychology, audiometry, pediatric, ophthalmology, endocrinology. *Faculty-student ratio:* 1:20. *Faculty qualifications:* 7 staff members have had specialized training in remedial reading; graduate level training has been had by 7 staff members in reading, by 5 staff members in speech, and by 7 staff members in learning disabilities; 1 staff member holds a Masters Degree in reading and speech.

West Texas State University
Department of Speech, Education and Psychology
Canyon, Texas 79016
Directors: Dr. Wendell Cain, Dr. Ruth Lowes

DIAGNOSTIC FACILITIES: *Diagnostic facilities offered for:* the aphasias, dyslexia (genetic or developmental), speech (developmental), minimal brain damage syndromes, slow learner. *Referral sources:* pediatrician, school – public and private, psychiatrist, psychologist. *Ages accepted:* 6 years to 16 years. *Waiting period for first appointment:* Autumn – 1 week, Spring – 1 week, Summer – 1 week. *Staff and orientation:* a total child, multi-discipline team approach: with emphasis in the psychological and educational areas. *Professional services available:* psychology, audiometry, visual training. *Average annual case load:* 206 – majority in the aphasias category.

TESTING FACILITIES: Strong testing program available.

SPECIAL INFORMATION: Emotional problems referred to psychiatric clinic in vicinity.

EDUCATIONAL FACILITIES: None available.

UTAH

Brigham Young University
Education Center
120 College Hall, BYU
Provo, Utah

DIAGNOSTIC FACILITIES: *Diagnostic facilities are offered for:* dyslexia (genetic or developmental), minimal brain damage syndromes, slow learner. *Referral sources:* pediatrician, school – public and private, psychiatrist, psychologist, parent. *Ages accepted:* 3 years to over 20 years. *Waiting period for first appointment:* Autumn – 1 month, Spring – 1 month, Summer – 2 weeks. *Staff and orientation:* a total child, multi-discipline team approach through consultation with emphasis in psychological and educational areas. *Professional services available:* neurology, psychology, audiometry, pediatric, ophthalmology, visual training, optometry, psychiatric, endocrinology. *Average annual case load:* 100—majority in the dyslexia category.

TESTING FACILITIES: Testing program available.

EDUCATIONAL FACILITIES: *Remedial/developmental facilities:* dyslexia (genetic or developmental), speech (developmental), minimal brain damage syndromes, slow learner, emotionally disturbed (moderate). *Instruction levels:* primary, elementary, junior and senior high, and adult rehabilitation. *Curriculum:* various classes a day; annual basis and Summer programs. *Waiting period for enrollment:* Autumn—1 month, Spring—1 month, Summer—2 weeks. *Average annual enrollment:* 275 students—majority in the dyslexia category. *Program limits:* no maximum time a student may be enrolled for a remedial program. *Staff:* majority of staff members have had 2 or more years practical experience.

SPECIAL INFORMATION: Educational programs vary greatly according to the need of each child. The goals of the center are: training of teachers and specialty workers; research into evaluational and treatment techniques for learning disability children; and service to children with special needs.

Northern Utah Mental Health Clinic
160 North Main Street
Logan, Utah

DIAGNOSTIC FACILITIES: *Diagnostic facilities offered:* minimal brain damage syndromes, slow learner, psychiatric disorders. *Referral sources:* pediatrician, school—public and private, psychiatrist, psychologist, parent. *Ages accepted:* all ages. *Waiting period for first appointment:* one month. *Staff and orientation:* a total child, multi-discipline team approach; with emphasis in the neurological, psychological, and psychiatric areas. *Professional services available:* neurology, psychology. *Average annual case load:* not given.

TESTING FACILITIES: Testing program available.

EDUCATIONAL FACILITIES: None available.

University of Utah
Speech and Hearing Center
1699 East 5th Street, South
Salt Lake City, Utah
Director: M. J. Macham, Ph.D.

DIAGNOSTIC FACILITIES: *Diagnostic facilities are offered for:* the aphasias, dyslexia (genetic or developmental), speech (developmental), minimal brain damage syndromes, slow learner, psychiatric disorders. *Referral sources:* pediatrician, neurologist, school—public and private, psychiatrist, psychologist, parent. *Ages accepted:* all ages. *Waiting period for first appointment:* Autumn—1 week, Spring—1 week, Summer—1 week. *Staff and orientation:* emphasis in the psychological and educational areas. *Professional services available:* neurology, psychology, audiometry, pediatric, ophthalmology, visual training, optometry, psychiatric, endocrinology, orthopedic, educational. *Average annual case load:* 194.

TESTING FACILITIES: Strong testing program available.

EDUCATIONAL FACILITIES: *Remedial/developmental programs offered:* the aphasias, dyslexia (genetic or developmental), speech (developmental), minimal brain damage syndromes, slow learner, emotionally disturbed (moderate and severe). *Instruction levels:* pre-school, primary, elementary, junior high, senior high, above 18—attending college (developmental reading), adult rehabilitation. *Curriculum:* tutorial only during the academic year; half day curriculum during Summer session. *Waiting time for enrollment:* waiting period for Autumn, Spring, and Summer sessions varies from a few days to a full quarter. *Average annual enrollment:* 75-100 students. *Program limits:* no maximum time a student may be enrolled for a remedial program. *Staff:* majority of staff members have had 2 or more years practical experience.

University of Utah
Speech and Hearing Clinic
1699 East 5th South
Building 413
Salt Lake City, Utah
Director: Merlin J. Macham, Ph.D.

DIAGNOSTIC FACILITIES: *Diagnostic facilities offered:* the aphasias, dyslexia (genetic or developmental), speech (developmental), minimal brain damage syndromes. *Referral sources:* not given. *Ages accepted:* all ages. *Waiting period for first appointment:* Autumn – 3 weeks, Spring – 2 weeks, Summer – 2 weeks. *Staff and orientation:* emphasis in the psychological and educational areas. *Professional services available:* neurology, psychology, audiometry, pediatric, psychiatric, otolaryngology. *Average annual case load:* 100 – majority in the speech category.

TESTING FACILITIES: Testing program available.

EDUCATIONAL FACILITIES: *Remedial/developmental facilities:* the aphasias, dyslexia (genetic or developmental), speech (developmental), minimal brain damage syndromes. *Instruction levels:* pre-school, primary, elementary, junior and senior high, and adult rehabilitation. *Curriculum:* tutorial only; annual basis. *Waiting period for enrollment:* Autumn – 3 weeks, Spring – 2 weeks, Summer – 2 weeks. *Average annual enrollment:* 100 students – majority in the speech category. *Program limits:* no maximum time a student may be enrolled for a remedial program. *Staff:* majority of staff members have completed pertinent graduate courses and have had 2 or more years practical experience.

Youth Center
Utah State Hospital
Provo, Utah
Director: Eugene Faey, M.D.

EDUCATIONAL FACILITIES: *Remedial/developmental programs offered:* the aphasias, dyslexia (genetic or developmental), speech (developmental), minimal brain damage syndromes, slow learner, emotionally disturbed (moderate and severe). *Instruction levels:* primary, elementary, junior high, senior high. *Curriculum:* full day – full curriculum; annual basis. *Waiting period for enrollment:* no waiting period permitted, immediate enrollment *Average annual enrollment:* 60-70 students. *Individual tutoring:* presented as an adjunct to the curriculum.

TESTING FACILITIES: Testing program available.

FACULTY: School is oriented to inter-discipline cooperation. *Professional services available to faculty:* neurology, psychology, audiometry, ophthalmology, visual training, psychiatric, endocrinology (internal medicine). *Faculty-student ratio:* 1:8-1:10 (ratio reduced in younger age groups). *Faculty qualifications:* entire staff has had specialized training in remedial reading; entire staff has had graduate level training in reading and learning disabilities. 10% in speech; 1 member of the staff holds a Masters Degree in speech, and two in learing disabilities.

VERMONT

Children's Rehabilitation Center of the Vermont Association for the Crippled, Inc.
88 Park Street
Post Office Drawer 834
Rutland, Vermont 05701
Director: Miss Dorothy Smithson

DIAGNOSTIC FACILITIES: *Diagnostic facilities offered:* the aphasias, dyslexia (genetic or developmental), speech (developmental), minimal brain damage syndromes, slow learner. *Referral sources:* pediatrician, school – public and private, psychiatrist, psychologist, parent, public health nurse. *Ages accepted:* 3 years to 12 years. *Waiting period for first appointment:* Autumn—0-1 month; Spring—3-4 months; Summer—no services. *Staff and orientation:* a total child, multi-discipline team approach. *Professional services available:* neurology, psychology, audiometry, pediatric, ophthalmology, psychiatric, orthopedic. *Average annual case load:* 100.

TESTING FACILITIES: Strong testing program available.

EDUCATIONAL FACILITIES: *Remedial/developmental facilities:* the aphasias, dyslexia (genetic or developmental), minimal brain damage syndromes, slow learner. *Instruction levels:* pre-school, kindergarten, primary. *Curriculum:* half day, full day—full curriculum; annual basis. *Waiting period for enrollment:* waiting list. *Average annual enrollment:* 49 students. *Program limits:* no maximum time a student may be enrolled for a remedial program (not well equipped for adolescents). *Staff:* majority of staff have completed pertinent graduate courses and have had 2 or more years practical experience.

SPECIAL INFORMATION: The team of therapists and clinicians who do non-medical evaluations, also do therapy and teaching; thus the diagnostic approach is practical and undertaken only if it is expected that some remedial measure may be used following identification of the child's problem(s).

DeGoesbriand Memorial Hospital
Center for Disorders of Communication
Burlington, Vermont
Director: Frank J. Falck, Ph.D.

EDUCATIONAL FACILITIES: *Remedial/developmental programs offered:* the aphasias, dyslexia (genetic or developmental), speech (developmental), minimal brain damage syndromes, slow learner. *Instruction levels:* all ages. *Curriculum:* tutorial only, half day, and full day—full curriculum (1st grade only); annual basis. *Waiting period for enrollment:* varies. *Average annual enrollment:* 140 students—majority in the speech category. *Individual tutoring:* included automatically in students curriculum.

TESTING FACILITIES: Not given.

FACULTY: School is oriented to inter-discipline cooperation. *Professional services available to faculty:* neurology, psychology, audiometry, pediatric, ophthalmology, psychiatric, endocrinology. *Faculty-student ratio:* most 1:1; some classes—1:8. *Faculty qualifications:* 25% of staff have had specialized training in remedial reading; graduate level training has been had by 25% of staff in reading, by 75% of staff in speech, by 25% of staff in learning disabilities; Masters Degrees are held by 25% of staff for reading, by 50% of staff for speech.

Overlake Day School
545 South Prospect Street
Burlington, Vermont
Director: S. K. Robinson

EDUCATIONAL FACILITIES: *Remedial/developmental programs offered:* dyslexia (genetic or developmental), minimal brain damage syndromes, slow learner. *Instruction levels:* primary and elementary. *Curriculum;* full day—full curriculum; annual basis. *Waiting period for enrollment:* September-only admissions for full year. *Average annual enrollment:* 10 students. *Individual tutoring:* included automatically in students curriculum.

TESTING FACILITIES: Testing program available.

FACULTY: School is oriented to inter-discipline cooperation. *Professional services available to faculty:* neurology, psychology, audiometry, pediatric, ophthalmology, optometry, psychiatric. *Faculty-student ratio:* 1:4. *Faculty qualifications:* 15% of staff have had specialized training in remedial reading; graduage level training has been had by 10% of staff in reading, by 5% of staff in speech and learning disabilities; 5% of staff hold Masters Degrees in reading.

United Counseling Service of Bennington County, Inc.
Dewey Street
Bennington, Vermont
Director: Joseph LoPiccolo

DIAGNOSTIC FACILITIES: *Diagnostic facilities offered:* the aphasias, dyslexia (genetic or developmental), speech (developmental), minimal brain damage syndromes, slow learner, psychiatric disorders. *Referral sources:* pediatrician, school—public and private, psychiatrist, psychologist, parent, open referral. *Ages accepted:* all ages. *Waiting period for first appointment:* varies—no more than 2 months. *Staff and orientation:* a total child, multi-discipline team approach; with emphasis in the neurological, psychological, pediatric, psychiatric areas. *Professional services available:* neurology, psychology, pediatric, psychiatric. *Average annual case load:* 137—majority in the psychiatric category.

TESTING FACILITIES: Strong testing program available.

EDUCATIONAL FACILITIES: None available.

SPECIAL INFORMATION: Primarily work in psychiatric. Diagnostic screening facility for language and learning disorders with referral for more specialized studies and/or treatment.

VIRGINIA

Glagdin School and Camp, Inc.
Box 143, Route 4
Leesburg, Virginia
Director: Agnes Saiter

EDUCATIONAL FACILITIES: *Remedial/developmental programs:* dyslexia (genetic or developmental), minimal brain damage syndromes, slow learner, emotionally disturbed (moderate). *Instruction levels:* primary, elementary, junior high. *Curriculum:* tutorial only, full day—full curriculum. *Waiting period for enrollment:* varies. *Average annual enrollment:* 22 students—majority in the emotionally disturbed category. *Individual tutoring:* presented as an adjunct to the curriculum.

TESTING FACILITIES: Testing program available—included with admission.

FACULTY: Orientation of school not given. *Professional services available to faculty:* psychology. *Faculty-student ratio:* 1:8. *Faculty qualifications:* one-third of staff has had specialized training in remedial reading; one-third of staff has had graduate level training in reading

SPECIAL REQUIREMENTS: 5-day boarding school.

SPECIAL INFORMATION: Students' problems vary—some have no learning problems. Summer camps offer individual tutoring and developmental reading.

Hampton Roads Reading Improvement Center
530 East Queen Street
Hampton, Virginia
Director: Nancy Sherman

EDUCATIONAL FACILITIES: *Remedial/developmental programs offered:* dyslexia (genetic or developmental), slow learner, emotionally disturbed (moderate). *Instruction levels:* primary, elementary, junior and senior high, above 18-college preparatory. *Curriculum:* tutorial only; annual basis. *Waiting period for enrollment:* seldom have a waiting period—after testing, students are absorbed into program. *Average annual enrollment:* 37 students—majority in the dyslexia category. *Individual tutoring:* included automatically in students curriculum.

TESTING FACILITIES: Strong testing program available.

FACULTY: School orientation not given. *Professional services available to faculty:* neurology, psychology, psychiatric. *Faculty-student ratio:* 1:1. *Staff qualifications:* entire staff has had specialized training in remedial reading; 2 members of staff have had graduate level training in reading, and 2 in learning disabilities; 1 staff member holds a Masters Degree in reading.

Medical College of Virginia
Department of Neurology
Seizure Central Clinic (Adult)
1200 East Broad Street
Richmond, Virginia
Director: Dr. Carey Suter

DIAGNOSTIC FACILITIES: *Diagnostic facilities offered:* the aphasias, minimal brain damage syndromes, slow learner. *Referral sources:* pediatrician, psychiatrist, psychologist. *Ages accepted:* all ages. *Waiting period for first appointment:* Autumn – 1-4 weeks. *Staff and orientation:* emphasis in the neurological area. *Professional services available:* neurology, psychology, audiometry, pediatric, ophthalmology, psychiatric. *Average annual case load:* 100.

TESTING FACILITIES: Testing program with referrals.

EDUCATIONAL FACILITIES: None available.

SPECIAL INFORMATION: Facility demonstrates special interest in brain damaged children, EEG research and the organic aspects of "soft neurological signs." Evaluations are available both on a clinic and private basis with complete resources available for further studies and treatment of cases available.

Old Dominion College
School of Education
Child Study Center
Hampton Blvd.
Norfolk, Virginia 23508

DIAGNOSTIC FACILITIES: *Diagnostic facilities are offered for:* the aphasias, dyslexia (genetic or developmental), speech (developmental), minimal brain damage syndromes, slow learner. *Referral sources:* pediatrician, school – public and private, psychiatrist, psychologist, parent. *Ages accepted:* 3 years to over 20 years; (16-20 years – stutterers) (above 20 years – voice problem and adult aphasiacs). *Waiting period for first appointment:* diagnostics in speech and hearing is about 1 month at all sessions. *Staff and orientation:* a total child, multi-discipline team approach is being developed; with emphasis on psychological, educational and pediatric on call and with neurological and psychiatric on referral. *Professional services available:* psychology, audiometry, visual training, optometry, and reading specialist. Referral on neurology, pediatric, ophthalmology, psychiatric and endocrinology. *Average annual case load:* 140 – majority in speech (developmental).

TESTING FACILITIES: Strong testing program with outside referrals.

EDUCATIONAL FACILITIES: *Remedial/developmental programs offered:* the aphasias, dyslexia (genetic or developmental), speech (developmental), slow learner, emotionally disturbed (moderate). *Instruction levels:* pre-school, primary, elementary, and above 18 – attending college (developmental reading and speech defects). *Curriculum:* half day school program; annual basis. (Full-day, full curriculum beginning in the Fall of 1967 for retarded children.) *Waiting time for enrollment:* 2 months waiting period for speech therapy; 2 months waiting period for Fall classes. *Average annual enrollment:* 100 students – majority in slow learner category. *Program limits:* children in regular classes attend for one year (semester). No maximum time a student may be enrolled for a remedial program in speech therapy. *Staff:* majority of staff members have completed pertinent graduate courses and have had 2 or more years practical experience.

SPECIAL INFORMATION: Facility is primarily concerned with teacher training in the areas of emotionally disturbed, mental retarded, visually impaired, speech, and hearing.

Tidewater Rehabilitation Institute
Diagnostic Special Education School
855 West Brambleton Avenue
Norfolk, Virginia
Director: Evelyn M. Hellinger, Ed. D.

EDUCATIONAL FACILITIES: *Remedial/developmental programs offered:* the aphasias, dyslexia (genetic or developmental), speech (developmental), minimal brain damage syndromes, and slow learner, emotionally disturbed (moderate) if a secondary disability. *Instruction levels:* pre-school, primary, elementary, and over 18-pre-vocational training for mentally retarded. *Curriculum:* full day—full curriculum; annual basis. *Waiting time for enrollment:* no waiting period at this time—new program and facilities. *Average annual enrollment:* figures not available at this time. *Individual tutoring:* no information given.

TESTING FACILITIES: Testing program in the planning stage, will include medical and educational evaluations.

FACULTY: School oriented to inter-discipline cooperation. *Professional services available to faculty:* psychology, audiometry, physical therapy, occupational therapy, audiology, speech therapy, physical medicine. *Faculty-student ratio:* 1:10. *Faculty qualifications:* 2 members of staff have had specialized training in remedial reading; 1 staff member has had graduate level training in reading, 2 in speech and education of the deaf, and 3 in learning disabilities (as part of special education); 2 members of staff hold Masters Degrees in Speech, and 3 in Special Education (which includes learning disabilities).

SPECIAL INFORMATION: School will open with the September session 1967, plans are to serve children (3 years to 13 years) with a variety of handicaps, specializing in education for the child with learning disabilities.

University of Richmond
Psychology Department
Center for Psychological Services
Post Office Box 38
Richmond, Virginia 23173
Director: Jean N. Dickinson

DIAGNOSTIC FACILITIES: *Diagnostic facilities offered:* minimal brain damage syndromes, slow learner, psychiatric disorders. *Referral sources:* pediatrician, school—public and private, psychiatrist, psychologist, parent, guidance counselor. *Ages accepted:* 6 years to 16 years. *Waiting period for first appointment:* 1 month. *Staff and orientation:* emphasis in the psychological and educational areas. *Professional services available:* psychology. *Average annual case load:* 90.

TESTING FACILITIES: Testing program available.

EDUCATIONAL FACILITIES: *Remedial/developmental facilities:* slow learner. *Instruction level:* elementary, junior and senior high. *Curriculum:* tutorial only; semester basis, plus weekly hour appointment. *Waiting period for enrollment:* Autumn—none; Spring—waiting period till Summer; Summer—waiting period till Fall. *Average annual enrollment:* 28-35 students. *Program limits:* no maximum time a student may be enrolled for a remedial program. *Staff:* majority of staff tutors are currently enrolled in graduate school and have had less than 2 years practical experience; and are under the continuous supervision of the director.

University of Virginia
Speech and Hearing Center
Department of Speech Pathology and Audiology
109 Cabell Hall
Charlottesville, Virginia 22903
Director: Helen G. Burr, Ph.D.

DIAGNOSTIC FACILITIES: *Diagnostic facilities offered:* the aphasias, dyslexia (genetic or developmental), speech (developmental), minimal brain damage syndromes. *Referral sources:* pediatrician, school—public and private, psychiatrist, psychologist, parent. *Ages accepted:* all ages. *Waiting period for first appointment:* Autumn—1 month, Spring—1 month, Summer—1 month. *Staff and orientation:* a total child, multi-discipline team approach (related services readily available). *Professional services available:* neurology, psychology, audiometry, pediatric, ophthalmology, visual training, optometry, psychiatric, endocrinology. *Average annual case load:* not given.

TESTING FACILITIES: Not listed.

EDUCATIONAL FACILITIES: *Remedial/developmental facilities:* the aphasias, dyslexia (genetic or developmental), speech (developmental), minimal brain damage syndromes. *Instruction levels:* pre-school, primary, elementary, junior and senior high, and adult rehabilitation. *Waiting period for enrollment:* Autumn—1 month, Spring—1 month, Summer—1 month. *Average annual enrollment;* not given. *Program limits:* no maximum time a student may be enrolled for a remedial program. *Staff:* majority of staff have had 2 or more years practical experience.

WEST VIRGINIA

West Virginia University
Division of Clinical Studies
Child Study Center
Morgantown, West Virginia
Director: Dr. Arreta Jaranko

EDUCATIONAL FACILITIES: *Remedial/developmental programs offered:* dyslexia (genetic or developmental), minimal brain damage syndromes. *Instruction levels:* primary, elementary, junior and senior high, above 18-college preparatory. *Curriculum:* tutorial only and full day—full curriculum; annual basis. *Waiting period for enrollment:* none. *Average annual enrollment:* 20. *Individual tutoring:* included automatically in students curriculum, if necessary.

TESTING FACILITIES: Strong testing program available.

FACULTY: School is oriented to inter-discipline cooperation. *Professional services available to faculty:* neurology, psychology, audiometry, pediatric, ophthalmology, visual training, optometry, psychiatric, endocrinology. *Faculty-student ratio:* not given. *Faculty qualifications:* entire staff has had specialized training in remedial reading; graduate level training has been had by 100% of staff in reading, 50% of staff in speech, and 75% of staff in learning disabilities; entire staff holds Masters Degrees in reading.

SPECIAL INFORMATION: Center is expanding facilities to include research and experimentation to help the training of graduate students in clinical work.

WASHINGTON

Children's Orthopedic Hospital and Medical Center
Retarded Children's Clinic
4800 Sand Point Way, N.E.
Seattle, Washington 98105
Director: E. Franklin Stone, Jr., M.D.

DIAGNOSTIC FACILITIES: *Diagnostic facilities offered for:* the aphasias, dyslexia (genetic or developmental), speech (developmental), minimal brain damage syndromes, slow learner, psychiatric disorders. *Referral sources:* pediatrician, school—public and private, psychiatrist, psychologist, parent, any agency. *Ages accepted:* 3 years to 16 years. *Waiting period for first appointment:* 3-6 months waiting period for Autumn, Winter, Spring and Summer. *Staff and orientation:* a total child, multi-discipline team approach. *Professional services available:* neurology, psychology, audiometry, pediatric, ophthalmology, psychiatric, endocrinology, social service. *Average annual case load:* 60—majority in minimal brain damaged category.

TESTING FACILITIES: Strong testing program available.

EDUCATIONAL FACILITIES: None available.

Marian School
Fort Wright College
Spokane, Washington 99204
Director: Sister M. Virginia Claire Ed.D.

EDUCATIONAL FACILITIES: *Remedial/developmental programs:* minimal brain damage syndromes, slow learner. *Instruction levels:* pre-school, primary, elementary, and junior high. *Curriculum:* full day—full curriculum; annual basis. *Waiting period for enrollment:* 2 weeks (while processing information). *Average annual enrollment:* 43 students—majority in the slow learner category. *Program limits:* no maximum time a student may be enrolled for a remedial program. *Staff:* director has Ed.D. in special education; other teachers have had long teaching experience and they are in their second-year experience in special education.

Seattle Seguin School
113 Madrona Place, East
Seattle, Washington
Director: Jerome Hellmuth

EDUCATIONAL FACILITIES: *Remedial/developmental programs:* the aphasias, dyslexia (genetic or developmental), speech (developmental), minimal brain damage syndromes, slow learner, emotionally disturbed (moderate). *Instruction levels:* pre-school, primary, elementary, junior high. *Curriculum:* full day—full curriculum; annual basis. *Waiting period for enrollment:* 2-4 weeks. *Average annual enrollment:* 25 students. *Individual tutoring:* presented as an adjunct to the curriculum.

TESTING FACILITIES: Testing program available with off-campus referral.

FACULTY: School is oriented to inter-discipline cooperation. *Professional services available to faculty:* neurology, psychology, audiometry, pediatric, ophthalmology, visual training, optometry, psychiatric, endocrinology. *Faculty-student ratio:* 1:3—1:4. *Faculty qualifications:* entire staff has had specialized training in remedial reading.

Speech and Hearing Clinic
Department of Speech—Speech Correction
E.W.S.E.
Cheney, Washington
Director: D. H. Breitenfeldt

DIAGNOSTIC FACILITIES: *Diagnostic facilities are offered for:* the aphasias, dyslexia (genetic or developmental), speech (developmental), minimal brain damage syndromes. *Referral sources:* pediatrician, school—public and private, psychiatrist, psychologist, parent. *Ages accepted:* all ages. *Waiting period for first appointment:* Autumn—2 months, Spring—2 months, Summer—2 months. *Staff and orientation:* a total child, multi-discipline team approach; with emphas in the neurological and educational areas. *Professional services available:* neurology, psychology, audiometry. *Average annual case load:* 115—majority in the developmental speech category.

TESTING FACILITIES: Testing program available.

EDUCATIONAL FACILITIES: *Remedial/developmental programs offered:* the aphasias, dyslexia (genetic or developmental), speech (developmental), minimal brain damage syndromes. *Instruction levels:* pre-school, primary, elementary, junior high, senior high, above 18-attending college (developmental reading), adult rehabilitation. *Curriculum:* tutorial; half day; annual basis. *Waiting period for enrollment:* Autumn—2 months, Spring—2 months, Summer—2 months. *Average annual enrollment:* 95 students—majority in the speech category. *Program limits:* no maximum time a student may be enrolled for a remedial program. *Staff:* majority of staff members have had 2 or more years practical experience.

University of Washington
Department of Pediatrics
Division of Child Health
4701 24th Avenue, N.E.
Seattle, Washington
Director: Robert W. Deisher, M.D.

DIAGNOSTIC FACILITIES: *Diagnostic facilities offered:* the aphasias, dyslexia (genetic or developmental), speech (developmental), minimal brain damage syndromes, slow learner. *Referral sources:* pediatrician, school—public and private, psychiatrist, psychologist, parent. *Ages accepted:* 3 years to 20 years. *Waiting period for first appointment:* Autumn —1-2 months, Spring—2-3 months, Summer—3-6 months. *Staff and orientation:* a total child multi-discipline team approach. *Professional services available:* neurology, psychology, audiometry, pediatric, ophthalmology, psychiatric, endocrinology. *Average annual case load:* 106—majority in the minimal brain damaged category.

TESTING FACILITIES: Not given.

EDUCATIONAL FACILITIES: *Remedial/developmental facilities:* speech (developmental), minimal brain damage syndromes, slow learner, emotionally disturbed (moderate and severe). *Instruction level:* pre-school, primary, elementary, junior high. *Curriculum:* half day and full day—full curriculum; annual basis. *Waiting period for enrollment:* Autumn—2 months, Spring—2 months, Summer—2 months. *Average annual enrollment:* 46-48 students—majority in the slow learner category. *Program limits:* 2-3 years is the maximum time a student may be enrolled for a remedial program. *Staff:* majority of staff have completed pertinent graduate courses and have had 2 or more years practical experience.

University of Washington
Department of Pediatrics
Division of Child Health
Child Development Program
4701 24th Street, N.E.
Seattle, Washington
Director: Robert Deisher, M.D.

DIAGNOSTIC FACILITIES: *Diagnostic facilities are offered for:* the aphasias, dyslexia (genetic or developmental), speech (developmental), minimal brain damage syndromes, slow learner. *Referral sources:* pediatrician, school—public and private, psychologist, parent. *Ages accepted:* 3 years to 20 years—above 20 years occasionally. *Waiting period for first appointment:* Autumn—1 month, Spring—4-6 months, Summer—3 months. *Staff and orientation:* a total child, multi-discipline team approach; with emphasis in the neurological, psychological, and pediatric areas. *Professional services available:* neurology, psychology, audiometry, pediatric, ophthalmology, psychiatric, endocrinology, educational, and social. *Average annual case load:* 220—majority in the slow learner and minimal brain damaged syndromes categories.

TESTING FACILITIES: Not given.

EDUCATIONAL FACILITIES: *Remedial/developmental programs offered for:* the aphasias, dyslexia (genetic or developmental), speech (developmental), minimal brain damage syndromes, slow learner, emotionally disturbed (moderate and severe). *Instruction levels:* all ages—from pre-school through adult rehabilitation. *Curriculum:* tutorial; half day; annual basis. *Waiting period for enrollment:* Autumn, Spring, and Summer—6-9 months waiting time. *Average annual enrollment:* less than 50 students. *Program limits:* remedial program limited to 4 months (exceptions in rare cases only). *Staff:* majority of staff members have had 2 or more years practical experience.

SPECIAL INFORMATION: Program does not remediate; clients are enrolled for short periods during which a variety of educational procedures are tried. When an effective procedure is demonstrated to increase the rate of acquisition of academic or behavioral skill, data is communicated to the referral agent.

WISCONSIN

The Cardinal Stritch College
Graduate Division
Reading Clinic
6801 N. Yates Road
Milwaukee, Wisconsin 53217
Director: Sister Mary Julitta, O.S.F.

DIAGNOSTIC FACILITIES: *Diagnostic facilities are offered for:* minimal brain damage syndromes, slow learner. *Referral sources:* pediatrician, school—public and private, psychiatrist, psychologist, parent, agency. *Ages accepted:* 3 years to 6 years (only on occasion), 6 years to over 20 years. *Waiting period for first appointment:* Autumn—1-6 months, Spring—1-7 months, Summer—1-4 months. *Staff and orientation:* emphasis on education. *Professional services available:* neurology, psychology, ophthalmology, visual training, optometry, psychiatric, and off-campus referrals. *Average annual case load:* 500-600.

TESTING FACILITIES: Strong testing program available, and off-campus referrals if needed.

SPECIAL INFORMATION: Clinic will test all referrals.

EDUCATIONAL FACILITIES: *Remedial/developmental programs offered:* speech (developmental) if reading is major problem, minimal brain damage syndromes, slow learner (not below 80 I.Q.), emotionally disturbed (moderate and severe) if recommended by psychiatrist. *Instruction levels:* primary, elementary, junior high, senior high, above 18-attending college (developmental reading), adult rehabilitation. *Curriculum:* tutorial or 2-3 in class; annual basis. *Waiting time for enrollment:* varies. *Average annual enrollment:* 700-800 students. *Program limits:* no maximum time a student may be enrolled for a remedial program. *Staff:* entire full-time staff members have completed pertinent graduate courses and have had 2 or more years practical experience.

Marquette University
Department of Education
Center for Reading Services
1834 W. Wisconsin Avenue
Milwaukee, Wisconsin
Director: L. L. VanGilder

DIAGNOSTIC FACILITIES: *Diagnostic facilities offered:* the aphasias, dyslexia (genetic or developmental), speech (developmental). *Referral sources:* Speech Department of university. *Ages accepted:* not given. *Waiting period for first appointment:* not given. *Staff and orientation:* emphasis in the educational area. *Professional services available on referral:* neurology, psychology, audiometry, pediatric, ophthalmology, visual training, optometry, psychiatric. *Average annual case load:* not given.

TESTING FACILITIES: Testing program for reading—laboratory purposes only.

SPECIAL INFORMATION: Center is primarily for teacher-training in laboratory and graduate courses.

EDUCATIONAL FACILITIES: *Remedial/developmental facilities* offered in university Speech Department: speech (developmental). *Instruction levels:* primary, elementary, junior and senior high, above 18—attending college, adult rehabilitation. *Waiting period for enrollment:* Autumn—6-12 months; Spring—6-12 months; Summer—6-12 months (waiting period for primary through senior high). *Average annual enrollment:* not given. *Program limits:* no maximum time a student may be enrolled for a remedial program. *Staff:* majority of staff have completed pertinent graduate courses and have had 2 or more years practical experience.

Marquette University
Department of Speech
Speech and Hearing Rehabilitation Center
1317 West Wisconsin Avenue
Milwaukee, Wisconsin
Director: Prof. A. J. Sokolnicki

DIAGNOSTIC FACILITIES: *Diagnostic facilities offered:* the aphasias, dyslexia (genetic or developmental), speech (developmental), minimal brain damage syndromes. *Referral sources:* pediatrician, school—public and private, psychiatrist, psychologist, parent, referrals from any source accepted. *Ages accepted:* all ages. *Waiting period for first appointment:* Autumn—3 months; Spring—2 months; Summer—4 months. *Staff and orientation:* emphasis in the educational area. *Professional services available:* audiometry, speech, language. *Average annual case load:* not given.

TESTING FACILITIES: Testing program available.

EDUCATIONAL FACILITIES: *Remedial/developmental facilities:* the aphasias, dyslexia, (genetic or developmental), speech (developmental), minimal brain damage syndromes. *Instruction levels:* all ages. *Curriculum:* tutorial only; annual basis. *Waiting period for enrollment:* Autumn—3 months; Spring—2 months; Summer—4 months. *Average annual enrollment:* not given. *Program limits:* no maximum time a student may be enrolled for a remedial program. *Staff:* majority of staff members have completed pertinent graduate courses and have had 2 or more years practical experience.

SPECIAL INFORMATION: Center is a training institution—including student (graduate and undergraduate), speech therapists, supervised by staff members with Masters or Ph.D. Degrees. Clinic evaluates all aspects of speech and language—at all age levels.

Speech and Hearing Rehabilitation Center
Department of Communicative Disorders
905 University Avenue
Madison, Wisconsin
Director: Claude S. Hayes, Ph.D.

DIAGNOSTIC FACILITIES: *Diagnostic facilities offered:* the aphasias, dyslexia (genetic or developmental), speech (developmental), minimal brain damage syndromes, slow learner. *Referral sources:* pediatrician, school—public and private, psychiatrist, psychologist, parent. *Ages accepted:* all ages. *Waiting period for first appointment:* Autumn—1-12 weeks, Spring—1-12 weeks, Summer—1-12 weeks. *Staff and orientation:* emphasis in the spelling, hearing, language, and psychometric areas. *Professional services available:* audiometry; any other by referral. *Average annual case load:* not given.

TESTING FACILITIES: Hearing and speech testing program available.

EDUCATIONAL FACILITIES: *Remedial/developmental facilities:* the aphasias, dyslexia (genetic or developmental), speech (developmental), minimal brain damage syndromes, slow learner, emotionally disturbed (moderate). *Instruction levels:* all ages. *Curriculum:* tutorial only; annual basis. *Waiting period for enrollment:* Autumn—none; Spring—none; Summer—0-2 months. *Average annual enrollment:* not given. *Program limits:* no maximum time a student may be enrolled for a remedial program. *Staff:* staff members are Ph.D.s' supervisors are all Masters.

University of Wisconsin
Milwaukee Branch
Department of Educational Psychology
Psycho-Educational Clinic
2513 E. Hartford Avenue
Milwaukee, Wisconsin
Director: Dr. Ronald H. Lingren

DIAGNOSTIC FACILITIES: *Diagnostic facilities are offered for:* dyslexia (genetic or developmental), minimal brain damage syndromes, the slow learner, general behavior problem.

Referral sources: pediatrician, school—public, psychologist, parent (with knowledge of school). *Ages accepted:* 3 years to 16 years. *Waiting period for first appointment:* Autumn —2-3 weeks, Spring—2-3 weeks, Summer—2-3 weeks. *Staff and orientation:* emphasis in psychological and educational areas. *Professional services available:* professional services available through further referral—neurology, pediatric. *Annual case load:* not given.

TESTING FACILITIES: Strong testing program available.

EDUCATIONAL FACILITIES: None available.

University of Wisconsin
Milwaukee Branch
Department of Exceptional Education
Special Learning Disabilities Laboratory
Milwaukee, Wisconsin
Director: Francis X. Blair, Ph.D.

EDUCATIONAL FACILITIES: *Remedial/developmental programs offered for:* the aphasias, dyslexia (genetic or developmental), speech (developmental), minimal brain damage syndromes. *Instruction levels:* pre-school, primary, elementary. *Curriculum:* tutorial only, half day sessions, full day—full curriculum. *Waiting time for enrollment:* Autumn—6-8 weeks, Spring—6-8 weeks, Summer—6-8 weeks. *Average annual enrollment:* 25-30 in special classes; 15 in dividual remediation. *Program limits:* no maximum time a student may be enrolled for a remedial program. *Staff:* majority of staff have had 2 or more years practical experience.

SPECIAL INFORMATION: Project is used for research, demonstration, and teacher training.

University of Wisconsin
Reading Clinic
3203 N. Downer Avenue
Milwaukee, Wisconsin
Director: Dr. Arthur Schoeller

EDUCATIONAL FACILITY: *Remedial/developmental programs offered:* the aphasias (with language disorders laboratory), dyslexia (genetic or developmental), emotionally disturbed (moderate), general reading disability. *Instruction levels:* primary, elementary, junior high, senior high. *Curriculum:* tutorial only, annual basis. *Waiting time for enrollment:* September —9 months, January—6 months, Summer program—6 months. *Average annual enrollment:* 105-111 students, majority in general reading disability. *Individual tutoring:* included automatically in students curriculum.

TESTING FACILITIES: Strong testing program, with referrals made.

FACULTY: School orientated to inter-discipline cooperation. *Professional services available to faculty:* neurology, psychology, audiometry, pediatric. *Faculty-student ratio:* not given. *Faculty qualifications:* all of the staff have had specialized training in remedial reading, and training at graduate level in reading; a few have had graduate level training in learning disabilities.

Wisconsin State University
Department of Speech Pathology and Audiology
Speech and Hearing Clinic
Stevens Point, Wisconsin
Director: Dr. Gerald F. Johnson

DIAGNOSTIC FACILITIES: *Diagnostic facilities are offered for:* the aphasias, dyslexia (genetic or developmental), speech (developmental), minimal brain damage syndromes, slow learner. *Referral sources:* pediatrician, school—public and private, psychiatrist, psychologist, parent, variety of sources. *Ages accepted:* all ages. *Waiting period for first appointment:* Autumn—2 weeks, Spring—4 weeks, Summer—1 week. *Staff and orientation:* a total child, multi-discipline team approach; with emphasis in the educational area. *Professional services available:* neurology, psychology, audiometry, pediatric, ophthalmology, visual training, optometry, psychiatric. *Average annual case load:* 92—majority in the speech (developmental) category.

TESTING FACILITIES: Testing program available.

EDUCATIONAL FACILITIES: None available.